Lecture Notes in Artificial Intelligence   10632

Subseries of Lecture Notes in Computer Science

More information about this series at http://www.springer.com/series/1244

Félix Castro · Sabino Miranda-Jiménez
Miguel González-Mendoza (Eds.)

Advances in Soft Computing

16th Mexican International Conference
on Artificial Intelligence, MICAI 2017
Enseneda, Mexico, October 23–28, 2017
Proceedings, Part I

 Springer

Editors
Félix Castro
Universidad Autónoma del Estado de
Hidalgo
Pachuca, Mexico

Miguel González-Mendoza
Tecnológico de Monterrey
Atizapán de Zaragoza, Mexico

Sabino Miranda-Jiménez
INFOTEC Aguascalientes
Aguascalientes, Mexico

ISSN 0302-9743   ISSN 1611-3349   (electronic)
Lecture Notes in Artificial Intelligence
ISBN 978-3-030-02836-7   ISBN 978-3-030-02837-4   (eBook)
https://doi.org/10.1007/978-3-030-02837-4

Library of Congress Control Number: 2018958468

LNCS Sublibrary: SL7 – Artificial Intelligence

This Springer imprint is published by the registered company Springer Nature Switzerland AG
The registered company address is: Gewerbestrasse 11, 6330 Cham, Switzerland

In memoriam
Dr. José Negrete Martínez

Preface

The Mexican International Conference on Artificial Intelligence (MICAI) is a yearly international conference series that has been organized by the Mexican Society of Artificial Intelligence (SMIA) since 2000. MICAI is a major international artificial intelligence forum and the main event in the academic life of the country's growing artificial intelligence community.

We dedicate this set of two volumes to the bright memory of Dr. José Negrete Martínez, the founder of the SMIA back in 1986, its first president, whose contribution to the promotion of artificial intelligence in our country is difficult to overestimate.

MICAI conferences publish high-quality papers in all areas of artificial intelligence and its applications. The proceedings of the previous MICAI events have been published by Springer in its *Lecture Notes in Artificial Intelligence* series, as volumes 1793, 2313, 2972, 3789, 4293, 4827, 5317, 5845, 6437, 6438, 7094, 7095, 7629, 7630, 8265, 8266, 8856, 8857, 9413, 9414, 10061, and 10062. Since its foundation in 2000, the conference has been growing in popularity and improving in quality.

With MICAI 2017, we celebrated the 30th anniversary of the SMIA, which was officially registered in 1987. Accordingly, MICAI 2017 featured a round table with the participation of a number of former presidents of the SMIA, including its founder Dr. José Negrete Martínez; this happened to be one of his last public appearances.

The proceedings of MICAI 2017 are published in two volumes. The first volume, *Advances in Soft Computing*, contains 30 papers structured into four sections:

- Neural Networks
- Evolutionary Algorithms and Optimization
- Hybrid Intelligent Systems and Fuzzy Logic
- Machine Learning and Data Mining

The second volume, *Advances in Computational Intelligence*, contains 30 papers structured into three sections:

- Natural Language Processing and Social Networks
- Intelligent Tutoring Systems and Educational Applications
- Image Processing and Pattern Recognition

This two-volume set will be of interest for researchers in all areas of artificial intelligence, students specializing in related topics, and for the general public interested in recent developments in artificial intelligence.

The conference received 203 submissions for evaluation from 23 countries: Argentina, Belgium, Brazil, Chile, Colombia, Cuba, Ecuador, France, India, Iran, Ireland, Malaysia, Mexico, Morocco, Pakistan, Paraguay, Peru, Portugal, Russia, South Africa, Spain, Ukraine, and USA. Of these submissions, 61 papers were selected for publication in these two volumes after the peer-reviewing process carried out by the international Program Committee. Thus, the acceptance rate was 30%.

The international Program Committee consisted of 192 experts from 19 countries: Argentina, Benin, Brazil, Canada, Colombia, Cuba, Finland, France, Greece, Israel, Italy, Japan, Mexico, Portugal, Singapore, Spain, UK, USA, and Uruguay.

MICAI 2017 was honored by the presence of renowned experts, who gave excellent keynote lectures:

- Pierre Baldi, University of California, Irvine, USA
- Hamido Fujita, Iwate Prefectural University, Japan
- Thamar Solorio, University of Houston, USA
- Eduardo Morales Manzanares, INAOE, Mexico
- Jeff Dean, Google, USA

The technical program of the conference also featured eight tutorials:

- "Artificial Hydrocarbon Networks and Their Applications," by Hiram Eredín Ponce Espinosa
- "Building a Digital Ecosystem Using FIWARE," by Nestor Velasco-Bermeo, Miguel González Mendoza, and Jesus Favela
- "Computational Biology," by Gabriel Del Rio and Carlos Brizuela
- "Data Science: A Quick Introduction," by Mauricio Alonso Sánchez Herrera
- "Introduction to Data Mining with Python," by Mario Garcia Valdez
- "Sentiment Analysis," by Alexander Gelbukh
- "Similarity, Correlation and Association Measures in Data Analysis: New Looks and New Measures," by Ildar Batyrshin
- "The Wavelet Transform in Soft Computing," by Oscar Herrera Alcántara

Three workshops were held jointly with the conference:

- HIS 2017: 10th Workshop on Hybrid Intelligent Systems
- WIDSSI 2017: Third International Workshop on Intelligent Decision Support Systems for Industry
- WILE 2017: 10th Workshop on Intelligent Learning Environments

The authors of the following papers received the Best Paper Awards based on the paper's overall quality, significance, and originality of the reported results:

- Best paper: "On the Many-Objective Pickup and Delivery Problem: Analysis of the Performance of Three Evolutionary Algorithms," by Abel García-Nájera, Antonio López-Jaimes, and Saúl Zapotecas-Martínez (Mexico)
- Best student paper: "Human Activity Recognition on Mobile Devices Using Artificial Hydrocarbon Networks," by Hiram Ponce, Guillermo González, Luis Miralles-Pechuán, and Lourdes Martínez-Villaseñor (Mexico)

The latter paper was selected among all papers of which the first author was a full-time student, excluding the paper that received the best paper award.

In addition, at MICAI 2017 the winners of the national contest of theses on artificial intelligence, organized by the Mexican Society of Artificial Intelligence (SMIA), were announced:

- Best PhD thesis, first place: "Image Classification Through Text Mining Techniques," by Adrián Pastor López Monroy with his advisors Manuel Montes-y-Gómez, Hugo Jair Escalante, and Fabio A. González
- Best PhD thesis, second place: "Hardware Acceleration of Frequent Itemsets Mining on Data Streams," by Lázaro Bustio Martínez with his advisors René Cumplido and Raudel Hernandez-León
- Best PhD thesis, third place: "Evolución Diferencial par Resolver Problemas de Optimización Dinámica con Restricciones," by María Yaneli Ameca Alducin with her advisors Nicandro Cruz Ramírez and Efrén Mezura Montes
- Best MSc thesis, first place: "Redes Neuronales de Tercera Generación Aplicadas al Reconocimiento de Imaginación de Movimientos en Registros de Electroencefalografía," by Ruben Isaac Cariño Escobar with his advisors Roberto Antonio Vázquez Espinoza de los Monteros and Josefina Gutiérrez Martínez
- Best MSc thesis, second place: "Distinción de Estados de Actividad e Inactividad Lingüística para Interfaces Eerebro Computadora," by Luis Alfredo Moctezuma Pascual with his advisors Maya Carrillo Ruiz and Alejandro A. Torres Garcia
- Best MSc thesis, third place (shared): "Clasificación de Patrones de Bandeo Obtenidos Mediante Western Blot para el Diagnóstico de Cáncer de Mama," by Diana María Sánchez Silva with her advisors Héctor Gabriel Acosta Mesa and Tania Romo González de la Parra
- Best MSc thesis, third place (shared): "Multimodal Sentiment Analysis in Social Media using Deep Learning with Convolutional Neural Networks," by Navonil Majumder with his advisor Alexander Gelbukh

The cultural program of the conference included tours to the La Bufadora natural attraction and the tour of wine production route.

We want to thank all people involved in the organization of this conference. In the first place, these are the authors of the papers published in this book: It is their research effort that gives value to the book and to the work of the organizers. We thank the track chairs for their hard work, the Program Committee members, and additional reviewers for their great effort spent on reviewing the submissions.

We would like to thank Dr. Juan Manuel Ocegueda Hernández, Rector of the Universidad Autónoma de Baja California, and Dr. Silvio Guido Lorenzo Marinone Moschetto, Director General of the Centro de Investigación Científica y de Educación Superior de Ensenada, along with all the members of their teams, for their invaluable help in the organization of the conference. We express our great gratitude to Dr. Blanca Rosa García Rivera, Dr. Juan Iván Nieto Hipólito, and Dr. Juan Crisóstomo Tapia Mercado for all the support provided to this event. We are deeply grateful to the student assistants from UABC and CICESE, who were very helpful at all stages of the organization. We are deeply grateful to the conference staff and to all members of the Local Committee headed by Dora Luz Flores Gutiérrez, Everardo Gutiérrez López, and Carlos Alberto Brizuela Rodríguez. The entire submission, reviewing, and selection process, as well as preparation of the proceedings, was supported free of charge by the

EasyChair system (www.easychair.org). Finally, yet importantly, we are very grateful to the staff at Springer for their patience and help in the preparation of this volume.

February 2018

Félix Castro
Sabino Miranda-Jiménez
Miguel González-Mendoza

Organization

MICAI 2017 was organized by the Mexican Society of Artificial Intelligence (SMIA, Sociedad Mexicana de Inteligencia Artificial) in collaboration with the Universidad Autónoma de Baja California (UABC), the Centro de Investigación Científica y de Educación Superior de Ensenada (CICESE), the Universidad Autónoma del Estado de Hidalgo (UAEH), the Centro de Investigación e Innovación en Tecnologías de la Información y Comunicación (INFOTEC), the Tecnológico de Monterrey CEM, the Centro de Investigación en Computación del Instituto Politécnico Nacional (CIC-IPN), and the Universidad Autónoma Metropolitana Azcapotzalco (UAM).

The MICAI series website is www.MICAI.org. The website of the Mexican Society of Artificial Intelligence, SMIA, is www.SMIA.org.mx. Contact options and additional information can be found on these websites.

Conference Committee

General Chair

Miguel González Mendoza	Tecnológico de Monterrey CEM, Mexico

Program Chairs

Félix Castro	Universidad Autónoma del Estado de Hidalgo, Mexico
Sabino Miranda Jiménez	INFOTEC, Mexico
Miguel González Mendoza	Tecnológico de Monterrey CEM, Mexico

Workshop Chairs

Obdulia Pichardo Lagunas	Instituto Politécnico Nacional, Mexico
Noé Alejandro Castro Sánchez	Centro Nacional de Investigación y Desarrollo Tecnológico, Mexico

Tutorials Chair

Félix Castro Espinoza	Universidad Autónoma del Estado de Hidalgo, Mexico

Doctoral Consortium Chairs

Miguel Gonzalez Mendoza	Tecnológico de Monterrey CEM, Mexico
Antonio Marín Hernandez	Universidad Veracruzana, Mexico

Keynote Talks Chair

Sabino Miranda Jiménez	INFOTEC, Mexico

Publication Chair

Miguel Gonzalez Mendoza   Tecnológico de Monterrey CEM, Mexico

Financial Chair

Ildar Batyrshin   Instituto Politécnico Nacional, Mexico

Grant Chairs

Grigori Sidorov   Instituto Politécnico Nacional, Mexico
Miguel Gonzalez Mendoza   Tecnológico de Monterrey CEM, Mexico

Organizing Committee Chairs

Dora Luz Flores Gutiérrez   Universidad Autónoma de Baja California, Mexico
Everardo Gutiérrez López   Universidad Autónoma de Baja California, Mexico
Carlos Alberto Brizuela   Centro de Investigación Científica y de Educación
  Rodríguez   Superior de Ensenada, Mexico

Area Chairs

Machine Learning

Eduardo Morales   Instituto Nacional de Astrofísica, Óptica y Electrónica,
  Manzanares   Mexico
Raul Monroy Borja   Tecnológico de Monterrey CEM, Mexico

Natural Language Processing

Sabino Miranda Jiménez   INFOTEC, Mexico
Esaú Villatoro   Universidad Autónoma Metropolitana Cuajimalpa,
                              Mexico

Evolutionary and Evolutive Algorithms

Hugo Jair Escalante   Instituto Nacional de Astrofísica, Óptica y Electrónica,
  Balderas   Mexico
Hugo Terashima Marín   Tecnológico de Monterrey CM, Mexico

Neural Networks

Angel Kuri Morales   Instituto Tecnológico Autónomo de México, Mexico
Pilar Gómez Gil   Instituto Nacional de Astrofísica, Óptica y Electrónica,
                              Mexico

Computer Vision and Robotics

José Martínez Carranza   Instituto Nacional de Astrofísica, Óptica y Electrónica,
                              Mexico
Daniela Moctezuma   Centro de Investigación en Ciencias de Información
                              Geoespacial, Mexico

Hybrid Intelligent Systems

Carlos Alberto Reyes Garcia	Instituto Nacional de Astrofísica, Óptica y Electrónica, Mexico
Juan Jose Flores	Universidad Michoacana, Mexico

Intelligent Applications

Gustavo Arroyo	Instituto Nacional de Electricidad y Energias Limpias, Mexico
Humberto Sossa	Instituto Politécnico Nacional, Mexico

Program Committee

Rocío Abascal-Mena	Universidad Autónoma Metropolitana Cuajimalpa, Mexico
Giner Alor-Hernández	Tecnológico de Orizaba, Mexico
Matias Alvarado	CINVESTAV, Mexico
Nohemi Alvarez Jarquin	Centro de Investigación en Geografía y Geomática Ing. Jorge L. Tamayo, A.C., Mexico
Gustavo Arechavaleta	CINVESTAV-Saltillo, Mexico
García Gamboa Ariel Lucien	Tecnológico de Monterrey CEM, Mexico
Gustavo Arroyo	Instituto Nacional de Electricidad y Energías Limpias, Mexico
Maria Lucia Barrón-Estrada	Instituto Tecnológico de Culiacán, Mexico
Rafael Batres	Tecnológico de Monterrey, Mexico
Ildar Batyrshin	Instituto Politécnico Nacional, Mexico
Edmundo Bonilla	Instituto Tecnológico de Apizaco, Mexico
Maricela Claudia Bravo Contreras	Universidad Autónoma Metropolitana, Mexico
Davide Buscaldi	LIPN, Université Paris 13, Sorbonne Paris Cité, France
Felix Calderon	Universidad Michoacana de San Nicolas de Hidalgo, Mexico
Hiram Calvo	Instituto Politécnico Nacional, Mexico
Nicoletta Calzolari	Istituto di Linguistica Computazionale – CNR, Italy
Erik Cambria	Nanyang Technological University, Singapore
Sergio Daniel Cano Ortiz	Universidad de Oriente, Cuba
Jesus Ariel Carrasco-Ochoa	Instituto Nacional de Astrofísica, Óptica y Electrónica, Mexico
Victor Carrera	Instituto Nacional de Astrofísica, Óptica y Electrónica, Mexico
Mario Castelan	CINVESTAV-Saltillo, Mexico
Oscar Castillo	Instituto Tecnológico de Tijuana, Mexico
Felix Castro Espinoza	Universidad Autónoma del Estado de Hidalgo, Mexico

Miguel Gonzalez-Mendoza	Tecnológico de Monterrey CEM, Mexico
Mario Graff	INFOTEC, Mexico
Fernando Gudiño	Universidad Nacional Autónoma de México, Mexico
Miguel Angel Guevara Lopez	University of Minho, Portugal
Octavio Gutierrez	Instituto Tecnológico Autónomo de México, Mexico
Andrés E. Gutiérrez-Rodríguez	Tecnológico de Monterrey, Mexico
Rafael Guzman Cabrera	Universidad de Guanajuato, Mexico
Yasunari Harada	Waseda University, Japan
Jean-Bernard Hayet	Centro de Investigación en Matemáticas, Mexico
Jorge Hermosillo	Universidad Autónoma del Estado de México, Mexico
Yasmin Hernandez	Instituto Nacional de Electricidad y Energías Limpias, Mexico
José Alberto Hernández	Universidad Autónoma del Estado de Morelos, Mexico
José-Crispín Hernández	Instituto Tecnológico de Apizaco, Mexico
Francisco J. Hernandez-Lopez	Centro de Investigación en Matemáticas, Mexico
Oscar Herrera	Universidad Autónoma Metropolitana Azcapotzalco, Mexico
Pablo H. Ibarguengoytia	Instituto de Investigaciones Eléctricas, Mexico
Angel Kuri-Morales	Instituto Tecnológico Autónomo de México, Mexico
Carlos Lara-Alvarez	Centro de Investigación en Matemáticas, Mexico
Yulia Nikolaevna Ledeneva	Universidad Autónoma del Estado de México, Mexico
Eugene Levner	Ashkelon Academic College, Israel
Fernando Lezama	Instituto Nacional de Astrofísica, Óptica y Electrónica, Mexico
Rodrigo Lopez Farias	IMT Institute for Advanced Studies Lucca, Italy
Omar Jehovani López Orozco	Instituto Tecnológico Superior de Apatzingán, Mexico
A. Pastor López-Monroy	Instituto Nacional de Astrofísica, Óptica y Electrónica, Mexico
Octavio Loyola-González	Tecnológico de Monterrey, Mexico
Andrea Magadan	Centro Nacional de Investigación y Desarrollo Tecnológico, Mexico
Yazmin Maldonado	Instituto Tecnológico de Tijuana, Mexico
Isaac Martín de Diego	Universidad Rey Juan Carlos, Spain
José Martínez Carranza	Instituto Nacional de Astrofísica, Óptica y Electrónica, Mexico
José Francisco Martínez-Trinidad	Instituto Nacional de Astrofísica, Óptica y Electrónica, Mexico
Anabel Martinez-Vargas	Universidad Politécnica de Pachuca, Mexico
Miguel Angel Medina Pérez	Instituto Nacional de Astrofísica, Óptica y Electrónica, Mexico
Patricia Melin	Instituto Tecnológico de Tijuana, Mexico
Ivan Vladimir Meza Ruiz	Universidad Nacional Autónoma de México, Mexico

Efrén Mezura-Montes	Universidad Veracruzana, Mexico
Sabino Miranda-Jiménez	INFOTEC, Mexico
Daniela Moctezuma	CONACYT, CentroGeo, Mexico
Raul Monroy	Tecnologico de Monterrey CEM, Mexico
Manuel Montes-y-Gómez	Instituto Nacional de Astrofísica, Óptica y Electrónica, Mexico
Marco Morales	Instituto Tecnológico Autónomo de México, Mexico
Eduardo Morales Manzanares	Instituto Nacional de Astrofísica, Óptica y Electrónica, Mexico
Annette Morales-González	CENATAV, Cuba
Alicia Morales-Reyes	Instituto Nacional de Astrofísica, Óptica y Electrónica, Mexico
Masaki Murata	Tottori University, Japan
Antonio Neme	Universidad Autónoma de la Ciudad de México, Mexico
C. Alberto Ochoa-Zezatti	Universidad Autónoma de Ciudad Juárez, Mexico
Diego Oliva	Universidad de Guadalajara, Spain
José Luis Oliveira	University of Aveiro, Portugal
Fernando Ornelas	Universidad Michoacana de San Nicolás de Hidalgo, Mexico
Jose Ortiz Bejar	Universidad Michoacana de San Nicolás de Hidalgo, Mexico
José Carlos Ortiz-Bayliss	Tecnológico de Monterrey, Mexico
Ivandre Paraboni	University of Sao Paulo, Brazil
Alvaro Pardo	Universidad Católica del Uruguay, Uruguay
Miguel Perez	Instituto Nacional de Electricidad y Energías Limpias, Mexico
Airel Pérez Suárez	CENATAV, Cuba
Humberto Pérez-Espinosa	CICESE-UT3, Mexico
Obdulia Pichardo-Lagunas	Instituto Politécnico Nacional, Mexico
Garibaldi Pineda	The University of Manchester, UK
Raul Pinto Elias	Centro Nacional de Investigación y Desarrollo Tecnológico, Mexico
Hiram Ponce Espinosa	Universidad Panamericana, Mexico
Soujanya Poria	Nanyang Technological University, Singapore
Belem Priego-Sanchez	Benemérita Universidad Autónoma de Puebla, Mexico; Université Paris 13, France; Universidad Autónoma Metropolitana Azcapotzalco, Mexico
Luis Puig	Universidad de Zaragoza, Spain
Vicenc Puig	Universitat Politècnica de Catalunya, Spain
J. R. G. Pulido	The University of Colima, Mexico
Juan M. Ramírez-Cortés	Instituto Nacional de Astrofísica, Óptica y Electrónica, Mexico
Gabriela Ramírez-De-La-Rosa	Universidad Autónoma Metropolitana Cuajimalpa, Mexico
Juan Ramirez-Quintana	Instituto Tecnológico de Chihuahua, Mexico

Juan Manuel Rendon-Mancha	Universidad Autónoma del Estado de Morelos, Mexico
Orion Reyes	University of Alberta Edmonton, Canada
Carlos Alberto Reyes García	Instituto Nacional de Astrofísica, Óptica y Electrónica, Mexico
José A. Reyes-Ortiz	Universidad Autónoma Metropolitana, Mexico
Roger Rios-Mercado	Universidad Autónoma de Nuevo León, Mexico
Noel Enrique Rodriguez Maya	Instituto Tecnológico de Zitácuaro, Mexico
Hector Rodriguez Rangel	University of Oregon, USA
Katya Rodriguez-Vazquez	Universidad Nacional Autónoma de México, Mexico
Alejandro Rosales	Tecnológico de Monterrey, Mexico
Jose Sanchez Del Rio	IMDEA Materiales, Spain
Cuauhtemoc Sanchez-Ramirez	Tecnológico de Orizaba, Mexico
Christian Sánchez-Sánchez	Universidad Autónoma Metropolitana, Mexico
Guillermo Santamaria	CONACYT, Instituto Nacional de Electricidad y Energías Limpias, Mexico
Oliver Schuetze	CINVESTAV-IPN, Mexico
Carlos Segura	Centro de Investigación en Matemáticas, Mexico
Ángel Serrano	Universidad Rey Juan Carlos, Spain
Grigori Sidorov	Instituto Politécnico Nacional, Mexico
Jesus Antonio Sosa Herrera	CentroGEO, Mexico
Juan Humberto Sossa Azuela	Instituto Politécnico Nacional, Mexico
Efstathios Stamatatos	University of the Aegean, Greece
Eric S. Tellez	CONACYT, INFOTEC, Mexico
Hugo Terashima	Tecnológico de Monterrey, Mexico
Esteban Tlelo-Cuautle	Instituto Nacional de Astrofísica, Óptica y Electrónica, Mexico
Luis Torres	General Electric, Mexico
Alejandro Antonio Torres García	Tecnológico de Monterrey, Mexico
Nestor Velasco-Bermeo	Tecnológico de Monterrey CEM, Mexico
Esau Villatoro-Tello	Universidad Autónoma Metropolitana, Mexico
Aline Villavicencio	Universidade Federal do Rio Grande do Sul, Brazil
Francisco Viveros Jiménez	Instituto Politécnico Nacional, Mexico
Carlos Mario Zapata Jaramillo	Universidad Nacional de Colombia, Colombia
Saúl Zapotecas Martínez	Universidad Autónoma Metropolitana Cuajimalpa, Mexico
Ramón Zatarain	Instituto Tecnológico de Culiacán, Mexico
Alisa Zhila	Target, USA
Carlos Zozaya	Grupo BAL, Mexico

Additional Reviewers

Maria-Yaneli Ameca-Alducin
Ildar Batyrshin
Jan Burchard
Jingcao Cai
Katy Castillo-Rosado
Barbara Cervantes
Sankha Deb
David Estévez
Alexander Gelbukh
Lázaro Janier González-Soler
Betania Hernandez Ocaña
Pablo H. Ibarguengoytia
Azah Mohamed
Gianluca Morganti
Rosa María Ortega-Mendoza

Daile Osorio Roig
Ferdinando Pezzella
Eduarda Portela
Marcela Quiroz-Castellanos
Alberto Reyes
Jorge Rodríguez-Ruiz
Alfonso Rojas
Manuel Schmitt
Ricardo Sousa
Yasushi Tsubota
Francisco Viveros Jiménez
Lunche Wang
Lei Wang
Rolf Wanka
Rodrigo Wilkens

Organizing Committee

Chairs

Dora Luz Flores Gutiérrez   Universidad Autónoma de Baja California, Mexico
Everardo Gutiérrez López   Universidad Autónoma de Baja California, Mexico
Carlos Alberto Brizuela   Centro de Investigación Científica y de Educación
    Rodríguez   Superior de Ensenada, Mexico

Members

David Cervantes Vasquez
Manuel Castañón Puga
Omar Álvarez Xochihua
Evelio Martínez Martínez
José Ángel González Fraga
Adrian Enciso Almanza
José Manuel Valencia Moreno
Christian Xavier Navarro Cota
Sergio Omar Infante Prieto
Yolanda Angélica Baez López
Eunice Vargas Viveros
Luz Evelia López Chico
Ariel Arturo Quezada Pina, Universidad Autónoma de Baja California, Mexico

Contents – Part I

Hybrid Intelligent Systems and Fuzzy Logic

Machine Learning and Data Mining

Contents – Part II

Intelligent Tutoring Systems and Educational Applications

Image Processing and Pattern Recognition

Neural Networks

Versatility of Artificial Hydrocarbon Networks for Supervised Learning

Hiram Ponce$^{(\boxtimes)}$ and Ma Lourdes Martínez-Villaseñor

Facultad de Ingeniería, Universidad Panamericana,
Augusto Rodin 498, 03920 Mexico City, Mexico
{hponce,lmartine}@up.edu.mx

Abstract. Surveys on supervised machine show that each technique has strengths and weaknesses that make each of them more suitable for a particular domain or learning task. No technique is capable to tackle every supervised learning task, and it is difficult to comply with all possible desirable features of each particular domain. However, it is important that a new technique comply with the most requirements and desirable features of as many domains and learning tasks as possible. In this paper, we presented artificial hydrocarbon networks (AHN) as versatile and efficient supervised learning method. We determined the ability of AHN to solve different problem domains, with different data-sources and to learn different tasks. The analysis considered six applications in which AHN was successfully applied.

Keywords: Artificial organic networks · Machine learning
Versatility · Interpretability

1 Introduction

Supervised machine learning techniques are being applied today to tackle a vast diversity of problems with commercial, academic, and industrial applications. There are many fields in which supervised learning performs well to gain new knowledge, for example: web mining, decision support systems in diverse domains, forecasting, and diagnosis [31]. Surveys on supervised machine learning [8,15,27] show that each technique has strengths and weaknesses that make each of them more suitable for a particular domain or learning task. For example, neural networks and support vector machines are recognized to have better prediction accuracy when dealing with multi-dimensions and continuous features [8]. On the other hand, the interpretability of decision trees and classification rules is better than the comprehensibility in so called black-box methods [5]. Hence, there is no technique that performs the best in all domains, with all types of data, and for all learning tasks [32].

Accuracy of the model is commonly used to evaluate which learning technique is more suitable for the resolution of a particular problem. Nevertheless, other features are also desirable in supervised machine learning over different

© Springer Nature Switzerland AG 2018
F. Castro et al. (Eds.): MICAI 2017, LNAI 10632, pp. 3–16, 2018.
https://doi.org/10.1007/978-3-030-02837-4_1

domains and applications. For example, from the user perspective, the lack of comprehensibility is a major issue for adoption of a medical diagnosis system [13].

No technique is capable to tackle every supervised learning task, and it is difficult to comply with all possible desirable features of each particular domain. However, it is necessary to have versatile machine learning techniques with the ability to solve a great diversity of problems.

The aim of this paper is to present artificial hydrocarbon networks (AHN) as a versatile and efficient supervised machine learning technique. We are considering the versatility of a supervised learning technique regarding the use: (i) in different domains, (ii) with different data-sources, and (iii) for different learning tasks. In order to show the versatility and efficiency of AHN, we reviewed six notable applications of artificial hydrocarbon networks already reported in literature. We compared AHN with other most commonly used supervised learning techniques with the purpose of identifying its strengths and weaknesses. The comparison includes: decision trees, neural networks, naïve Bayes, k-nearest neighbors and support vector machines. We revise seven desirable features of supervised learning methods in comparison with those of AHN, namely accuracy, tolerance to missing values, tolerance to noise, variety of attributes, regression, classification and interpretability.

The rest of the paper is as follows. Section 2 discusses related work in supervised machine learning. A brief description of artificial hydrocarbon networks technique is presented in Sect. 3. The analysis of six applications of artificial hydrocarbon networks for classification and regression tasks is presented in Sect. 4. We discuss the results in Sect. 5. Conclusions and directions for future research are described in Sect. 6.

2 Features of Supervised Learning Methods

Although the selection of learning algorithm given a classification or regression task, is often based on the empirical comparison in terms of accuracy, other features of the techniques must be taken into account for particular applications. Most commonly highlighted properties in literature are: robustness in terms of accuracy and precision [31]; tolerance to missing values, noise, and irrelevant values; interpretability; speed of learning; dealing with different types of attributes; dealing with overfitting [8].

In sensor-based applications, noise and missing values in input features can be found due to different causes. Sensors can be broken, switched off, miscalibrated or misplaced. These issues make it difficult to obtain accurate models for real problems [14]. Robustness of machine learning techniques capable of dealing with noisy data is very important for sensor-based applications.

Interpretability, also called comprehensibility, is a very important requirement in decision support systems mainly when the consequences of errors are critical, for example in financial or medical domains. If the expert does not understand how the model is making its prediction, he/she will not trust the system.

The users will not rely in the application, and will therefore be reluctant to use it [13].

It is well known that there is often a trade-off between predictive power, speed of learning, and comprehensibility. Neural networks and support vector machines are more accurate in general, but also more time consuming when classifying [8,27]. Decision trees and rule-based classifiers are less accurate, but more interpretable and easier to understand by experts [5,13]. Naïve Bayes is less accurate, but quicker [8,27]. Therefore, it is important that a new technique comply with the most requirements and desirable features of as many domains and learning tasks as possible. It is important that a supervised learning technique is versatile.

Versatility in literature can be considered regarding different aspects. In [12], the author referred to versatility of deep learning having many potential applications in biomedicine. Tsochantaridis *et al.* [28] proved that their method to generalize multiclass support vector machine learning is versatile reporting results on a number of learning tasks in different problems. Grinke *et al.* [6] considered versatility in terms of the adaptive behaviors of complex robots generated by their neural mechanisms. These are just some examples of the great diversity of approaches to consider versatility in the machine learning community.

We considered that a supervised learning technique is versatile, when it is able to function effectively in different domains, with different data-sources, and for different learning tasks.

3 Artificial Hydrocarbon Networks

Artificial hydrocarbon networks (AHN) is a supervised learning method inspired on the structure and the inner chemical mechanisms of organic molecules [25]. This method was firstly proposed by Ponce and Ponce [22] as an implementation of their more general technique namely artificial organic networks (AON) [25].

Figure 1 shows a graphical interpretation of artificial hydrocarbon networks. In a nutshell, the purpose of the AHN method is to package information, from a set of instances, in basic units known as *molecules*. These molecules –composed of hydrogen and carbon atoms– are described by nonlinear functions, and they can be related among them using chemical heuristics resulting in complex units of information so-called *compounds*. Moreover, a set of compounds can be combined together, linearly, producing *mixtures*. To this end, the mixture constitutes a model [25].

3.1 Overview of the Learning Algorithm

Given an input vector $x \in \mathbb{R}^n$ of n features, a molecule φ_k is defined as (1); where, k is the order of the molecule (e.g. the number of hydrogen atoms attached), $\sigma_r \in \mathbb{R}$ is called the carbon value, and $H_i \in \mathbb{C}^n$ is a vector representing the ith hydrogen atom attached [25,26]. Thus, the graph-model of a molecule in AHN

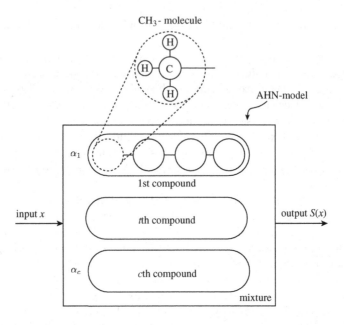

Fig. 1. Diagram example of artificial hydrocarbon networks.

is represented by up to four hydrogen atoms and one carbon atom (Fig. 1).

$$\varphi_k(x) = \sum_{r=1}^{n} \sigma_r \prod_{i=1}^{k \leq 4} (x_r - H_{i,r}) \tag{1}$$

Two or more unsaturated molecules, e.g. $k < 4$, can be joined together forming a compound $\psi_t(x; \varphi_{k_1}^{(1)}, \ldots, \varphi_{k_m}^{(m)})$ of m molecules, as shown in Fig. 2. Different approaches have been implemented for a compound [23, 25, 26]. One of the most used implementations is the linear and saturated hydrocarbon compound [24] strategy. This strategy assumes that all molecules in the compound are of order $k = 2$, except the first and last molecules with $k = 3$, shaping a chain of molecules $\varphi_{k_j}^{(j)}$ with full hydrogen values. Thus, a linear and saturated hydrocarbon compound ψ_t is expressed as (2); where, $\Sigma_j = \{x | \arg\min_j(x - \mu_j) = j\}$ represents that an input x belongs to the domain of the jth molecule, and $\mu_j \in \mathbb{R}^n$ is the center of the jth molecule [25].

$$\psi_t(x) = \begin{cases} \varphi_3^{(1)}(x) & x \in \Sigma_1 \\ \varphi_2^{(2)}(x) & x \in \Sigma_2 \\ \ldots & \ldots \\ \varphi_2^{(m-1)}(x) & x \in \Sigma_{m-1} \\ \varphi_3^{(m)}(x) & x \in \Sigma_m \end{cases} \tag{2}$$

As reported in [25, 26], the center of molecules μ_j are calculated using a chemical heuristic that allows to determine the distance between molecules, e.g.

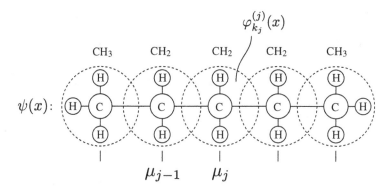

Fig. 2. Graph-model representation of a hydrocarbon compound.

intermolecular distances, based on the error of the estimates in molecules. First, the molecular parameters σ_r and H_i of the m molecules are computed using the least squares estimates (LSE) method, also storing the error produced by each molecule, E_j. At each step of the learning method, the centers μ_j are then updated by applying the gradient descendent method with rule (3) [25]; where, $0 < \eta < 1$ is the learning rate. $E_0 = 0$ is employed as the initial condition.

$$\mu_j = \mu_j - \eta(E_{j-1} - E_j) \tag{3}$$

Finally, a set of c compounds can be mixed up in definite ratios so-called *stoichiometric coefficients* or simply weights, $\alpha_t \in \mathbb{R}$, resulting in a mixture $S(x; \psi_1, \ldots, \psi_c)$ as shown in (4) [25,26].

$$S(x) = \sum_{t=1}^{c} \alpha_t \psi_t(x) \tag{4}$$

Different modifications to the AHN-algorithm have been proposed [18,24–26]. For illustrative purposes, we select Algorithm 1 to show the simple learning method of AHN [26]. A full description of the method can be found in [25], and a numerical example for computing the AHN-algorithm can be found in [20].

4   AHN for Supervised Learning

In this section, we review six notable applications of artificial hydrocarbon networks reported in literature. Particularly, we aim to highlight the versatility of AHN in terms of: (i) different domains, (ii) different data-sources, and (iii) different learning tasks. Table 1 summarizes the description of each application related to these versatility criteria, and Table 2 shows the summary of the metrics reported in the applications.

Table 1. Related versatility criteria of the reported applications.

Case number	Problem domain	Source data	Learning task
4.1	Audio filtering	Audio signals	Regression & clustering
4.2	Online sales predictions	Consumer information	Regression & prediction
4.3	Face recognition	Images	Classification & feature extraction
4.4	Human activity recognition	Sensor signals	Classification
4.5	Robotics control	Controlled variables	Regression & inference
4.6	Breast cancer diagnosis	Tissue properties	Classification & interpretation

Table 2. Summary of the metrics reported in the applications.

Case number	Metrics
4.1	AHN-filter: 2.33 (recording), 8.39 (mic), 6.13 (mobile) SNR
	FIR-filter: 0.86 (recording), 1.45 (mic), 1.92 (mobile) SNR
4.2	AHN: 5,828 RMSE
	Cubic splines: 5,870 RMSE
	Model trees: 5,995 RMSE
	Neural networks: 6,323 RMSE
	Random forest: 6,439 RMSE
4.3	AHN: 90% accuracy (no comparison)
4.4	AHN: 99.49% accuracy
	Deep learning: 99.27% accuracy
	Random forest: 98.72% accuracy
	Decision trees: 97.99% accuracy
	Neural networks: 92.58% accuracy
4.5	AHN-controller: 5.0° error in steady-state (noise)
	Type II Mamdani-controller: 5.5° error in steady-state (noise)
4.6	AHN: 97.85% accuracy, medium interpretability
	Neural networks: 95.33% accuracy, low interpretability
	Support vector machines: 98.09% accuracy, low interpretability
	Decision trees: 69.23% accuracy, high interpretability
	Rule-based: 95.00% accuracy, high interpretability

Algorithm 1. Simple AHN-algorithm

Input: data tuples $(x_1, \ldots, x_n, y)$, number of molecules m, number of compounds c and learning rate η
Output: molecular parameters $\{H, \sigma, \mu\}$ and weights of compounds α

for $t = 1$ **to** c **do**
$\quad \psi_t(x) \leftarrow$ initialize a m-molecule compound
$\quad \mu_j \leftarrow$ randomly generate a set of molecular centers
$\quad$ **while** not reach a stop criterion **do**
$\quad\quad \Sigma_j \leftarrow$ do a partition of the input x using μ_j
$\quad\quad$ **for** $j = 1$ **to** m **do**
$\quad\quad\quad \{H_j, \sigma_j\} \leftarrow$ using LSE of $\varphi_{k_j}^{(j)}(x)$ with $x \in \Sigma_j$
$\quad\quad\quad E_j \leftarrow$ calculate the error between $\varphi_{k_j}^{(j)}(x)$ and $y \in \Sigma_j$
$\quad\quad$ **end for**
$\quad\quad \mu_j \leftarrow \mu_j - \eta(E_{j-1} - E_j)$
$\quad$ **end while**
$\quad \psi_t(x) \leftarrow$ update the compound using all $\varphi_{k_j}^{(j)}(x)$, H_j, σ_j and μ_j
end for
$\alpha_t \leftarrow$ using LSE over $\sum_{t=1}^{c} \alpha_t \psi_t(x)$ with all $\psi_t(x)$
return $\{H, \sigma, \alpha, \mu\}$

4.1 Audio Filtering

A major problem in audio signal applications is the addition of noise that interfere with the original signal resulting in poor performance of audio. As a consequence, it causes non-intelligibility of audio, from the perspective of human ears, and imprecise data information that pollutes important features in audio signals. Thus, a tradeoff between noise supresion and signal distortion should be done. Different approaches and techniques have been proposed, such as [4,30]: analog filters, digital linear filters, digital nonlinear filters, digital adaptive nonlinear filters, among others.

In [24], authors propose an adaptive artificial hydrocarbon network as a digital audio filter. The methodology of the proposal is as follows. First, a noisy audio signal is divided in batches with fixed window size. Each batch or window is also divided in n non-fixed size partitions which are, indeed, determined by an artificial hydrocarbon network. Actually, each molecule in AHN represents a partition in the fixed batch. Three experiments were conducted in both artificial and real noisy audio signals. Authors reported better performance of the adaptive AHN in comparison with a classical finite impulse response (FIR) filter, widely employed in audio denoising. The signal-to-noise ratio (SNR) value was measured. In the three experiments, the AHN-filter resulted better for SNR $(2.33, 8.39$ and $6.13)$ in contrast with the FIR-filter $(0.86, 1.45$ and $1.92)$ [24]. It can be concluded that the AHN-filter denoise audio signals in a better way (Tables 1 and 2).

4.2   Online Sales Prediction

Online retail sales prediction and online advertising have become very important for decision-making on pricing, advertising responsiveness, product demand, among others [3]. Predict the number of sales promotes an effective planning of all business processes. However, historical data of online sales can contain uncertain and imprecise data. In order to overcome the above problem, game theory, simulation and statistical methods have been used to predict online sales. In particular, simulation methods are based on supervised learning models proving effectiveness. For example, Ponce *et al.* [19] proposed a predictive model based on artificial hydrocarbon networks for monthly online sales using a data set of consumer products. Twelve AHN-models were developed, one per month. For experimentation, 70% of data were used for training and 30% for testing. Results reported in their work validated that the AHN-models reached the less root-mean squared error (RMSE) metric in comparison with other ten supervised machine learning methods employed as benchmark. Actually, AHN, cubic-splines, model-trees, Bayesian neural networks and random forests ranked in the top five –in this particular order– of the analysis [19]. See Table 1 for details on the versatility of AHN in online retail sales prediction.

4.3   Face Recognition

Face recognition is a challenging problem in computer vision due to position, illumination, environmental and instrumental noise, pose, etc. that affect the performance of algorithms [29]. Several face recognition algorithms have been proposed in literature, for example: background removal, illumination normalization, artificial neural networks, discrete cosine transform, and others. But in practice, the above variables draw undesirable performance in methods.

In [25], the authors proposed a face recognition system based on the metadata of artificial hydrocarbon networks aiming to minimize timing of feature matching when using discrete cosine transform as the basis of the feature extraction process. In a nutshell, the methodology considers to firstly pre-process RGB-color images by transforming them into grayscale images. Then, the discrete cosine transform (DCT) is computed in order to extract values that represent the image. Later on, a set of these values (corresponding to images of a given subject in different poses) is used to train an artificial hydrocarbon network. Metadata of AHN, such as centers as well as lower and upper bounds of molecules, are stored and treated as features of the subject. Lastly, given a new unknown image, a feature extraction based on the latter methodology is obtained and compared with the stored features. Applying simple matching algorithms such as the Euclidean classifier, a subject is identified. Authors reported 90% of accuracy in the AHN-based face recognition system when using a dataset of 10 different subjects in 5 poses [25]. A summary of the versatility details of this case is shown in Tables 1 and 2.

4.4 Human Activity Recognition

Derived from the great advances in wearable sensors and the common use of smartphones, physical human activity recognition (HAR) based on sensors is a growing area of interest [7,20]. Monitoring personal activities results in various applications to deliver proactive and personalized services: pervasive and mobile computing, surveillance-based security, context-aware computing, health and ambient assistive living, among others [1]. Current research in human activity recognition based on sensors considers several issues. For instance, noise in data, imprecise activity labeling, support new users and variations of the same subject in a user-specific approach, handle new or irrelevant activities, are common problems in HAR. Thus, different approaches have been proposed to tackle this problem.

In [18] and [20], authors proposed the usage of artificial hydrocarbon networks as a flexible and suitable approach for physical activity recognition using wearable sensors. The proposed methodology considered the following steps: obtain all sensor signals in the wearable device, pre-process signals in windows of fixed size, extract features, reduce the number of features, detect unknown activities, train and build activity AHN-models, and use AHN-models for activity classification. The AHN-classifier was compared with different supervised machine learning methods. Results reported in the work proved that the HAR classifier with artificial hydrocarbon networks performs statistically equal to a HAR classifier with deep learning. At last, the work reported that AHN-classifier performed high accuracy (99.49%) when performing with different users and in different activity performance [20] (Table 2).

4.5 Intelligent Control Systems for Robotics

Navigation of mobile robots is still a challenging problem [2]. Particularly, uncertain and dynamical environments push robots to be adaptable and robust for dealing with these circumstances. Different control strategies have been proposed in literature. Precisely, intelligent control has been considered in those robotics problems: fuzzy controllers, neuro-fuzzy controllers, support vector machines-based controllers, nature-inspired controllers, etc. [11,16]. Additionally, minimizing the number of sensors is also an issue in mobile robots. For instance, vision-based robotics systems are the most promising efforts when dealing with sensor minimization. In that sense, authors in [21] proposed an artificial organic controller with optical flow feedback for mobile robot navigation. The proposed system considered a closed-loop control system in which the control law was performed with an ensemble of fuzzy inference systems and artificial hydrocarbon networks, and the feedback loop was implemented with a vision-based system that computes the relative velocity of objects in image sequences.

The proposed ensemble of fuzzy inference systems and artificial hydrocarbon networks, namely fuzzy-molecular inference system (FMI) [21,23], has been implemented for intelligent control that deals with uncertain and imprecise data. Results reported in literature have proved that FMI-based controllers perform slightly better and with less computational resources than type-II fuzzy controllers [23]. In terms of the mobile robot navigation, results showed that the FMI performs well for dynamical object avoidance [21]. Thus, hybridization of AHN with other techniques improves the quality of responses in a given domain. Table 1 shows the versatility characterization of this domain and the performance reported is shown in Table 2.

4.6 Breast Cancer Detection and Interpretation

Support decision systems are very important in the medical application domain. Typically, experts in the field must rely in the computer system to support critical decisions. A key issue in those systems is the interpretability or comprehensibility of the model in order to understand the underlying decision process [9,10]. If the clinician does not undertand it, then it will be difficult to trust in the system. Then, most medical systems are designed to be interpretable as well as accurate.

For instance, in [17], authors proposed a breast cancer classifier based on artificial hydrocarbon networks and a methodology to deliver interpretable models using AHN. Their proposal considered to build the AHN-model using a training data set of tissue samples. Results showed that the AHN-model can be converted into a binary tree that produces a set of rules, easily to read and understand. The accuracy reported falls in 97.8% which is very competitive with other blackbox-like machine learning classifiers (e.g. 91.8% mean accuracy) built for the same data set [17] (see Table 2).

Table 3. Comparative chart of supervised learning methods. Symbols: ($\checkmark$) = lowest, ($\checkmark\checkmark$) = medium and ($\checkmark\checkmark\checkmark$) = highest satisfaction.

Features	AHN	DT	NN	NB	kNN	SVM
Accuracy	$\checkmark\checkmark\checkmark$	$\checkmark\checkmark$	$\checkmark\checkmark\checkmark$	$\checkmark$	$\checkmark\checkmark$	$\checkmark\checkmark\checkmark$
Tolerance (missing values)	$\checkmark$	$\checkmark\checkmark\checkmark$	$\checkmark$	$\checkmark\checkmark\checkmark$	$\checkmark$	$\checkmark\checkmark$
Tolerance (noise)	$\checkmark\checkmark\checkmark$	$\checkmark\checkmark$	$\checkmark\checkmark$	$\checkmark\checkmark\checkmark$	$\checkmark$	$\checkmark\checkmark$
Variety of attributes	$\checkmark\checkmark$	$\checkmark\checkmark\checkmark$	$\checkmark\checkmark$	$\checkmark\checkmark$	$\checkmark\checkmark$	$\checkmark\checkmark$
Regression	$\checkmark\checkmark\checkmark$	$\checkmark$	$\checkmark\checkmark$	$\checkmark$	$\checkmark\checkmark$	$\checkmark\checkmark$
Classification	$\checkmark\checkmark\checkmark$	$\checkmark\checkmark\checkmark$	$\checkmark\checkmark\checkmark$	$\checkmark\checkmark\checkmark$	$\checkmark\checkmark$	$\checkmark\checkmark\checkmark$
Interpretability	$\checkmark\checkmark$	$\checkmark\checkmark\checkmark$	$\checkmark$	$\checkmark\checkmark\checkmark$	$\checkmark\checkmark$	$\checkmark$

5 Discussion

In terms of the versatility criteria depicted in Table 1, it can be seen that artificial hydrocarbon networks can be used for different problem domains, with different data-sources and for different learning tasks. Although the AHN-models, built for the cases reviewed above, report high performance and accuracy, they depend on the specific requirements of domains. For example, offline intelligent systems are suitable for breast cancer diagnosis or face recognition in which pre-processing data and training time are not issues. But domains such as human activity recognition demand online and real-time intelligent systems in which artificial hydrocarbon networks have limitations, as reported in [20]. Besides, Table 1 summarizes different data-sources used in AHN. It should be noted that in most of the domains, pre-processing and/or feature extraction are required beforehand, like image and signal processing. To this end, artificial hydrocarbon networks can perform different learning tasks (Table 1). In [25], authors report that this method is mainly for regression tasks. However, tasks like classification, clustering, prediction and feature extraction are also well handled by artificial hydrocarbon networks.

We also compared AHN with other supervised learning methods: decision trees (DT), neural networks (NN), naïve Bayes (NB), k-nearest neighbors (kNN) and support vector machines (SVM). Based on theoretical and empirical studies [8,25], Table 3 compares features in supervised learning methods. Seven features were considered: accuracy, tolerance to missing values, tolerance noise, variety of attributes, regression, classification and interpretability.

Particularly to artificial hydrocarbon networks, accuracy is highly performed in different domains, as shown in Sect. 4. However, this accuracy is very dependent to the optimal choice of hyper-parameters (i.e. number of molecules, number of compounds, learning rate). Literature reports the usage of cross-validation in AHN to increase accuracy [18–20]. Other supervised learning methods with high accuracy are neural networks and support vector machines. In terms of tolerance, AHN is very suitable when handling noisy data, as explained in several works [18,24,25]. In general, naïve Bayes is tolerant as well (see Table 3). Nevertheless, AHN is poorly tolerant to missing values, but it can be afforded using pre-processing techniques as in [19].

Considering variety of attributes as handling discrete, binary and continuous data, Table 3 shows that decision trees is the best method for using different attributes. For instance, AHN is better for continuous data [25], NN, SVM and kNN do not consider discrete data, and naïve Bayes is not suitable for continuous data [8]. On the other hand, artificial hydrocarbon networks is mainly designed for regression purposes, as explained before. But, classification is also performed well as shown in Table 2. As noted in Table 3, AHN is the only method that ranks highest in both regression and classification.

Analyzing the above features and looking closer to the learning algorithm (see Sect. 3), AHN presents similarities with neural networks and support vector machines. However, AHN has interpretability as an additional feature that NN and SVM do not. Although interpretability in AHN is currently being studied, previous works suggests that artificial hydrocarbon networks can be converted into binary trees or list of rules [17]. If this interpretability is theoretically proved, then AHN will also be similar to decision trees.

Finally, artificial hydrocarbon networks fulfills different features desired in supervised machine learning over different domains and data-sources, but also performs different learning tasks as regression, classification and even clustering (Table 1). Thus, AHN reveals versatility for supervised learning.

6 Conclusions

In this paper, we presented artificial hydrocarbon networks as a versatile and efficient supervised learning method. We determined the ability of AHN to solve different problem domains, with different data-sources and to learn different tasks. The analysis considered six applications in which AHN was successfully applied. We also compared artificial hydrocarbon networks with other classical supervised learning methods, concluding that AHN performs different learning tasks such as regression, classification and clustering.

As discussed earlier, interpretability and tolerance to missing values should be key future research directions on artificial hydrocarbon networks. But also, the ability to handle a huge amount of data and to implement online and real-time intelligent systems should be improved as well.

References

1. Avci, A., Bosch, S., Marin-Perianu, M., Marin-Periauni, R., Havinga, P.: Activity recognition using inertial sensing for healthcare, wellbeing and sports applications. In: 23rd International Conference on Architecture of Computing Systems, pp. 1–10 (2010)
2. Barrera, A.: Mobile Robots Navigation. InTechOpen, London (2010)
3. Beheshti-Kashi, S., Karimi, H.R., Thoben, K.D., Lutjen, M., Teucke, M.: A survey on retail sales forecasting and prediction in fashion markets. Syst. Sci. Control. Eng.: Open Access J. 3(1), 154–161 (2015)
4. Diniz, P.S.R.: Adaptive Filtering Algorithms and Practical Implementation. Springer, New York (2008). https://doi.org/10.1007/978-1-4614-4106-9
5. Freitas, A.A.: Comprehensible classification models: a position paper. ACM SIGKDD Explor. Newsl. 15(1), 1–10 (2014)
6. Grinke, E., Tetzlaff, C., Wörgötter, F., Manoonpong, P.: Synaptic plasticity in a recurrent neural network for versatile and adaptive behaviors of a walking robot. Front. Neurorobotics 9(11), 1–15 (2015)
7. Kim, E., Helal, S., Cook, D.: Human activity recognition and pattern discovery. IEEE Pervasive Comput. 9, 48–53 (2010)
8. Kotsiantis, S.B., Sotiris, B., Zaharakis, I., Pintelas, P.: Supervised machine learning: a review of classification techniques. In: Proceedings of the 2007 Conference on Emerging Artificial Intelligence Applications in Computer Engineering, pp. 3–24 (2007)
9. Letham, B., Rudin, C.: Interpretable classifiers using rules and Bayesian analysis: building a better stroke prediction model. Technical report 609, Department of Statistics, University of Washington, August 2013
10. Letham, B., Rudin, C., MacCormick, T.H., Madigan, D.: An interpretable stroke prediction model using rules and Bayesian analysis. In: 27th AAAI Conference on Artificial Intelligence, pp. 65–67. MIT (2013)

11. Llorca, D., et al.: Autonomous pedestrian collision avoidance using a fuzzy steering controller. IEEE Trans. Intell. Transp. Syst. **12**(2), 390–401 (2011)
12. Mamoshina, P., Vieira, A., Putin, E., Zhavoronkov, A.: Applications of deep learning in biomedicine. Mol. Pharm. **13**(5), 1445–1454 (2016)
13. Martens, D., Vanthienen, J., Verbeke, W., Baesens, B.: Performance of classification models from a user perspective. Decis. Support Syst. **51**(4), 782–793 (2011)
14. Nettleton, D.F., Orriols-Puig, A., Fornells, A.: A study of the effect of different types of noise on the precision of supervised learning techniques. Artif. Intell. Rev. **33**, 275–306 (2010)
15. Palmer, J., Chakravrty, A.: Supervised machine learning, Chap. 15, pp. 231–246. Wiley (2015)
16. Ponce Espinosa, H.E. (ed.): Nature-Inspired Computing for Control Systems. SSDC, vol. 40. Springer, Cham (2016). https://doi.org/10.1007/978-3-319-26230-7
17. Ponce, H., Martínez-Villasenor, M.L.: Interpretability of artificial hydrocarbon networks for breast cancer classification. In: 2017 International Joint Conference on Neural Networks, pp. 3535–3542. IEEE (2017)
18. Ponce, H., Martínez-Villasenor, M.L., Miralles-Pechuán, L.: A novel wearable sensor-based human activity recognition approach using artificial hydrocarbon networks. Sensors **16**(7), 1033 (2016)
19. Ponce, H., Miralles-Pechúan, L., de Lourdes Martínez-Villaseñor, M.: Artificial hydrocarbon networks for online sales prediction. In: Lagunas, O.P., Alcántara, O.H., Figueroa, G.A. (eds.) MICAI 2015. LNCS (LNAI), vol. 9414, pp. 498–508. Springer, Cham (2015). https://doi.org/10.1007/978-3-319-27101-9_38
20. Ponce, H., Miralles-Pechuán, L., Martínez-Villasenor, M.L.: A flexible approach for human activity recognition using artificial hydrocarbon networks. Sensors **16**(11), 1715 (2016)
21. Ponce, H., Moya-Albor, E., Brieva, J.: A novel artificial organic controller with hermite optical flow feedback for mobile robot navigation, Chap. 6, pp. 145–169. InTechOpen (2016)
22. Ponce, H., Ponce, P.: Artificial organic networks. In: 2011 IEEE Conference on Electronics, Robotics and Automotive Mechanics, pp. 29–34. IEEE (2011)
23. Ponce, H., Ponce, P., Molina, A.: Artificial hydrocarbon networks fuzzy inference system. Math. Probl. Eng. **2013**, 13 (2013)
24. Ponce, H., Ponce, P., Molina, A.: Adaptive noise filtering based on artificial hydrocarbon networks: an application to audio signals. Expert. Syst. Appl. **41**(14), 6512–6523 (2014)
25. Ponce-Espinosa, H., Ponce-Cruz, P., Molina, A.: Artificial Organic Networks: Artificial Intelligence Based on Carbon Networks. Studies in Computational Intelligence, vol. 521. Springer, Cham (2014). https://doi.org/10.1007/978-3-319-02472-1
26. Ponce, H., Ponce, P., Molina, A.: The development of an artificial organic networks toolkit for LabVIEW. J. Comput. Chem. **36**(7), 478–492 (2015)
27. Singh, Y., Bhatia, P.K., Sangwan, O.: A review of studies on machine learning techniques. Int. J. Comput. Sci. Secur. **1**(1), 70–84 (2007)
28. Tsochantaridis, I., Hofmann, T., Joachims, T., Altun, Y.: Support vector machine learning for interdependent and structured output spaces. In: Proceedings of the 21st International Conference on Machine Learning ICML 2004, pp. 104–111 (2004)
29. Varadarajan, K.K., Suhasini, P.R., Manikantan, K., Ramachandran, S.: Face recognition using block based feature extraction with CZT and Goertzel-algorithm as a preprocessing technique. Procedia Comput. Sci. **46**, 1458–1467 (2015)
30. Winder, S.: Analog and Digital Filter Design. Newnes/ElsevierScience, Woburn (2002)

31. Witten, I.H., Frank, E., Hall, M.A., Pal, C.J.: Data Mining: Practical Machine Learning Tools and Techniques. Morgan Kaufmann, Burlington (2016)
32. Wolpert, D.H.: The supervised learning no-free-lunch theorems. In: World Conference on Soft Computing (2001)

Human Activity Recognition on Mobile Devices Using Artificial Hydrocarbon Networks

Hiram Ponce[1]([✉]), Guillermo González[1], Luis Miralles-Pechuán[2],
and Ma Lourdes Martínez-Villaseñor[1]

[1] Facultad de Ingeniería, Universidad Panamericana,
Augusto Rodin 498, 03920 Mexico City, Mexico
{hponce,0147901,lmartine}@up.edu.mx
[2] Centre for Applied Data Analytics Research (CeADAR),
University College Dublin, Belfield, Dublin 4, Ireland
luis.miralles@ucd.ie

Abstract. Human activity recognition (HAR) aims to classify and identify activities based on data-driven from different devices, such as sensors
or cameras. Particularly, mobile devices have been used for this recognition task. However, versatility of users, location of smartphones, battery,
processing and storage limitations, among other issues have been identified. In that sense, this paper presents a human activity recognition
system based on artificial hydrocarbon networks. This technique have
been proved to be very effective on HAR systems using wearable sensors, so the present work proposes to use this learning method with the
information provided by the in-sensors of mobile devices. Preliminary
results proved that artificial hydrocarbon networks might be used as an
alternative for human activity recognition on mobile devices. In addition,
a real dataset created for this work has been published.

Keywords: Artificial organic networks · Human activity recognition
Classification · Machine learning · Sensors · Mobile

1 Introduction

In recent years, mobile and biometric technology has grown and intertwined
with people lives. We increasingly rely on mobile devices and sensors that we
carry around at all times, they offer valuable information and commodities in
an instant. This growing potential has been exploited in areas such as entertain-
ment, productivity and even health. These new technologies have introduced
the possibility of developing and testing more efficient and robust human activity recognition algorithms and techniques [5]. The human activity recognition
or HAR process aims to classify and identify activities based on collected data
from different devices such as sensors or cameras, this data is interpreted with
different pattern recognition techniques [8].

© Springer Nature Switzerland AG 2018
F. Castro et al. (Eds.): MICAI 2017, LNAI 10632, pp. 17–29, 2018.
https://doi.org/10.1007/978-3-030-02837-4_2

The true importance of HAR comes from all of its uses in different areas. Examples of this are patient monitoring for adequate treatment and health monitoring, health risks during a certain activity or even security. Complex activity recognition is still an open research area that offers many challenges involving the intricate patterns generated and the techniques used for their recognition.

There are multiple ways to recognize human activities, involving vision and image data or sensor data. When the activity recognition is based on visual data, images are collected through cameras and are later processed to highlight interesting features that will help with pattern recognition. The other type of recognition is based on sensor data, this type of HAR is divided in wearable sensors and mobile device's sensors. While wearable sensors might offer a more detailed and accurate measurement, mobile devices are the more widespread and affordable solution and offer a complete package of sensors and communication capabilities. The almost ubiquitous use of smartphones, unobstruviness, and ease of usability provide a perfect platform for data recollection for HAR purposes.

Recently, authors in [12,13] have proved the usage of artificial hydrocarbon networks (AHN) – a supervised learning method inspired on the structure and the inner chemical mechanisms of organic molecules – in human activity recognition systems using wearable sensors. This learning method contributed to perform high accurate models to recognize activities even in presence of noise (in both environmental and sensor miscallibration). Moreover, in these studies, artificial hydrocarbon networks have been proved to be statistically similar to the output response of deep learning approaches, and with less computational efforts. However, AHN has not been proved to be efficient in mobile devices with unique sensor location in human bodies.

In that sense, this work aims to propose the implementation of a human activity recognition system, for mobile devices, using artificial hydrocarbon networks. The methodology follows three steps: data collection, AHN-model training, and HAR system testing. In addition, the contribution of this paper considers: (i) a new public dataset for the HAR community using mobile devices, and (ii) the exploration of artificial hydrocarbon networks to accurately classify human activities from data-driven collected by mobile devices.

The rest of the paper is as follows. Section 2 gives a general explanation of the related work. Section 3 further explains the artificial hydrocarbon networks method. Section 4 describes the methodology proposed in this work, and Sect. 5 presents and discusses preliminary results. Finally, Sect. 6 concludes the paper and discusses future work.

2   Related Work

Interest in human activity recognition systems and applications has been growing since 1980. Traditionally research in this area is done with two main approaches: vision based and sensor based.

In vision based activity recognition, RGB cameras, motion capture systems, and more recently range or depth sensors are used for activity recognition. Each of these modalities has pros and cons [3]. RGB video and depth cameras are easy to use, cost effective, and provide rich information. Nevertheless, when using cameras subject has to be in the field of view, algorithms to analyze image sequences are computationally expensive, and depending on the type of camera, they might be sensitive to lighting and illumination conditions, or require calibration.

Wearable sensors are also available and cost effective, and they can provide vast information working anywhere. However the main issues of this approach are that subjects must wear the sensors for extended time, obtrusiveness, location of the sensors, and energy consumption [8].

In recent years, mobile phone has become the perfect platform for data recollection given the ubiquity and ease of use of these devices. Activity recognition from smartphone sensors information is unobtrusive, doesn't require installation nor calibration, and it does not disturb or limit the persons activities [5]. Activity recognition with smartphones has drawbacks also: battery, processing and storage limitations, and user behavior are the most frequently mentioned.

Recent works [22,23] show that supervised and unsupervised classification techniques have been used for HAR purposes with smartphones. Similarly, these techniques have also been used in wearable sensors approaches [18]. It is difficult to compare the suitability of classification techniques for HAR being that the related works present great variability in: (a) type of model to be analyzed, (b) recollection method, (c) subjects used, (d) activities considered, (e) type, location and orientation of sensors or devices, (f) feature extraction and model configurations. Public databases with large, diverse, standardized, with high quality, and good documented can help to leverage the research in HAR. These data sets will also help to perform comparisons, and determine the suitability of a classification technique for HAR.

Some databases for HAR have been published with wearable sensors information [20,24] or based on depth sensors [9]. In recent years multimodal databases have also been created and published like Berkeley MHAD dataset [11] and University of Rzeszow fall detection (URFD) dataset [7], among others. Datasets with information collected with mobile phone are also public, for example see [1,6]. Nevertheless, to our knowledge, very few datasets have been published for HAR with information collected with mobile phones. Kwapisz et al. [6] published a dataset containing data collected from accelerometers using cell phone in controlled laboratory conditions. Anguita et al. [1] presented a database recorded of 30 subjects carrying smartphones.

Although several datasets have been created, and a few have been published for all approaches, some problems and limitations with HAR data sets are still challenging. Data sets are not always publically available, standardized or clearly documented. Experimentation with some data sets are not always replicable due to unrealistic assumptions or methodology problems [10].

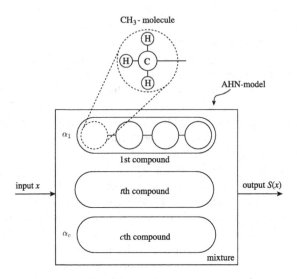

Fig. 1. Schematic of artificial hydrocarbon networks.

3   Overview of Artificial Hydrocarbon Networks

Artificial hydrocarbon networks (AHN) is a supervised learning method inspired on the structure and the inner chemical mechanisms of organic molecules [14,16], as part of a more general technique namely artificial organic networks [16]. Artificial hydrocarbon networks aims to package information, from a set of instances, in basic units known as *molecules*. These molecules, composed of hydrogen and carbon atoms, are described by nonlinear functions, and they can be related among them using chemical heuristics resulting in complex units of information so-called *compounds*. Moreover, a set of compounds can be combined together, linearly, producing *mixtures*. To this end, the mixture constitutes a model [16]. Figure 1 shows a graphical interpretation of artificial hydrocarbon networks.

Given an input vector $x \in \mathbb{R}^n$ of n features, a molecule φ_k is defined as (1); where, k is the order of the molecule (e.g. the number of hydrogen atoms attached), $\sigma_r \in \mathbb{R}$ is called the carbon value, and $H_i \in \mathbb{C}^n$ is a vector representing the ith hydrogen atom attached [16,17].

$$\varphi_k(x) = \sum_{r=1}^{n} \sigma_r \prod_{i=1}^{k \leq 4} (x_r - H_{i,r}) \qquad (1)$$

Two or more unsaturated molecules, e.g. $k < 4$, can be joined together forming a compound $\psi_t(x; \varphi_{k_1}^{(1)}, \ldots, \varphi_{k_m}^{(m)})$ of m molecules. This work proposes to use the linear and saturated hydrocarbon compound [15] strategy. It assumes that all molecules in the compound are of order $k = 2$, except the first and last molecules with $k = 3$, shaping a chain of molecules $\varphi_{k_j}^{(j)}$ with full hydrogen values. Thus, a linear and saturated hydrocarbon compound ψ_t is expressed as (2);

where, $\Sigma_j = \{x \mid \arg\min_j(x - \mu_j) = j\}$ represents that an input x belongs to the domain of the jth molecule, and $\mu_j \in \mathbb{R}^n$ is the center of the jth molecule [16].

$$\psi_t(x) = \begin{cases} \varphi_3^{(1)}(x) & x \in \Sigma_1 \\ \varphi_2^{(2)}(x) & x \in \Sigma_2 \\ \dots & \dots \\ \varphi_2^{(m-1)}(x) & x \in \Sigma_{m-1} \\ \varphi_3^{(m)}(x) & x \in \Sigma_m \end{cases} \tag{2}$$

As reported in [16,17], the center of molecules μ_j are calculated using a chemical heuristic that allows to determine the distance between molecules, e.g. intermolecular distances, based on the error of the estimates in molecules. First, the molecular parameters σ_r and H_i of the m molecules are computed using the least squares estimates (LSE) method, also storing the error produced by each molecule, E_j. At each step of the learning method, the centers μ_j are then updated by applying the gradient descendent method with rule (3) [16]; where, $0 < \eta < 1$ is the learning rate. $E_0 = 0$ is employed as the initial condition.

$$\mu_j = \mu_j - \eta(E_{j-1} - E_j) \tag{3}$$

Finally, a set of c compounds can be mixed up in definite ratios so-called *stoichiometric coefficients* or simply weights, $\alpha_t \in \mathbb{R}$, resulting in a mixture $S(x; \psi_1, \dots, \psi_c)$ as shown in (4) [16,17].

$$S(x) = \sum_{t=1}^{c} \alpha_t \psi_t(x) \tag{4}$$

Different modifications to the AHN-algorithm have been proposed [12,15–17]. In this work, we select a simple learning method of AHN [17], as shown in Algorithm 1. A full description of the method can be found in [16], and a numerical example for computing the AHN-algorithm can be found in [13].

4   Description of the Proposal

This section describes the human activity recognition system for mobile devices using AHN, and the process of data acquisition and presentation in a dataset. Lastly, it describes the implementation of the system in a real mobile device.

4.1   Artificial Hydrocarbon Networks for Human Activity Recognition

In this paper, we propose a classifier based on artificial hydrocarbon networks, or AHN-classifier for short, as a human activity recognition model. Currently, it considers two steps: training and testing.

Firstly, consider a previously collected and processed dataset (see next subsection), such that this dataset is organized in Q samples with n features of the

---

Algorithm 1. Simple AHN-algorithm

Input: data tuples $(x_1, \ldots, x_n, y)$, number of molecules m, number of compounds c and learning rate η
Output: molecular parameters $\{H, \sigma, \mu\}$ and weights of compounds α

for $t = 1$ **to** c **do**
    $\psi_t(x) \leftarrow$ initialize a m-molecule compound
    $\mu_j \leftarrow$ randomly generate a set of molecular centers
    while not reach a stop criterion **do**
        $\Sigma_j \leftarrow$ do a partition of the input x using μ_j
        for $j = 1$ **to** m **do**
            $\{H_j, \sigma_j\} \leftarrow$ using LSE of $\varphi_{k_j}^{(j)}(x)$ with $x \in \Sigma_j$
            $E_j \leftarrow$ calculate the error between $\varphi_{k_j}^{(j)}(x)$ and $y \in \Sigma_j$
        end for
        $\mu_j \leftarrow \mu_j - \eta(E_{j-1} - E_j)$
    end while
    $\psi_t(x) \leftarrow$ update the compound using all $\varphi_{k_j}^{(j)}(x)$, H_j, σ_j and μ_j
end for
$\alpha_t \leftarrow$ using LSE over $\sum_{t=1}^{c} \alpha_t \psi_t(x)$ with all $\psi_t(x)$
return $\{H, \sigma, \alpha, \mu\}$

---

form x_i for all $i = 1, \ldots, n$, and each sample with an associated label y_j representing the j-th activity in the set of all possible human activities, Y, for all $j = 1, \ldots, J$; where J is the number of different activities to be recognized by the system. Thus, each sample of the dataset is form as $(x_1, \ldots, x_n, y_j)^q, \forall q = 1, \ldots, Q$. It is remarkable to say that this work does not support unknown activities.

In the training phase, the artificial hydrocarbon networks based classifier is proposed to have the same number of molecules m that the number of different activities J, such that $m = J$. Then, one saturated and linear compound is used for this model, i.e. the number of compounds $c = 1$. Algorithm 1 is set with these attributes, as well as the learning rate $0 < \eta < 1$ is set manually. To this end, the training data Σ considers a random subset of the dataset. The remaining data samples are collected in the testing set.

Once the AHN-algorithm ends to train the AHN-classifier, the testing phase considers to validate that the obtained model classifies with high accuracy. In that sense, the testing set is used to compute the estimated output values $\hat{y}$, and accuracy and F-score measures are calculated. Finally, the trained AHN-classifier, ahn, is used to estimate the human activity using (5).

$$\hat{y} = ahn(x_1, \ldots, x_n) \tag{5}$$

Table 1. Example of a CSV file in the proposed dataset: X represents the number of subject, A represents the number of attempt, and Activity refers to the activity performed.

SXA_Activity.csv											
Timestamp	Accelerometer			Gyroscope			Magnetic field			Linear acc.		
	x	y	z	x	y	z	x	y	z	x	y	z
81747	−6.2	1.5	11.8	−0.6	0.4	1.3	27.5	6.8	−33.9	−3.6	−3.1	3.2
81748	−7.7	−0.6	−12.0	−0.4	0.4	−1.0	28.4	12.4	16.9	−4.1	1.2	−8.6
81749	3.9	−9.8	−1.2	1.7	2.8	−2.4	−14.5	23.9	22.0	1.8	0.6	−2.5

4.2 Description of the Dataset

We develop an original and public dataset in order to train, test and validate the AHN-classifier. The dataset was collected to be used in human activity recognition with a mobile device, and it can be accessed from GitHub[1].

The dataset is a collection of four different activities: *jumping, walking, laying-on* and *running*. These activities were performed by four subjects, so the dataset uses a personal model type [10]. Each subject performed each activity three times, and the raw sensors signals were stored in a separate CSV file. The in-sensors of the mobile employed during the activities are: 3-axis accelerometer, 3-axis gyroscope, 3-axis magnetic field, and 3-axis linear accelerometer. Table 1 shows an example of a CSV file. Tables 2 and 3 summarize the technical specifications of the mobile device and the application for retrieval purposes, and the profile of the subjects, respectively.

Each attempt was performed: for walking, laying-on and running during 5 min, and for jumping during 2 min. All activities were performed outdoors, in a plain terrain with dimensions $7 \times 5 \, m^2$, and the mobile device was located at the left pocket of the subjects' pants in vertical position. This dataset contains not-a-number (NaN) values since the application used for retrieving data does not guarantee the measurement of all sensor signals. Once the attempt ends, the information was stored in a CSV file in the internal memory. After that, the file was exported to a computer via USB cable. No other processing was done over the dataset.

4.3 Experimentation

We implement the AHN-based human activity recognition system for mobile devices in order to validate the proposal. The HAR system considers the following steps: data acquisition, windowing, feature extraction, activity model processing, and classification.

For this implementation, we used the public dataset from the previous subsection. First, we collected together all information from the four subjects in a

---

[1] HAR_Mobile dataset link: https://github.com/hiramponce/HAR_Mobile.

Table 2. Technical specifications of the mobile device.

Specification	Description
Mobile	
Model	Huawei NXT-L09
Processor	HiSilicon Kirin 950
Memory	32 GB internal with 3 GB RAM
Battery	Li-Po 4000 mAh
Application	
Application	Sensorstream IMU + GPS V1.0
Sampling frequency	5 Hz
Storage media	Internal memory

Table 3. Profile of the subjects.

Subject	Age	Gender	Height (m)	Weight (kg)
1	22	Male	1.85	75
2	28	Female	1.57	49
3	55	Male	1.75	75
4	29	Female	1.68	54

single file, and we added one column with the target value: jumping (1), laying-on (2), running (3) and walking (4). The timestamp column was omitted. We pre-processed this dataset to handle the NaN-values by replacing them with the mean value of its corresponding feature.

Then, we applied windowing over the dataset. Currently, we selected windows of 20 s in size without overlapping, i.e. 100 samples per window. Based on the state-of-the-art [2,12,13], we extracted 13 features in time domain and 8 features in frequency domain: mean, standard deviation, root mean square, variance, maximal vs. minimal amplitude, median, number of zero-crossing, skewness, kurtosis, first quartile, third quartile, interquartile range, autocorrelation, mean frequency, median frequency, root mean square frequency, entropy, Shannon spectral entropy, spectral flatness measure, mode frequency and peak frequency. To this end, a feature dataset was computed with 21 features per raw signal. In this work, feature reduction was not performed.

Lastly, we conduct different experiments regarding to compare the performance of the AHN-classifier in contrast with other 10 well-known machine learning methods [4,8,18,21]. In that sense, the following experimentation considered two steps:

– *Best model configuration.* This experiment computes the best model configuration based on each machine learning method, including the AHN-classifier. The feature dataset is partitioned in two subsets: 70% for training set and 30%

Table 4. Benchmark of the best model configuration, sorted by accuracy.

Model	Accuracy (%)	F-score (%)
Artificial hydrocarbon networks	96.65	96.41
Random forest	96.64	97.94
Multivariate adaptive regressing splines	96.64	97.77
Booted logistic regression	96.62	97.90
C5.0 decision trees	94.63	96.62
Rule-based classifier	94.63	96.62
Penalized discriminant analysis	93.96	96.11
Naive Bayes	93.29	95.19
k-nearest neighbors	89.26	92.94
Support vector machines	74.50	81.85
Artificial neural networks	51.01	–

for testing set. We use 10-fold cross-validation and 5 repetitions for training each model, and the accuracy metric is employed.

– *User-specific approach.* A new attempt from one subject is retrieved. This attempt considers to perform all the activities continuously, one per minute. Using an active learning approach, the AHN-classifier is firstly adjusted with new information from the user, in order to accurately estimate the activities. The percentage of the training set is computed to determine the minimum volume of new data required to learn the performance of this user.

It is important to notice that the classification task is performed using the voting scheme [19] which consideres to determine the mode of the estimation during several attempts. In this case, we use 3 estimations from the machine learning model before the notification to the user.

5 Results and Discussion

This section presents preliminary results of the AHN-based human activity recognition system for mobile devices.

First, the best model configuration of the AHN-classifier was built. In Table 4 is summarized the performance of the AHN-classifier and other 10 well-known machine learning based models. The accuracy and the F-score were measured. In this case, the performance of AHN-classifier was 96.65% in accuracy and 96.41% in F-score, ranking in the first position in comparison with the other methods. Random forest, multivariate adaptive regression splines and booted logistic regression were the best three positions below AHN. The confusion matrix of the AHN-classifier is shown in Fig. 2. As it can be seen, the AHN-classifier detected *walking* without error, and *laying-on* was the most over-predicted activity. To

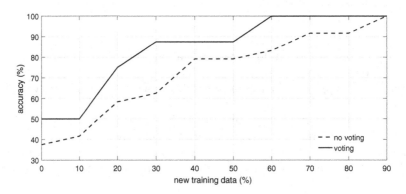

target values

		jumping	laying-on	running	walking
	jumping	33	3	0	0
predicted values	laying-on	1	42	2	0
	running	0	0	46	0
	walking	0	0	0	52

Fig. 2. Confusion matrix of the AHN-classifier obtained from the best model configuration.

Fig. 3. Accuracy of the AHN-classifier built in dependance of the percentage of new training data: (dashed line) with no voting scheme, and (solid line) with voting scheme.

this ends, it is important to say that these preliminary results show that the AHN-classifier is competitive as well as the other methods.

In this work, a user-specific approach was selected [8]. Thus, the second experiment aims to determine the influence of the amount of new data training in order to adjust the AHN-classifier to an specific user. In that sense, one subject was selected from Table 3 and this user performed the four activities in sequence and in a whole attempt. Once the feature dataset was computed from this data, the AHN-classifier was retrained with different percentages of new training data. The remaining data was used as the testing set.

Figure 3 shows the accuracy of the AHN-classifier (i.e. the same model built in the previous experiment) before and after the voting scheme, in comparison with the percentage of new training data occupied. As shown, the voting scheme increases the accuracy of the output response. Particularly at 30% of new training data, the AHN-classifier predicts with high accuracy after the voting scheme

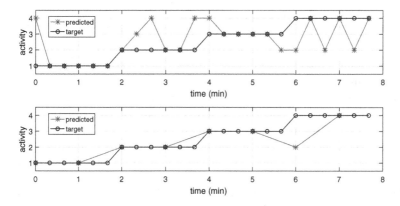

Fig. 4. Output response of the AHN-classifier built with 30% new training data: (top) response with no voting, and (bottom) response with voting scheme.

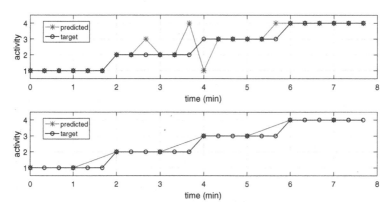

Fig. 5. Output response of the AHN-classifier built with 60% new training data: (top) response with no voting, and (bottom) response with voting scheme.

(87.5%). In addition, the AHN-classifier predicts with the best accuracy when 60% of new training data or more is used. Figure 4 shows the output response of the AHN-classifier re-built with 30% of new training data, and Fig. 5 shows the same response when the model was re-built with 60% of new training data.

From the above results, it can be seen that there is no neccessary to re-train the AHN-classifier intensively, since 30% of new training data is enough to obtain high accuracy in the performance. In addition, the voting scheme is relevant to the process since it can compute better responses. To this end, these preliminary results offer valuable insights to the usage of the AHN-classifier as an alternative in human activity recognition for mobile devices.

6 Conclusions and Future Work

In this paper, we proposed to use artificial hydrocarbon networks in a human activity recognition system specifically for mobile devices. As shown in the preliminary results, the AHN-classifier performed high accuracy, 96.65%, in contrast with other well-known machine learning methods. Also, a user-specific experiment confirmed that at least 30% of new data can be used for re-trained the AHN-classifier to compute correct output responses for a particular user. It is important when the HAR system should be customized to new users. To this end, a public dataset was collected and disposed to the community aiming to contribute with new data sets for benchmark and test support.

For future work, we are considering to create a larger dataset with more subjects and measurements. In addition, related functions such as detection of unknown activities and feature reduction will be added. We are also considering to develop a real-time AHN-based HAR system for mobile devices.

References

1. Anguita, D., Ghio, A., Oneto, L., Parra, X., Reyes-Ortiz, J.L.: A public domain dataset fro human activity recognition using smartphones. In: European Symposium on Artificial Neural Networks, Computational Intelligence and Machine Learning (2013)
2. Bulling, A., Blanke, U., Schiele, B.: A tutorial·on human activity recognition using body-worn inertial sensors. ACM Comput. Surv. (CSUR) **46**(3), 1–33 (2014)
3. Chen, C., Jafari, R., Kehtarnavaz, N.: A survey of depth and inertial sensor fusion for human action recognition. Multimed. Tools Appl. **76**(3), 4405–4425 (2017)
4. Dohnálek, P., Gajdoš, P., Moravec, P., Peterek, T., SnáŠel, V.: Application and comparison of modified classifiers for human activity recognition. Przegląd Elektrotechniczny **89**(11), 55–58 (2013)
5. Incel, O., Kose, M., Ersoy, C.: A review and taxonomy of activity recognition on mobile phones. BioNanoScience **3**(2), 145–171 (2013)
6. Kwapisz, J.R., Weiss, G.M., Moore, S.A.: Activity recognition using cell phone accelerometers. In: Proceedings on the Fourth International Workshop on Knowledge Discovery from Sensor Data (2010)
7. Kwolek, B., Kepski, M.: Human fall detection on embedded platform using depth maps and wireless accelerometer. Comput. Methods Programs Biomed. **117**(3), 489–501 (2014)
8. Lara, O.D., Labrador, M.A.: A survey on human activity recognition using wearable sensors. IEEE Commun. Surv. Tutor. **15**(3), 1192–1209 (2013)
9. Li, W., Zhang, Z., Liu, Z.: Action recognition based on a bag of 3D points. In: Computer Vision and Pattern Recognition Workshops, pp. 9–14 (2010)
10. Lockhart, J.W., Weiss, G.M.: Limitations with activity recognition methodology and data sets. In: Proceedings of the 2014 ACM International Joint Conference on Pervasive and Ubiquitous Computing: Adjunct Publication, pp. 747–756 (2014)
11. Ofli, F., Chaudhry, R., Kurillo, G., Vidal, R., Bajcsy, R.: Berkeley MHAD: a comprehensive multimodal human action database. In: IE Workshop on Applications of Computer Vision, pp. 53–60 (2013)

12. Ponce, H., Martínez-Villasenor, M.L., Miralles-Pechuán, L.: A novel wearable sensor-based human activity recognition approach using artificial hydrocarbon networks. Sensors **16**(7), 1033 (2016)
13. Ponce, H., Miralles-Pechuán, L., Martínez-Villasenor, M.L.: A flexible approach for human activity recognition using artificial hydrocarbon networks. Sensors **16**(11), 1715 (2016)
14. Ponce, H., Ponce, P.: Artificial organic networks. In: 2011 IEEE Conference on Electronics, Robotics and Automotive Mechanics, pp. 29–34. IEEE (2011)
15. Ponce, H., Ponce, P., Molina, A.: Adaptive noise filtering based on artificial hydrocarbon networks: an application to audio signals. Expert Syst. Appl. **41**(14), 6512–6523 (2014)
16. Ponce-Espinosa, H., Ponce-Cruz, P., Molina, A.: Artificial organic networks. Artificial Organic Networks. SCI, vol. 521, pp. 53–72. Springer, Cham (2014). https://doi.org/10.1007/978-3-319-02472-1_3
17. Ponce, H., Ponce, P., Molina, A.: The development of an artificial organic networks toolkit for LabVIEW. J. Comput. Chem. **36**(7), 478–492 (2015)
18. Preece, S.J., Goulermas, J.Y., Kenney, L.P.J., Howard, D., Meijer, K., Crompton, R.: Activity identification using body-mounted sensors-a review of classification techniques. Physiol. Meas. **30**(4), 1–33 (2009)
19. Reiss, A.: Personalized mobile physical activity monitoring for everyday life. Ph.D. thesis, Technical University of Kaiserslautern (2014)
20. Roggen, D., et al.: OPPORTUNITY: towards opportunistic activity and context recognition systems. In: 3rd IEEE Workshop on Autononomic and Opportunistic Communications (2009)
21. Roggen, D., et al.: Collecting complex activity datasets in highly rich networked sensor environments. In: Seventh International Conference on Networked Sensing Systems (INSS), Kassel, Germany, pp. 233–240. IEEE (2010)
22. Shoaib, M., Bosch, S., Incel, O.D., Scholten, H., Havinga, P.J.M.: A survey of online activity recognition using mobile phones. Sensors **15**(1), 2059–2085 (2015)
23. Su, X., Tong, H., Ji, P.: Activity recognition with smartphone sensors. Tsinghua Sci. Technol. **19**(3), 235–249 (2014)
24. Yang, A.Y., Jafari, R., Sastry, S.S., Bajcsy, R.: Distributed recognition of human actions using wearable motion sensor networks. J. Ambient. Intell. Smart Environ. **1**(2), 103–115 (2009)

Road Perspective Depth Reconstruction from Single Images Using Reduce-Refine-Upsample CNNs

José E. Valdez-Rodríguez$^{(\boxtimes)}$, Hiram Calvo$^{(\boxtimes)}$, and Edgardo M. Felipe-Riverón

Centro de Investigación en Computación, Instituto Politécnico Nacional,
J.D. Bátiz e/M.O. de Mendizábal, 07738 Mexico City, Mexico
jvaldezr1000@alumno.ipn.mx, {hcalvo,edgardo}@cic.ipn.mx

Abstract. Depth reconstruction from single images has been a challenging task due to the complexity and the quantity of depth cues that images have. Convolutional Neural Networks (CNN) have been successfully used to reconstruct depth of general object scenes; however, these works have not been tailored for the particular problem of road perspective depth reconstruction. As we aim to build a computational efficient model, we focus on single-stage CNNs. In this paper we propose two different models for solving this task. A particularity is that our models perform refinement in the same single-stage training; thus, we call them Reduce-Refine-Upsample (RRU) models because of the order of the CNN operations. We compare our models with the current state of the art in depth reconstruction, obtaining improvements in both global and local views for images of road perspectives.

Keywords: Depth reconstruction · Convolutional Neural Networks
One stage training · Embedded refining layer · Stereo matching

1 Introduction

Reconstructing depth from a single image (opposed to stereoscopic images) is a challenging task due to the depth cues that it contains, such as shadows, perspective, motion blur, etc. [1]. In this work we focus on reconstructing depth in images with predominant perspective, such as those of roads and motorways. This kind of images needs to be analyzed by autonomous mobile robots or cars when only a 2D view is available to calculate their displacement [2–4]. Previous works in depth reconstruction have tackled the general problem of estimating the component of depth in a wide range of images, mainly focusing on objects against a solid or a complex background, or city buildings and people, for example. To our knowledge, there are no specific works devoted to the problem of reconstructing depth for images where perspective plays a predominant role.

We thank Instituto Politécnico Nacional (SIP, COFAA, EDD, EDI and BEIFI), and CONACyT for their support for this research.

© Springer Nature Switzerland AG 2018
F. Castro et al. (Eds.): MICAI 2017, LNAI 10632, pp. 30–40, 2018.
https://doi.org/10.1007/978-3-030-02837-4_3

Additionally, several models in the state of the art propose multi-stage networks that require separate training for each one of their stages, making the process of training them more time consuming.

In this paper we propose two Convolutional Neural Networks (CNN) capable of reconstructing depth from a single image that require only one training stage. The models proposed in this work are capable of reconstructing depth both in a global and a local view [1]. This paper is organized as follows: in Sect. 2 we describe related work this research is based on, Sect. 3 describes the proposed method, Sect. 4 shows results obtained from our proposal and a comparison with the state of the art, and finally in Sect. 5 the conclusions of this work are drawn.

2 Related Work

Depth reconstruction from a single image has been tackled by different methods. Although using CNNs has recently become one of the best techniques, using CNNs to solve the problem of depth reconstruction can be still considered at a development stage due to the complexity of the design of these networks.

One of the first works to use this technique can be found in Eigen, Puhrsch and Fergus [5]. They propose using two CNNs: the first one estimates depth at global view, and the second one refines the local view. They establish a CNN architecture to be applied to depth estimation and propose a loss function. Eigen and Fergus [6] use three CNNs, one for each stage to estimate depth from a single image. The first network estimates depth at a global view; the second network tries to estimate depth at half the resolution of the input image, and a third one refines or estimates depth at a local level. They propose a new loss function. Liu, Shen and Lin [7] present a single CNN that uses a pre-processed input based on superpixels. They complement their work using a probabilistic method to improve their results. Then, from the same team, Liu, Shen, Lin and Reid [8] change the architecture of their network maintaining the stage of improvement of the image. Finally, Afifi and Hellwich [9] use a single CNN in regression mode to estimate depth with a different loss function.

In general, the discussed architectures are similar, being the main changes between them the loss function, the activation functions, the number of filters per layer, and the size of the filter. Different databases have been used to train and test their neural networks, making it difficult to directly compare their performances. Despite of this, one of works that is considered to achieve the best results in the state of the art is Afifi and Hellwich [9]. Additionally, their architecture is based on a single-stage training CNN. They present results of reconstructing depth of chair images against different backgrounds. As we were interested on evaluating the performance of this method on images with perspective, we reimplemented their CNN model as seen in Fig. 1. In region A the reduce operation is performed through four Residual blocks and a Convolutional layer. In region B the upsample operation is carried out through two Residual Blocks and one Convolutional layer. In Sect. 3 we will give more details of these operations.

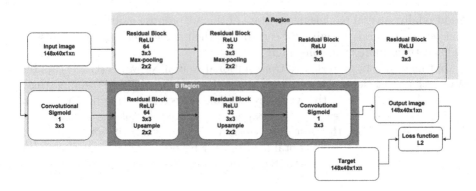

Fig. 1. CNN model by Afifi and Hellwich [9].

In the next section we present our proposal. Similar to Afifi and Hellwich's CNN, our architecture is based on a single CNN, but, among other differences, we add local refinement in the same training stage.

3   Proposed Method

In this section we present our Convolutional Neural Network (CNN) models, we have decided to name them as Reduce-Refine-Upsample (RRU) due to the operations that are performed in each stage of the CNN. Because, to our knowledge, there are no public datasets available for this task, to perform training in our models we opted for creating our own dataset from the object tracking section of *The KITTI Vision Benchmark Suite* [10]. This dataset contains 15000 outdoor scenes given as stereoscopic images. This dataset does not contain the target depth maps, so that we built the target depth maps using different algorithms such as *Semiglobal stereo matching* [11] and *Blockmatching stereo algorithm* [12]. In Fig. 2 we can observe a brief comparison between the stereo matching algorithms tested to obtain the target depth map. Finally, we decided to use the *Efficient large-scale stereo matching* [13] due to the quality and the evaluation received by Menze and Geiger [14]. This algorithm receives pairs of stereo images as described in Fig. 3 and its result is the target depth map.

Fig. 2. Target depth map comparison with different stereo matching methods, (A) Stereoscopic images, (B) Semiglobal Matching, (C) Blockmatching method, (D) Large-Scale matching method.

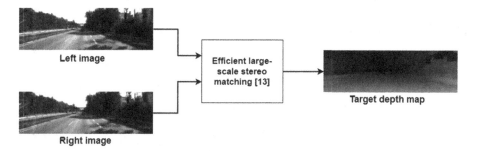

Fig. 3. Target depth map creation.

Our models were built with *Convolutional layers* [15], *Residual Block* [16], *Max-pooling and Upsample* [17] layers. We also add biases to every layer. In Fig. 4 we can observe a representation of a layer in our CNN models.

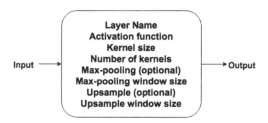

Fig. 4. Single layer representation

Model 1. The block diagram of this model is presented in Fig. 5. The input image is the left image of the dataset and the target image is the depth map obtained from the stereo matching algorithm. In region A we can see the Reduction operation which tries to reconstruct depth at global view; it consists of four Residual Blocks with kernel size of 3 × 3 and the activation function *Rectified Linear Unit* (ReLU) [18], the residual block is used because we tried to avoid weights with zero value. We use Max-pooling only on the first two Residual Blocks to reduce image resolution and reconstruct depth at different image sizes. At the end of Region A we use a convolutional layer with a sigmoid activation function to limit output to values between 0 and 1.

In region B we perform the Upsample operation which tries to recover the original size of the input image; we use two Residual Blocks with kernel size 3 × 3 and activation function ReLU to perform this operation. Finally region C tries to estimate depth at local view, joining the output of region A and two convolutional layers with max-pooling. The refining method in this model was taken from the work of Xu et al. [20], the output of the model is given by the convolutional layer with kernel size 3×3 and a sigmoid activation function in region B.

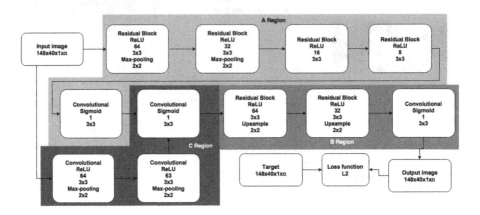

Fig. 5. Reduce-Refine-Upsample CNN Model 1

Model 2. This model is presented in Fig. 6. In the same way that the previous model, the input image is the left image of the dataset and the target image is the depth map obtained from the stereo matching algorithm. In region A we can see the Reduction operation which attempts to reconstruct depth at global view; it consists of four Residual Blocks with kernel size of 3×3 and activation function ReLU. The residual block is used because we tried to avoid weights with zero value. We use Max-pooling only on the first two Residual Blocks to reduce image resolution and reconstruct depth at different image sizes. At the end we use a convolutional layer with a sigmoid activation function to limit output to values between 0 and 1. In region B we perform the Upsample operation which tries to recover the original size of the input image.

We use two Residual Blocks with kernel size 3×3 and activation function ReLU to carry out this operation. The output of region B is given by the convolutional layer with kernel size 3×3 and a sigmoid activation function. Finally region C attempts to refine depth with local information, joining the output of region B and the input image, followed by four Convolutional layers with kernel size 3×3 and activation function ReLU. In this model we adapted the last convolutional layer to be sigmoid—this layer is then the output of the model. The refining method in this model was taken from the work of Dosovitskiy et al. [19].

Resuming, the main difference between our models and Afifi's is the refinement stage. Afifi's model does not perform this stage and according to Eigen and Fergus [6] it is necessary for achieving better results in local view. Our models perform this operation and additionally it is performed in a single training stage. The main differences between our models are the refinement method and the order of the operations, because the number an size of the kernels are similar in both models, also the activation functions are similar.

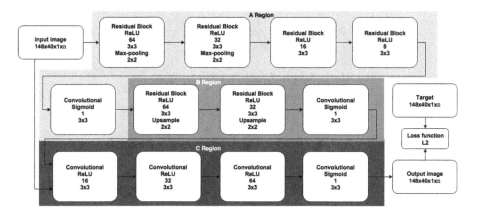

Fig. 6. Reduce-Refine-Upsample CNN Model 2

Loss Function. To train our CNN model we have to minimize an objective loss function. This loss function measures the global error between the target image and the depth reconstruction given by the CNN. We use the *L2* norm as the loss function, and it is used by both models. The L2 norm can be calculated as show in Eq. 1.

$$L2 = \frac{1}{2n} \sum_{i=1}^{n} \|y(i) - y'(i)\|_2^2 \tag{1}$$

where:

$y' = Reconstructed\ depth\ map$
$y = Target\ depth\ map$
$n = Number\ of\ images\ per\ batch$

Error Measures. To evaluate our method we used several error measures in order to be able to (roughly) compare with related work:

Root Mean Square Error:

$$RMSE = \sqrt{\frac{1}{|T|} \sum_{y' \epsilon |T|} (y - y')^2} \tag{2}$$

Mean Cuadratic Error:

$$MCE = \frac{1}{|T|} \sum_{y' \epsilon |T|} (y - y')^2 \tag{3}$$

Logaritmic Root Mean Square Error:

$$RMSELOG = \sqrt{\frac{1}{|T|} \sum_{y' \epsilon |T|} (log(y) - log(y'))^2} \tag{4}$$

Logaritmic Root Mean Square Error Scale Invariant:

$$RMSELOGSI = \frac{1}{|T|} \sum_{y' \epsilon |T|} (log(y) - log(y'))^2 \tag{5}$$

Absolute Relative Difference:

$$ARD = \frac{1}{|T|} \sum_{y' \epsilon |T|} \frac{|y - y'|}{y'} \tag{6}$$

Squared Relative Difference:

$$SRD = \frac{1}{|T|} \sum_{y' \epsilon |T|} \frac{\|y - y'\|^2}{y'} \tag{7}$$

where:

y' = *Reconstructed depth map*
y = *Target depth map*
T = *Number of pixels on the images*

4   Experiments and Results

In this section we describe the results of our models. We trained them with Backpropagation (BP) [21] and Stochastic Gradient Descent (SGD) [22]. We used 1,000 iterations and batch size of 40. From the dataset we used 12,482 left images and its respective target depth map for training and 2,517 for testing. Both input and output images have a size of 148 × 40 pixels, giving $/T/ = 5920$ and $n = 40$ due to the batch size.

We implemented our models with the Python toolbox, *Tensorflow* [23] which can be trained on a GPU for swift performance. We trained our models on a GPU NVIDIA GTX 960; it took two days for training and less than a second for testing a single image.

As we explained in Sect. 2, we implemented as well the model proposed by Afifi and Hellwich [9] because they only use one training stage on their model;

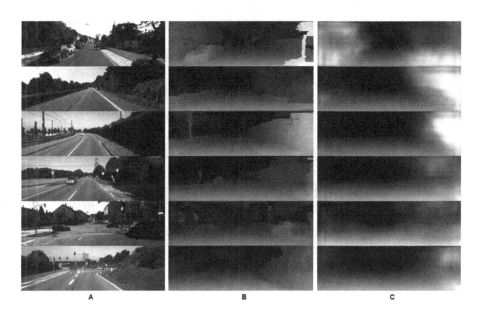

Fig. 7. Sample output of CNN by Afifi and Hellwich [9] on our dataset. (A) Input image, (B) Target depth map y, (C) Result of the CNN y'.

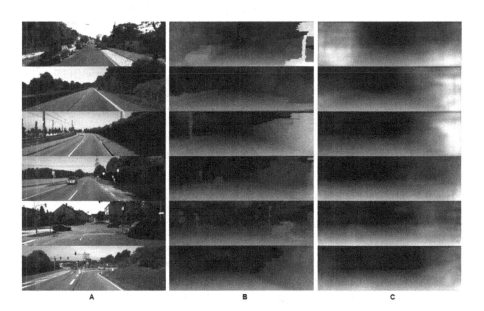

Fig. 8. Sample output of Model 1. (A) Input image, (B) Target depth map y, (C) Result of the CNN y'.

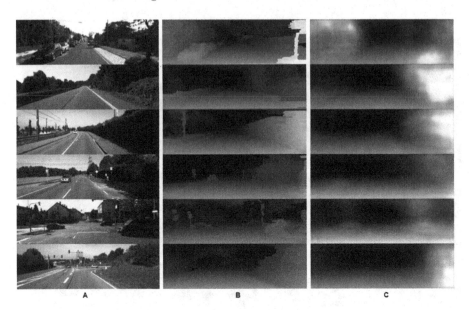

Fig. 9. Sample output of Model 2. (A) Input image, (B) Target depth map y, (C) Result of the CNN y'.

their model can be trained with the L2 norm and still obtain better results than the rest of the related work without using an additional CNN.

In Fig. 7 we can observe the result from the implementation of [9]. In Figs. 8 and 9 we present a sample of the results from our models 1 and 2, respectively.

Qualitatively comparing results shown in previous figures, it can be seen that our models are capable of reconstructing depth at global view, with slightly better attention to details in local view than previous proposals. For global view we refer to the image in general avoiding small details and for local view we refer to small details such as cars, pedestrians, etc. For a quantitative analysis, in Table 1 we present the error measures of both our models and the reimplemented model. RMSE, MCE and ARD measure the global view error in the images, while

Table 1. Error comparisons between our approach and the state of the art

	State of the art [9]	Model 1	Model 2
RMSE	0.1496	**0.1218**	0.1348
MCE	0.0260	**0.0166**	0.0213
RMSELOG	0.3377	**0.3239**	0.3260
RMSELOGSI	0.2068	0.1980	**0.1931**
ARD	9.8658	9.5285	**9.3036**
SRD	45.4089	46.6177	**43.5062**

and RMSLOG, RMSLOGSI and SRD measure the local view error. Comparing our methods with the state of the art, we obtain better results with both models, but Model 1 yields better performance at global view while Model 2 performs better at local view.

5   Conclusions and Future Work

We have presented two CNN models that require only a single-stage training and perform refinement in the same stage. We adapted an existing dataset of stereoscopic images to develop a resource oriented to test depth reconstruction on road images with perspective. We used this dataset to test our models and compared their performance with the current state of the art in depth reconstruction. We found that the use of a residual block instead of convolutional layers improves results. Using upsample layers improves quantitative results as well, although this may not be directly attested in some cases when examining results qualitatively—some objects appear to be blurred and less defined because of this layer. The perspective of the image takes an important role on the reconstruction of depth. Quantitatively, local depth can be estimated with our models, but this still needs to be validated with other datasets.

As a future work we plan to experiment with different kernel sizes, different loss functions and activation functions to further improve our proposed models.

References

1. Howard, I.P.: Perceiving in Depth, Volume 1: Basic Mechanisms. Oxford University Press, Oxford (2012)
2. Bills, C., Chen, J., Saxena, A.: Autonomous MAV flight in indoor environments using single image perspective cues. In: 2011 IEEE International Conference on Robotics and Automation (ICRA), pp. 5776–5783. IEEE (2011)
3. Kundu, A., Li, Y., Dellaert, F., Li, F., Rehg, J.M.: Joint semantic segmentation and 3D reconstruction from monocular video. In: Fleet, D., Pajdla, T., Schiele, B., Tuytelaars, T. (eds.) ECCV 2014. LNCS, vol. 8694, pp. 703–718. Springer, Cham (2014). https://doi.org/10.1007/978-3-319-10599-4_45
4. Häne, C., Sattler, T., Pollefeys, M.: Obstacle detection for self-driving cars using only monocular cameras and wheel odometry. In: 2015 IEEE/RSJ International Conference on Intelligent Robots and Systems (IROS), pp. 5101–5108. IEEE (2015)
5. Eigen, D., Puhrsch, C., Fergus, R.: Depth map prediction from a single image using a multi-scale deep network. In: Advances in neural information processing systems, pp. 2366–2374 (2014)
6. Eigen, D., Fergus, R.: Predicting depth, surface normals and semantic labels with a common multi-scale convolutional architecture. In: Proceedings of the IEEE International Conference on Computer Vision, pp. 2650–2658 (2015)
7. Liu, F., Shen, C., Lin, G.: Deep convolutional neural fields for depth estimation from a single image. In: Proceedings of the IEEE Conference on Computer Vision and Pattern Recognition, pp. 5162–5170 (2015)

8. Liu, F., Shen, C., Lin, G., Reid, I.: Learning depth from single monocular images using deep convolutional neural fields. IEEE Trans. Pattern Anal. Mach. Intell. **38**, 2024–2039 (2016)
9. Afifi, A.J., Hellwich, O.: Object depth estimation from a single image using fully convolutional neural network. In: 2016 International Conference on Digital Image Computing: Techniques and Applications (DICTA), pp. 1–7. IEEE (2016)
10. Geiger, A., Lenz, P., Urtasun, R.: Are we ready for autonomous driving? The KITTI vision benchmark suite. In: Conference on Computer Vision and Pattern Recognition (CVPR) (2012)
11. Hirschmuller, H.: Stereo processing by semiglobal matching and mutual information. IEEE Trans. Pattern Anal. Mach. Intell. **30**, 328–341 (2008)
12. Konolige, K.: Small vision systems: hardware and implementation. In: Shirai, Y., Hirose, S. (eds.) Robotics Research, pp. 203–212. Springer, London (1998)
13. Geiger, A., Roser, M., Urtasun, R.: Efficient large-scale stereo matching. In: Kimmel, R., Klette, R., Sugimoto, A. (eds.) ACCV 2010. LNCS, vol. 6492, pp. 25–38. Springer, Heidelberg (2011). https://doi.org/10.1007/978-3-642-19315-6_3
14. Menze, M., Geiger, A.: Object scene flow for autonomous vehicles. In: Conference on Computer Vision and Pattern Recognition (CVPR) (2015)
15. LeCun, Y., et al.: Handwritten digit recognition with a back-propagation network. In: Advances in Neural Information Processing Systems, pp. 396–404 (1990)
16. He, K., Zhang, X., Ren, S., Sun, J.: Deep residual learning for image recognition. In: Proceedings of the IEEE Conference on Computer Vision and Pattern Recognition, pp. 770–778 (2016)
17. Zeiler, M.D., Fergus, R.: Visualizing and understanding convolutional networks. In: Fleet, D., Pajdla, T., Schiele, B., Tuytelaars, T. (eds.) ECCV 2014. LNCS, vol. 8689, pp. 818–833. Springer, Cham (2014). https://doi.org/10.1007/978-3-319-10590-1_53
18. Arora, R., Basu, A., Mianjy, P., Mukherjee, A.: Understanding deep neural networks with rectified linear units. arXiv preprint arXiv:1611.01491 (2016)
19. Dosovitskiy, A., et al.: FlowNet: learning optical flow with convolutional networks. In: Proceedings of the IEEE International Conference on Computer Vision, pp. 2758–2766 (2015)
20. Xu, N., Price, B., Cohen, S., Huang, T.: Deep image matting. arXiv preprint arXiv:1703.03872 (2017)
21. LeCun, Y.A., Bottou, L., Orr, G.B., Müller, K.-R.: Efficient BackProp. In: Montavon, G., Orr, G.B., Müller, K.-R. (eds.) Neural Networks: Tricks of the Trade. LNCS, vol. 7700, pp. 9–48. Springer, Heidelberg (2012). https://doi.org/10.1007/978-3-642-35289-8_3
22. LeCun, Y., Bottou, L., Bengio, Y., Haffner, P.: Gradient-based learning applied to document recognition. Proc. IEEE **86**, 2278–2324 (1998)
23. Abadi, M., et al.: TensorFlow: large-scale machine learning on heterogeneous systems (2015). tensorflow.org

Fast Learning for Accurate Object Recognition Using a Pre-trained Deep Neural Network

Víctor Lobato-Ríos$^{(\boxtimes)}$, Ana C. Tenorio-Gonzalez, and Eduardo F. Morales

Instituto Nacional de Astrofísica, Óptica y Electrónica, Tonantzintla, Mexico
{vlobato,catanace17,emorales}@inaoep.mx

Abstract. Object recognition is a relevant task for many areas and, in particular, for service robots. Recently object recognition has been dominated by the use of Deep Neural Networks (DNN), however, they required a large number of images and long training times. If a user asks a service robot to search for an unknown object, it has to deal with selecting relevant images to learn a model, deal with polysemy, and learn a model relatively quickly to be of any use to the user. In this paper we describe an object recognition system that deals with the above challenges by: (i) a user interface to reduce different object interpretations, (ii) downloading on-the-fly images from Internet to train a model, and (iii) using the outputs of a trimmed pre-trained DNN as attributes for a SVM. The whole process (selecting and downloading images and training a model) of learning a model for an unknown object takes around two minutes. The proposed method was tested on 72 common objects found in a house environment with very high precision and recall rates (over 90%).

1 Introduction

Object recognition is an open research area based on obtaining models able to identify one kind of object from another. This task has several applications, for example, for service robotics, which must be capable of finding, ideally, any object requested by a user. However, accomplishing this assignment involves many problems such as the great variety of existing objects of the same kind, *e.g.*, four chairs are depicted in Fig. 1, every one of them has unique characteristics that make it different from the others, but at the end, all of them are chairs.

On the other hand, also the polysemy problem must be considered. This problem happens when a word has more than one meaning, *e.g.*, the word "mouse" can refer both, the animal or the computer device. Then, for these cases a robot can not only learn the general concept, it must learn the precise meaning of the concept according to what the user requested.

Therefore, given all the possible requests that a user can ask and all the meanings for each request, it is intractable to train a model for this unthinkable amount of concepts. Instead, models able to differentiating the correct meaning

© Springer Nature Switzerland AG 2018
F. Castro et al. (Eds.): MICAI 2017, LNAI 10632, pp. 41–53, 2018.
https://doi.org/10.1007/978-3-030-02837-4_4

Fig. 1. Chairs with different characteristics. Images retrieved from: https://www.pinterest.com.mx

of the user's request and learning quickly any object's characteristics in order to recognize them are necessary.

Nowadays, the most accurate methods to recognize objects are those using Deep Neural Networks (DNN). Since Krizhevsky *et al.* (2012) [1] won the ILSVRC-2012 with their DNN called AlexNet, many modifications to this network and also new architectures have been proposed in order to improve the object recognition performance [2–8], however, training these networks takes months. Imagine an scenario where the user requests a service robot to find an unknown object. In this case, the robot must learn a model of that object as quickly as possible in order to recognize it and fulfill the user's request.

This research proposes an object recognition system suitable for service robots and focused on both, polysemy and fast learning. The first is managed through an interface where the user can refine his/her request until it is clear the type of object that must be learned. The latter is dealt through transfer learning and downloading the training images directly from Internet. The output of one of the DNN's last layers is used as the attributes to train a Support Vector Machine (SVM) with images that are downloaded on-the-fly to recognize new concepts.

Summarizing, the proposed system allows users to specify what they want and uses transfer learning for quickly learning accurate models for recognizing previously unknown objects.

The rest of the article is organized as follows. In Sect. 2 related work is revised. In Sect. 3 our object recognition system is presented in detail. In Sect. 4 the experiments and the results obtained are described. Finally, in Sect. 5 the conclusions and the future work of this research are discussed.

2   Related Work

DNNs have been used in the last years for solving different recognition tasks. The most common DNNs are the AlexNet, CaffeNet [3], VGG (with its variants) [4,5] and Inception v3 [8]. The four DNNs have been pre-trained using ImageNet, and these models and the networks ready to be trained are available for implementing.

Training a DNN from scratch can take several weeks in the best cases. Because of that, previous works have tried to speed-up the DNN's training time using different techniques, such as: optimization [9–11], Fourier domain [12], networks compressing [13,14] and fine-tuning [15,16], among others.

For the latter mentioned methods, fine-tuning is the faster way to train a network accomplishing the task in less than an hour. This approach is based on the idea of retrained the last layers of the network maintaining the rest without changes. The use of outputs of intermediate layers as attributes has been previously studied. This method can be considered as transfer learning [17] due to it uses the features transferred from the unaltered part of the network as the input for layers to be retrained.

Fine-tuning have been successfully used classifying images from completely different domains such as land segmentation [16,18], emotion recognition [19] or medical images [20]. However, the retraining time required by this method remains useless if we need an on-line training system that can be used by service robots. In order to decrease the time to retrain a network, the proposed system is based on the transfer learning idea, obtaining a layer output as the attributes of a SVM which can be quickly retrained.

Some works, based on the same principle as our system, are shown in Table 1. They use a DNN's layer output as the SVM's attributes, however, they present some differences with our system. The characteristics analyzed for each work listed in Table 1 are: the DNN used; if the training happens off-line or on-line; the classifier receiving the transfered features; and, the application.

Table 1. Related works using transfer learning

	DNN	Training	Transfer learning	Application
Ng et al. (2015) [19]	AlexNet and VGG-CNN-M	Off-line	Double fine-tuning	Emotions recognition
Codella et al. (2015) [21]	CaffeNet	Off-line	Sparse Coding + SVM	Melanoma recognition
Akilan et al. (2017) [22]	AlexNet, VGG-16 and Inception v3 (all together)	Off-line	SVM	Object and action recognition
D'Innocente et al. (2017) [23]	Re-trained AlexNet and Inception v3	Off-line	SVM	Objects recognition
Our system	Inception v3	On-line	SVM	Home objects recognition

As can be seen, the applications for all the works presented in Table 1 are recognition tasks, however all of them, except us, are re-trained off-line. Codella et al. (2015) [21] added the features transfered from the DNN to the features obtained from a Sparse Coding for the SVM's input features, while Akilan et al. (2017) [22] used a system combining the outputs of three DNNs as SVM's attributes. These methods need much more processing time.

On the other hand, D'Innocente et al. (2017) [23] presented the most closely related work to our system, however, they need to retrain the complete DNN to accomplish the object recognition task. Also, the images used for training our system are directly downloaded on-the-fly from Internet.

Summarizing, the main advantage of our system against related work is its capacity to be retrained on-line with images selected on-the-fly without losing accuracy in the recognition of new objects.

3 Object Recognition System

The proposed object recognition system is composed by six steps as shown in Fig. 2. At the beginning, the system receives as input the concept of the object to be recognized and then the process starts.

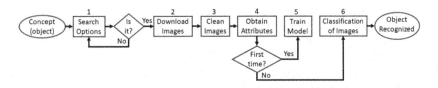

Fig. 2. Flowchart of the object recognition system

Step 1 searches images, of the concept requested by the user, to train the system using *Google Images*. In order to deal with polysemy, an interface, depicted in Fig. 3, is shown to the user with possible options related with the concept in order to filter the search if needed. The user must select the most related option with his/her request or introduce a more specific concept if all the options are unsuitable. When the new concept or a filter is selected the interface shows the new possible options considering the refined search.

Figure 3(a) shows an example when the requested concept is "mouse". As can be seen, the example images consider both, animals and computer devices. However, if the filter "computer" is selected, the search is refined and now all the example images correspond to computer devices as shown in Fig. 3(b)

Step 2 uses the concept selected in the previous step as the search string to download 100 images from *Google Images* to train the system. As the previous step considers the concept's polysemy, the downloaded images are expected to be more related with the concept that must be learned.

Step 3 consists of "cleaning" the downloaded images, i.e., making the format and size of the images suitable to be used in next steps. For Steps 4, 5 and 6, three methods were explored: the pre-trained *Iv3* deep neural network; a SVM classifier using images' color and shape features as attributes; and a SVM classifier using an output layer from *Iv3* as attributes. These methods are explained in detail below.

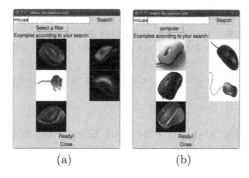

(a)   (b)

Fig. 3. Interface used to show users the example images according to his/her request: (a) when the concept "mouse" is requested; (b) when the filter "computer" is added to the original request

3.1 Pre-trained Iv3 Deep Neural Network (*Iv3* Method)

The Iv3 model is a deep neural network with 42 layers, a representation of this network is depicted in Fig. 4. This model is available in the open source software library *TensorFlow* (TF), where it has been trained for the ImageNet Large Visual Recognition Challenge using the data from 2012. For this task, the Iv3 should classify images into 1000 classes considering daily life objects, animals, food, or means of transport, among others.

Fig. 4. Inception v3 general architecture

For the proposed object recognition system, the pre-trained Iv3 model has been selected over other commonly used DNN models such as AlexNet, CaffeNet, and VGG. Iv3 requires less computational resources [7], which makes it feasible for being used in on-line applications, as the implemented in this work. Furthermore, it outperforms the object recognition precision achieved by the other DNN models [22].

The Iv3 model is obtained from TF and it deals with the Steps 4, 5 and 6 of the proposed object recognition system. First, for Step 4, it obtains the attributes for the images from Step 3. For this method, the images need both, being in *jpg* format and having a size of 299×299 pixels. Then, since the model is pre-trained, Step 5 is not needed. Finally, the last 3 layers of the model perform the classification using the attributes obtained from Step 4 in the dropout and fully connected layers, and in the *Softmax* classifier for 1,000 classes. Therefore, using this method, it is possible to recognize the objects belonged to the classes for which the model was trained.

3.2 SVM Classifier Using Color and Shape Features (*Color* + *Shape* + *SVM* Method)

This method implements the last three steps of the proposed system. For Step 4, histograms of oriented gradients [24] and dominant color identification features of objects are extracted.

Using these features as attributes, a SVM is trained in Step 5. Finally, the SVM is used to predict classes in Step 6 and, therefore, to recognize objects obtaining the shape and color features of the images tested. This method can be applied to any requested object.

3.3 SVM Classifier Using Iv3 (*Iv3* + *SVM* : *All* Method)

This method uses the Iv3 model to obtain the images' attributes for Step 4 of the object recognition system. As it was mentioned above, Iv3 has 42 layers and the last 3 (dropout, fully connected and *Softmax* layers) are used to perform the classification. It has been previously analysed how the features used to describe images on a DNN goes from the most general to the most specific as the DNN's output is closer [17]. Moreover, it has been proved that better results are obtained transferring features from the DNN's layers before the fully connected layers [23].

In this regard, the input vector for the Iv3 model's dropout layer, which has a size of 2,048, is considered as the set of attributes which describes an image independently of its domain. Therefore, for this method, Step 4 trims the Iv3 network just after the last average pool layer and interprets the resulting vector as the image descriptors that will be used as the attributes for training a SVM classifier in Step 5, as shown in Fig. 5.

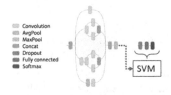

Fig. 5. SVM replacing the last three layers of the Inception v3 architecture

After training, images can be processed using the Iv3 model to obtain their attributes and the trained SVM will be used as Step 6 of the object recognition system. For this method, since the attributes are obtained from the Iv3 model, the images also need both, being in *jpg* format and having a size of 299 × 299 pixels. Applying this method it is also possible to recognize any object requested by the user.

Binary Classification (*Iv3 + SVM : Binary* Method). For this method it is also proposed a variant where the model is trained for only two classes, a positive and a negative, where the positive class examples are those representing the searched object and the negative class examples are those representing any other object different to the positive class.

Therefore, for this variant, Step 4 remains the same, Step 5 will always be performed for two classes and Step 6 will say whether or not the object is the one it has been searching for.

4   Experiments and Results

The performance of the proposed object recognition system depends on the accuracy of the classification. Therefore, the first experiment conducted was a classification task comparing the precision, recall and f-measure obtained by the three methods proposed against the *Iv3* method when classifying 72 classes. These objects were selected by 7 independent users that were asked to suggest 10 objects that can be found by a service robot in a house environment, and complemented with objects from the Semantic Robot Vision Challenge 2009 and ImageCLEF2014.

A dataset of 5,670 images obtained from *Google Images* (80 images per class) was created for this task. Implementation of the Iv3 model was accomplished through *TensorFlow*. On the other hand, the SVM was implemented using Sklearn from the Scikit package for Python. The classification using the SVM was performed applying a 5 fold-cross validation (80% examples for training, 20% examples for testing).

The classes involved in the experiment are restrained to objects that can be found in a house. Some of these 72 classes are among the 1,000 classes used to train the Iv3 model, but not all of them. In Table 2 are shown all the classes involved in the experiment. These classes are divided into three groups according with their correspondence with the classes considered by the Iv3 model.

In the first column are the classes with a Direct Correspondence (DC) between our classes and the Iv3 classes, *i.e.*, those classes that are the same in both groups.

In the second column are the classes with an Indirect Correspondence (IC) between both groups, *i.e.*, those of the 72 classes representing a more general class than others considered by the Iv3 model, *e.g.*, the classes "tennis", "sandals", "boots", or "heels", considered by the Iv3 model, are represented with our class "Shoe", therefore, if the Iv3 model classifies an example as any kind of "Shoe", it will be considered as correct because all are shoes.

Finally, in the third column are the classes with No Correspondence between both groups (NC). Therefore, these classes are not considered in the results reported for the $Iv3$ method.

Table 2. Classes with a direct correspondence (DC), an indirect correspondence (IC) and without correspondence (NC)

DC classes	IC classes		NC classes	
Pen	Apple	Shirt	Book	Blanket
Cellphone	Shoe	Sock	Spoon	Milk
Towel	Coffee	Cup	Fork	Soap
Tv remote	Clothe	Knife	Glass of water	Pumpkin
Broom	Laptop	Coat	Coke	Dinosaur toy
Mop	Bread	Bottle	Key	CD
Backpack	Bed sheet	Toy car	Scissor	DVD
Pillow	Handbag	Potato chips	Comb	Video game
Glasses	Food	Phone	Bible	Toy
Orange	Chair	Bookshelf	Cell charger	Cracker
Paddle	Medicine		Baby bottle	Cookie
Soccer ball	Ac remote		Headphone	Extinguisher
Frying pan	Tablet		Nail clipper	Potty
Printer	Plate		Inhaler	Softener
Trash	Jacket		Cosmetic bag	
Fridge	Hand cream		Fly swatter	

The average results for precision, recall and f-measure obtained by each method are shown in Table 3. From the second to the fifth columns the results for the $Iv3$, $Color + Shape + SVM$, $Iv3 + SVM : All$ and $Iv3 + SVM : Binary$ methods are presented, respectively.

As can be seen, the best results are obtained by the $Iv3 + SVM : Binary$ method. This method has a performance of at least 90% for the three measurements and for all the groups of classes. The latter lead us to make some remarks.

First of all, the performance of the $Iv3 + SVM : Binary$ method is slightly better for the DC and IC classes than the NC classes, however, this difference is lower than 3% for precision, recall and f-measure. This proves that the method is consistent whether the recognized objects have or not a correspondence with the classes for which the Iv3 model was trained. This is important because it means that we can quickly learn highly accurate models for objects found in house environments using features of a DNN that was not necessarily trained on those objects.

Also, it should be noted that there is a significant increase in performance when using a binary classification. The classification precision for the $Iv3$ method was improved in almost 10% for the AC classes (DC + IC classes), whereas the recall was improved in more than 20%. Although the $Iv3$ was trained for 1,000 classes and we are comparing with classifiers of 72 classes, we expect the robot to be using mainly binary classifiers.

Table 3. Average precision, recall and f-measure for the four methods

Group of classes	Measurement	$Iv3$	Color + Shape + SVM	$Iv3$ + SVM : All	$Iv3$ + SVM : Binary
AC (DC+IC)	Precision	0.894	0.085	0.884	0.986
	Recall	0.703	0.122	0.851	0.932
	F-Measure	0.770	0.075	0.865	0.958
DC	Precision	0.926	0.060	0.913	0.987
	Recall	0.755	0.160	0.873	0.934
	F-Measure	0.822	0.070	0.892	0.959
IC	Precision	0.874	0.100	0.866	0.985
	Recall	0.671	0.100	0.838	0.931
	F-Measure	0.738	0.079	0.849	0.957
NC	Precision	—	0.091	0.802	0.967
	Recall	—	0.087	0.819	0.898
	F-Measure	—	0.077	0.807	0.930

On the other hand, the $Iv3 + SVM : All$ method have a 1% lower precision than the $Iv3$, which means that substituting the last layers of the pre-trained DNN by a SVM does not decrease considerably the classification precision. Furthermore, the f-measure increase almost 10% using the $Iv3+SVM : All$ method, due to the better recall results. Furthermore, the $Iv3+SVM : All$ has the advantage to be easily re-trained for recognizing any object among a group.

The performance for both methods, $Iv3$ and $Iv3+SVM : All$, is quite similar, however, statistical significance of differences was computed and proved using a χ^2 test with a 2×2 contingency table and $\alpha = 0.05$, obtaining a $p - value <$ 0.0001 for the AC, DC and IC groups of classes. This test assumes unpaired data which corresponds to our situation since the training sets were different for each method.

Finally, it was surprising the $Color + Shape + SVM$ method's poor performance. During some previous experiments with cleaner images and fewer classes, this method showed a good performance. However, our dataset from *Google Images* contains images that are not exactly related with the classes or that have many different views, and these could be some of the factors causing the drop of the method's performance.

Given the outcomes of the first experiment, the $Iv3+SVM$: $Binary$ method was selected to complete our object recognition system. The Iv3 model is the top of the object recognition solutions until now, and the main goal of our experiment was not to propose a better object recognition system, but instead, to demonstrate that applying our method it is feasible to recognize, with a high precision, an unknown object using transfer learning from a pre-trained DNN.

On the other hand, the second experiment conducted consists of measuring the execution time elapsed by the entire object recognition system using our selected method. The results of this experiment are shown in Table 4. The second column of the table depicts the number of images involved in every step of the system and the third column shows the average time elapsed for each step after 10 complete runs.

The object recognition system runs on Python 2.7.12 over Ubuntu 16.04. The computer used for the experiments has four Intel Core i7-6500U processors at 2.50 GHz and 8 Gb RAM. The Internet connection speed for downloads was 10 Mb/s.

Table 4. Execution time for the entire object recognition system using the $Iv3+SVM$: $Binary$ method

	Images involved	Iv3 + SVM : Binary
Step 1: Search options	6	14.04 ± 2.81 s
Step 2: Download images	80	77.23 ± 3.29 s
Step 3: Clean images	80 → 75	2.16 ± 0.06 s
Step 4: Obtain attributes	150	33.40 ± 1.00 s
Step 5: Train the model	150	0.12 ± 0.02 s
Step 6: Classify images	1	1.10 ± 0.32 s
Total time		128.06 ± 3.50 s

The first step involves 6 example images used to show what the user can expect according to his/her search string. The Step 1 duration will vary depending on the Internet connection speed, but in our case, it will remain less than 20 s whichever the object to be searched or the filters applied.

The second step involves the images used to learn a concept, for our experiments, we used 80 images. Again, the duration of this step depends on the Internet connection speed, in our case, the images were approximately downloaded at a rate of 1 image per second. The images' size and the number of images used for the model training impact on the time required to finish this step. However, for our experiments, 80 images were enough to obtain high classification rates as it was shown in the first experiment.

The third step consists of cleaning the 80 downloaded images, since *TensorFlow* works only with *jpg* format images. Images from *Google Images* have different formats and not all of them can be retrieved correctly. For each one of the 10 runs of our experiment, the cleaning step removed 5 images that were unusable. Therefore, at the end of the step, there are 75 images ready to be processed in order to obtain their attributes. The time consumed by this step was very constant along all runs, and it was always less than 2.3 s.

The $Iv3 + SVM : Binary$ method starts working on Step 4 where attributes from the 75 downloaded and cleaned images must be obtained. These examples are labeled as the positive class. On the other hand, 75 negative class examples are selected from images of the 72 classes involved in our first experiment. If the positive class is among our 72 classes, its examples are discarded from the dataset. The time rate to retrieve the images' attributes using the Iv3 DNN was on average 2.25 images per second. Therefore, using this method, it is possible to create, in less than 35 s, a data set able to train an accurate object recognition system.

Step 5 is the faster on the entire system as the SVM requires less than 0.15 s to be trained. Therefore, aggregating Steps 4 and 5, our system is able to learn a new concept in less than 36 s, and then, recognize what was learned with at least 96% of precision.

Finally, once the concept was learned, the system is ready to search the required object. Thus, our system will take less than 1.5 s evaluating an object in order to determine if it is or it is not the requested object.

Overall, the proposed system is able to learn an accurate model of a completely unknown object using images from Internet in roughly two minutes.

5   Conclusions and Future Work

Object recognition is a relevant task in computer vision and in particular for robotics. The field has been recently dominated by Deep Neural Networks achieving impressive results over a large number of objects. Training DNN models, however, require a large number of samples and take very long training times. If we want a robot to search for an unknown object it has to select relevant images and quickly induce an adequate model to be useful for the user. In this paper we described a system that downloads relevant images from Internet, with the aid of a user interface, and leverages the use of DNNs to quickly learn a model using the outputs of pre-trained intermediate layers as features of a fast classifier. It is shown that the proposed system can learn a model for an unknown object in about two minutes with high performance measures, even in objects that were not used for training the original DNN.

As future work, we will like to use a real robot to search for unknown objects, suggested by independent users, in a house environment.

References

1. Krizhevsky, A., Sutskever, I., Hinton, G.E.: Imagenet classification with deep convolutional neural networks. In: Advances in Neural Information Processing Systems, pp. 1097–1105 (2012)
2. Sermanet, P., Eigen, D., Zhang, X., Mathieu, M., Fergus, R., LeCun, Y.: OverFeat: integrated recognition, localization and detection using convolutional networks. arXiv preprint arXiv:1312.6229 (2013)
3. Jia, Y., et al.: Caffe: convolutional architecture for fast feature embedding. In: Proceedings of the 22nd ACM International Conference on Multimedia, pp. 675–678. ACM (2014)
4. Simonyan, K., Zisserman, A.: Very deep convolutional networks for large-scale image recognition. arXiv preprint arXiv:1409.1556 (2014)
5. Chatfield, K., Simonyan, K., Vedaldi, A., Zisserman, A.: Return of the devil in the details: delving deep into convolutional nets. arXiv preprint arXiv:1405.3531 (2014)
6. Ouyang, W., et al.: DeepID-Net: deformable deep convolutional neural networks for object detection. In: Proceedings of the IEEE Conference on Computer Vision and Pattern Recognition, pp. 2403–2412 (2015)
7. Szegedy, C., et al.: Going deeper with convolutions. In: Proceedings of the IEEE Conference on Computer Vision and Pattern Recognition, pp. 1–9 (2015)
8. Szegedy, C., Vanhoucke, V., Ioffe, S., Shlens, J., Wojna, Z.: Rethinking the inception architecture for computer vision. In: Proceedings of the IEEE Conference on Computer Vision and Pattern Recognition, pp. 2818–2826 (2016)
9. Jaderberg, M., Vedaldi, A., Zisserman, A.: Speeding up convolutional neural networks with low rank expansions. arXiv preprint arXiv:1405.3866 (2014)
10. Lebedev, V., Ganin, Y., Rakhuba, M., Oseledets, I., Lempitsky, V.: Speeding-up convolutional neural networks using fine-tuned CP-decomposition. arXiv preprint arXiv:1412.6553 (2014)
11. Zhang, X., Zou, J., He, K., Sun, J.: Accelerating very deep convolutionalnetworks for classification and detection. IEEE Trans. Pattern Anal. Mach. Intell. **38**(10), 1943–1955 (2016)
12. Mathieu, M., Henaff, M., LeCun, Y.: Fast training of convolutional networks through FFTs. arXiv preprint arXiv:1312.5851 (2013)
13. Kim, Y.-D., Park, E., Yoo, S., Choi, T., Yang, L., Shin, D.: Compression of deep convolutional neural networks for fast and low power mobile applications. arXiv preprint arXiv:1511.06530 (2015)
14. Chen, W., Wilson, J., Tyree, S., Weinberger, K., Chen, Y.: Compressing neural networks with the hashing trick. In: International Conference on Machine Learning, pp. 2285–2294 (2015)
15. Carneiro, G., Nascimento, J., Bradley, A.P.: Unregistered multiview mammogram analysis with pre-trained deep learning models. In: Navab, N., Hornegger, J., Wells, W.M., Frangi, A.F. (eds.) MICCAI 2015. LNCS, vol. 9351, pp. 652–660. Springer, Cham (2015). https://doi.org/10.1007/978-3-319-24574-4_78
16. Castelluccio, M., Poggi, G., Sansone, C., Verdoliva, L.: Land use classification in remote sensing images by convolutional neural networks. arXiv preprint arXiv:1508.00092 (2015)
17. Yosinski, J., Clune, J., Bengio, Y., Lipson, H.: How transferable are features in deep neural networks? In: Advances in Neural Information Processing Systems, pp. 3320–3328 (2014)

18. Penatti, O.A., Nogueira, K., dos Santos, J.A.: Do deep features generalize from everyday objects to remote sensing and aerial scenes domains? In: Proceedings of the IEEE Conference on Computer Vision and Pattern Recognition Workshops, pp. 44–51 (2015)
19. Ng, H.-W., Nguyen, V.D., Vonikakis, V., Winkler, S.: Deep learning for emotion recognition on small datasets using transfer learning. In: Proceedings of the ACM International Conference on Multimodal Interaction, pp. 443–449. ACM (2015)
20. Litjens, G., et al.: A survey on deep learning in medical image analysis. arXiv preprint arXiv:1702.05747 (2017)
21. Codella, N., Cai, J., Abedini, M., Garnavi, R., Halpern, A., Smith, J.R.: Deep learning, sparse coding, and SVM for melanoma recognition in dermoscopy images. In: Zhou, L., Wang, L., Wang, Q., Shi, Y. (eds.) MLMI 2015. LNCS, vol. 9352, pp. 118–126. Springer, Cham (2015). https://doi.org/10.1007/978-3-319-24888-2_15
22. Akilan, T., Wu, Q.J., Yang, Y., Safaei, A.: Fusion of transfer learning features and its application in image classification. In: IEEE 30th Canadian Conference on Electrical and Computer Engineering, pp. 1–5. IEEE (2017)
23. D'Innocente, A., Carlucci, F.M., Colosi, M., Caputo, B.: Bridging between computer and robot vision through data augmentation: a case study on object recognition. arXiv preprint arXiv:1705.02139 (2017)
24. Dalal, N., Triggs, B.: Histograms of oriented gradients for human detection. In: IEEE Computer Society Conference on Computer Vision and Pattern Recognition, vol. 1, pp. 886–893. IEEE (2005)

Introducing a Classification Model Based on SVM for Network Intrusion Detection

Ghodratolah Dastfal[1], Samad Nejatian[2,3(✉)], Hamid Parvin[1,4], and Vahideh Rezaie[3,5]

[1] Department of Computer Engineering, Nourabad Mamasani Branch,
Islamic Azad University, Nourabad, Mamasani, Iran
[2] Department of Electrical Engineering, Yasooj Branch,
Islamic Azad University, Yasooj, Iran
nejatian@iauyasooj.ac.ir
[3] Young Researchers and Elite Club, Yasooj Branch,
Islamic Azad University, Yasooj, Iran
[4] Young Researchers and Elite Club, Nourabad Mamasani Branch,
Islamic Azad University, Nourabad, Mamasani, Iran
[5] Department of Mathematic, Yasooj Branch,
Islamic Azad University, Yasooj, Iran

Abstract. Intrusion Detection Systems are designed to provide security into computer networks. In this article, we used rough sets theory for feature selection to enhance support vector machine in intrusion detection. Testing and evaluation of the proposed method has been performed mainly on NSL-KDD data sets as a corrected version of KDD-CUP99. Experimental results indicate that the proposed method shows a good performance in providing high precision, intrusion detection readout, less error notification rate and more detailed detection compared to its basic and simpler methods.

Keywords: Intrusion detection · Support vector machine · Data size reduction
Feature selection · IDS

1 Introduction

There are three main reasons to use intrusion detection systems [1]: (a) Legal and controlling problems, (b) Specification and definition for types of attacks, and (c) Overall implementation of in-depth-defense.

Generally speaking, malwares are potential risks and threats to global security, which also are spreading in terms of their number and variety, on a daily basis [2]. In addition to damage to users' computers, malwares can have an access to users' privacy and therefore steal the confidential information of them. Unfortunately, due to the vulnerability of the application, most valid software packs originate unwanted intrusion of the malwares and this endangers users' privacy even by applying a legal software pack.

© Springer Nature Switzerland AG 2018
F. Castro et al. (Eds.): MICAI 2017, LNAI 10632, pp. 54–66, 2018.
https://doi.org/10.1007/978-3-030-02837-4_5

The present paper is organized as follows:

In the first section, an introduction and overview of the research will be presented. In the second section, it will mention to tasks has been done in this field and there will be a review of the related literature. In the third section, details of the proposed method, such as feature selection techniques used in SVM algorithm for intrusion detection systems will be provided. In the fourth section, details of implementing the proposed method, data sets and tools for detection are given. Then, the evaluation method will be discussed. At the end of this article, the results of the tests will be offered. Eventually in the fifth section, a general conclusion will be presented about the contents of this article and there will be a review of new horizons and offering suggestions for future research on the subject.

2   A Review of Previous Work

Artificial intelligence has been used in many applications [3–6]. Data mining is one of the branches of artificial intelligence. Extraction of knowledge from a large amount of data is named data mining [10]. Based on our different expectations, different data mining tasks emerged. The most important category of tasks in data mining is supervised learning tasks [3–6]. Data mining is one of the branches of artificial intelligence. Extraction of knowledge from a large amount of data is named data mining [3–20].

Zhang and Sun employed Tabu Search (TS) for pattern selection [21]. TS is applied on a primitive set (solution), and during the search process, some solutions are identified as tabu (which means that solution should not be changed); other solutions will be evaluated (non-taboo solutions) in order to find the best solution (by a classifier). Procedure of finding a solution from all solutions is the assessment of neighboring sets in which only a different element with Si is replaced by a better organized subset and when this process is completed, S is the best solution found so far.

According to direct computation of decision level separation methods are implemented in another category of studies that is based on the maximum margin separation of data of two data classes and other categories. In this category of researches, it is attempted to gain a decision level in order to classify the data in which such a decision level creates the maximum margin of separation between two classes. Two popular methods in this area are references [22] and [23]. In [22], the aim is to determine the distance-based separation function with a maximum distance of each data class in Baanakh space. For this purpose, Lipschitz functions have been used where a fixed Lipschitz function indicates the separation margin value. Finding the suitable Lipschitz function for real data is a difficult task, and the current solutions are weak in terms of performance. In this regard the results of its implementation are not satisfactory in terms of performance. In another method of SVM [23], a linear decision level in Hilbert space is proposed with the aim of considering maximum margin of separator between two classes of data, with the assistance of optimization procedures. In this method, the problem of finding the decision level has turned into a quadratic programming problem. Regarding issues of high-volume, such as Intrusion Detection, a part of current challenges is solving this planning problem [24]. Although Support Vector Machines have a potential ability to classify the data in intrusion detection, they cannot be used solely in intrusion detection systems. Based on the conducted studies, some cases affect the efficiency of these systems. When the number of normal data inputs in the training time is more than attack data, these machines will be able to work more accurately; which it is not always possible. On one hand, the number for the aspects of network traffic features is significant in training time, as well as the system performance. In many training data sets (such as KDDCUP99 [25]), of 41 features, it is possible to select some of the key features of machines and employ them in machine training. In [26], a combination of support vector machine, the Simulated Annealing (SA) and the decision tree is used to detect the attacks. The SA is used in optimization problems. At the beginning, SVM and SA are used to select the best features and furthermore to take advantage of the decision tree and SA to generate decision rules. These phases will be performed in a cycle and will be continued until the termination condition is not established. The output of these algorithm of selected features, gives the best accuracy in the evaluation set and decision rules. Kuang et al. [26], proposed a new hybrid model for SVM, consisting of kernel principal component analysis (KPCA) in combination with genetic algorithm (GA) for the problem of intrusion detection. In this model, KPCA is used to reduce the feature vectors size and the run-time as well. Furthermore, to reduce noises caused by different features and improve the SVM performance, an improved kernel function (N-RBF) is proposed. GA is employed to optimize the penalty factor, C, kernel parameters, σ, and ε for SVM. The results for applying this method indicate an increase in prediction accuracy, acceleration of convergence speed and a better generalization in comparison to other similar algorithms. Similarly, the authors in [27], used the combination of KPCA and the Improved Chaotic Particle Swarm Optimization Method (ICPSO) to deal with the intrusion detection problem. In this model, ICPSO is used to optimize above parameters. Using this method in dataset of NSL-KDD, has led to the improvement of similar results.

3   Instruments and Methods

Today, the use of classifiers in applications with large data is inevitable. Using classifiers is ever-increasing in many fields such as in biology, satellite images with large scale and hyperspectral [28] and web pages on the Internet. Nowadays, the development in methods of classification to be used in these fields is a real challenge. In this context (from an application view point in terms of bulky and large-scale data) non-parametric classification techniques without learning stage (without optimization) as SVM are of a high importance. Considering the importance of their application, studies are focused on new category of applications. In regard to these problems, large projects in recent years been defined in combination with fields having wide variety of data such as malware detection. It is worthy to note some applications mentioned in [29, 30].

3.1   Feature Selection

The feature selection problem is one of the problems that have been raised in the context of machine learning and statistical identification of the template. This problem is important in many applications, such as categorization, since in these applications, there are features, many of which have little or no use, or have not much information. If no removing be conducted on these features, it does not lead to a problem in terms of information, however, the computational rate of this application will be increased and moreover it causes a lot of useless information to be saved, along with useful data. In intrusion detection systems, it is difficult to analyze and classify due to the fact that the amount of data that the system needs to check and monitor a network is too much. Thus, an intrusion detection system should reduce the amount of data to be processed so that the complexity of relationships exists between some features to be deleted or lower [31]. Since the increase in number of features increases the computational cost of the system, designing and implementing systems with the least number of features is necessary.

One of the desired data mining concepts based on that we can extract and select features is *rough sets theory* which is discussed in the next section.

3.2 Rough Set Theory

Rough Set Theory (RST), an intelligent mathematical tool to deal with uncertainty and ambiguity, first time was presented in 1982 by Professor Pawlak [32]. This theory is considered as a new mathematical method to analyze intelligent data and data mining. After about three decades of laying the foundation of Rough set theory, its applicable methods have reached a certain accomplishment and in recent years, there is a considerable growth of this theory and its applications all around the universe. The concept of set theory is based on this assumption that every member of the Universal Series, U, contains certain information (data, knowledge), that these traits are described by some Qualities (Q). This information can be observed in the data table, where each of the rows, pointing to various objects and each column represents a property of the object. If in the data table, sets of feature Q divided into conditional features of C and determining features of D, in a way that $Q = C \cup D$, it will be called S's Decision table. Correlations that have been used in the rest of this section, all are given from the reference [33].

Every subset of X, of the Universal Series, may be interpreted in terms of partitioned sets accurately or approximately. The subset of X, may be specified by two normal sets called upper and lower approximations. According to Eq. (1), the bottom approximation X, is formed of the entire partitioned collection properly in X (the elements X, X is definitely belongs to) (Fig. 1).

$$P(X) = \{x \in U : I_p(x) \subseteq X\} \tag{1}$$

where, $I_p(x)$ represents the equivalence relationship on U, which is calculated according to Eqs. 2 and 3. $P \subseteq Q$ is an infinite subset of features.

$$I_p = \{(u,v) \in U \times U | \forall a \in p, (a(u) = a(v)) \cup (a(u) = *) \cup (a(v) = *)\} \tag{2}$$

$$I_p(x) = \{v \in U | (u,v) \in I_p \tag{3}$$

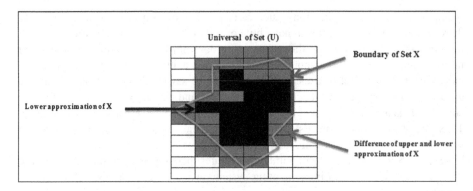

Fig. 1. An ideal approximation set X in U.

Based on the Eq. (4), high approximation of X consists of all partitioned sets that bear non-empty subscription with X (x elements may have belonged to X).

$$\overline{P(x)} = \{x \in U : I_p(x) \cap X \neq \emptyset\} \tag{4}$$

If $(i = 1, \ldots, n)yi$, are partitions of the set U to D variables, the top and down of P approximations can be generalizable to two sets of $P(Y) = \{P(y1), \ldots, P(yn)\}$.

$POSp(D)$ is called, quality division and based on Eq. (5), this parameter indicates all correct classified objects to all objects in a universal set U. Based on Eq. (6), $sig(a, P, D, U)$ shows the importance degree of variable a.

$$POS_p(D) = \frac{\sum_{i=1}^{n} |P(Y_i)|}{|U|} \tag{5}$$

$$sig(a, P, D, U) = POS_{p \cup \{a\}}(D) - POS_p(D) \tag{6}$$

The discernibility matrix is calculated based Eqs. (7), (8) and (9). This matrix is used to find the smallest subset of appropriate features.

$$M_P = \begin{cases} m_p(i,j) & \min\{|\partial_p(x_i)|, |\partial_p(x_j)| = 1\} \\ \emptyset & else \end{cases} \tag{7}$$

Where in Eq. (7), $\partial p(x)$ is known as a decision function. If $|\partial p(x)| = 1$ for each instance of a universal set U, then S is compatible and otherwise incompatible.

$$\partial_p(x) = \{i | i = D(y), y = I_p(x)\} \tag{8}$$

$$m_p(i,j) = \begin{cases} b | (b \in P) \cap (b(x_i) \neq *) \cap (b(x_j) \neq *) \cap (b(x_i) \neq (x_j)) & D(x_i) = \neq D(x_j) \\ \emptyset & else \end{cases} \tag{9}$$

$$1 \leq i, j \leq n = |U|.$$

Once the smallest subset of convenient features is found, all features that do not exist in the subtracted collection will be removed from the feature set. Then these features will be ranked based on their importance level. Then, features will be classified based on how important they are. A feature's importance level is remarked in a basis that to what extent one feature is significant during the course of classification. This criterion is determined based on characteristics of feature dependency. In this thesis, Rough set theory is used to incorporate similar features and reducing their number. Using this set theory increases the processing speed and attack detection rates. Details of the proposed method are presented in the next section.

3.3   The Improved Support Vector Machine with Rough Set Theory

The kernel function acts as a key for mapping of two-dimensional space onto a higher-dimensional one. This function, determines the form of final separator. Therefore, it is logical that this function should be transformed for the purpose of getting to a better type of the data. This means that the SVM improvement is associated with variation of the SVM kernel function.

On one hand, the use of all available parameters of the network packs to evaluate and detect attacks patterns increases processing overhead, prolongs diagnosis process and thus the reduces the efficiency of intrusion detection systems. As mentioned before, the aim of having feature selection is to find a subset that will maximize the classification measures, such as the classification accuracy. Since removing worthless and useless input data simplifies the problem and accelerates more accurate and fast intrusion detection, the feature selection is a very important subject in feature selection.

In the model presented in this paper, the rough set theory is used for feature selection. In [34], the ability to detect attacks has been described in intrusion detection systems and results have indicated that the rough set theory has a high classification accuracy and it performs classification task faster. In [35], the Rough set theory method is used in intrusion detection and shown its efficiency in feature selection. In this paper the presented intrusion detection system, utilizes the rough set theory in order to develop a weighing generalizable kernel in combination with SVM algorithm to create a new model for increasing the attack detection speed and selecting a new combinatorial kernel function which in turn leads to enhance a high performance and reducing the computer sources, such as memory and processing time. Using important parameters for classification, leads to a better accuracy and significantly reduces training time and testing as well.

3.4   Using Rough Set as the Weighted Kernel of SVM

So far, many SVM kernel functions have been introduced for different applications. The most common ones were the linear function, polynomial function, sigmoid function and the radial basis function. The major weakness of these kernels is the lack of differences between the characteristics of a given data set. By attention to general form of the kernel function SVM, $K(x_i, x)$; we will see all features of the training and testing data sets are treated the same. Equal treatment with all features may not work and will have an adverse effect on the accuracy of SVM. A possible solution for this problem, is adding weights to the kernel function based on the importance level of various features. The weights are used to measure the importance of each feature. A general form of a new kernel function is formulated in a $K(wx_i, wx)$ form. In this case, the nonlinear separator function with weights of features will be in the form of Eq. (10):

$$f(x) = \left\{ sgn \left(\sum_{i=1}^{l} \alpha_i y_i K(wx_i, wx) + b \right) \right.$$ (10)

Where, I is the number of subtracted features and w is a vector containing the weights of all the features of data sets. This $\vec{w}$ vector is considered as a diagonal matrix (Eq. 11).

$$\vec{w} = \begin{bmatrix} w_0 & \cdots & 0 \\ \vdots & \ddots & \vdots \\ 0 & \cdots & w_l \end{bmatrix}.$$ (11)

The improved SVM model pursues the main following objectives:

- The reduction of redundant features to increase the speed of intrusion detection.
- Applying the features information of SVM classification to improve the accuracy of intrusion detection.

Generally, the robust nature of the support vector machine along with the structure of detracting the feature vector, developing a mathematical accord and having the rough sets feature, is one of the proposed method properties that provides the objectivity of accuracy and timing of the algorithm in order to have smart intrusion detection.

4 Experimental Result

In this section, in order to discriminate strengths and weaknesses of the proposed method as well as an analysis of its performance in comparison to basic methods, NSL-KDD-CUP99 data set is used to evaluate it; for this purpose, several tests with the aim of evaluating different parameters have been arranged so that its features are investigated. The results of these experiments with the analysis of the proposed method work, all are presented in this section. At first, while presenting details of the proposed system, the data sets used, and the data preprocessing condition will be reviewed. Then, the tests and the evaluation parameters will be presented and eventually, the tests' results with proper analyses and the comparison of other basic methods will be offered.

4.1   Details of the Proposed System

To evaluate the proposed method, NSL-KDD [27] data set is used. This dataset contains selected records of KDD-CUP99 [36] in which the existing problems, such as duplicate records in the data set have been eliminated. Since 1999, KDD-CUP99 dataset was the most beneficiary dataset for evaluating the anomaly detection methods and network intrusion. This data set is developed by Stolfo et al. [37], based on an application for evaluation of intrusion detection systems, called DARPA'98 [38].

The proposed intrusion detection system in this study has five components including data set, normalization, feature selection, support vector machine and the post-processing. Figure 2 shows the structure of the proposed intrusion detection system.

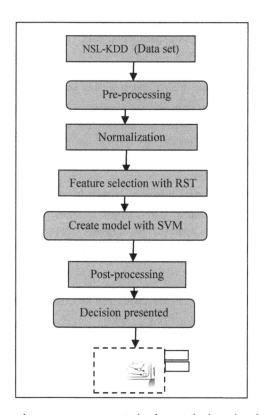

Fig. 2. The proposed system components to implement the intrusion detection function.

4.2   The Evaluation of Results

To train the proposed system, 2,000,000 records of KDDTrain+ set were randomly selected without-replacement in such a way that it includes 24 types of detected attacks, and to test it, also 700,000 records of KDDTest+ set were selected in such a way that 14 unknown new attacks to be included in addition to the 24 known attacks. After selecting the important features, the input data decreased by about 80%.

Of advantages of feature selection in proposed method are less time in training and support vector machine test and therefore computational costs and as a result less computer sources such as memory and processor time which deemed to be necessary for attack detection. For this reason, training and test duration are computed in two modes: presence of feature and lack of feature.

These times are calculated in milliseconds (ms). Comparison of Precision, recall and *F*-score based on attack modes are shown for each class of 41 features and eight features in Tables 1, 2, 3 and 4, respectively. What is evident is that, recall and *F*-scale of intrusion detection system will also increase by selecting feature of precision. In all 5 classes of attacks, detection percentage is higher when we use 8 features compared to using 41 features of datasets. This specifically will be in higher state for detection percentage of U2R and R2L classes. Also, the system uses the most important features of a higher power to detect new and unknown attacks that has not been faced in training process and it is contained only in experimental data.

Table 1. Training and testing time of SVM model without and with using the selection feature

	41 features	8 features	Time reduction
Training time	28384654 ms	8489850 ms	70.09%
Testing time	2348220 ms	377124 ms	83.94%

Table 2. SVM attack detection accuracy for each attack class

	Normal	DoS	PRB	U2R	R2L
41 features	76.71%	97.72%	99.86%	53.49%	63.39%
8 features	96.65%	97.29%	99.87%	55.86%	99.04%

Table 3. SVM attack detection recall for each attack class

	Normal	DoS	PRB	U2R	R2L
41 features	97.99%	86.27%	97.65%	40.07%	53.55%
8 features	98.39%	84.10%	98.50%	46.40%	65.40%

Table 4. SVM attack detection F-measure for each attack class

	Normal	DoS	PRB	U2R	R2L
41 features	86.05%	91.63%	98.74%	45.81%	58.05%
8 features	97.51%	90.11%	99.18%	50.69%	78.77%

In this part, the performance of SVM is compared to Multi Layer Perceptron (MLP) Artificial Neural Network and Back-Propagation algorithm (BP). The BP Learning algorithm is based on Steepest Descent algorithm (SD). Setting the network parameters is carried out in accordance with the error signals which will be calculated based on presentation of each pattern to the network. MATLAB software is used to implement this method. The comparison of Precision, recall and F-score, is showed in Figs. 3, 4 and 5 based on order of attack modes for each class of 41 features and eight features for the support vector machine and neural networks, respectively. As it is shown, the percentage of the mentioned criteria is almost higher than the neural network for both 41 and 5 features of the SVM.

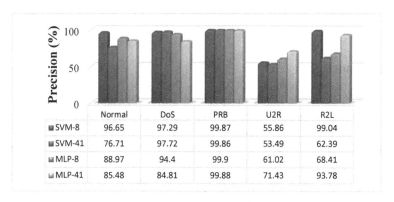

	Normal	DoS	PRB	U2R	R2L
SVM-8	96.65	97.29	99.87	55.86	99.04
SVM-41	76.71	97.72	99.86	53.49	62.39
MLP-8	88.97	94.4	99.9	61.02	68.41
MLP-41	85.48	84.81	99.88	71.43	93.78

Fig. 3. Comparison of attack detection accuracy rate in the different classes for different methods

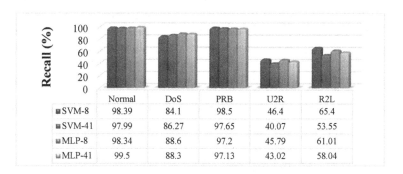

	Normal	DoS	PRB	U2R	R2L
SVM-8	98.39	84.1	98.5	46.4	65.4
SVM-41	97.99	86.27	97.65	40.07	53.55
MLP-8	98.34	88.6	97.2	45.79	61.01
MLP-41	99.5	88.3	97.13	43.02	58.04

Fig. 4. Comparison of attack detection recall rate in the different classes for different methods

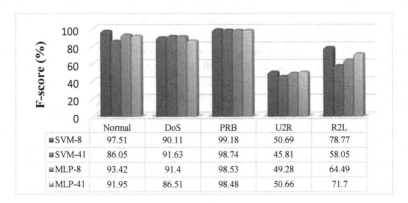

Fig. 5. Comparison of attack detection F-measure rate in the different classes for different methods

5 Conclusion

Intrusion detection methods are divided into two categories, misuse detection and anomaly detection. In misuse detection, pre-made intrusion samples in a form of law are kept. So that each model encompasses different types of a certain intrusion and if such a model occurs in the system, the intrusion will be announced. In anomaly detection method, by specifying the behavior as normal for the studied subject (user, host or the entire system), any deviation from this behavior is considered as abnormal that can be a possibility of an attack. In this thesis, the network-based intrusion detection system was evaluated based on anomaly method of Rough sets theory and support vector machine uses. Rough sets theory is known as one of the most widely used methods in the discovery of knowledge in information systems. This set theory is an extended version of classical theories and is based on approximation concept. Using all existing methods in connected network in order to evaluate and discover attacks' models, due to the fact that some of these features are unrelated and redundant, leads to the scoria increase and the rater makes errors, and utilizing all features prolongs the detection process and reduce intrusion detection system performance. The use of feature selection methods is beneficial because of managing and reducing computation time. In this article, we reviewed some of the basic concepts of the Rough set theory and the explanation of some of its applications as well as showing how to reduce data from a variety of attacks conducted by this theory. The Rough set theory, by discovering dependencies on different data and using equivalence rules can lead to the reduction of redundant data in the data set of the Intrusion Detection System. Then, different layers of this system, including data sets, data preprocessing, feature selection, support vector machines and post-processing, were evaluated separately. To train and test the proposed model, NSL-KDD datasets were used. Among the advantages of the proposed model, is reducing the cost of computing and, as a result, computer resources such as memory and CPU time reduction, which is necessary to detect attacks. Also, by selecting the feature in the proposed model, the accuracy level, recall and F-Measure intrusion detection system increases. Additionally, the SVM performance was compared with the one of MLP neural network. The results indicated that the SVM had a higher performance than the neural network. The high performance of SVM to neural network could be for the following reasons:

- Feature Selection in SVM is less complex than the neural networks. Gamma and margin parameters are set in SVM while in neural networks, the number of hidden layers, neurons, transfer functions, etc., must be specified. Inappropriate parameter selection causes problems in neural networks.
- SVM implements the principle of minimum structural risk.

References

1. Endorf, C., Eugene, S., Mellander, J.: Intrusion Detection & Prevention. McGraw-Hill, New York (2004)
2. Santos, I., Sanz, B., Laorden, C., Brezo, F., Bringas, P.G.: Opcode-sequence-based semi-supervised unknown malware detection. Comput. Intell. Secur. Inf. Syst. **6694**, 50–57 (2011)
3. Alishvandi, H., Gouraki, G.H., Parvin, H.: An enhanced dynamic detection of possible invariants based on best permutation of test cases. Comput. Syst. Sci. Eng. **31**(1), 53–61 (2016)
4. Parvin, H., Minaei-Bidgoli, B., Alinejad-Rokny, H.: A new imbalanced learning and dictions tree method for breast cancer diagnosis. J. Bionanosci. **7**(6), 673–678 (2013)
5. Parvin, H., Alinejad-Rokny, H., Minaei-Bidgoli, B., Parvin, S.: A new classifier ensemble methodology based on subspace learning. J. Exp. Theor. Artif. Intell. **25**(2), 227–250 (2013)
6. Parvin, H., Minaei-Bidgoli, B., Alinejad-Rokny, H., Punch, W.F.: Data weighing mechanisms for clustering ensembles. Comput. Electr. Eng. **39**(5), 1433–1450 (2013)
7. Parvin, H., Alizadeh, H., Minaei-Bidgoli, B.: A New method for constructing classifier ensembles. JDCTA **3**(2), 62–66 (2009)
8. Parvin, H., Alinejad-Rokny, H., Asadi, M.: An ensemble based approach for feature selection. J. Appl. Sci. Res. **7**(9), 33–43 (2011)
9. Parvin, H., Alizadeh, H., Minaei-Bidgoli, B., Analoui, M.: CCHR: combination of classifiers using heuristic retraining. In: International Conference on Networked Computing and Advanced Information Management (NCM 2008) (2008)
10. Parvin, H., Alizadeh, H., Fathy, M., Minaei-Bidgoli, B.: Improved face detection using spatial histogram features. In: IPCV 2008, pp. 381–386 (2008)
11. Parvin, H., Alinejad-Rokny, H., Parvin, S.: A classifier ensemble of binary classifier ensembles. Int. J. Learn. Manag. Syst. **1**(2), 37–47 (2013)
12. Parvin, H., Minaei-Bidgoli, B.: A clustering ensemble framework based on elite selection of weighted clusters. Adv. Data Anal. Classif. **7**(2), 181–208 (2013)
13. Alizadeh, H., Minaei-Bidgoli, B., Parvin, H.: Optimizing fuzzy cluster ensemble in string representation. IJPRAI **27**(2), 1350005 (2013)
14. Parvin, H., Beigi, A., Mozayani, N.: A clustering ensemble learning method based on the ant colony clustering algorithm. Int. J. Appl. Comput. Math. **11**(2), 286–302 (2012)
15. Alizadeh, H., Minaei-Bidgoli, B., Parvin, H.: To improve the quality of cluster ensembles by selecting a subset of base clusters. J. Exp. Theor. Artif. Intell. **26**(1), 127–150 (2014)
16. Alizadeh, H., Minaei-Bidgoli, B., Parvin, H.: Cluster ensemble selection based on a new cluster stability measure. Intell. Data Anal. **18**(3), 389–408 (2014)

17. Minaei-Bidgoli, B., Parvin, H., Alinejad-Rokny, H., Alizadeh, H., Punch, W.F.: Effects of resampling method and adaptation on clustering ensemble efficacy. Artif. Intell. Rev. **41**(1), 27–48 (2014)

18. Parvin, H., Minaei-Bidgoli, B.: A clustering ensemble framework based on selection of fuzzy weighted clusters in a locally adaptive clustering algorithm. Pattern Anal. Appl. **18**(1), 87–112 (2015)

19. Parvin, H., Mirnabibaboli, M., Alinejad-Rokny, H.: Proposing a classifier ensemble framework based on classifier selection and decision tree. Eng. Appl. Artif. Intell. **37**, 34–42 (2015)

20. Parvin, H., Mohammadi, M., Rezaei, Z.: Face identification based on Gabor-wavelet features. Int. J. Digit. Content Technol. Appl. **6**(1), 247–255 (2012)

21. Bhutan, M.H., Bhattacharyya, D.K., Kalita, J.K.: Network anomaly detection: methods, systems and tools. IEEE Commun. Surv. Tutor. **16**(1), 303–336 (2014)

22. Luxburg, U.V., Bousquet, O.: Distance-based classification with Lipschitz functions. J. Mach. Learn. Res. **5**, 669–695 (2004)

23. Cortes, C., Vapnik, V.: Support-vector network. Mach. Learn. **20**, 273–297 (1995)

24. Zhang, J., Perdisci, R., Lee, W., Luo, X., Sarfraz, U.: Building a scalable system for stealthy P2P-botnet detection. IEEE Trans. Inf. Forensics Secur. **9**(1), 27–38 (2014)

25. KDD Cup (1999), October 2007. http://kdd.ics.uci.edu/databases/kddcup99/kddcup99.html

26. Kuang, F., Xu, W., Zhang, S.: A novel hybrid KPCA and SVM with GA model for intrusion detection. Appl. Soft Comput. **18**, 178–184 (2014)

27. NSL-KDD data set for network-based intrusion detection systems, March 2009. http://nsl.cs.unb.ca/NSL-KDD/

28. Keshavarz, A., Ghassemian, H., Dehghani, H.: Hierarchical classification of hyperspectral images by using SVMs and neighborhood class property. In: IEEE IGARSS2005, pp. 3219–3222 (2005)

29. Woniakeyot, M., Graña, M., Corchado, E.: A survey of multiple classifier systems as hybrid systems. Inf. Fusion **16**, 45–90 (2014)

30. Bijani, S., Robertson, D.: A review of attacks and security approaches in open multi-agent systems. Artif. Intell. Rev. 1–30 (2012)

31. Chebrolu, S., Abraham, A., Thomas, J.P.: Feature deduction and ensemble design of intrusion detection systems. Comput. Secur. **24**, 295–307 (2005)

32. Pawlak, Z.: Rough sets. Int. J. Comput. Inf. Sci. **11**(5), 341–356 (1982)

33. Zhou, J., Hu, L., Wang, F., Lu, H., Zhao, K.: An efficient multidimensional fusion algorithm for IOT data based on partitioning. Tsinghua Sci. Technol. **18**, 369–378 (2013)

34. Zhang, L., Zhang, G., Yu, L., Bai, Y.: Intrusion detection using rough set classification. J. Zhejiang Univ. Sci. **5**(9), 1076–1086 (2004)

35. Chen, R.C., Cheng, K., Hsieh, C.F.: Using rough set and support vector machine for network intrusion detection system. In: Proceedings of the 1st Asian Conference on Intelligent Information and Database Systems, Washington, DC, USA (2009)

36. Tavallaee, M., Bagheri, E., Lu, W., Ghorbani, A.A.: A detailed analysis of the KDD CUP 99 data set. In: Proceeding of the 2009 IEEE Symposium on Computational Intelligence in Security and Defense Application (CISDA) (2009)

37. Stolfo, S.J., Fan, W., Prodromidis, A., Chan, P.K., Lee, W.: Cost-sensitive modeling for fraud and intrusion detection: results from the JAM project. In Proceedings of the 2000 DARPA information survivability conference and exposition (2000)

38. Lippmann, R., Haines, J., Fried, D., Korba, J., Das, K.: The 1999 DARPA off-line intrusion detection evaluation. Comput. Netw. **34**, 579–595 (2000)

Evolutionary Algorithms and Optimization

On the Many-Objective Pickup and Delivery Problem: Analysis of the Performance of Three Evolutionary Algorithms

Abel García-Nájera[✉], Antonio López-Jaimes, and Saúl Zapotecas-Martínez

Departamento de Matemáticas Aplicadas y Sistemas,
Universidad Autónoma Metropolitana Unidad Cuajimalpa,
Av. Vasco de Quiroga 4871, Col. Santa Fe Cuajimalpa,
05300 Ciudad de México, Mexico
{agarcian,alopez,szapotecas}@correo.cua.uam.mx

Abstract. Many-objective optimization focuses on solving optimization problems with four or more objectives. Effort has been made mainly on studying continuous problems, with interesting results and for which several optimizers have been proposed. Nevertheless, combinatorial problems have not received as much attention, making this an open research area. An important result on continuous problems states that the problem does not necessarily becomes more difficult while more objectives are considered, but, does this result hold for combinatorial problems? This investigation takes this subject on by studying a many-objective combinatorial problem, particularly, the pickup and delivery problem (PDP), which is an important combinatorial optimization problem in the transportation industry and consists in finding a collection of routes with minimum cost. Traditionally, cost has been associated with the number of routes and the total travel distance, however, some other objectives emerge in many applications, for example, travel time, workload imbalance, and uncollected profit. If we consider all these objectives equally important, PDP can be tackled as a many-objective problem. This study is concerned with the study of the performance of three multi-objective evolutionary algorithms on the PDP varying the number of objectives, in order to analyze the change of PDP's difficulty when the number of objectives is increased. Results show that the problem becomes more difficult to solve while more objectives are considered.

Keywords: Many-objective optimization
Pickup and delivery problem
Multi-objective evolutionary algorithms · Combinatorial optimization

1 Introduction

Many-objective optimization is a research area which considers problems with more than three objectives [2] and that has drawn the researcher's attention in

© Springer Nature Switzerland AG 2018
F. Castro et al. (Eds.): MICAI 2017, LNAI 10632, pp. 69–81, 2018.
https://doi.org/10.1007/978-3-030-02837-4_6

the past few years. This interest stems from the fact that several experimental and analytical studies have shown that the performance of well-known multi-objective evolutionary algorithms (MOEAs) based on Pareto dominance quickly degrades as the number of objectives to optimize increases. Effort has been led to the proposal of more robust algorithms in order to solve problems with four or more objective functions. Nonetheless, most of these studies have been focused on continuous problems, while combinatorial problems have received scarce attention [9,10].

From these studies we have learned that the main source of difficulty that makes a multi-objective optimization problem harder is the fact that the proportion of non-dominated solutions (i.e., equally good solutions according to Pareto dominance) in a population increases rapidly with the number of objectives. However, as pointed out by Schütze et al. [11], the increase in the number of non-dominated individuals is not a sufficient condition for an increment of the hardness of a problem, since in certain problems their difficulty is marginally increased when more objectives are added despite the exponential growth of the proportion of non-dominated solutions.

Ishibuchi et al. [5] analyzed the effect of adding objectives to a combinatorial optimization problem. They analyzed the performance of some representative MOEAs on a discretized version of the knapsack multi-objective problem. Contrary to what is observed in continuous many-objective problems, they found that NSGA-II and SPEA2 improved their performance when the number of objectives increased in this discretized problem. They argue that the source of this behavior is because the number of non-dominated solutions decreases when the knapsack problem is discretized, and therefore, the pressure selection does not decay as happens in many-objective continuous problems. This study is an evidence that results observed when the objectives are continuous cannot be directly applied for discrete objectives.

In addition to the previous study, Ishibuchi et al. [4] examined the behavior of NSGA-II, MOEA/D, SMS-EMOA, and HypE, which are three classes of MOEAs, on many-objective knapsack problems. Their experimental results are consistent with well-known performance deterioration of Pareto dominance-based algorithms. That is, NSGA-II is outperformed by the other algorithms. However, it was also shown that NSGA-II outperforms the other algorithms when objectives are highly correlated. MOEA/D shows totally different search behavior depending on the choice of a scalarizing function and its parameter value. Some MOEA/D variants work very well only on bi-objective problems while others work well on many-objective problems with four to ten objectives.

Therefore, an open research question is whether the same sources of difficulty observed in continuous spaces are the same in problems with discrete spaces. To this end, the pickup and delivery problem (PDP) is formulated as a many-objective problem in order to analyze the scalability of three MOEAs when more objectives are aggregated.

The PDP is part of the vehicle routing class of problems [6], which is known to be NP-hard [7]. The PDP considers transportation requests, which are defined between pairs of customers. The problem consists in designing a set of routes with minimum cost to service all transportation requests, where cost has traditionally been associated with the number of routes and the travel distance.

An additional distinctive feature of PDP is that it has both continuous and discrete objectives, e.g. the number of routes is discrete, while travel distance is a continuous objective. Hence, it is not trivial to predict the way in which PDP's difficulty is going to change when the number of objectives is varied.

In summary, we study the performance of three MOEAs on the many-objective PDP using different objectives settings, in order to analyze the change of the PDP's difficulty when the number of objectives is increased.

The remainder of this paper is organized as follows. Section 2 introduces the main concepts of multi-objective optimization and explains the performance metrics that are used here to test algorithm performance. Section 3 describes the many-objective PDP. The multi-objective optimizers used in this study are briefly described in Sect. 4. Section 5 presents the experimental set-up and the analysis of the results. Finally, conclusions are given in Sect. 6.

2 Multi-objective Optimization Problems

Any multi-objective optimization problem can be defined, without loss of generality, as the problem of minimizing $\mathbf{f}(\mathbf{x}) = (f_1(\mathbf{x}), \ldots, f_m(\mathbf{x}))$, subject to $g_i(\mathbf{x}) \leq 0, \forall\ i \in \{1, \ldots, p\}$, and $h_j(\mathbf{x}) = 0, \forall\ j \in \{1, \ldots, q\}$, where $\mathbf{x} \in \mathcal{X}$ is a potential solution to the problem, $\mathcal{X}$ is the domain of feasible solutions, $\mathbf{f} : \mathcal{X} \rightarrow \mathbb{R}^m$ are the m objective functions, and the constraint functions $g_i, h_j : \mathcal{X} \rightarrow \mathbb{R}$ delimit the feasible search space.

We say that solution $\mathbf{x}$ *dominates* solution $\mathbf{y}$, written as $\mathbf{x} \prec \mathbf{y}$, if and only if $f_i(\mathbf{x}) \leq f_i(\mathbf{y}), \forall\ i \in \{1, \ldots, m\}$, and $\exists\ j : f_j(\mathbf{x}) < f_j(\mathbf{y})$. Consequently, solution $\mathbf{x} \in \mathcal{S} \subseteq \mathcal{X}$ is *non-dominated* with respect to $\mathcal{S}$ if there is no solution $\mathbf{y} \in \mathcal{S}$ such that $\mathbf{y} \prec \mathbf{x}$. Solution $\mathbf{x} \in \mathcal{X}$ is said to be *Pareto optimal* if it is non-dominated with respect to $\mathcal{X}$, and the *Pareto optimal set* is defined as $\mathcal{P}_s = \{\mathbf{x} \in \mathcal{X} \mid \mathbf{x} \text{ is Pareto optimal}\}$. Finally, the *Pareto front* is defined as $\mathcal{P}_f = \{\mathbf{f}(\mathbf{x}) \in \mathbb{R}^m \mid \mathbf{x} \in \mathcal{P}_s\}$.

In contrast, with single-objective problems, where one can straightforwardly compare the best solutions from the various approaches studied, multi-objective problems have to compare whole sets of solutions. Many performance indicators have been proposed in the literature, being two of them the *hypervolume* and the *generational distance*, which are explained next.

Hypervolume Indicator. The hypervolume performance metric $H(\mathcal{A}, \mathbf{z})$ concerns the size of the objective space defined by the approximation set $\mathcal{A}$, which is limited by setting a suitable reference point $\mathbf{z}$. Formally, for a two-dimensional objective space $\mathbf{f}(\mathbf{x}) = (f_1(\mathbf{x}), f_2(\mathbf{x}))$, each solution $\mathbf{x_i} \in \mathcal{A}$ delimits a rectangle defined by $(f_1(\mathbf{x_i}), f_2(\mathbf{x_i}))$ and the reference point $\mathbf{z} = (z_1, z_2)$, and the size of the union of all such rectangles is used as the measure. This concept can be extended to any number of dimensions to give the general hypervolume metric.

72   A. García-Nájera et al.

Generational Distance Indicator. In order to evaluate the convergence of the algorithms to the Pareto front, we adopted the generational distance indicator $\mathsf{GD}(\mathcal{A})$, which is defined by $\mathsf{GD}(\mathcal{A}) = 1/|\mathcal{A}| \left(\sum_{i=1}^{|\mathcal{A}|} d_i^2 \right)^{1/2}$, where d_i is the Euclidean distance between each solution $\mathbf{x_i} \in \mathcal{A}$ and the nearest member of $\mathcal{P}_f$.

3   The Many-Objective Pickup and Delivery Problem

The pickup and delivery problem considers a set $\mathcal{V} = \{0, 1, \ldots, N, N+1, \ldots, 2N\}$ of $2N + 1$ vertexes. Customers are represented by the vertexes in the subset $\mathcal{V}' = \mathcal{V} \setminus \{0\}$. Each customer $i \in \mathcal{V}'$ is geographically located at coordinates (x_i, y_i), and has an associated time window $[b_i, e_i]$, during which it has to be serviced, and a service time s_i required to load or unload goods. Customer subset $\mathcal{V}_{\mathcal{P}} = \{1, \ldots, N\}$ corresponds to the pickup locations, while customer subset $\mathcal{V}_{\mathcal{D}} = \{N+1, \ldots, 2N\}$ represents the delivery locations.

The set $\mathcal{O} = \{1, \ldots, N\}$ represents N transportation requests. Each transportation request $i \in \mathcal{O}$ specifies the size q_i of the load to be transported between locations $i \in \mathcal{V}_{\mathcal{P}}$ and $N + i \in \mathcal{V}_{\mathcal{D}}$, where the load will be picked up (origin) and delivered (destination), respectively.

The vertex 0 is located at (x_0, y_0), has a time window $[0, e_0 \geq \max \{e_i \mid i \in \mathcal{V}'\}]$, and service time $s_0 = 0$. This vertex is the base of a homogeneous fleet of vehicles which have capacity $Q \geq \max \{q_i \mid i \in \mathcal{O}\}$.

The aim of the problem is to find a set of routes which minimize the travel cost, subject to the following constraints: (*i*) Each route starts and ends at the base; (*ii*) Each customer is visited for service exactly once; (*iii*) Vehicles cannot arrive at customers locations after the end of their time windows; (*iv*) The vehicle load must not, at any time, be negative and must not exceed the vehicle capacity Q; (*v*) For each transportation request $j \in \mathcal{O}$, its pickup location i must be visited in the same route and before its corresponding delivery location $N + i$; and (*vi*) For each transportation request $j \in \mathcal{O}$, its delivery location $N + i$ must be visited in the same route and after its corresponding pickup location i.

The travel between vertexes i and j has associated costs, such as travel distance d_{ij} (relating to fuel cost) and travel time t_{ij} (relating to driver salary). However, in some applications, cost is improbably to be associated with whether distance or time, but with both. This is the reason why some previous studies have considered travel distance and travel time as independent sources of cost and optimized them simultaneously. That is, the PDP has been tackled as a multi-objective problem.

Moreover, we can identify additional objectives to be optimized in this problem. Since the use of a vehicle implies a leasing or maintenance, the number of vehicles used to attend the transportation requests can also be minimized. Regarding transportation requests, if we consider that each request has an associated profit and that they are optional to be attended, this means that the origin and destination customers associated to a request might not be visited, consequently, there is no profit collected from that request. This situation would involve the minimization of the uncollected profit. Finally, we can also take into account the workload balance, such that all routes have similar distances and duration. This leads to the minimization of the travel distance of the longest route, and to the minimization of the travel time that ends the latest.

4   Multi-objective Optimizers

In this section, the three multi-objective optimizers used in this study for solving the many-objective PDP are briefly described.

4.1   GN-MOEA

García-Nájera and Gutiérrez-Andrade [3] proposed a problem-specific multi-objective evolutionary algorithm (GN-MOEA) for minimizing three objectives of the PDP simultaneously, namely the number of routes, the travel distance, and the travel time. GN-MOEA uses an encoding of list of lists: a route is encoded as a list and a solution as a list of routes. They use the non-dominance sorting criterion to assign fitness to individuals. Solution similarity is used as a diversity measure. This is simply computed as the ratio of the number of arcs that are common in two solutions to the total number of arcs traversed in both solutions. This measure is used in the mating selection process, since one parent is selected according to the diversity measure and the other is selected according the fitness. These parents are selected by using the tournament selection method. Crossover aims at combining routes from both parents, while mutation exchanges transportation requests between routes, and removes transportation requests from one route and inserts them into another.

4.2   MOEA/D

MOEA/D [12] was selected because it is one of the current best multi-objective optimizers and has been shown to offer improved performance on problems closely related to the VRP. It works by explicitly decomposing the multi-objective problem defined in Sect. 2, with m objective functions f_i, into m scalar minimization subproblems j of the form $\phi(\mathbf{x}|\boldsymbol{\lambda}^j) = \sum_{i=1}^{m} \lambda_i^j f_i(\mathbf{x})$, where $\mathbf{x}$ is a problem solution, $\phi(\mathbf{x}|\boldsymbol{\lambda}^j)$ is the objective function of subproblem j, and $\boldsymbol{\lambda}^j = (\lambda_1^j, \ldots, \lambda_m^j)$ is the corresponding weight vector with positive components that sum to 1. Then, the optimal solution to each scalar problem is a Pareto optimal solution of the full problem, and using a uniform distribution of m weight vectors $\{\boldsymbol{\lambda}^j\}$ gives a set of m different Pareto optimal solutions. MOEA/D minimizes all m objective functions simultaneously in a single run by maintaining a population composed of the best solution found so far for each subproblem [12]. It also maintains an archive of the non-dominated solutions of the original multi-objective problem found during the search.

　　MOEA/D follows the same sequence of stages as any evolutionary algorithm, except that, after reproduction, the offspring is submitted to an improvement heuristic instead of the mutation stage. If the resulting offspring dominates any solutions in the archive, those solutions are removed from it. If no solution in the archive dominates the offspring, it is added to the archive. Further details can be found in the original publication of Zhang and Li [12].

4.3 NSGA-III

More recently, Deb and Jain [1] proposed NSGA-III, an improvement of its predecessor NSGA-II. This new algorithm was based on the original framework of its predecessor, in which a key element is the non-dominated sorting for survival selection. In this sorting method the combination of parents and offspring is classified into several non-dominated levels. Each level is composed of mutually non-dominated solutions. Once all solutions are classified, individuals of each level are selected to construct the population for the next generation. This process ends when the size of the population is N. If the number of individuals of the last level that completes the population exceeds N, then a secondary criterion is used. In NSGA-II the crowding distance was adopted. That is, those with the largest crowding distance are selected to fill the remaining spaces for the new population. The improvement introduced in NSGA-III is the criterion for selecting individuals from the last level. Instead of crowding distance, NSGA-III adopts a niche mechanism based on a set of predefined reference points. Each reference point defines a niche, so that solutions in less crowded niches are selected first to compose the new population. In order to create the set of reference points at each generation a hyper-plane using the extreme solutions of the current approximation of the Pareto front is computed.

5   Experimental Set-Up and Results

Our study has two main purposes. Firstly, to know the performance of the three MOEAs on solving a number of benchmark instances of the many-objective PDP, and secondly, to perform a many-objective analysis of the PDP. To this end, we carried out a series of experiments, which considered an increasing number of objectives to be optimized.

In order to have controlled experiments, we used the PDP benchmark set of Li and Lim [8][1]. This set includes 56 instances of size $N = 50$, and are divided into six categories: lc1, lc2, lr1, lr2, lrc1, and lrc2. Customers in categories lc1 and lc2 are located in clusters, in categories lr1 and lr2 are located randomly, and in categories lrc1 and lrc2 are located in both clusters and randomly. Categories lc1, lr1, and lrc1 consider wider time windows and larger vehicle capacities, while categories lc2, lr2, and lrc2 narrower time windows and smaller vehicle capacities.

All three algorithms were configured with the same crossover and mutation operators used in GN-MOEA. Crossover and mutation rates were set to 1.0 and 0.1 for the three algorithms. Population size in GN-MOEA and NSGA-III was set to 100 and in MOEA/D was set to 200. The number of generations was set to 500. We ran all three algorithms 30 times for each problem instance.

---

[1] Instances are publicly available from the web site https://www.sintef.no/projectweb/top/pdptw/li-lim-benchmark/. Last accessed: 7/1/2017.

Table 1. Number of instances in each category for which non-dominated solutions from GN-MOEA (G) and NSGA-III (N) cover a significantly larger hypervolume than those from the other for each objectives settings.

Instance category	RP		RPD		RPDT		RPDTd		RPDTdt	
	G	N	G	N	G	N	G	N	G	N
lc1 (9)	0	2	3	3	0	9	0	9	0	8
lc2 (8)	1	1	0	2	0	8	0	7	0	8
lr1 (12)	10	0	0	11	0	12	0	12	0	8
lr2 (11)	0	1	6	0	0	11	0	6	0	6
lrc1 (8)	8	0	0	6	0	8	0	8	0	5
lrc2 (8)	0	1	3	2	0	8	0	7	1	6
Total (56)	19	5	12	24	0	56	0	49	1	41

5.1 Analysis of the Hypervolume Indicator

To compute the hypervolume indicator, we require an appropriate reference point. From the 90 Pareto approximations for each instance (30 from each algorithm), we took the maximum value for each objective, and the reference point **z** was set 10% above each dimension's maximum value. For each instance and repetition, we took the non-dominated set and computed the hypervolume covered by those solutions. Then, we applied a statistical Wilcoxon rank-sum test (two-sample, one-tailed) to the three pairs of vectors of 30 hypervolume values (GN-MOEA and MOEA/D, GN-MOEA and NSGA-III, and MOEA/D and NSGA-III) to test the alternative hypothesis that the mean hypervolume delimited by the solutions from optimizer A is larger than that covered by the solutions from optimizer B. For each pair of algorithms A and B, we counted the number of instances for which the hypervolume delimited by the Pareto approximation from algorithm A is significantly larger than that covered by the non-dominated set from algorithm B and viceversa. The test employed has a significance level of 5%. The summary of the statistical test between GN-MOEA and NSGA-III is shown in Table 1. The first column of Table 1 show the instance category, and the number of instances comprising that category is shown between parenthesis. This Table has one main column for each combination of objectives, and each main column has two subcolumns, corresponding to the number of instances in each instance category for which non-dominated solutions from GN-MOEA (G) and from NSGA-III (N), respectively, covered a statistically larger hypervolume.

We can observe that, in the RP case, non-dominated solutions from GN-MOEA covered a significantly larger hypervolume than those from NSGA-III in 19 out of the 56 instances, and the latter outperformed the former in 5. However, the performance of NSGA-III improved for objectives settings RPD and $RPDT$, for which its non-dominated solutions covered a significantly larger hypervolume for nearly half of the instances and for all 56 instances, respectively. Nevertheless, the enhanced performance of NSGA-III decayed for objectives $RPDTd$ and

Table 2. Number of instances in each category for which non-dominated solutions from GN-MOEA (G) and NSGA-III (N) are significantly closer to the reference set than those from the other for each objectives settings.

Instance category	RP		RPD		$RPDT$		$RPDTd$		$RPDTdt$	
	G	N	G	N	G	N	G	N	G	N
lc1 (9)	3	0	0	8	0	9	0	9	9	0
lc2 (8)	1	0	2	0	0	8	2	4	6	1
lr1 (12)	8	0	0	10	0	12	0	6	5	1
lr2 (11)	1	1	2	4	0	10	0	1	8	1
lrc1 (8)	8	0	0	3	0	8	0	6	2	1
lrc2 (8)	0	0	1	3	0	8	0	6	7	0
Total (56)	21	1	5	28	0	55	2	32	37	4

$RPDTdt$. This would indicate that the problem becomes more difficult to solve while more objectives are being optimized, since the superior performance of NSGA-III displayed for three and four objectives was not maintained for five and six objectives.

In this case we only show the results for this pair of algorithms, since solutions from them largely surpassed those from MOEA/D and this situation does not provide additional valuable information to make conjectures.

5.2 Analysis of the Generational Distance Indicator

Since the optimal Pareto front is not known for the benchmark instances, a reference set for each instance was used for computing the generational distance GD, which was formed with the non-dominated solutions resulting from the union of all the approximation sets obtained by each algorithm at the end of every run.

After computing GD for each approximation set obtained by the four algorithms, the Wilcoxon rank-sum test (two-sample, one-tailed) was computed to determine which algorithm yielded the shorter generational distance. The alternative hypothesis is that the mean of GD generated by optimizer A is less than that of B was tested, considering a significance level of 5%. Table 2 presents a summary of the statistical tests, which structure is similar to that of Table 1.

From Table 2 we can observe that, in the RP case, non-dominated solutions from GN-MOEA are significantly closer to the reference set than those from NSGA-III in 21 out of the 56 instances, and those from NSGA-III are significantly closer only in one instance. As for the hypervolume, the performance of NSGA-III improved for objectives RPD and $RPDT$, for which its non-dominated solutions are significantly closer to the reference set for half of the instances and for 55 instances, respectively. However, again, the enhanced performance of the NSGA-III decayed for objectives $RPDTd$ and $RPDTdt$. Furthermore, for the latter case, not only the performance of NSGA-III decayed, but the non-dominated

Table 3. Success rate of GN-MOEA, MOEA/D, and NSGA-III in finding solutions with the minimum and maximum values for objective P.

	Minimum			Maximum		
	GN-MOEA	MOEA/D	NSGA-III	GN-MOEA	MOEA/D	NSGA-III
RP	100	100	100	65	87	61
RPD	99	99	47	61	85	63
$RPDT$	97	100	14	60	85	62
$RPDTd$	95	100	18	65	86	62
$RPDTdt$	93	100	7	62	85	62
%Decrease	7	0	93	5	2	0

solutions from GN-MOEA have a significantly shorter generational distance than those from NSGA-III for 37 instances. The performance of these algorithms is consistent with the one analyzed in the hypervolume indicator.

As for the hypervolume, we only show the results for this pair of algorithms, since non-dominated solutions from these algorithms widely outperformed those from MOEA/D and does not provide further information to the analysis.

5.3   Analysis of Objective P Extreme Values

From all the six objectives, we only know the minimum and maximum values for objective P, which are zero and the total possible profit, respectively. Using these values we can analyze whether the three optimizers are able to find those extreme values. For each instance and optimizer, we computed the success rate, that is, the per cent of the execution times that the algorithms found at least one solution with the minimum uncollected profit, and at least one solution with the maximum uncollected profit. Table 3 shows the success rate for the minimum and maximum uncollected profits.

From Table 3, we observe for the minimum value that the success rate of MOEA/D is very high, since for each objectives settings is 100%, on average, except for objectives settings RPD, which is 99%. The success rate of GN-MOEA is, on average, higher than 93% for all objectives settings. Contrastingly, the success rate of NSGA-III decayed 93%, since for objectives settings RP was 100% and for objectives settings $RPDTdt$ was 7%.

Regarding the maximum value, the success rate of the three algorithms was nearly constant, though that of MOEA/D was above 85%, which is 20% higher than those of GN-MOEA and NSGA-III.

The fact that NSGA-III is not able to maintain a high success rate in finding the minimum and maximum values, is an evidence that the problem becomes more difficult to solve while more objectives are considered. This is concordant to the previous analysis made of the two performance indicators.

Table 4. Average size of the non-dominated sets, grouped by instance category, from MOEA/D (M) and NSGA-III (N) for each objectives settings.

Instance category	RP		RPD		RPDT		RPDTd		RPDTdt	
	M	N	M	N	M	N	M	N	M	N
lc1 (9)	11	11	34	96	58	100	97	100	178	100
lc2 (8)	5	4	13	56	21	100	54	100	119	100
lr1 (12)	15	14	53	100	80	100	140	100	200	100
lr2 (11)	4	4	22	95	33	100	94	100	157	100
lrc1 (8)	15	14	46	100	65	100	111	100	196	100
lrc2 (8)	5	4	22	93	31	100	86	100	151	100

Table 5. Average execution time (in seconds), grouped by instance category, of GN-MOEA (G), MOEA/D (M) and NSGA-III (N) for each objectives settings.

Instance category	RP			RPD			RPDT			RPDTd			RPDTdt		
	G	M	N	G	M	N	G	M	N	G	M	N	G	M	N
lc1	91	59	65	33	60	26	45	61	25	43	60	25	46	64	33
lc2	128	84	108	35	90	35	53	88	44	58	84	45	72	86	53
lr1	88	51	50	46	54	31	49	53	25	46	56	24	46	56	23
lr2	176	107	145	61	119	72	75	116	77	83	116	73	82	124	52
lrc1	77	51	44	39	53	28	46	55	25	42	56	20	44	53	18
lrc2	169	88	127	53	90	54	56	91	64	67	87	67	71	90	53

5.4   Size of the Approximation Sets

Despite not being concluding data, the size of the approximation sets could give additional information of the algorithms' performance. In Table 4 we present the average approximation sets size, grouped by instance category, for non-dominated solutions from MOEA/D and NSGA-III. In this case, we do not present results for GN-MOEA since the size of the non-dominated sets are similar to those from NSGA-III. In this case, we can observe that, when optimizing three objectives, RPD, the size of the non-dominated sets found by NSGA-III is nearly maximum (100), and with four to six objectives, $RPDT$ to $RPDTdt$, the size is maximum. Contrastingly, the size of the non-dominated sets from MOEA/D never reaches the maximum (200), except for category lr1. This could be due to that vectors in MOEA/D are not well distributed because of the discrete objectives like the number of routes and uncollected profit.

5.5   Execution Time

Finally, in order to have supplementary information, we present in Table 5 the average execution time, grouped by instance category, of the three algorithms under study. First of all, we can see that the execution time of MOEA/D is nearly steady for each instance category, no matter which and how many objectives are being optimized. On the other hand, GN-MOEA and NSGA-III present the largest execution time for each instance category while optimizing two objectives. This is known for Pareto dominance-based algorithms, since, in this case, there are few solutions in each non-dominated front. For the remaining objectives settings, both algorithms present approximately the same execution time for instance categories lc1, lr1, and lrc1, but this is not the case for instance categories lc2, lr2, and lrc2, where both algorithms have a slightly increase in the execution time. In general, all three algorithms have a shorter execution time for instance categories lc1, l1, and lrc1 than for instance categories lc2, lr2, and lrc2. This is expected since the latter categories consider wider customer time windows and larger vehicle capacities, which allow more solutions to be feasible, consequently the algorithms have a higher probability to find feasible solutions and update the non-dominated set.

5.6   Final Remarks

As we have seen from the previous subsections, there is no constant performance of any algorithm for any metric, either hypervolume, generational distance, success rate of finding the minimum and maximum values for objective P, the number of non-dominated solutions, and the execution time. NSGA-III is probably one the most credible state-of-the-art many-objective algorithms, however, GN-MOEA, which was not design for solving the many-objective PDP, and MOEA/D, which is probably considered a not-anymore-state-of-the-art algorithm, are capable of surpassing NSGA-III in some metrics. With this analysis we can conjecture that the many-objective PDP becomes more difficult to solve while more objectives are considered, and that conclusions on continuous problems does not necessarily hold for combinatorial problems.

6   Conclusions

In this paper we have analyzed the many-objective PDP, namely the change of difficulty when the number of objectives is increased. To this end, we employed three multi-objective optimizers: GN-MOEA, which was previously designed to specifically solve the PDP, the well-known MOEA/D, which has been successful in a number of applications, and the state-of-the-art NSGA-III, which has proved to be a baseline optimizer for continuous many-objective problems. We ran a series of experiments to optimize six objectives in an aggregated manner.

   Our analysis is three-fold. First, we computed the hypervolume and the generational distance of the non-dominated solutions found by the three algorithms. We found that GN-MOEA and NSGA-III have an enhanced performance over MOEA/D for both indicators and for all objectives settings. However, the improved performance that NSGA-III showed over GN-MOEA for two to four objectives, deteriorated for five and six objectives.

Secondly, we computed the success rate of each algorithm in finding the minimum and maximum values for objective P. Regarding the minimum value, MOEA/D presented the best performance, finding the minimum value practically 100% of the times. Contrastingly, the success rate of NSGA-III degenerated from 100% for two objectives to 7% for six objectives.

Finally, we analyzed the number of non-dominated solutions in the Pareto approximations and the execution time of the three algorithms. In this case, we found that GN-MOEA and NSGA-III have similar performance due to they both are Pareto dominance-based algorithms. Something different was found for MOEA/D, since it is based on decomposition. Regarding the number of non-dominated solutions, while GN-MOEA and NSGA-II promptly filled the maximum number of non-dominated solutions (four objectives), MOEA/D did not, not even with six objectives. With respect to execution time, MOEA/D executed in practically the same time for each instance category, while GN-MOEA and NSGA-III took an increasing time when more objectives were considered.

After these interesting results, we believe that we can continue with our research by investigating why MOEA/D and NSGA-III are not able to find solutions to have similar performance metrics, that is, what are the properties of NSGA-III that make it a better solver when considering hypervolume and generational distance, and what are the characteristics of MOEA/D which make it find the extreme solutions.

References

1. Deb, K., Jain, H.: An evolutionary many-objective optimization algorithm using reference-point-based nondominated sorting approach, Part I: solving problems with box constraints. IEEE Trans. Evol. Comput. **18**(4), 577–601 (2014)
2. Farina, M., Amato, P.: On the optimal solution definition for many-criteria optimization problems. In: NAFIPS-FLINT International Conference 2002, pp. 233–238. IEEE (2002)
3. Garcia-Najera, A., Gutierrez-Andrade, M.A.: An evolutionary approach to the multi-objective pickup and delivery problem with time windows. In: 2013 IEEE Congress on Evolutionary Computation, pp. 997–1004. IEEE (2013)
4. Ishibuchi, H., Akedo, N., Nojima, Y.: Behavior of multiobjective evolutionary algorithms on many-objective knapsack problems. IEEE Trans. Evol. Comput. **19**(2), 264–283 (2015)
5. Ishibuchi, H., Yamane, M., Nojima, Y.: Difficulty in evolutionary multiobjective optimization of discrete objective functions with different granularities. In: Purshouse, R.C., Fleming, P.J., Fonseca, C.M., Greco, S., Shaw, J. (eds.) EMO 2013. LNCS, vol. 7811, pp. 230–245. Springer, Heidelberg (2013). https://doi.org/10.1007/978-3-642-37140-0_20
6. Laporte, G.: Fifty years of vehicle routing. Transport. Sci. **43**(4), 408–416 (2009)
7. Lenstra, J.K., Kan, A.H.G.R.: Complexity of vehicle routing and scheduling problems. Networks **11**(2), 221–227 (1981)
8. Li, H., Lim, A.: A metaheuristic for the pickup and delivery problem with time windows. In: 13th International Conference on Tools and Artificial Intelligence, vol. 1, pp. 160–167. IEEE Computer Society (2001)

9. López Jaimes, A., Coello Coello, C.A.: Many-objective problems: challenges and methods. In: Kacprzyk, J., Pedrycz, W. (eds.) Springer Handbook of Computational Intelligence, pp. 1033–1046. Springer, Heidelberg (2015). https://doi.org/10.1007/978-3-662-43505-2_51
10. von Lücken, C., Barán, B., Brizuela, C.: A survey on multi-objective evolutionary algorithms for many-objective problems. Comput. Optim. Appl. **58**(3), 707–756 (2014)
11. Schütze, O., Lara, A., Coello Coello, C.A.: On the influence of the number of objectives on the hardness of a multiobjective optimization problem. IEEE Trans. Evol. Comput. **15**(4), 444–455 (2011)
12. Zhang, Q., Li, H.: MOEA/D: a multiobjective evolutionary algorithm based on decomposition. IEEE Trans. Evol. Comput. **11**(6), 712–731 (2007)

An Evolutive Scoring Method for Cloud Computing Provider Selection Based on Performance Indicators

Lucas Borges de Moraes, Adriano Fiorese, and Rafael Stubs Parpinelli[✉]

Graduate Program in Applied Computing, Santa Catarina State University,
Joinville 89219-710, Brazil
lucasborges1292@gmail.com, {adriano.fiorese,rafael.parpinelli}@udesc.br

Abstract. The success of cloud computing paradigm has leveraged the emergence of a large number of new companies providing cloud computing services. This fact has been making difficult, for consumers, to choose which cloud providers will be the most suitable to attend their computing needs, satisfying their desired quality of service. To qualify such providers it is necessary to use metrics, such as performance indicators (PIs), useful for systematic and synthesized information collection. A genetic algorithm (GA) is a bio-inspired meta-heuristic tool used to solve various complex optimization problems. One of these complex optimization problems is to find the best set of cloud computing providers that satisfies a customer's request, with the least amount of providers and the lowest cost. Thus, this article aims to model, apply and compare results of a GA and a deterministic matching algorithm for the selection of cloud computing providers.

1 Introduction

Cloud computing has emerged as a service model capable of hosting and distributing, on demand, computing resources around the world via the Internet [1,2]. This service model abstracts from the consumer, the complex infrastructure and internal architecture of the service provider. Thus, to use the service, the consumer don't need to perform installations, configurations, software updates or purchase specialized hardware. Soon, this paradigm has brought the benefit of better use of computational resources [2], besides being a convenient service, easily accessible via the network and priced only for the time it is used [1].

This paradigm has become a good source of investment in both academia and industry and its success has motivated its adoption and deployment in every major known IT companies (e.g., Google, Amazon, Microsoft, Salesforce.com, IBM, etc.). Thus, a large number of new companies has been competitively created as providers of cloud computing services. This explosion in the number of providers does not essentially mean a guarantee of quality of service. With the increasing number of new providers, the task of choosing and selecting which

F. Castro et al. (Eds.): MICAI 2017, LNAI 10632, pp. 82–94, 2018.
https://doi.org/10.1007/978-3-030-02837-4_7

cloud providers are best suited to each customer's need has become a complex process. Measuring the quality of each provider and comparing them is not a trivial process, since there are usually many factors and criteria involved throughout this process (e.g., cost, latency, computational resources offered, availability, flexibility, reliability, etc.) [3–7].

Assessing the quality of a provider can be made by systematically measuring the individual quality of each of its associated performance indicators (PIs), reaching a certain value or ranking. Indicators are an effective and practical tool to systematically measure (assign value) to different aspects of an organization. Thus, each provider ("organization") will have a set of associated PIs. At the end of the assessment process, those providers that present the best assessed value through their PIs will be elect as the most suitable provider to attend the previously defined requirements.

After obtaining the necessary PIs, this quality calculation of each provider can be performed by a simple and intuitive matching algorithm, weighted by the importance of each PI, as proposed in [8]. The problem in using this matching approach is that a single provider may not be able to effectively attend all the defined requirements, i.e., a better solution would become a subset of all available providers. So, any non-empty subset would be a possible answer. The complexity of conducting an exhaustive search would be exponential to the number of providers involved in selection (2^n), disabling the use of an exhaustive search algorithm for a selection problem with a significantly large number of providers (n). It is in this scenario that the use of an heuristic/meta-heuristic search algorithm is highlighted. Therefore, this work will use a genetic algorithm.

The genetic algorithm, or simply GA, is a meta-heuristic search technique, bio-inspired, first introduced by John Holland in the 1970s [9]. Since then the GA has been used for real optimization problems of high complexity. Holland studied the natural evolution of the species and considered this a robust and powerful process that could be easily adapted to a computational algorithm capable of obtaining satisfactory solutions to complex optimization problems in an acceptable period of time. Thus, the objectives of this article are: To model a GA that is able to select one or more cloud providers (based on their known PIs) satisfying the customer's request with the lowest possible cost and with the smallest number of providers; and to compare the efficiency and the execution time of the GA and the deterministic matching algorithm described in [8].

This work is organized as follows: Sect. 2 presents an overview of the problem addressed in this work. Section 3 describes the methodology used to solve the problem described, as well as the modeling developed to specify a provider selection method using GA. So, Sect. 4 presents a set of experiments in a particular scenario to demonstrate and validate the operation of the developed approach. Finally, Sect. 5 elaborates on the final considerations.

2   The Problem of Selecting Cloud Computing Providers

Given a finite initial set P with n distinct cloud providers, each one with M distinct associated PIs, the problem is to choose the best subset of providers in

P, in order to attend a specific request of a cloud service consumer with the least possible amount of providers and with the lowest cost involved. The consumer request represents its computing needs to achieve its goals and must have all PIs of interest of the customer, with its respective value and desired importance. In practice, a third-party (e.g., the server where the selection method is hosted) initially has an extensive database containing a list of cloud computing providers. Each provider has a respective set of PIs, fed directly or indirectly by organizations such as brokers and/or cloud auditors [1] or maintained by the cloud providers themselves in order to create a cooperative and publicly accessible database. The existence of this database is an essential requirement for the GA to be able to identify the registered PIs and their values.

PIs are tools that enable a systematic summarized information collection about a particular aspect of an organization. They are metrics responsible for quantifying (assigning a value) the objects of study to be measured, allowing organizations to monitor and control their own performance over time. PIs should be carefully measured in periods of regular time so that they are representative to the characteristic they represent. Some PIs found in the literature are: Computer resources offered, cost of service, supported operating systems, security level, response time, availability, recoverability, accuracy, reliability, transparency, usability, customer support, etc. [4–7,10–13]. Cloud computing has a noticeable set of PIs organized in a hierarchical framework divided into seven major categories (accountability, agility, service assurance, financial, performance, security and privacy, usability), called Service Measurement Index (SMI), developed by Cloud Service Measurement Index Consortium (CSMIC) [14].

Indicators are classified into quantitative discrete or quantitative continuous, i.e., they can be expressed numerically and worked algebraically; and qualitative ordered or qualitative unordered, i.e., they have distinct states, levels or categories defined by an exhaustive and mutually exclusive set of sub classes, which may be ordered (possesses a logical gradation among its sub classes, giving idea of a progression) or not [15]. It is also possible to classify PIs according to the behavior of their utility function, i.e., how useful the PI becomes when its numerical value varies [15]: HB (Higher is Better - The highest possible values for this indicator are preferred), LB (Lower is Better - The smallest possible values for this indicator are preferred) and NB (Nominal is Best - A particular value is considered to be the best, higher and lower values are undesirable). A notably and relevant PI for selecting cloud providers is cost. Cost is a PI to be always considered, even if it is not informed by the customer in the request, since it is a value that is always desirable to minimize (LB).

Figure 1 presents the initial scenario comprising the provider selection problem based on its PIs. In this case, a total of m PIs of interest should be chosen by the customer according to its goals towards cloud providers. The customer will have a support interface, informing the available PIs and able to collect the selected one's weight.

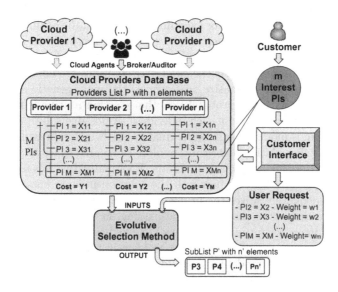

Fig. 1. Scenario of application of the selecting cloud providers problem.

The method loads a list with the n providers, each one with its M PIs, from the database, along with the customer request and the cost of each provider. These data will be used to calculate the fitness of each individual in the proposed GA. This calculation will be detailed later in Sect. 3.

3   Solution Methodology Using a Genetic Algorithm

This Section aims to describe the methodology used to modeling the problem of selecting cloud computing providers using a GA. The selection method is intended to support the decision-making process of a client who need to select suitable providers through the values of their PIs of interest. The structure containing the PIs of interest, with their respective desired values and weights, is called request.

The GA was first proposed by John Holland in the 1970 s. Is a bio-inspired technique based on the theory of evolution of the species of Charles Darwin, i.e., as the process of natural selection, adaptability (fitness), heredity, and genetic mutation are able to influence the changes and selection of genetic material that will be passed on to future generations of a population of individuals of same specie.

The GAs are probabilistic and populational, i.e., generate approximate solutions and work on a set of candidate solutions of a population for each generation (iteration of the algorithm). The GA looks for the best solution to a problem based on the adaptive value (fitness function) of its individuals. Each individual has a genetic coding (genotype), formed by a vector with different chromosomes.

Each chromosome is responsible for encoding a variable of the optimization problem. Each variable directly influences the quality of the problem solution and has a domain and a coding (e.g., binary, real, etc.). All variables must have the same encoding. In canonical GAs the candidate solutions are encoded in binary vectors of fixed size and emphasize crossover as the main genetic operator and apply the mutation with low probabilities, the selection routine is probabilistic and proportional to the fitness of each individual. A possible solution to an optimization problem is modeled as an individual in GA, which represents a point in the search space. Population algorithms explore the search space in parallel with the individuals that make up the population. Each individual has an associated fitness (phenotype), indicating how well the solution it represents, encoded by its genotype, adequately solves the problem in question. The greater the fitness, the greater the chances of that individual passing on his genetic load (portions of his chromosomes) for future generations. The highest fitness individual in the population represents the solution to the problem in that current generation.

For the proposed GA modelling, the individual uses a binary encoding, where the number of coded variables is equal to the total number of providers registered in the database of the method. Each variable represents a single bit, indicating whether that provider belongs to the solution set (bit 1) or not (bit 0). Figure 2 illustrates this modeling via an example with 10 hypothetical providers and the resulting solution set that this individual encodes.

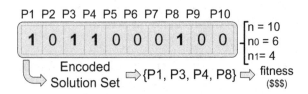

Fig. 2. Example of a possible solution encoded in a binary individual.

Thus, let be $I = \{bit(0|1)_{P_1}, bit(0|1)_{P_2}, ..., bit(0|1)_{P_n}\}$ the set representing an individual as a single binary vector with n bits, where bit 1 in the position i of that vector indicates provider P_i belongs to the solution set coded by that individual. Similarly, bit 0 informs that the ith provider in P doesn't belong to the solution set. This information will be used in the fitness function to generate a fitness value to GA. The search space is $2^n - 1$, since the whole code filled with 0 is not a valid solution (it indicates that no provider is part of the solution). The total cost of the individual is equal to the sum of the cost of all its encoded providers.

3.1 Fitness Function Modeling

The fitness of the individual is proportionally linked to the minimization of three factors: (i) the distance from the providers' PI values encoded in the individual (represented by bits 1 in its coding vector) to the customer request PI values, (ii) the total cost of the individual, and (iii) the amount of providers in the individual solution set. Thus, if the objective function of the problem is the sum of these components, fitness will be the minimization of this function, plus the application of penalties if the individual is invalid (does not fully comply with the requisition). Therefore, the objective function ($funcObj$) and the fitness function ($funcFit$) of the ith individual of the population are given respectively by Eqs. 1 and 2. The weight values of cost (w_c) and number of providers (w_n) ponder the importance of the lowest cost and the least amount of providers desired for the final solution.

$$funcObj_i = \frac{w_c * cost_i + w_n * numProv_i}{w_c + w_n} \tag{1}$$

$$funcFit_i = 1 - funcObj_i - penalty_i \tag{2}$$

The individual score depends on its encoding. Let $P = \{P_1, P_2, ..., P_n\}$ the set containing the n different providers available for selection in the database. Therefore, the individual i has a size encoding of n and if $n0_i$ represents the sum of all 0 bits in the encoding vector of i and $n1_i$ is the sum of all bits 1, the score given to the individual i by its number of providers ($numProv_i$) will be a value between 0 and 1, according Eq. 3.

$$numProv_i = \begin{cases} 1, \ (n0_i = n) \ \text{or} \ (n1_i = n) \\ \frac{(n1_i - 1)}{n}, \ \text{otherwise} \end{cases} \tag{3}$$

Note that the goal is to minimize the objective function, so the value 1 will prejudice the fitness of individual i. The extreme cases (encoding all filled with bits 0 or bits 1) are totally undesirable for the solution problem, since it is desired to minimize the amount of providers (although zero providers is not a possible solution to be considered). The extremes are penalized to the maximum (value 1), and a single provider would be the ideal quantity (value 0).

Let $cost_i = \{y_1, y_2, y_3, ..., y_n\}$ the respective costs associated with each of the n different providers of P. The cost of the ith individual Y_i, is equal to the sum of the costs of all providers that belong (bit 1) to its encoded solution set. If provider not belong (bit 0) to its encoded solution, it cost will be zero. The score given to a individual i, by its cost ($cost_i$), will be a value between 0 and 1, according to Eq. 4, with $j = 1, 2, ..., n$, $k = 1, 2, ..., n1_i$ and where I represents coded individual.

$$cost_i = \frac{Y_i}{\sum_{j=1}^{n} y_j} = \frac{\sum_{k=1}^{n} y_k \, [\, I_k = \text{bit}(1) \,]}{\sum_{j=1}^{n} y_j} \tag{4}$$

As the goal is to minimize the cost, maximum score (value 1) is given for the solution that encompasses all available providers (worst case) and minimum score (value 0) for the rare case of zero cost. Zero cost would be a provider that makes available its resources for free, something theoretically possible, but uncommon.

Penalties can be applied to each invalid individual that can be generated in the GA. Penalties significantly decrease the fitness value of the individual if it presents an inadequate solution to the problem. A penalized individual can't be given as a response to the problem. If this occurs then the algorithm did not find a valid solution with that number of generations. The penalty calculation can be seen in Eq. 2. It is calculated proportionally as a function of how much the solution infringes the problem restrictions. For the provider selection problem there are two constraints that need to be observed: if the individual is all zero (with all encoding filled with bits 0, that is, $n0_i = n$) and if the individual not satisfies all customer requested PIs. The first restriction is simple to circumvent. It is just to prevent the functions that generate the initial random population and those ones that modify the codification of the individual (genetic operators) of generating the all zero bits individual. The second restriction will proportionally penalize every individual i that does not attend all PIs of the request, according to Eq. 5. The ordered list w contains the weights of each PI_k and m is the number of customer interest PIs from the request.

$$penalty_i = \frac{\sum_{k=1}^{m} Attend(x_k, z_k, PI_k) * w_k}{\sum_{j=1}^{m} w_j} \tag{5}$$

A PI of the request is attended if at least one provider encoded in the individual attend it. Thus, given a PI belonging to some provider of the solution set encoded by the individual i, which stores a numerical value x, and the specified value requested by the customer is z, then Eq. 6 models PI's attendance, for all m PIs of the request.

$$Attend(x, z, PI) = \begin{cases} 0, \text{if } x \geq z \text{ and } PI \in HB \\ 0, \text{if } x \leq z \text{ and } PI \in LB \\ 0, \text{if } x = z \text{ and } PI \in NB \\ 1, \text{otherwise} \end{cases} \tag{6}$$

The fitness calculation (Eq. 2) is applied to every individual in the population for each generation of the algorithm (iteration), up to a predefined number of generations. At the end of the generations, the best fitness individual is sought. If it has not been penalized, it returns the providers encoded by the individual as the response to the problem, otherwise an error returns.

4   Experiments, Results, and Analysis

Algorithms were implemented in Java, JDK version 1.8, in the operational system Windows 7, 64 bits, with 4 gigabytes of RAM and AMD Phentom B93 2.8 Ghz processor. As GA is a probabilistic algorithm, 30 executions were performed for each selection instance for each explicit request. The weights for cost (w_c) and quantity of providers (w_n) on the fitness function have the same importance and will be 1 $(w_c = w_n = 1)$.

Table 1 presents the main parameters to apply to a canonical GA [9]. They are: population size, the probability of crossover, the probability of mutation and the number of iterations/generations, used as the stop condition. Therefore, for the proposed GA, the number of variables is always equal to the number of providers, n, registered in the method's database. Size of the population is 50 individuals and the number of iterations is 1000, generating a total of 50.000 fitness evaluations ($sizePop*numIt$). The selection routine used is called stochastic tournament and presents a parameter k which represents the size of the group that will compete for each iteration of the GA. The crossover routine used is the one-cut-point crossover, chosen randomly between 1 and n. The mutation routine used is the bit-flip mutation.

Table 1. List of parameters used by GA.

Parameter name	Acronym	Value
Population size	$sizePop$	50
Number of generations	$numIt$	1000
Probability of crossover	$Pcross$	95%
Probability of mutation	$Pmut$	1%
Stochastic tournament size	k	5

Table 2 informs the base data set used in the experiments. This set is fictitious and involves ten providers and six hypothetical quantitative PIs that could occur in real life (especially cost). Each PI has one type of associated behavior (HB, LB or NB) and one value for each provider.

Table 2. Hypothetical data base with providers and their PIs instantiated by the authors.

PIs	Type	P1	P2	P3	P4	P5	P6	P7	P8	P9	P10
PI 1	HB	4	2	8	4	2	8	16	4	2	8
PI 2	HB	10	20	30	25	40	30	20	20	15	20
PI 3	HB	2	1	3	1	4	2	8	2	2	4
PI 4	NB	2	1	3	2	1	2	4	2	2	1
PI 5	HB	85.80	88.80	90.00	95.50	98.00	99.00	99.99	92.00	95.00	98.50
Cost	LB	1.50	1.25	3.00	2.50	2.75	2.80	4.50	2.50	1.75	3.20

Table 3 informs five possible requests considering the database shown in Table 2. Note that not necessarily all registered PIs are useful to the customer. Request 5, for example, ignores PIs four and five, that is, their value does not matter to the customer. The cost is a special PI, which is not stated explicitly in the requisition, but is always taken into account in the fitness function. In this example each PI has exactly the same importance weight (1.0) as all others. The last line of the Table 3 presents the known answers (desired optimal) for each request. The most complex requests to be answered in this scenario are the third and fourth requests, since they require a set of 3 providers.

Table 3. Five hypothetical customer requests.

PIs	Req. 1	Req. 2	Req. 3	Req. 4	Req. 5
PI 1	4	4	16	16	4
PI 2	20	40	40	40	20
PI 3	2	4	8	4	1
PI 4	2	1	2	3	–
PI 5	90.0	95.0	99.0	–	–
Optimal	P8	P1 and P5	P1 and P5 and P7	P3 and P5 and P7	P4 or P8

Tests were performed for 10, 50 and 100 providers. Thus, the data in Table 2 were replicated 5 and 10 times, respectively, to 50 and 100 providers. The requests (Table 3) are the same for all three databases. The search space of possible solutions, with n providers, is $2^n - 1$, i.e., all possible combinations of providers to be tested. Thus, the search space for 10, 50 and 100 providers is 1023, $1.1259 * 10^{15}$ and $1.2676 * 10^{30}$, respectively. The average time to complete a fitness assessment was approximately 0.2 ms on the used computer. So, the estimated time for all fitness assessments for 10, 50 and 100 providers, are respectively 0.2046 s, 7140.41 years and $8.039 * 10^{18}$ years. Thus, the use of an exhaustive search algorithm becomes impractical for instances larger than 50 providers. Requests 4 and 5 have fewer PIs to be attended, so, their execution time is slightly less than 0.2 ms, but also not enable the use of an exhaustive search.

The developed GA will be compared with a deterministic and intuitive matching algorithm described in [8]. The matching algorithm is a logical/mathematical method capable of scoring an extensive list of cloud computing providers based on their PIs. Based on the scores, the algorithm is able to quickly select the provider that is the most suitable for each request. The score varies in the range of 0 to 1. The closer to 1, more adequate is that provider to satisfy the customer request. The method is divided into three stages: Elimination of incompatible providers, scoring of PIs (quantitative and/or qualitative) by level of importance and calculation of final provider score. The algorithm returns a list with the highest-ranked providers, containing their name, their suitability (percentage of how many PIs of the request has been attend), and the total time of this scoring process.

Table 4 presents the results obtained when applying the GA and the matching algorithm on the data set of Table 2, taking as input each of the five requisitions of Table 3. The GA was run 30 times with the parameters of the Table 1 and the deterministic matching algorithm, only once. The fitness in GA ranges from 0 to 1. Average and standard deviation of the fitness are calculated as well as average execution time and the hit percentage (based on the known response - last line Table 3) of GA and matching algorithm ("Mtc").

Table 4. Experiments developed for 10, 50 and 100 providers.

10 providers					
Request	Fitness	Hits (GA)	Hits (Mtc)	Time (GA)	Time (Mtc)
Req. 1	0.9520 ± 0.0	100%	100%	0.930 s	0.003 s
Req. 2	0.8733 ± 0.0	100%	0.0%	1.419 s	0.002 s
Req. 3	0.7232 ± 0.0	100%	0.0%	2.110 s	0.003 s
Req. 4	0.6844 ± 0.0	100%	0.0%	1.532 s	0.002 s
Req. 5	0.9520 ± 0.0	100%	100%	0.560 s	0.002 s
50 providers					
Request	Fitness	Hits (GA)	Hits (Mtc)	Time (GA)	Time (Mtc)
Req. 1	0.9904 ± 0.0	100%	100%	1.276 s	0.005 s
Req. 2	0.9747 ± 0.0	100%	0.0%	1.756 s	0.006 s
Req. 3	0.9446 ± 0.0	100%	0.0%	2.557 s	0.006 s
Req. 4	0.9369 ± 0.0	100%	0.0%	1.935 s	0.005 s
Req. 5	0.9901 ± 0.0015	96.67%	100%	0.799 s	0.004 s
100 providers					
Request	Fitness	Hits (GA)	Hits (Mtc)	Time (GA)	Time (Mtc)
Req. 1	0.9952 ± 0.0	100%	100%	1.900 s	0.005 s
Req. 2	0.9873 ± 0.0	100%	0.0%	2.461 s	0.005 s
Req. 3	0.9723 ± 0.0	100%	0.0%	3.366 s	0.006 s
Req. 4	0.9684 ± 0.0	100%	0.0%	2.655 s	0.004 s
Req. 5	0.9952 ± 0.0	100%	100%	1.217 s	0.004 s

It is noteworthy that for 50 and 100 providers there are multiple optimal possible solutions. Request 2, for example, for 50 providers, has as optimal answers: P1 and P5 or P11 and P15 or P21 and P25 or P31 and 35 or P41 and P45 or any combination between one of these providers terminated at 1 and 5. This factor increases the probability of GA converging to any of these optimal, justifying the exceptional GA performance observed in Table 4. The matching presents a minimal execution time and finds optimal solutions for simpler requests, but not very satisfactory for complex cases where more than one provider is required.

In order to eliminate the problem with multiple optimal solutions for 50 and 100 providers, the cost of the first 10 providers that compose each solution of the current request was arbitrarily lowered in −1, 00. Thus, Table 5 was obtained.

Table 5. Experiments developed for 50 and 100 providers with arbitrary decrease in cost in the first 10 providers to eliminate multiple optimal solutions.

50 providers			
Request	Fitness	Hits (GA)	Hits (Mtc)
Req. 1	0.9954 ± 0.0	100%	100%
Req. 2	0.9834 ± 0.0015	90.00%	0.0%
Req. 3	0.9586 ± 0.0013	93.33%	0.0%
Req. 4	0.9510 ± 0.0015	90.00%	0.0%
Req. 5	0.9941 ± 0.0041	90.00%	100%
100 providers			
Request	Fitness	Hits (GA)	Hits (Mtc)
Req. 1	0.9974 ± 0.0009	86.67%	100%
Req. 2	0.9917 ± 0.0007	90.00%	0.0%
Req. 3	0.9788 ± 0.0015	73.33%	0.0%
Req. 4	0.9751 ± 0.0014	70.00%	0.0%
Req. 5	0.9968 ± 0.0021	76.67%	100%

The execution time of the algorithms are almost the same as in the previous table and will be omitted.

With Table 5 it is possible to state that the GA is able to find very satisfactory answers, even for the most difficult cases (e.g., requests 3 and 4 with 100 providers) in an acceptable time. The matching algorithm is largely efficient for simple requests, but fails to find answers to complex requests with more than one provider.

5   Conclusion

The success and popularization of cloud computing has led to the emergence of numerous companies as providers of cloud services with a wide range of purposes (academic, industrial, commercial). These companies are significantly heterogeneous and offers different types of services, pricing policy, resources availability, quantity of computational resources, etc. Data representing a PI, metric that is responsible for quantitatively or qualitatively measuring a particular aspect of a provider. Choosing one or more providers has become a complex process, so an automated method of decision-making support has become necessary tool.

This work specified a GA modeling responsible for selecting the most appropriate set of providers to attend a customer request. The request must have the PIs of interest, the preferences of values for them and the weights of the PIs for the customer. This paper also presents the fitness function used by GA to perform such task, and, applies it to a specific case with hypothetical data with six PIs for 10, 50 and 100 providers. The GA is compared with an intuitive matching algorithm that presents a considerable low execution time. The major problem of the matching approach is that it is designed to return a single provider as response. This problem is solved by the proposed GA in acceptable execution time and converging satisfactorily.

As future work, it is desired to apply the GA for scenarios with real data, i.e., with cloud providers and PIs that already exist, assessing its practical effectiveness. Another improvement is to make the method able to consider PIs that need to be mandatory in the same provider. An example of this is PIs like amount of RAM, disk memory and number of CPU cores, which form a virtual machine that must necessarily belong to same provider. It is also intended to perform testing for vertical scalability, i.e., keeping number of providers constant and increasing continuously the number of PIs. A hybrid approach using GA and the matching algorithm together is also an interesting approach to be studied.

References

1. Hogan, M.D., Liu, F., Sokol, A.W., Jin, T.: Nist Cloud Computing Standards Roadmap. NIST Special Publication 500 Series (2013). Accessed September 2015
2. Zhang, Q., Cheng, L., Boutaba, R.: Cloud computing: state-of-the-art and research challenges. J. Internet Serv. Appl. **1**, 7–18 (2010)
3. Sundareswaran, S., Squicciarin, A., Lin, D.: A brokerage-based approach for cloud service selection. In: 2012 IEEE Fifth International Conference on Cloud Computing, pp. 558–565 (2012)
4. Garg, S.K., Versteeg, S., Buyya, R.: A framework for ranking of cloud computing services. Futur. Gener. Comput. Syst. **29**, 1012–1023 (2013)
5. Baranwal, G., Vidyarthi, D.P.: A framework for selection of best cloud service provider using ranked voting method. In: 2014 IEEE International Advance Computing Conference (IACC), pp. 831–837 (2014)
6. Wagle, S., Guzek, M., Bouvry, P., Bisdorff, R.: An evaluation model for selecting cloud services from commercially available cloud providers. In: 7th International Conference on Cloud Computing Technology and Science, pp. 107–114 (2015)
7. Shirur, S., Swamy, A.: A cloud service measure index framework to evaluate efficient candidate with ranked technology. Int. J. Sci. Res. **4**, 1957–1961 (2015)
8. Moraes, L., Fiorese, A., Matos, F.: A multi-criteria scoring method based on performance indicators for cloud computing provider selection. In: 19th International Conference on Enterprise Information Systems (ICEIS 2017), vol. 2, pp. 588–599 (2017)
9. Holland, J.H.: Adaptation in Natural and Artificial Systems: An Introductory Analysis with Applications to Biology, Control, and Artificial Intelligence. MIT Press, Bradford Books (1975)
10. Karim, R., Ding, C., Miri, A.: An end-to-end QoS mapping approach for cloud service selection. In: 2013 IEEE Ninth World Congress on Services, pp. 341–348. IEEE (2013)
11. Achar, R., Thilagam, P.: A broker based approach for cloud provider selection. In: 2014 International Conference on Advances in Computing, Communications and Informatics (ICACCI), pp. 1252–1257 (2014)
12. Souidi, M., Souihi, S., Hoceini, S., Mellouk, A.: An adaptive real time mechanism for IaaS cloud provider selection based on QoE aspects. In: 2015 IEEE International Conference on Communications (ICC), pp. 6809–6814. IEEE (2015)

13. Alves, G., Silva, C., Cavalcante, E., Batista, T., Lopes, F.: Relative QoS: a new concept for cloud service quality. In: 2015 IEEE Symposium on Service-Oriented System Engineering (SOSE), pp. 59–68. IEEE (2015)
14. CSMIC: Service measurement index framework. Technical report, Carnegie Mellon University, Silicon Valley, Moffett Field, California (2014). Accessed November 2016
15. Jain, R.: The Art of Computer Systems Performance Analysis: Techniques for Experimental Design, Measurement, Simulation, and Modeling. John Wiley & Sons, Littleton (1991)

A Fast and Efficient Method for #2SAT via Graph Transformations

Marco A. López[3], J. Raymundo Marcial-Romero[1(✉)], Guillermo De Ita[2], and Rosa M. Valdovinos[1]

[1] Facultad de Ingeniería, UAEM, Washington, D.C., USA
{jrmarcialr,rvaldovinosr}@uaemex.mx
[2] Facultad de Ciencias de la Computación, BUAP, Puebla, Mexico
deita@cs.buap.mx
[3] Facultad de Ingeniería, UAEM, Toluca, Mexico
mlopezm158@alumno.uaemex.mx

Abstract. In this paper we present an implementation (markSAT) for computing #2SAT via graph transformations. For that, we transform the input formula into a graph and test whether it is which we call a cactus graph. If it is not the case, the formula is decomposed until cactus sub-formulas are obtained. We compare the efficiency of markSAT against sharpSAT which is the leading sequential algorithm in the literature for computing #SAT obtaining better results with our proposal.

1 Introduction

Given a Boolean formula F, $SAT(F)$ consists on deciding whether F has a model, e.g. whether there exists an assignment to the variables of F whose evaluation with respect to propositional logic is true. If F is in two Conjunctive Normal Form (2-CNF), then $SAT(F)$ can be computed in polynomial time [1]. However if F is given in k-CNF, $(k > 2)$ then $SAT(F)$ is NP-Complete. On the other hand, $\#SAT(F)$ consists on counting the number of models that F has. In this way $\#SAT(F)$ belongs to the $\#P$-Complete class even if F is in 2-CNF, denoted as #2SAT [2].

Even though #2SAT is #P-Complete, there are instances which can be solved in polynomial time [3]. For example, if the graph which represents the input formula is acyclic, then #2SAT can be solved in polynomial time.

Actually, the algorithms to solve $\#SAT(F)$ for any F in k-CNF decompose the formula in sub-formulas until some criteria are met in order to determine their models. Nowadays, the algorithm with the smallest time complexity reported in the literature for 2-CNF formulas was given by Wahlström [4]. He reported a time complexity of $O(1.2377^n)$ where n is the number of variables of the input formula. Schmitt et al. [5] present an algorithm for #SAT where the criteria to decompose the input formula consists on choosing a clause, however their algorithm does not improve the bound given by Wahlström for #2SAT.

On the other hand, the implementations for $\#SAT(F)$ is focusing on searching strategies which allow solving $\#SAT(F)$ efficiently although the number of

© Springer Nature Switzerland AG 2018
F. Castro et al. (Eds.): MICAI 2017, LNAI 10632, pp. 95–106, 2018.
https://doi.org/10.1007/978-3-030-02837-4_8

variables increases. The leading sequential implementations are relsat [6] and sharpSAT [7]. Additionally, a parallel implementation, called countAntom [8] has been proposed.

In this paper we present a method which transforms the input formula F into a graph. If an intersected cycle is found, the formula is decomposed applying the Schmitt's rule. The process is iterated until no intersected cycles are found. For each subgraph of F, generated during the decomposition, without intersected cycles, a linear time algorithm is applied to compute $\#2SAT(G_i)$. We experimentally show that our proposal is faster than sharpSAT. It is worth to mention that the use of Schmitt et al. algorithm instead of Wahlström is given as the stop criteria based on cycles rather than variables, so in the worst case the time complexity of our algorithm coincides with the obtained by Schmitt et al.

2   Preliminaries

Let $X = \{x_1, \ldots, x_n\}$ be a set of n Boolean variables. A literal is either a variable x_i or a negated variable $\overline{x}_i$. As usual, for each $x_i \in X$, we write $x_i^0 = \overline{x}_i$ and $x_i^1 = x_i$. A clause is a disjunction of different literals (sometimes, we also consider a clause as a set of literals). For $k \in N$, a k-clause consist on exactly k literals and, a $(\leq k)$-clause is a clause with at most k literals. A variable $x \in X$ appears in a clause c if either the literal x^1 or x^0 is an element of c.

A Conjunctive Normal Form (CNF) F is a conjunction of clauses (we also call F a Conjunctive Form). A k-CNF is a CNF which contains clauses with at most k literals.

We use $\nu(Y)$ to express the set of variables involved in the object Y, where Y could be a literal, a clause or a Boolean formula. $Lit(F)$ is the set of literals which appear in a CNF F, i.e. if $X = \nu(F)$, then $Lit(F) = X \cup \overline{X} = \{x_1^1, x_1^0, \ldots, x_n^1, x_n^0\}$. We also denote $\{1, 2, \ldots, n\}$ by $[[n]]$.

An assignment s for F is a Boolean function $s : \nu(F) \rightarrow \{0, 1\}$. An assignment can be also considered as a set which does not contain complementary literals. If $x^\epsilon \in s$, being s an assignment, then s turns x^ϵ true and $x^{1-\epsilon}$ false, $\epsilon \in \{0, 1\}$. Considering a clause c and assignment s as a set of literals, c is satisfied by s if and only if $c \cap s \neq \emptyset$, and if for all $x^\epsilon \in c$, $x^{1-\epsilon} \in s$ then s falsifies c.

If $F_1 \subset F$ is a formula consisting of some clauses of F, then $\nu(F_1) \subset \nu(F)$, and an assignment over $\nu(F_1)$ is a partial assignment over $\nu(F)$.

Let F be a Boolean formula in CNF, F is satisfied by an assignment s if each clause in F is satisfied by s. F is contradicted by s if any clause in F is contradicted by s. A model of F is an assignment for $\nu(F)$ that satisfies F. We denote as $SAT(F)$ the set of models for the formula F.

Given a CNF F, the SAT problem consists on determining if F has a model. The #SAT problem consists of counting the number of models of F defined over $\nu(F)$. In this case #2-SAT denotes #SAT for formulas in 2-CNF.

2.1   The Signed Primal Graph of a 2-CNF

There are some graphical representations of a CNF (see e.g. [9]), in this work the signed primal graph of a 2-CNF is used.

Let F be a 2-CNF, its signed primal graph (constraint graph) is denoted by $G_F = (V(F), E(F))$, with $V(F) = \nu(F)$ and $E(F) = \{\{\nu(x), \nu(y)\} : \{x, y\} \in F\}$. That is, the vertices of G_F are the variables of F, and for each clause $\{x, y\}$ in F there is an edge $\{\nu(x), \nu(y)\} \in E(F)$. For $x \in V(F)$, $\delta(x)$ denotes its degree, i.e. the number of incident edges to x. Each edge $c = \{\nu(x), \nu(y)\} \in E$ is associated with an ordered pair (s_1, s_2) of signs, assigned as labels of the edge connecting the literals appearing in the clause. The signs s_1 and s_2 are related to the literals x^ϵ and y^δ, respectively. For example, the clause $\{x^0, y^1\}$ determines the labelled edge: "$x \overset{-}{\underset{+}{=}} y$" which is equivalent to the edge "$y \overset{+}{\underset{-}{=}} x$".

Formally, let $S = \{+, -\}$ be a set of signs. A graph with labelled edges on a set S is a pair (G, ψ), where $G = (V, E)$ is a graph, and ψ is a function with domain E and range S. $\psi(e)$ is called the label of the edge $e \in E$. Let $G = (V, E, \psi)$ be a signed primal graph with labelled edges on SxS. Let x and y be vertices in V, if $e = \{x, y\}$ is an edge and $\psi(e) = (s, s')$, then $s(resp.s')$ is called the adjacent sign to $x(resp.y)$. A 2-CNF F is a path, cycle, or a tree if its signed primal graph G_F represents a path, cycle, or a tree, respectively. We will omit the signs on the graph if all of them are $+$.

Note that a signed primal graph of a 2-CNF can be a multigraph since two fixed variables can be involved in more than one clause of the formula, forming so parallel edges. Furthermore, a unitary clause is represented by a loop (an edge to join a vertex to itself). A polynomial time algorithm to process parallel edges and loops to solve #SAT has been shown in [10] and is presented in Sect. 3 for completeness.

Let $\rho : 2\text{-CNF} \to G_F$ be the function whose domain is the space of Boolean formulae in 2-CNF and codomain is the set of multi-graphs, ρ is a bijection. So any 2-CNF formula has a unique signed constraint graph associated via ρ and viceversa, any signed constraint graph G_F has a unique formula associated.

3   Computing #2SAT According to the Topology of the Signed Primal Graph

In this section we briefly summarize the main results already reported at [10] for completeness. We describe simple topologies of a graph representing a 2-CNF formula F and how it is computed the value #2SAT(F). We begin with simple topologies as acyclic graphs.

Let f_i be a family of clauses of the formula F built as follows: $f_1 = \emptyset$; $f_i = \{C_j\}_{j<i}$, $i \in [\![m]\!]$. Let $SAT(f_i) = \{s : s \text{ satisfies } f_i\}$, $A_i = \{s \in SAT(f_i) : x_i^1 \in s\}$, $B_i = \{s \in SAT(f_i) : x_i^0 \in s\}$. Let $\alpha_i = |A_i|$; $\beta_i = |B_i|$ and $\mu_i = |SAT(f_i)| = \alpha_i + \beta_i$.

For every vertex $x \in G_F$ a pair (α_x, β_x) is computed, where α_x indicates how many times the variable x can take the value 'true' and β_x the number of times that x can take value 'false' into the F model's set.

Path Case. Notice that if F is a path $n = |\upsilon(F)| = m+1$, $f_i \subset f_{i+1}$, $i \in [\![m-1]\!]$.

$$F = \{C_1, C_2, \ldots, C_m\} = \{\{x_1^{\epsilon_1}, x_2^{\delta_1}\}, \{x_2^{\epsilon_2}, x_3^{\delta_2}\}, \ldots, \{x_m^{\epsilon_m}, x_{m+1}^{\delta_m}\}\},$$

where $\delta_i, \epsilon_i \in \{0,1\}$, $i \in \llbracket m \rrbracket$. The pairs (α_i, β_i) associated to each vertex x_i, $i = 2, \ldots, m$ are computed according to the signs (ϵ_i, δ_i) of the literals in the clause c_i by the following recurrence equation:

$$(\alpha_i, \beta_i) = \begin{cases} (\beta_{i-1} & , \alpha_{i-1} + \beta_{i-1}) \text{ if } (\epsilon_i, \delta_i) = (-,-) \\ (\alpha_{i-1} + \beta_{i-1}, \beta_{i-1} &) \text{ if } (\epsilon_i, \delta_i) = (-,+) \\ (\alpha_{i-1} & , \alpha_{i-1} + \beta_{i-1}) \text{ if } (\epsilon_i, \delta_i) = (+,-) \\ (\alpha_{i-1} + \beta_{i-1}, \alpha_{i-1} &) \text{ if } (\epsilon_i, \delta_i) = (+,+) \end{cases} \tag{1}$$

The first pair is $(\alpha_1, \beta_1) = (1,1)$ since x_1 can be true or false for satisfying f_1.

Note that as $F = f_m$ then $\#SAT(F) = \mu_m = \alpha_m + \beta_m$.

Parallel Edges Case. Suppose, that two clauses are $c_k = (x_{i-1}^{\epsilon_k}, x_i^{\delta_k})$ and $c_j = (x_{i-1}^{\epsilon_j}, x_i^{\delta_j})$, which involve variables x_{i-1} and x_i. Then, we compute the values for (α_i, β_i) associated to the node x_i, according to the signs (ϵ_k, δ_k) and (ϵ_j, δ_j) as:

$$(\alpha_i, \beta_i) = \begin{cases} (\alpha_{i-1}, \alpha_{i-1}) \text{ if } (\epsilon_k, \delta_k) = (1,1) \text{ and } (\epsilon_j, \delta_j) = (1,0) \\ (\mu_{i-1}, 0 \quad) \text{ if } (\epsilon_k, \delta_k) = (1,1) \text{ and } (\epsilon_j, \delta_j) = (0,1) \\ (\beta_{i-1}, \alpha_{i-1}) \text{ if } (\epsilon_k, \delta_k) = (1,1) \text{ and } (\epsilon_j, \delta_j) = (0,0) \\ (\alpha_{i-1}, \beta_{i-1}) \text{ if } (\epsilon_k, \delta_k) = (1,0) \text{ and } (\epsilon_j, \delta_j) = (0,1) \\ (0 \quad, \mu_{i-1}) \text{ if } (\epsilon_k, \delta_k) = (1,0) \text{ and } (\epsilon_j, \delta_j) = (0,0) \\ (\beta_{i-1}, \beta_{i-1}) \text{ if } (\epsilon_k, \delta_k) = (0,1) \text{ and } (\epsilon_j, \delta_j) = (0,0) \end{cases} \tag{2}$$

Let F be a 2-CNF such that three clauses in F involve the same variables, then the value of (α_i, β_i) is computed by recurrence (3).

$$(\alpha_i, \beta_i) = \begin{cases} (0 \quad, \alpha_{i-1}) \text{ if } \{(x_{i-1}, x_i), (x_{i-1}, \overline{x}_i), (\overline{x}_{i-1}, \overline{x}_i)\} \subseteq F \\ (\mu_{i-1}, 0 \quad) \text{ if } \{(x_{i-1}, x_i), (x_{i-1}, \overline{x}_i), (\overline{x}_{i-1}, x_i)\} \subseteq F \\ (\beta_{i-1}, \alpha_{i-1}) \text{ if } \{(x_{i-1}, x_i), (\overline{x}_{i-1}, x_i), (\overline{x}_{i-1}, \overline{x}_i)\} \subseteq F \\ (\alpha_{i-1}, \beta_{i-1}) \text{ if } \{(\overline{x}_{i-1}, x_i), (x_{i-1}, \overline{x}_i), (\overline{x}_{i-1}, \overline{x}_i)\} \subseteq F \end{cases} \tag{3}$$

Of course, four parallel edges among the same endpoints indicate that the 2-CNF F is unsatisfiable and then $\#2SAT(F) = 0$.

Unitary Clauses Case. A unitary clause represents a loop in the signed primal graph of a 2-CNF. When (α_i, β_i) is computed over a node x_i which has a loop edge, recurrence (4) is applied.

$$(\alpha_i, \beta_i) = \begin{cases} (0, \beta_i) \text{ if } (x_i^0) \in U \\ (\alpha_i, 0) \text{ if } (x_i^1) \in U \end{cases} \tag{4}$$

Since an unitary clause uniquely determines the value of its variable. Furthermore, when both $(x_i^1) \in U$ and $(x_i^0) \in U$ then the original formula is unsatisfiable. Both of them, parallel edges and unitary clauses can be considered in a pre-processing step of the formula, before to apply the general algorithm presented in Sect. 5.

Acyclic Graphs Case. Let F be a 2-CNF formula where its associated signed primal graph G_F is acyclic, which may contain loops and parallel edges, then we can assume G_F as a rooted tree, a traversal of the graph allows to built a rooted tree. A tree has three kinds of nodes: a root node, interior nodes and leaf nodes. We denote with (α_v, β_v) the pair associated with the node v ($v \in G_F$). We compute #2SAT(F) while we are traversing G_F in post-order with the following algorithm.

Algorithm Count_Models_for_trees_loops_parallel(G_F)
Input: G_F - a tree graph which may contain parallel edges and loops.
Output: The number of models of F
Procedure:
Traversing G_F in post-order, and when a node $v \in G_F$ is visit, assign:

1. $(\alpha_v, \beta_v) = (1,1)$ if v is a leaf node in G_F.
2. If v is a parent node with a list of child nodes associated, i.e., $u_1, u_2, ..., u_k$ are the child nodes of v, as we have already visited all child nodes, then each pair $(\alpha_{u_j}, \beta_{u_j})$ $j = 1, ..., k$ has been determined. Let $e_1 = v^{\epsilon_1} u_1^{\delta_1}, e_2 = v^{\epsilon_2} u_2^{\delta_2}, ..., e_k = v^{\epsilon_k} u_k^{\delta_k}$ be the edges connecting v with each of its child nodes. A pair $(\alpha_{e_j}, \beta_{e_j})$ is computed for each edge e_j based on recurrence (1) where α_{e_j-1} is α_{u_j} and β_{e_j-1} is β_{u_j} for $j = 1, ... k$. Then, let $\alpha_v = \prod_{j=1}^{k} \alpha_{e_j} + \beta_v$ and $\beta_v = \prod_{j=1}^{k} \beta_{e_j}$. Notice that this step includes the case when v has just one child node.
3. if v has parallel edges apply recurrence (2) or (3)).
4. if v has a loop apply recurrence (4)
5. If v is the root node of G_F then return $(\alpha_v + \beta_v)$.

This procedure returns the number of models for F in time $O(n + m)$ which is the necessary time for traversing G_F in post-order.

Simple Cycles Case. Let $C_n = (V, E)$ be a simple cycle graph, so $|V| = n = |E| = m$, i.e. every vertex in V has degree two. We decompose the cycle C_n as: $P_n \cup \{v_1^{\epsilon_1}, v_n^{\epsilon_2}\}$, where $P_n = (V, E')$, $E' = \{c_1, ..., c_{n-1}\}$. P_n is the internal path of the cycle, and $c_n = \{v_1^{\epsilon_1}, v_n^{\epsilon_2}\}$ is called the cycle *frond edge*.

In order to process the number of models of C_n based on the P_n models, two *computing threads* or just *threads* are used. A computing thread is a sequence of pairs $(\alpha_i, \beta_i), i = 1, ..., n$ used for counting the number of models on a path graph. One thread, called the main thread L_m, is used for computing #2SAT(P_n). Since L_m counts the assignments where both $v_1^{\epsilon_1-1}$ and $v_1^{\epsilon_2-1}$ appear, they need to be removed from the models of C_n due to $c_n = \{v_1^{\epsilon_1}, v_n^{\epsilon_2}\}$ belongs to C_n, so a second thread L_s is used for computing $|\{s \in \#2SAT(P_n) : v_1^{\epsilon_1-1} \in s \wedge v_n^{\epsilon_2-1} \in s\}|$, e.g. the number of assignments where both $v_1^{\epsilon_1-1}$ and $v_1^{\epsilon_2-1}$ appear, these assignments are going to be subtracted from counting #2SAT(P_n) in orden to compute #2SAT(C_n). The main thread L_m begins counting with the pair $(\alpha_1, \beta_1) = (1,1)$, since the models where both v_1^0 and v_1^1 appear are counted. On the other hand, L_s begins with the pair $(\alpha_1, \beta_1) = (0, 1)$ since just the assignments where $v_1^{\epsilon_1 - 1}$ appears need to be counted. If the last pair of L_s is (α_n', β_n'), just the value for β_n' is considered since β_n' holds the number of assignments where $v_n^{\epsilon_2 - 1}$ appears. Therefore, if $L_m = (\alpha_n, \beta_n)$ and $L_s = (\alpha_n', \beta_n')$ then $\#2SAT(C_n) = \alpha_n + \beta_n - \beta_n'$. The time complexity of this procedure is $O(2m)$ where m is the number of clauses of the cycle.

4   Counting #2SAT for Cactus Formulas

A Spanish version of the algorithm for cactus graphs has been submitted to IEEE Transactions on Latin America, the submitted version can be consulted at (http://arxiv.org/abs/1702.08581). For that here we highlight the main idea. A cactus formula is one whose signed primal graph is cactus. A cactus graph is one where each pair of simple cycles intersect in at most one node, e.g. each pair of cycles are independent or have a singleton intersection. The algorithm for counting models in cactus graphs combines the procedures described in Sect. 3. The steps of the procedure and its description is presented below.

1. Store the input formula in a dynamically allocation table.
2. Built a spanning tree using a depth first search strategy.
3. Count over the tree in a postorder traversal considering the edges that form simple cycles.

Dynamically Allocation Table. The dynamically allocation table is built as follows. Let x_i be a variable of the formula F. The index of the i-th row represents the variable x_i. For each clause $\{x_i^{\epsilon_1}, x_j^{\epsilon_2}\}$ a triple $(j, \epsilon_1, \epsilon_2)$ is stored at the i-th row. A mirror table is also built in order to speed up the tree construction. The second table stores the triple $(i, \epsilon_1, \epsilon_2)$ at the j-th row.

Spanning Tree Construction. From the tables, tuples of the form (Tree, Cotree) are built. If the input formula can be decomposed in more than one tuple (Tree, Cotree), it means that the input formula has several components (subformulas which do not have common variables), hence the number of models of the input formula can be computed using the product of the models of its subformulas. The indices of the tables are visited in order to build a node of the spanning tree, if during the traversal an edge which forms a simple cycle is found this is stored in the Cotree structure. Additionally, the fact that a literal or its negations appears in a clause is stored in the node of the tree (cotree).

Counting over the Tree and Its Cotree. The correctness of counting over the (Tree, Cotree) structure has been reported in [11]. In summary, to each vertex x_i of the tree, a tuple (α_i, β_i) is associated where α_i denotes the number of models where x_i is true and β_i the number of models where β_i is false relative to the vertices already visited in the tree. When a vertex x_i which belongs to an edge $e = \{x_i, x_j\}$ of the cotree is reached, a second pair $(\alpha_{i_2}, \beta_{i_2})$ is associated to each vertex until reaching x_j in the tree. Since the graph is cactus, at most two pairs can co-exists during the execution of the algorithm. A postorder traversal over the tree computing the pairs gives the number of models of the input formula [12].

To each leaf of the tree the pair $(1, 0)$ is associated, which is the initial value if the formula is considered as a single literal. If the leaf starts a fundamental cycle the pair $(0,1)$ is also counted. When an interior node is visited, a clause $\{x^{\epsilon_1}, y^{\epsilon_1}\}$ has been considered, hence the models are computed according to recurrence (1).

Both the allocation table construction and the tree construction takes m steps each one. The counting procedure traverse also each edge of the tree, hence the time complexity of the algorithm is $O(3m)$ which is linear according to the number of clauses.

5   Counting for General 2-CNF Formulas

Schmitt et al. [5] algorithm works as follows: let F be a boolean formula, choose at random a clause $c = \{x_i^{\epsilon_1}, x_j^{\epsilon_2}\} \in F$, in order to satisfy F either $x_i^{\epsilon_1}$ or $x_j^{\epsilon_2}$ must be true. Hence three possible cases can be derived in orden to satisfy c, $(s(x_i^{\epsilon_1}) = 1$ and $s(x_j^{\epsilon_2}) = 1)$ or $(s(x_i^{\epsilon_1}) = 1$ and $s(x_j^{\epsilon_2}) = 0)$ or $(s(x_i^{\epsilon_1}) = 0$ and $s(x_j^{\epsilon_2}) = 1)$.

Each case generates a subformula F_k of F, $k = 1, 2, 3$ where Boolean values for the variables $x_i^{\epsilon_1}$ and $x_j^{\epsilon_2}$ can be fixed for reducing the input formula. This process is iterated until some criteria are met in order to decide the number of models of each subformula. In the method presented in this paper (called markSAT), two variants of Schmith algorithm are considered. Firstly, the clause chosen for decomposing the input formula is one that when is transformed to its signed primal graph, forms an intersected cycle, e.g. a witness that the graph is not cactus. Secondly, our process is iterated until cactus subgraphs are obtained.

Table 1. Results of comparing markSAT against sharpSAT.

| | Variables | Clauses | | Time in seconds | | | |
| | | | | sharpSAT | | markSAT | |
		Instance 1	Instance 2	Instance 1	Instance 2	Instance 1	Instance 2
1	100	4,950	2,475	0.031	0.028	0.011	0.006
2	200	19,900	9,950	0.051	0.038	0.042	0.022
3	500	124,750	62,375	**0.283**	0.151	0.285	0.143
4	1,000	499,500	249,750	1.674	0.834	1.166	0.597
5	2,000	1,999,000	999,500	11.889	5.786	4.850	2.445
6	5,000	12,497,500	6,248,750	171.442	82.970	30.870	15.558
7	6,000	17,997,000	8,998,500	293.078	141.755	49.694	22.752
8	6,500	21,121,750	10,560,875	371.091	179.876	58.447	26.448

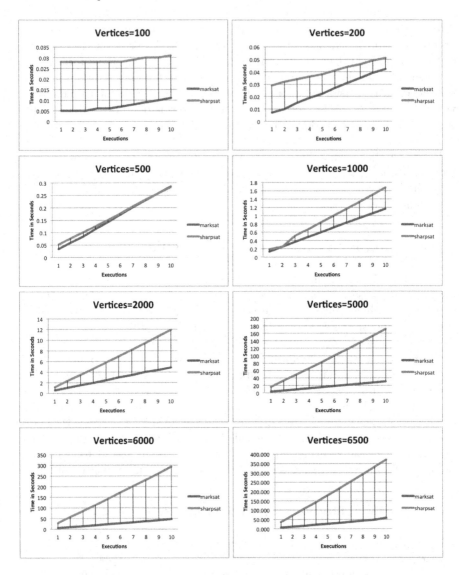

Fig. 1. Time comparison between sharpSAT and markSAT. From left to right and top to bottom number of vertices 100, 200, 500, 1000, 2000, 5000, 6000 and 6500 respectively. Each graphic denotes 10 executions with different number of edges, as described in Tables 2 and 3.

To make a comparison we built formulas with a range of 100 to 6500 variables and between 2,495 and 21,121,750 clauses. The standard format used to store the formulas was DIMACS (http://logic.pdmi.ras.ru/basolver/dimacs. html). Table 1 shows the time comparisons between markSAT and sharpSAT methods. Clauses that represent parallel edges in the graph can be counted by

Table 2. Formulas with 100, 200, 500 and 1000 variables. The number of clauses goes from 495 to 499,500.

Instance	Variables	Clauses	Time in seconds	
			sharpSAT	markSAT
100_10	100	495	0.028	0.005
100_20	100	990	0.028	0.005
100_30	100	1,485	0.028	0.005
100_40	100	1,980	0.028	0.006
100_50	100	2,475	0.028	0.006
100_60	100	2,970	0.028	0.007
100_70	100	3,465	0.029	0.008
100_80	100	3,960	0.030	0.009
100_90	100	4,455	0.030	0.010
100_100	100	4950	0.031	0.011
200_10	200	1,990	0.029	0.007
200_20	200	3,980	0.032	0.010
200_30	200	5,970	0.034	0.015
200_40	200	7,960	0.036	0.019
200_50	200	9,950	0.038	0.022
200_60	200	11,940	0.041	0.027
200_70	200	13,930	0.044	0.031
200_80	200	15,920	0.046	0.035
200_90	200	17,910	0.049	0.039
200_100	200	19,900	0.051	0.042
500_10	500	12,475	0.052	0.033
500_20	500	24,950	0.076	0.059
500_30	500	37,425	0.101	0.084
500_40	500	49,900	0.125	0.114
500_50	500	62,375	0.151	0.143
500_60	500	74,850	0.176	0.171
500_70	500	87,325	0.205	0.201
500_80	500	99,800	0.232	0.230
500_90	500	112,275	0.258	0.257
500_100	500	124,750	0.283	0.285
1000_10	1,000	49,950	0.189	0.131
1000_20	1,000	99,900	0.247	0.250
1000_30	1,000	149,850	0.512	0.368
1000_40	1,000	199,800	0.670	0.483
1000_50	1,000	249,750	0.834	0.597
1000_60	1,000	299,700	1.003	0.717
1000_70	1,000	349,650	1.167	0.832
1000_80	1,000	399,600	1.331	0.944
1000_90	1,000	449,550	1.507	1.055
1000_100	1,000	499,500	1.674	1.166

Table 3. Formulas with 2,000, 5,000, 6,000 and 6,500 variables. The number of clauses goes from 199,900 to 21,121,750.

Instance	Variables	Clauses	Time in seconds	
			sharpSAT	markSAT
2000_10	2,000	199, 900	1.162	0.558
2000_20	2,000	399, 800	2.298	1.023
2000_30	2,000	599, 700	3.465	1.491
2000_40	2,000	799, 600	4.594	1.963
2000_50	2,000	999, 500	5.786	2.445
2000_60	2,000	1, 199, 400	6.940	2.941
2000_70	2,000	1, 399, 300	8.172	3.381
2000_80	2,000	1, 599, 200	9.375	3.959
2000_90	2,000	1, 799, 100	10.666	4.352
2000_100	2,000	1, 999, 000	11.889	4.850
5000_10	5,000	1, 249, 750	16.314	3.614
5000_20	5,000	2, 499, 500	32.796	6.496
5000_30	5,000	3, 749, 250	49.208	9.403
5000_40	5,000	4, 999, 000	66.069	12.495
5000_50	5,000	6, 248, 750	82.970	15.558
5000_60	5,000	7, 498, 500	100.173	18.631
5000_70	5,000	8, 748, 250	117.360	21.662
5000_80	5,000	9, 998, 000	134.945	24.827
5000_90	5,000	11, 247, 750	153.102	27.760
5000_100	5,000	12, 497, 500	171.442	30.870
6000_10	6,000	1, 799, 700	27.923	5.248
6000_20	6,000	3, 599, 400	56.106	9.404
6000_30	6,000	5, 399, 100	84.246	13.693
6000_40	6,000	7, 198, 800	112.913	18.087
6000_50	6,000	8, 998, 500	141.755	22.752
6000_60	6,000	10, 798, 200	171.544	26.847
6000_70	6,000	12, 597, 900	200.839	31.258
6000_80	6,000	14, 397, 600	230.728	35.959
6000_90	6,000	16, 197, 300	261.389	41.961
6000_100	6,000	17, 997, 000	293.078	46.694
6500_10	6,500	2, 112, 175	35.212	6.069
6500_20	6,500	4, 224, 350	70.990	11.053
6500_30	6,500	6, 336, 525	106.997	16.075
6500_40	6,500	8, 448, 700	142.817	21.254
6500_50	6,500	10, 560, 875	179.876	26.488
6500_60	6,500	12, 673, 050	216.774	31.536
6500_70	6,500	14, 785, 225	254.181	37.294
6500_80	6,500	16, 897, 400	292.413	42.579
6500_90	6,500	19, 009, 575	331.912	47.816
6500_100	6,500	21, 121, 750	371.091	58.447

our cactus procedure as well as unitary clauses, hence complete graphs have the maximum number of cycles (instance 1 in Table 1). We reduce the number of edges (clauses) by a factor of 10% in each execution. In column (4) of Table 1 we report graphs (formulas) with 50% of edges (clauses) with respect to a complete graph (Instance 2). Each formula was randomly created. As it can be analyzed in fifteen of the sixteen cases the execution time of our proposal overcomes sharpSAT.

Additionally, we tested our implementation with eighty different instances compared against sharpSAT. We begin with a formula which represents a complete graph and we removed 10% of the clauses in each execution. The name of the Instance XXX_YY in column 1 of Tables 2 and 3 means that there are XXX number of variables with YY% number of clauses with respect to $n * (n-1)/2$ where $n = |XXX|$ is the number of variables of the formula. Figure 1 shows graphically the results. The instances and the comparison table with the eighty formulas can be downloaded at (http://sc.uaemex.mx/rmarcial/markSAT).

6 Conclusions

In this paper, we have presented an implementation for counting models of 2-CNF formulas. Our implementation combines two procedures, the first decomposes the input formula choosing a clause and the second counts on cactus graphs (formulas). From results, we show that our implementation overcome sharpSAT in terms of processing time, the leading sequential implementation in the literature. In fact the time complexity in the worst case remains as the one established by Schmitt et al. [5].

We thanks the Universidad Autónoma del Estado de México for the sponsorship under the project 4315/2017/CI and CONACYT for the first author scholarship to carry on a Master degree.

References

1. Ita Luna, G.: Polynomial classes of boolean formulas for computing the degree of belief. In: Lemaître, C., Reyes, C.A., González, J.A. (eds.) IBERAMIA 2004. LNCS (LNAI), vol. 3315, pp. 430–440. Springer, Heidelberg (2004). https://doi.org/10.1007/978-3-540-30498-2_43
2. Brightwell, G., Winkler, P.: Counting linear extensions. Order **8**(3), 225–242 (1991)
3. Paulusma, D., Slivovsky, F., Szeider, S.: Model counting for cnf formulas of bounded modular treewidth. Algorithmica **76**(1), 168–194 (2016)
4. Wahlström, M.: A tighter bound for counting max-weight solutions to 2SAT instances. In: Grohe, M., Niedermeier, R. (eds.) IWPEC 2008. LNCS, vol. 5018, pp. 202–213. Springer, Heidelberg (2008). https://doi.org/10.1007/978-3-540-79723-4_19
5. Schmitt, M., Wanka, R.: Exploiting independent subformulas: a faster approximation scheme for #k-sat. Inf. Process. Lett. **113**(9), 337–344 (2013)

6. Bayardo Jr., R.J., Schrag, R.C.: Using CSP look-back techniques to solve real-world sat instances. In: Proceedings of the Fourteenth National Conference on Artificial Intelligence and Ninth Conference on Innovative Applications of Artificial Intelligence, AAAI 1997/IAAI 1997, pp. 203–208. AAAI Press (1997)

7. Thurley, M.: sharpSAT – counting models with advanced component caching and implicit BCP. In: Biere, A., Gomes, C.P. (eds.) SAT 2006. LNCS, vol. 4121, pp. 424–429. Springer, Heidelberg (2006). https://doi.org/10.1007/11814948_38

8. Burchard, J., Schubert, T., Becker, B.: Laissez-faire caching for parallel #SAT solving. In: Heule, M., Weaver, S. (eds.) SAT 2015. LNCS, vol. 9340, pp. 46–61. Springer, Cham (2015). https://doi.org/10.1007/978-3-319-24318-4_5

9. Szeider, S.: On fixed-parameter tractable parameterizations of SAT. In: Giunchiglia, E., Tacchella, A. (eds.) SAT 2003. LNCS, vol. 2919, pp. 188–202. Springer, Heidelberg (2004). https://doi.org/10.1007/978-3-540-24605-3_15

10. De Ita, G., Bello López, P., González, M.C.: New polynomial classes for #2SAT established via graph-topological structure. Eng. Lett. **15**, 250–258 (2007)

11. Marcial-Romero, J.R., De Ita Luna, G., Hernández, J.A., Valdovinos, R.M.: A parametric polynomial deterministic algorithm for #2SAT. In: Sidorov, G., Galicia-Haro, S.N. (eds.) MICAI 2015. LNCS (LNAI), vol. 9413, pp. 202–213. Springer, Cham (2015). https://doi.org/10.1007/978-3-319-27060-9_16

12. Bondy, J.A., Murty, U.S.R.: Graph Theory, 3rd printing edn. Springer, Heidelberg (2008)

AL-DDoS Attack Detection Optimized with Genetic Algorithms

Jan Quequezana-Buendia and Julio Santisteban[(✉)]

Universidad Católica San Pablo, Arequipa, Peru
{jan.quequezana,jsantisteban}@ucsp.edu.pe
http://www.ucsp.edu.pe

Abstract. Application Layer DDoS (AL-DDoS) is a major danger for Internet information services, because these attacks are easily performed and implemented by attackers and are difficult to detect and stop using traditional firewalls. Managing to saturate physically and computationally the information services offered on the network. Directly harming legitimate users, to deal with this type of attacks in the network layer previous approaches propose to use a configurable statistical model and observed that when being optimized in various configuration parameters Using Genetic Algorithms was able to optimize the effectiveness to detect Network Layer DDoS (NL-DDoS), however this method is not enough to stop DDoS at the level of application because this level presents different characteristics, that is why we propose a new method Configurable and optimized for different scenarios of Attacks that effectively detect AL-DDoS.

Keywords: DDOS · Genetic algorithms · Variances analysis · Security

1 Introduction

The approach proposed by Kim *et al.* [3] proposes to use a configurable statistical model. Observe that being optimized in several configuration parameters using Genetic Algorithms it was able to optimize the effectiveness to detect attacks NL-DDoSc. However this method is not sufficient to detect attacks DDoS at the application level because this level has different characteristics [5].

HTTP-based attacks AL-DDoS will probably not be detected by TCP anomaly mechanisms due to successful TCP connections [5]. The absence of heavy traffic peaks is a common feature in (AL-DDoS) [1].

Traffic patterns are relatively quiet during most attacks AL-DDoS and there is difficulty distinguishing them from *Flash Events* (FE), i.e. sudden increases in requests made by legitimate users. On the other hand, AL-DDoS attacks resemble normal web traffic [2]. The present paper presents a statistical model proposed by Kim *et al.* [3] optimized with Genetic Algorithms as a basis to develop a new model taking into account various characteristics of the application layer and obtain a configurable method for To detect attacks AL-DDoS.

© Springer Nature Switzerland AG 2018
F. Castro et al. (Eds.): MICAI 2017, LNAI 10632, pp. 107–117, 2018.
https://doi.org/10.1007/978-3-030-02837-4_9

In order to migrate the model proposed by Kim *et al.* [3] to the application layer. We need to consider additional factors specific to this layer. We propose to use as traffic matrix indexes The IP addresses for the rows and the URI accessed for the columns.

On the other hand, the *twindow* that Kim *et al.* [3] represented the number of packets that the model processes in the network layer, will now represent the time the model processes packets in the layer *twindow* length will be static and depends on the traffic flow being processed by the model, when the traffic flow that is entering is high, *twindow* should be shorter and vice versa.

The Traffic Matrix must have a reasonable size n so that the traffic matrix is processed in real time.

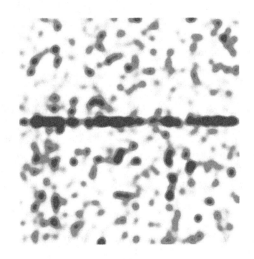

Fig. 1. Traffic matrix without AL-DDoS attack *variance* = 0.016.

Detection Method. When the AL-DDoS attacks are increased, the number of requests in the URI from legitimate IP addresses increases, the variance of the array was higher during AL-DDoS attacks compared to normal conditions, because when these types of attacks are performed, more requests are condensed at certain points in the array. A normal condition has more dispersion in the matrix.

Index Function. The indexes of rows and columns are represented by the IPs and URI respectively. To obtain decimal indexes from these two characteristics we will use the hash function CRC32, then the module of these values will be obtained with respect to the size n of the Traffic Matrix.

$$Row = (crc32(IP) \rightarrow decimal) \bmod n$$
$$Column = (crc32(URI) \rightarrow decimal) \bmod n$$

Fig. 2. Traffic matrix with AL-DDoS attack *variance* = 9.

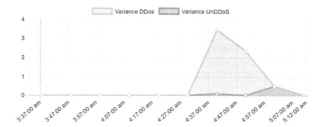

Fig. 3. Transition from normal to flood status by analysing variances.

Traffic Matrix's Variance. The Eq. (1) allows you to obtain the variance of a Traffic Matrix every time you have finished processing packages during a *twindow*.

$$V = \frac{1}{k} \sum_{j=0}^{n} \sum_{i=0}^{n} (M_{(i,j)} - \mu)^2, if M_{(i,j)} \neq 0 \tag{1}$$

$$\mu = \frac{1}{k} \sum_{j=0}^{n} \sum_{i=0}^{n} (M_{(i,j)})^2, if M_{(i,j)} \neq 0$$

M represents the traffic matrix, n the size of the matrix, k the number of indices in the traffic matrix that are not empty.

Matrix of Traffic in Normal State. It can be observed that the traffic matrix under normal conditions Fig. 1 has several dispersion points and presents a variance evaluation of 0.016 and there is a slightly uniform distribution.

Transition from Normal State Flooding. The variance obtained from the traffic matrices along each *twindow* cycle will not show how a transition from a normal state to a flood happens, this can be observed in Fig. 3 in which they obtain variances below 0.05 in 6 *twindow* before moving to a flood condition that results in variances greater than 1.

Traffic Matrix in State of Flooding. The traffic matrix characterizes a different behavior in flood conditions. This can be observed in the Fig. 2 which shows a diffuse and elevated distribution. This behavior is derived from flooding *botnets*.

2   Optimization of the Model Using Genetic Algorithms

Lee *et al.* [4] managed to optimize the model proposed by Kim *et al.* [3] to detect DDoS-NL attacks using genetic algorithms. It was observed that there are three variables to be optimized (i) the size of the traffic matrix n, (ii) the window time to process network packets (*twindow*), (iii) and the detection threshold (*dThreshold*) to distinguish a normal condition from an attack.

We will apply the same optimization to the new detection model proposed for AL-DDoS attacks, for this we will define a new evaluation function. We will use the same genetic representation (Binary) as if crossing percentages (0.6) and mutation (0.06). Used by Lee *et al.* [4] and we will add new genetic operators.

Evaluation Function. The evaluation function *feval* that we will use. Is defined by the $VS (VS = \{V_1, V_2, ..., V_m\})$, where m represents the number of times that *twindow* has been made through. Along a set of access records in the application layer for a period of time (*stime*) where $stime > twindow$, a value that is obtained in the Eq. (2).

$$feval = \frac{1}{m} \sum_{i=0}^{m} (V_i - \bar{V})^2 \tag{2}$$

$$\bar{V} = \frac{1}{m} \sum_{i=0}^{m} V_i$$

Selection Methods. We will use three methods of selection with the intention of obtaining three different types of behaviour that we should explore (stochastic, deterministic-stochastic, deterministic), among these selection criteria that satisfy the desired behaviours we have Roulette selection (*rt*), Stochastic surplus selection (*rs*), Selection by tournament (*tr*).

Crossing Methods. In order to extend the optimization made by Lee *et al.* [4] we will add new crossing methods that are about genetic algorithms of Binary representation. Which allow the exploration and exploitation for individuals in the population, The aggregate crossing methods are Cross-Point (*one*), Two-Point Crossing, and Uniform Crossing (*uni*).

Probability Setting. The configuration of probabilities of genetic manipulation that we will use will be those posed by the Lee *et al.* [4] investigation. Configuration parameters are Probability of crossing in 0.6 and Probability of mutation in 0.05, which prevented the optimization from ending at a local maximum.

Table 1. Configuration for genetic algorithm

Configuration	Value
Individuals	10
Iterations	25
Elitism	Activated
Percentage crossing	0.6
Percentage of mutation	0.05
Representation	Binary
Evaluation function	*feval*
Crossing methods	*one—two—uni*
Selection methods	*rs—rt—tr*
Limits *twindow*	[60, 1800]
Limits *n* matrix	[400, 1000]
Decimal precision	0

3 Tests and Results

Optimization Stage. Different tests were done combining the different methods of Crossing and Selection, each of these combinations were realized 20 times and the average of the behaviour of each configuration were obtained which were captured in different curves of monitoring (*Online—Offline—Best-so-Far*).

Curve Online. In the Fig. 4 we visualize the rapid attainment of good solutions and the convergence of the population, each point of the curve is given by:

$$v_{on}(t) = \frac{1}{t+1} \sum_{i=0}^{t} \bar{feval}(X_t) \tag{3}$$

where $\bar{feval}(X_t)$ is the mean of the evaluations of all individuals $x_i \in X_t$, for the generation t ($t = 0$ is the initial population).

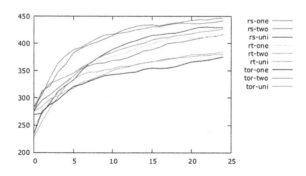

Fig. 4. Curvas monitoreo *online*

It is observed that the combination using tournament selection and two-point crossing (*tor—two*) obtains optimal individuals quickly, followed by stochastic surplus selection with two-point crossing (*rs—two*) and uniform crossing (*rs—uni*) respectively.

Curve Offline. In the Fig. 5 we visualize the attainment a good solutions no matter the time taken to find them, each point of the curve is given by:

$$v_{off}(t) = \frac{1}{t+1} \sum_{i=0}^{t} feval(x_{best}, t) \tag{4}$$

where $feval(x_{best}, t)$ is the evaluation of the best element of the generation t, ($t = 0$ is the initial population).

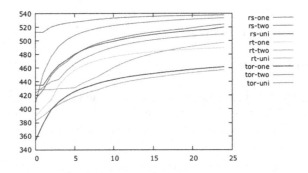

Fig. 5. Curves monitoring *offline*

It is observed that the combination using stochastic surplus selection with two point crossing (*rs—two*). It gets the best individuals throughout the whole evolution. Followed by the two-point crossbreed selection (*tr—two*) and stochastic leftover cross-point selection (*rs—one*).

Curve Best-so-far. In the Fig. 6 we observe the values $x_{best}(t)$ during the generations 0 at $t = 24$:

$$v_{best}(t) = feval(x_{best}, t) \tag{5}$$

where $feval(x_{best}, t)$ is the evaluation of the best element of the t generation.

It is observed that the combination using stochastic surplus selection and uniform cross-over (*rs—uni*) obtained the best individual, followed by the selection of stochastic surpluses with one-point crossing (*rs—one*) Tournament selection with a two-point cross (*tr—two*).

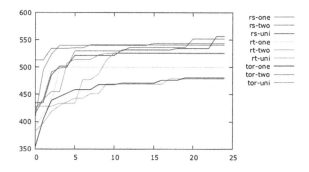

Fig. 6. Curves monitoring *best-so-far*

Table 2. Features of the dataset used [6].

Item	Experimental	NASA	ClarckNet
Duration	1 day	1 month	2 weeks
Start date	December 6/15	July 1/95	August 28/95
Data size (MB)	279.2 MB	205.2 MB	327.5 MB
Total requests	3,628,774	1,891,714	3,328,587
Petitions/day (avg)	3,628,774	56,748	237,756
Total bytes transferred	6,072.32 MB	62,489 MB	27,647 MB
Bytes transferred/day (avg)	6,072.32 MB	1,024.4 MB	1,974.8 MB

4 Experiments

Experimental Dataset. This experiment was performed on December 6, 2015 and we used a dedicated server hosted data center Iliad DC3 is located in Vitry-sur-Seine at 61 rue Julian Grimau, 6 km from Paris (France), has a 200 Mb/s bandwidth, 2 GB DDR2 memory, 1@1.6 Ghz x64 kernel, VT, installed nginx web server on port 8080 with default configuration, then implemented AL-DDoS attacks using code Javascript attack reported by Cloudflare, below:

```
function imgflood () {
var TARGET = '195.154.7x.xx:8080'
var URI = '/index.php?'
var pic = new Image()
var rand = Math.floor(Math.random() * 1000)
pic.src = 'http://'+TARGET+URI+rand+'=val'
}
setInterval(imgflood, 10)
```

We retrieved the access log generated by the nginx web server and used it in our DDoS detection method, the configuration we used is the optimal individual discovered after the optimization using genetic algorithms. The results can

Table 3. Attacks performed using AL-DDoS (Javascript) in the experimental dataset.

Date	Duration	Requests (avg)	Total requests
06/12/2015 12:00	30 min	60/min	138,214
06/12/2015 20:00	15 min	300/min	828,571
07/12/2015 04:00	60 min	600/min	2,282,518

Table 4. Results in the dataset experimental.

Date	Variance	Variance detection	Requests totals	Requests detected	Effectiveness	Attack
06/12/2015 13:00	1.063	0.107	49161	48210	98%	1st
06/12/2015 13:10	2.036	0.133	96139	93655	97%	1st
06/12/2015 20:00	5.505	0.266	490419	466286	95%	2nd
06/12/2015 20:10	3.726	0.156	371083	356936	96%	2nd
07/12/2015 04:10	1.085	0.214	138797	135193	97%	3rd
07/12/2015 04:20	21.102	2.36	925922	804156	86%	3rd
07/12/2015 04:30	16.211	1.913	764953	679185	88%	3rd
07/12/2015 04:40	9.618	0.921	204631	188959	92%	3rd
07/12/2015 04:50	9.651	0.897	127534	118685	93%	3rd
07/12/2015 05:00	10.387	0.9514	88921	83118	93%	3rd
07/12/2015 05:10	2.772	0.123	34734	33767	97%	3rd

be seen in the Table 4; This data allowed us to determine that our method of detecting AL-DDoS attacks has an effectiveness of 93.81%, in addition we determined that the larger the dataset the effectiveness decreases to 86% this occurs because the size of The matrix is not suitable to characterize large variations in the data set; On the other hand it was observed that the data characterized by our matrix offer variances according to the behavior of the bandwidth reported by the data center, this data can be observed in Fig. 7.

NASA Dataset. In this experiment we used the log of HTTP accesses made on the NASA server, the characteristics of this dataset can be observed in the Table 2. It was determined to use an array of size $n = 500$, $twindow = 7200$ s and an approximate detection threshold $dThreshold = 1$, after applying this configuration the obtained results as far as the variance and the detection can be observed In the Fig. 8, in which is observed that the model detects constant variations and little adequate for the traffic flow of the previous days, the variations were observed between the days 11,12,13,14,23,24 of the first month analysed.

We produced the Table 5 that characterizes the behaviour of this type of traffic source and what amount of requests we can identify as attackers.

ClarkNet Dataset. In this experiment we used the ClarkNet web server dataset [6].

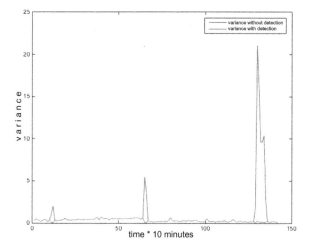

Fig. 7. Representation of the variance over time in the data set experimental. Representation of AL-DDoS experimental attacks.

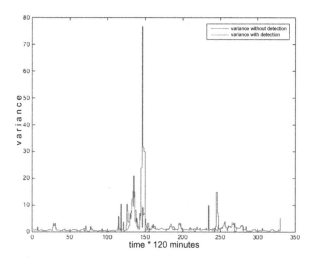

Fig. 8. Representation of the variance over time in the data set NASA-HTTP. Representation of NASA-HTTP AL-DDoS attacks.

In this experiment we learned to use an array of size $n = 500$, $twindow = 7200\,\mathrm{s}$ and a detection threshold of $dThreshold = 2$, after applying that configuration it was decided to mix both sets of data to be processed. The results obtained in terms of variance and detection can be observed in Fig. 9. In which it is observed that the traffic presented by this server is constant and exceeded the limit of the detection threshold. This is an opportunity for which we define that this is a false positive. Because based on previous experiences we observe

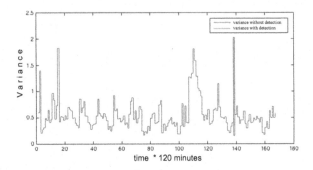

Fig. 9. Representation of the variance over time, in CLarckNet-HTTP data. Representation of AL-DDoS attacks Clark Net-HTTP

Table 5. Results in the dataset NASA-HTTP.

Variance without detection	Variance with detection	Requests totals	Requests detected	Percentage of attackers	Attack
0.575	0.575	4005	0	0%	No
0.580	0.580	6488	0	0%	No
1.792	*0.546*	*5846*	*806*	*13.78%*	*Si*
...	...	...	...	...	...
0.529	0.529	5436	0	0%	No
0.340	0.340	4214	0	0%	No
1.479	1.515	8490	1304	15.35%	Si
1.590	1.157	11604	2200	18.95%	Si

that when it comes to DDoS attacks are observed high increases in the variance and in this experiment barely shows some points outside the established limit.

5   Conclusion

The migration of the model proposed by Kim *et al.* [3] is a basis for detecting AL-DDoS attacks. Making various modifications that allow to capture characteristics of the application layer. Our proposal includes characterization of network traffic in a square matrix of dynamic size and the use of detection thresholds that can be optimized using genetic algorithms and the evaluation function that allows determining which configuration is most optimal to obtain a high degree of effectiveness.

From the experiments we can conclude that our proposed model to detect AL-DDoS gives us an efficiency of over 90%, besides being a light model and easy configuration for different types of scenarios. The model can be implemented in any type scenario without requiring many computational requirements and can certainly mitigate large-scale AL-DDoS attacks. Plus it has the advantage of being configurable for various types of attacks using genetic algorithms.

References

1. Application-layer denial of service (2011). http://forums.juniper.net/t5/Security-Mobility-Now/Application-layer-Denial-of-Service/ba-p/103306
2. Using Human Behavioral Analysis to Stop DDOS at Layer 7 (2012). http://hwww.networkcomputing.com/security/using-human-behavioral-analysis-to-stop/240007110
3. Kim, T.H., Kim, D.S., Lee, S.M., Park, J.S.: Detecting DDoS attacks using dispersible traffic matrix and weighted moving average. In: Park, J.H., Chen, H.-H., Atiquzzaman, M., Lee, C., Kim, T., Yeo, S.-S. (eds.) ISA 2009. LNCS, vol. 5576, pp. 290–300. Springer, Heidelberg (2009). https://doi.org/10.1007/978-3-642-02617-1_30
4. Lee, S.M., Kim, D.S., Lee, J.H., Park, J.S.: Detection of DDoS attacks using optimized traffic matrix. Comput. Math. Appl. **63**(2), 501–510 (2012)
5. Prabha, S., Anitha, R.: Mitigation of application traffic DDoS attacks with trust and AM based HMM models. Int. J. Comput. Appl. IJCA **6**(9), 26–34 (2010)
6. Bottomley, L., Balbach, S., Arlitt, M., Williamson, C.: The Internet Traffic Archive (2000). http://ita.ee.lbl.gov/EPA-HTTPNASA-HTTPClarkNet-HTTP

A Quartile-Based Hyper-heuristic for Solving the 0/1 Knapsack Problem

Fernando Gómez-Herrera$^{(\boxtimes)}$, Rodolfo A. Ramirez-Valenzuela,
José Carlos Ortiz-Bayliss$^{(\boxtimes)}$, Ivan Amaya, and Hugo Terashima-Marín

Escuela de Ingeniería y Ciencias, Tecnologico de Monterrey, Monterrey, Mexico
gomezhyuuga@acm.org, rodolfo@ramirezvalenzuela.com,
{jcobayliss,iamaya2,terashima}@itesm.mx

Abstract. This research describes three novel heuristic-based approaches for solving the 0/1 knapsack problem. The knapsack problem, in its many variants, arises in many practical scenarios such as the selection of investment projects and budget control. As an NP-hard problem, it is not always possible to compute the optimal solution by using exact methods and, for this reason, the problem is usually solved by using heuristic-based strategies. In this document, we use information of the distributions of weight and profit of the items in the knapsack instances to design and implement new heuristic-based methods that solve those instances. The solution model proposed in this work is two-fold: the first part focuses on the generation of two new heuristics, while the second explores the combination of solving methods through a hyper-heuristic approach. The heuristics proposed, as well as the hyper-heuristic model, were tested on a heterogeneous set of knapsack problem instances and compared against four heuristics taken from the literature. One of the proposed heuristics proved to be highly competent with respect to heuristics available in the literature. By using the hyper-heuristic, a solver that dynamically selects heuristics based on the problem features, we improved the results obtained by the new heuristics proposed and, achieved the best results among all the methods tested in this investigation.

Keywords: Heuristics · Hyper-heuristics · Knapsack problem
Quartile

1 Introduction

Combinatorial optimization arises in a large number of events in real-world problems. Among those problems, the knapsack problem (KP) (including all its variants) is one of the most challenging ones due to its relevance and impact, in both academic and industrial settings. The KP states the following: given a set of items, each with a weight and a profit, determine which items to include in a knapsack so that the weight is less or equal than a given limit, and the total profit is as large as possible. This version of the problem is usually referred to

© Springer Nature Switzerland AG 2018
F. Castro et al. (Eds.): MICAI 2017, LNAI 10632, pp. 118–128, 2018.
https://doi.org/10.1007/978-3-030-02837-4_10

as the 0/1 KP, since the items are indivisible. The KP is classified as an NP-hard problem [10]. Then, in the worst case, this problem cannot be solved in a reasonable time.

The KP is the root of several interesting problems such as operations research and polynomial factorization. It is also widely used in daily life tasks. For instance, while a person is doing his luggage for an incoming trip, the airlines usually give a maximum capacity to carry in the flight. Then, determining the items the passenger may carry during the journey can be seen as a simple KP. Other real-world applications that may be modeled as KPs include load balancing problems [13], project selection problems [17] and capital budgeting problems [7].

The many different strategies that can be used to solve the KP are mainly classified into two large groups: exact methods and approximated ones. As the name indicates, the solutions obtained by exact methods are exact and optimal. Solutions obtained by approximated methods are usually suboptimal, as they approximate the solution by making some assumptions to simplify the solving process. Due to the computational resources and the problem complexity, exact methods have limited applications since they have proved to be inefficient, particularly for large problems.

The aim of this paper is to explore the use of quartile-based information of the distributions of weight and profit of the items in the KP instances to produce competitive heuristic-based methods that outperform other heuristics when tested on instances with different features. Two main contributions are derived from this investigation:

1. Two new heuristics that select the next item to pack by using quartile-based information of the distributions of weight and profit of the items.
2. A hyper-heuristic –a high-level heuristic– that is capable of selecting one suitable heuristic according to the current problem state. This hyper-heuristic outperforms the rest of the heuristics considered for this work (even the new ones proposed in this investigation).

The paper is organized as follows. Section 2 presents the basics of the KP and several approaches that have commonly been used solve the problem. The methodology followed throughout this investigation is described in Sect. 3. Section 4 carefully describes the heuristics used and the solution model proposed in this work. In Sect. 5 we present the experiments conducted and the results obtained, as well as their analysis and discussion. Finally, we present the conclusion and future work in Sect. 6.

2   Background

Solving the KP requires a technique that selects, among the many different groups of items that can be formed, the one that maximizes the sum of the profits in the knapsack without exceeding its capacity [22]. Among the many different methods to solve the KP we can mention: tabu search [1,3,6,18], scatter search [11], local search [12], and ant colony optimization [4,8,9].

There is always a trade-off between the quality of the solution and consumption of resources. For example, some techniques rely on auxiliary lists that increase the use of the memory [18]. To avoid the high consumption of computational resources, heuristic-based methods are commonly used to solve the KP, since they consume fewer resources and lead to good-quality solutions faster than exact methods. Unfortunately, heuristic-based methods pay the price of simplicity by not guaranteeing that the optimal solution will always be found.

Some innovative approaches for solving the KP have been developed in recent years. For example, some probabilistic models include Cohort Intelligence (CI) [14], which is a new emerging technique inspired in human social interactions like learning from each other experiences. Because CI modeling involves dealing with the probability of constraints that change along with the distribution of the problem items, it is capable of jumping out of local minima. Another recent work for solving the KP involves Greedy Degree and Expectation Efficiency (GDEE) [15], which uses a technique similar to the work described in this document. The authors divide the items by a set of partitions: current item regions, candidate regions and unknown regions. This is done by a dynamic rearrangement of the items using a static objective function based on a greedy strategy. Their experiments are done by using fifteen instances from the Standard Test Case Libraries (STCL) and, for each solution, the best profit, worst profit and running time are provided. Hybrid heuristics have also proven to be useful for solving this problem. For example, by using Mean Field Theory [2], the authors generate a probabilistic model capable of replacing a difficult distribution of items by an easier one.

Another solving approach that has become popular in the last decade for other optimization problems is hyper-heuristics [20,21]. These high-level heuristic-based strategies provide a set of guidelines or strategies to develop heuristic optimization. Some authors describe hyper-heuristics simply as "heuristics to choose heuristics". Hyper-heuristics [23], particularly selection ones, are high-level heuristics that control a set of low-level heuristics and decide when and where to apply each low-level heuristic based on the problem state at the moment of the decision.

Most of the recent work on hyper-heuristics has focused on two hyper-heuristic approaches [5]: selection hyper-heuristics and generation ones. Selection hyper-heuristics generate a strategy that chooses, among a set of available heuristics, the one that best suits the current problem characterization. Solving a problem by using a hyper-heuristic implies applying one heuristic at the time, based on the features of the problem state. By applying such a heuristic, the problem state will change, and then the process will be repeated until the problem is solved.

3   Methodology

The process followed in this research is divided into three steps: data collection, model definition and experimentation.

Data collection. A total of 400 KP instances were used to test the heuristic-based methods considered for this investigation. All the instances were solved by each of the methods. More details on the instances considered for this investigation can be found in Sect. 5.

Model definition. The heuristic methods proposed in this investigation use quartile-based information to select the next item to pack. By using the information from the quartiles, we propose to split the items into three groups. For example, if we consider the weight, the sets that can be formed are $Q1_W$ (which contains the lightest 25% of the items), $Q4_W$ (which contains the heaviest 25% of the items), and IQR_W (which contains the remaining 50% of the items). Three sets of items can be generated in a similar way by considering the profit of the items: $Q1_P$, IQR_P and $Q4_P$. A graphical example of this division of the items is depicted in Fig. 1. By using this intuitive conception of rules, we proposed two heuristics for solving the KP: QBH-01 and QBH-02 (both heuristics will be explained in Sect. 4.1). This investigation goes beyond the proposal of two new heuristics, as it also proposes a third heuristic-based approach: a hyper-heuristic (QBHH) that selectively applies QBH-01 and QBH-02, as well as one usually competent heuristic already defined in the literature, max profit.

Experimentation. In this stage, we tested our heuristic-based methods on each of the 400 instances. Related to the hyper-heuristic model, we also explored the arrangement of the selection rules in order to find which one of the new heuristics should take priority on the decision process. Two different metrics were used to evaluate the performance of the methods considered for this investigation: the local win rate (LWR) and the global win rate (GWR). LWR is a tournament-based-metric that initializes a counter of 'wins' to zero. Then, each test instance is solved and the method that obtains the maximum profit for that instance (considering only the results of the other available solvers), increases its counter by one. Thus, this metric records the fraction of instances where a method obtains the best results compared to the other methods tested. It is worth mentioning that, in some cases, two or more methods may obtain the best profit. In such cases, the counters of both methods are increased, as they both obtained the best result. GWR extends LWR by incorporating the profit of the optimal solution into the calculation. Just as in LWR, GWR uses the number of 'wins', but in a completely different fashion. It uses a threshold as a parameter and also the profit of the optimal solution[1]. The concept of winning for this metric is related to how close

---

[1] As the reader may have already noticed, GWR requires to know the optimal solution for the instances used for testing the methods. Given the sizes of the instances studied in this work, the optimal solution was found through dynamic programming. Unfortunately, this metric might not be useful for other instances, as for some of them it could be unfeasible to obtain the optimal solution.

a solution is to the optimal one. Then, a method is the winner of a given instance if $P_h \geq \theta \times P^*$, where P_h is the profit of the solution produced by the method being evaluated, $\theta \in [0, 1]$ is a threshold value, and P^* is the profit of the optimal solution. For example, $\theta = 0.99$ means that the method wins only if it obtains a profit at least large as 99% of P^*. By setting $\theta = 1$ we consider winners only the methods that obtain the optimal solution. For this work, we used two values for θ: $\theta = 0.99$ and $\theta = 1$.

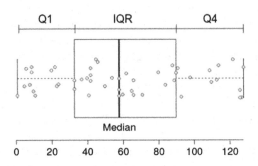

Fig. 1. Boxplot showing the sets constructed by using the distribution of the items according to the quartiles.

4   Solution Model

This section describes the heuristics considered for this investigation, how they work and how they are combined into a selection hyper-heuristic.

4.1   Heuristics

All the heuristics considered for this investigation work as follows. They pack one item at the time, according to one particular criterion. The process is repeated until no more items can be packed into the knapsack. Because the criteria are different, they give place to many different strategies. For example:

Default. Packs the next item that fits within the current capacity of the knapsack.
Max profit. Packs the item with the highest profit.
Max profit per weight. Packs the item with the highest ratio of profit over weight.
Min weight. Packs the item with the minimum weight.

Please note that for this work, any item that exceeds the capacity of the knapsack is removed from the list of available items. This removal procedure is invoked every time a heuristic is to be applied. Thus, the heuristics only work with items that fit into the knapsack.

4.2 Quartile-Based Heuristics

This work not only relies on existing heuristics, but proposes two new ones which are based on a combination of previously defined criteria.

QBH-01. This heuristic selects first the item with the highest profit from 'light' items (the item with the highest profit in $Q1_W$). It then selects the item from those whose weight is not "very low" nor "very high" (items in IQR_W). Finally, QBH-01 selects, from these two items, the one with the largest profit and packs it into the knapsack.

QBH-02. This heuristic follows the rationale "if there is an item with large profit and it is not too heavy, then take it". Thus, this heuristic selects the item that maximizes the profit among all the items with profits larger than $\bar{p} + \sigma_p$ and weights in IQR_W. Where $\bar{p}$ is the mean of the profit distribution and σ_P is the standard deviation of the profit distribution.

4.3 A Quartile-Based Hyper-heuristic

In this section, we describe a novel selection hyper-heuristic approach for solving the KP. The general idea is to define a high-level heuristic that controls single heuristics such as QBH-01, QBH-02 and max profit. The core of the hyper-heuristic model, the module that selects which heuristic to apply, uses a fixed sequence of heuristics, which are applied only when certain conditions are satisfied.

Figure 2 presents the pseudo-code for QBHH. In a graphical way, the behaviour of the hyper-heuristic is depicted in Fig. 3.

The hyper-heuristic proposed in this investigation was obtained empirically, based on the observations of the solving methods and their performance on the instances used in this work. As the reader may observe, QBHH mainly relies on the two quartile-based heuristics proposed in this investigation, QBH-01 and QBH-02; and only when these heuristics fail to select an item, based on their particular criteria, max profit is used.

To clarify the process followed by the hyper-heuristic when a KP instance is solved, Fig. 4 presents an example of the iterations and how the distributions of weight and profit of the items change throughout the solving process.

5 Experiments and Results

We trained and tested the heuristic-based methods on a set of KP instances with different features. These instances are grouped into four groups of 100 instances each. The instances are balanced with respect to four existing heuristics, so the arrangement of the items inside each group is designed to favour different heuristics. Each instance considered for this investigation contains 50 items with a capacity of 50 units of weight. The items have at most 20 units of weight. The profits of the items range from 1 and 128. The instances used in this investigation are available at http://bit.ly/KnapsackInstances.

Knapsack ← ∅
Items ← $\{I_1, I_2, \ldots I_n\}$
while (Knapsack.Weight < Capacity) **and** (Items.Size > 0) **do**
    for each item ∈ Items **do**
        if item.Weight + Knapsack.Weight > Capacity **then**
            Items.Remove(item)
        end if
    end for
    x ← max(item.Profit) ∈ $Q1_W$
    y ← max(item.Profit / item.Weight) ∈ IQR_W
    if x **and** y **then**
        Knapsack.Add(max(x.Profit, y.Profit))   ▷ QBH-01
    end if
    x ← item ∈ Items | item.Profit > $\sigma_p + \bar{p}$ **and** item.Weight ∈ IQR_W
    if x **then**
        Knapsack.Add(x)   ▷ QBH-02
    end if
    x ← max(item.Profit) ∈ Items
    Knapsack.Add(x)   ▷ Max profit
end while

Fig. 2. An algorithmic description of QBHH. Comments on the right indicate the heuristic used by each rule.

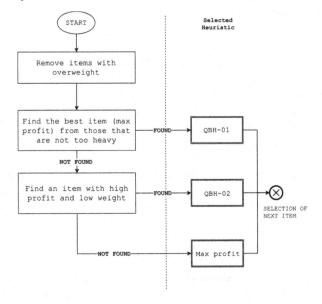

Fig. 3. High-level description of QBHH. The process depicted in this figure is repeated until no more items can be packed into the knapsack. Every time an item is selected, the process starts over and, by doing so, the attributes of the problem change as well as the sets that group the items by using the quartiles. Whenever QBH-01 and QBH-02 fail to find an item to pack based on their respective criteria, they select the next item to pack according to the max profit heuristic.

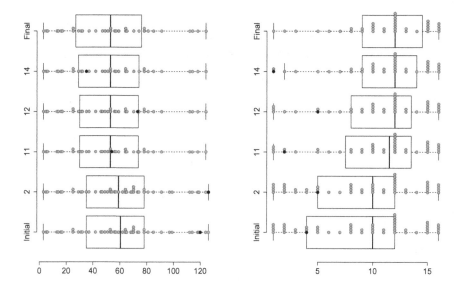

Fig. 4. Example of how the distribution of weight and profit of the items changes as the solving process takes place by using QBHH. Left and right figures represent the profit and weight distributions at different iterations of the solving process, respectively. Black circles indicate the selected item for that iteration. The left axis labels indicate the current iteration of the selection process. The 'Initial' and 'Final' labels indicate the status of the distribution at the initial state and at the end of the solving process, respectively.

Table 1. Comparison of the different methods considered for this investigation by using the metrics LWR, GWR ($\theta = 0.99$) and GWR ($\theta = 1$). The best performer for each metric is highlighted in bold.

Method	LWR	GWR ($\theta = 0.99$)	GWR ($\theta = 1$)
Default	14.25%	9.50%	5.75%
Max profit	24.00%	24.25%	22.25%
Max profit per weight	24.25%	25%	19.75%
Min weight	23.75%	21.00%	12.50%
QBH-01	45.75%	44.25%	35.50%
QBH-02	20.25%	21.25%	18.00%
QBHH	**49.50%**	**49.00%**	**38.25%**

Table 1 shows the performance of the different heuristic-based methods studied in this investigation by using the three metrics previously described. From the simple heuristics, QBH-01 is clearly the best option, as it obtains the best results by using the three metrics. The second quartile-based heuristic proposed in this investigation, QBH-02, performed poorly on this set of instances. By combining the quartile-based heuristics into a hyper-heuristic we obtained the best performer of the methods in this investigation: QBHH. When the metric LWR is considered, the hyper-heuristic wins in almost 50% of the instances, which is more than twice the best heuristic taken from the literature, max profit per weight. The performance of QBHH represents a small improvement in performance with respect to QBH-01, but a large one for any of the other heuristics (around 20% for any of the metrics). The fact that QBHH relies mainly on QBH-01 explains this behaviour, as the first rule tries to apply QBH-01 and, only if it is unable to find an item, it tries QBH-02 – which proved a poor performer when applied in isolation.

A deeper analysis on the process conducted by QBHH shows that the hyper-heuristic applies QBH-01 to pack around 86% of the items in the instance set. The proportion of items that are packed by using QBH-02 and max profit drops to 6.76% and 7.46%, respectively.

5.1 Discussion

Does the order of the heuristics in the hyper-heuristic process affect the performance of the hyper-heuristic? Aiming at answering this question we inverted the order of QBH-01 and QBH-02 in QBHH. By changing the order of the heuristics (so that the first available heuristic was QBH-02 instead of QBH-01) the performance of the hyper-heuristic decreased by half. This behaviour is interesting, as the same heuristic, used at a different position of the sequence, leads to very different results.

As part of a further analysis, we replaced QBH-02 by max profit per weight, and use it as a second option in the sequence of available heuristics for the hyper-heuristic. The rationale for this change was to explore how the second best of the heuristics could fit into the hyper-heuristic model. Contrary to what we expected, the performance was significantly below the one shown by the original sequence QBH-01/QBH-02/max profit.

6 Conclusion and Future Work

This work describes two new heuristics for solving the KP. These heuristics use the information of the distributions of weight and profit of the items in the problem to decide which item to pack next. Specifically, these new heuristics (QBH-01 and QBH-02) split the items into three groups by feature, based on the quartile-information of the distributions. Although the idea seems simple, the results proved that one of these heuristics, QBH-01, outperformed four heuristics taken from the current literature in any of the three metrics considered for this work. Regarding QBH-02, its performance (when applied in isolation) was below our expectations and their results were rather poor.

Trying to improve the performance of the solving methods, we intuitively proposed a way to combine QBH-01, QBH-02 and max-profit to further improve the solution process. The hyper-heuristic obtained outstanding results, outperforming all the other heuristics –even QBH-01.

There are various interesting paths which may be worth exploring in the future. The first one is related to how the quartile-based heuristics are defined. For example, the boundaries for selection might be automatically generated by using genetic programming or a similar approach. The hyper-heuristic itself is another field of opportunity. For this work, we proposed the sequence of heuristics by empirical reasons but various methods for producing hyper-heuristics have been proposed in the last years [16,19]. It will be an interesting future work to use one or more of such models to define the sequence of heuristics to apply.

Acknowledgments. This research was supported in part by CONACyT Basic Science Projects under grant 241461 and ITESM Research Group with Strategic Focus in intelligent Systems.

References

1. Amuthan, A., Thilak, K.D.: Survey on Tabu search meta-heuristic optimization. In: 2016 International Conference on Signal Processing, Communication, Power and Embedded System (SCOPES), pp. 1539–1543, October 2016
2. Banda, J., Velasco, J., Berrones, A.: A hybrid heuristic algorithm based on mean-field theory with a simple local search for the quadratic knapsack problem. In: 2017 IEEE Congress on Evolutionary Computation (CEC), pp. 2559–2565, June 2017
3. Barichard, V., Hao, J.K.: Genetic Tabu search for the multi-objective knapsack problem. Tsinghua Sci. Technol. 8(1), 8–13 (2003)
4. Burke, E., Kendall, G.: Search Methodologies: Introductory Tutorials in Optimization and Decision Support Techniques. Springer, Heidelberg (2005). https://doi.org/10.1007/0-387-28356-0
5. Burke, E.K., Hyde, M., Kendall, G., Ochoa, G., Özcan, E., Woodward, J.R.: A classification of hyper-heuristic approaches. In: Gendreau, M., Potvin, J.Y. (eds.) Handbook of Metaheuristics, pp. 449–468. Springer, Boston (2010). https://doi.org/10.1007/978-1-4419-1665-5_15
6. Chou, Y.H., Yang, Y.J., Chiu, C.H.: Classical and quantum-inspired Tabu search for solving 0/1 knapsack problem. In: 2011 IEEE International Conference on Systems, Man, and Cybernetics, pp. 1364–1369, October 2011
7. Cui, X., Wang, D., Yan, Y.: AES algorithm for dynamic knapsack problems in capital budgeting. In: 2010 Chinese Control and Decision Conference, pp. 481–485, May 2010
8. Dorigo, M., Stützle, T.: The Ant Colony Optimization Metaheuristic, pp. 25–64. MIT Press, Cambridge (2004)
9. Gagliardi, E.O., Dorzán, M.G., Leguizamón, M.G., Peñalver, G.H.: Approximations on minimum weight pseudo-triangulation problem using ant colony optimization metaheuristic. In: 2011 30th International Conference of the Chilean Computer Science Society, pp. 238–246, November 2011
10. Garey, M.R., Johnson, D.S.: Computers and Intractability: A Guide to the Theory of NP-Completeness. W. H. Freeman & Co., New York (1979)
11. Hifi, M., Otmani, N.: A first level scatter search for disjunctively constrained knapsack problems. In: 2011 International Conference on Communications, Computing and Control Applications (CCCA), pp. 1–6, March 2011

12. Jaszkiewicz, A.: On the performance of multiple-objective genetic local search on the 0/1 knapsack problem - a comparative experiment. IEEE Trans. Evol. Comput. **6**(4), 402–412 (2002)
13. Kiss, Z.I., Hosu, A.C., Varga, M., Polgar, Z.A.: Load balancing solution for heterogeneous wireless networks based on the knapsack problem. In: 2015 38th International Conference on Telecommunications and Signal Processing (TSP), pp. 1–6, July 2015
14. Kulkarni, A.J., Shabir, H.: Solving 0–1 knapsack problem using cohort intelligence algorithm. Int. J. Mach. Learn. Cybern. **7**(3), 427–441 (2016)
15. Lv, J., Wang, X., Huang, M., Cheng, H., Li, F.: Solving 0–1 knapsack problem by greedy degree and expectation efficiency. Appl. Soft Comput. J. **41**, 94–103 (2016)
16. Maashi, M., Özcan, E., Kendall, G.: A multi-objective hyper-heuristic based on choice function. Expert Syst. Appl. **41**(9), 4475–4493 (2014)
17. Naldi, M., Nicosia, G., Pacifici, A., Pferschy, U., Leder, B.: A simulation study of fairness-profit trade-off in project selection based on HHI and knapsack models. In: 2016 European Modelling Symposium (EMS), pp. 85–90, November 2016
18. Niar, S., Freville, A.: A parallel Tabu search algorithm for the 0–1 multidimensional knapsack problem. In: Proceedings 11th International Parallel Processing Symposium, pp. 512–516, April 1997
19. Ortiz-Bayliss, J.C., Terashima-Marín, H., Conant-Pablos, S.E.: Combine and conquer: an evolutionary hyper-heuristic approach for solving constraint satisfaction problems. Artif. Intell. Rev. **46**(3), 327–349 (2016)
20. Özcan, E., Bilgin, B., Korkmaz, E.E.: A comprehensive analysis of hyper-heuristics. Intell. Data Anal. **12**(1), 3–23 (2008)
21. Ren, Z., Jiang, H., Xuan, J., Hu, Y., Luo, Z.: New insights into diversification of hyper-heuristics. IEEE Trans. Cybern. **44**(10), 1747–1761 (2014)
22. Sapra, D., Sharma, R., Agarwal, A.P.: Comparative study of metaheuristic algorithms using knapsack problem. In: 2017 7th International Conference on Cloud Computing, Data Science Engineering - Confluence, pp. 134–137, January 2017
23. Terashima-Marín, H., Flores-Alvarez, E.J., Ross, P.: Hyper-heuristics and classifier systems for solving 2D-regular cutting stock problems. In: Proceedings of the 7th annual conference on Genetic and evolutionary computation, pp. 637–643. ACM (2005)

Extending the Pareto-Dominance Based MOEAs Framework for Overlapping Community Detection

Darian Horacio Grass-Boada[1(✉)], Airel Pérez-Suárez[1], Rafael Bello[2], and Alejandro Rosete[3]

[1] Advanced Technologies Application Center (CENATAV), Havana, Cuba
{dgrass,asuarez}@cenatav.co.cu

[2] Department of Computer Science, Universidad Central "Marta Abreu" de Las Villas, Santa Clara, Cuba
rbellop@uclv.edu.cu

[3] Facultad de Ingeniería Informática, Universidad Tecnológica de la Habana "José Antonio Echeverría" (Cujae), Havana, Cuba
rosete@ceis.cujae.edu.cu

Abstract. The detection of communities in Social Networks has been successfully applied in several contexts. Taking into account the high computational complexity of this problem as well as the drawbacks of single-objective approaches, community detection has been recently addressed as Multi-objective Optimization Evolutionary Algorithms (MOEAs); however, most of the algorithms following this approach only detect disjoint communities. In this paper, we extend the general Pareto-dominance based MOEAs framework for discovering overlapping communities. The experimental evaluation of our proposal over four real-life networks showed that it is effective for overlapping community detection.

Keywords: Social networks analysis
Overlapping community detection · Multi-objective optimization

1 Introduction

In the analysis of complex networks, a given network is said to have a *community structure* if its vertices can be organised into groups of vertices (i.e., communities) such that nodes belonging to the same community are densely interconnected but spare connected with the remaining nodes in the network [1]. Specifically, in the content of Social Network Analysis, the detection of communities plays an important role and it has been received a lot of attention nowadays [2].

The community detection problem has an NP-hard nature [1]. Therefore, most reported approaches define an objective function that captures the notion of community and then, they use heuristics in order search for a set of communities optimising this function. Nevertheless, single-objective optimization approaches

© Springer Nature Switzerland AG 2018
F. Castro et al. (Eds.): MICAI 2017, LNAI 10632, pp. 129–141, 2018.
https://doi.org/10.1007/978-3-030-02837-4_11

has two main drawbacks: (a) the optimization of only one function confines the solution to a particular community structure, and (b) returning one single partition may not be suitable when the network has many potential structures. Taking into account these limitations, many community detection algorithms model the problem as a Multi-objective Optimization Problem.

A multi-objective community detection problem aims to search for a partition P^* of a network N such that:

$$F(P^*) = min_{P \in \Omega} (f_1(P), f_2(P), \ldots, f_r(P)), \tag{1}$$

where P is a partition of N, Ω is the set of feasible partitions, r is the number of objective functions and f_i is the ith objective function. With the introduction of the multiple objective functions, which are commonly contradictory to each other, there is usually no absolute optimal solution but several solutions being *Pareto optimal* [1]. A solution (i.e., a set of communities) is said to be Pareto optimal iff there is no other solution dominating it. Let $S_1, S_2 \in \Omega$ be two solutions. S_1 is said to dominate S_2 iff it fulfils the following two conditions: (i) $\forall i = 1 \ldots r, f_i(S_1) \leq f_i(S_2)$, and (ii) $\exists j = 1 \ldots r$ such that $f_j(S_1) < f_j(S_2)$. A commonly used way to solve a multi-objective community detection problem and looking for the set of Pareto optimal solutions is by using MOEAs.

Although the MOEAs-based community detection algorithms reported in the literature have been attained good results, most of them constraint communities to be disjoint; however, it is known that most real-world networks have overlapping community structure [3]. The space of feasible solutions in the overlapping community detection problem is more complicated than that of the disjoint case; thus, it results challenged to apply MOEA for discovering overlapping community structures in social networks. To the best of our knowledge, only the Pareto-dominance based MOEAs proposed in [2,4–7] addressed the overlapping community detection problem.

In this paper, we extend the general Pareto-dominance based MOEAs framework for discovering overlapping communities. In order to accomplish this purpose, we assume the communities detected by a Pareto-dominance based MOEAs as seed clusters and we introduce four steps, named *preprocessing*, *expansion*, *improving* and *merging*, which aim to build the final overlapping communities. The *preprocessing* step removes from the original network those edges that do not represent strong connections, in order to produce better seed clusters. On the other hand, the remaining three introduced steps allow our proposal to detect overlapping zones in the network, to improve the overlapping quality of these zones, and to merge communities having high overlapping, respectively.

Our experimental evaluation over four classical real-life social networks, compares our proposal against the state-of-the-art related algorithms in terms of the accuracy they attain, according to the NMI external evaluation measure [8]. The experimental results showed that our proposal is promising and effective for overlapping community detection in social networks.

The remainder of this paper is organised as follows: Sect. 2 briefly describes the related work. In Sect. 3, we introduce our proposal whilst Sect. 4 presents its experimental evaluation over four classical real-life networks. Finally, Sect. 5 gives the conclusions and future work directions.

2   Related Work

The problem of detecting the communities existing in a social network is similar to the problem of graph clustering [9]. According to Mukhopadhyay *et al.* in [10], any clustering algorithm following a MOEAs approach must include the following four steps: (1) generating an initial population of chromosomes (i.e., solutions to the problem at hand), taking into account a predefined representation, (2) applying the evolutionary operators over the current population for building the next generation; this step allows MOEAs to move through the solution space, (3) evaluating the current and new populations by using a predefined set of objective functions, and (4) applying a predefined heuristic for keeping and improving the best solutions found so far. Usually, steps b, c and d are repeated a predefined number of times or until a specific stop criterium is fulfilled.

The first algorithm using MOEAs for detecting overlapping communities is MEA_CDPs [2] which uses an undirected representation of the solution and the NSGA-II optimization framework with the reverse operator, in order to search for the solutions optimising three objective functions. On the other hand, iMEA_CDPs [5] also uses NSGA-II and the same representation of MEA_CDPs but it proposes to employ the PMX operator and the simple mutation operator as evolutionary operators, for looking for solutions optimising two objective functions.

IMOQPSO [6] uses a center-based representation of the solution that is built from the eigenvectors extracted from the line graph associated to the original network. This algorithm uses a combination of QPSO and HSA as its optimization framework, in order to search for solutions optimising two objective functions. On the other hand, OMO [4] employs a representation based on adjacencies between edges of the network and two objective functions. This algorithm uses the NSGA-II framework, together with the two-point crossover and the random gene mutation as crossover and mutation evolutionary operators, respectively.

Another related algorithm is MCMOEA [7] which first detects the set of maximal cliques of the network and then it builds the maximal-clique graph. Starting from this transformation, MCMOEA uses a representation based on labels and the MOEA/D optimization framework in order to detect the communities optimising the two objective functions.

3   Proposal

There are different MOEAs classes. Similar to most of the related algorithms, our proposal follows a Pareto-dominance based MOEAs approach, which in turn follows the same steps described by Mukhopadhyay *et al.* The main idea of our proposal is to do not build overlapping communities directly but rather using the first three steps of any algorithm *A* following the general Pareto-dominance based MOEAs approach for producing in each iteration a set of disjoint seed clusters, and then to process these seeds in order to build the final overlapping communities, by using three steps we propose to include in this general approach.

For building the disjoint seed clusters the steps 1 and 2 of the Pareto-dominance based MOEAs framework are employed; each seed cluster represent the set of vertices an overlapping community does not share with any other community in the network. In order to build seed clusters as cohesive as possible, we introduce the *preprocessing* step prior to step 1. The *preprocessing* step aims to build a transformed network that does not contain those edges of the original network which, from our point of view, do not represent strong connections. The above mentioned steps 1 and 2 are performed over this transformed network.

Once the current population (CP) of chromosomes is built, the set of disjoint seeds represented by each chromosome is processed, considering the original network, by using the introducing *expansion, improving* and *merging* steps. These three steps aim to detect overlapping zones of the network, to locally improve each overlapping zone detected and to reduce the redundancy existing in the solutions, respectively. The overlapping communities resulting from this process constitutes the current overlapping population (COP). Following, the fitness of each solution in CP and COP is computed using the step 3 of the Pareto-dominance based MOEAs framework. For evaluating each set of disjoint seeds in CP we employ the objectives functions defined by the algorithm A. On the other hand, for evaluating each solution $S_i \in COP$ we employ as objective functions the *intra* and *inter* factors of the overlapping Modularity used in [11]:

$$Intra(S_i) = 1 - \left(\sum_{j=1}^{|S_i|} \sum_{v,w \in C_j} \frac{A_{v,w}}{2 \cdot m \cdot O_v \cdot O_w} \right) \tag{2}$$

$$Inter(S_i) = \sum_{j=1}^{|S_i|} \sum_{v,w \in C_j} \frac{|N(v)| \cdot |N(w)|}{4 \cdot m^2 \cdot O_v \cdot O_w}, \tag{3}$$

where $C_j \in S_i$ is a community, $A_{v,w}$ is 1 if there is an edge between vertices v and w in the original network; otherwise, $A_{v,w}$ is 0. O_v and O_v are the number of communities to which v and w belong, respectively; m is the total number of edges in the network, $N(v)$ is the set of adjacent vertices of vertex v and $|\cdot|$ refers to the cardinality of a given set.

Finally, for addressing the step (4) we employ the same mechanism used by the algorithm A in order to keep and to improve the best set of disjoint seeds in CP. Additionally, in this step we use an archive mechanism defined by PESA-II [1], for keeping and improving the best overlapping solutions in COP.

Following, the *preprocessing, expansion, improving* and *merging* steps are explained in details.

3.1   Preprocessing Step

Let $G = \langle V, E \rangle$ a network where V is the set of vertices and E the set of edges between those vertices. As it was mentioned a seed cluster should contain the vertices that the overlapping community associated with that seed does not share with any other community. Taking into account the basic notion of community, we use G and a new relation between vertices in order to build a transformed network $G' = \langle V, E' \rangle$ containing only edges that represent strong connections.

From our point of view, two vertices of G' should be related if the number of neighbours they share in G is greater than the number of neighbours they do not share. We will say that a vertex $v_j \in V$ is related with a vertex $v_i \in V$, denoted as $v_i R v_j$, iff $|N(v_i) \cap N(v_j)| > \frac{1}{2} \cdot |N(v_j)|$. The set built from all the vertices related to a vertex v_i form the so called *similarity class* of v_i, denoted as $[v_i]_R$.

For building $G' = \langle V, E' \rangle$ we compute $[v_i]_R$ for each $v_i \in V$ and then, for each pair of vertices $v_i, v_j \in V$ we add an undirected edge (v_i, v_j) in E' if $v_j \in [v_i]_R$ or $v_i \in [v_j]_R$.

3.2   Expansion Step

Overlapping vertices are supposed to be those vertices that belong to more than one community and in order to be correctly located inside a community they need to have edges with vertices inside those communities. For detecting overlapping zones we soften the criterium used for building the seed clusters. For accomplishing this purpose, each seed S_i is processed for determining which vertices outside S_i share a significant number of their adjacent vertices with vertices inside S_i, considering $G = \langle V, E \rangle$.

Let S_i be a seed cluster and $\partial S_i \subseteq S_i$ the set of vertices of S_i having neighbours outside S_i. The strength of ∂S_i, denoted as $Str(\partial S_i)$, is computed as the ratio between the number of edges ∂S_i has with vertices inside S_i, and the number of edges ∂S_i has with vertices inside and outside S_i.

The strategy for expanding seed S_i is as follows: (1) determining the set L of vertices $v \notin S_i$ having at least one adjacent in ∂S_i, such that $Str(\partial S'_i) - Str(\partial S_i) > 0$, where $S'_i = S_i \cup \{v\}$, (2) applying the roulette wheel selection method over L, where the probability of selecting a vertex $v \in L$ is computed by using the increase v produces in $Str(\partial S_i)$, and (3) repeat steps 1–2 while $L \neq \emptyset$.

3.3   Improving Step

Let Z be an overlapping zone detected by the expansion step and $C_Z = \{C_1, C_2, \ldots, C_m\}$ the set of communities that set up Z. Let $v \in Z$ be an overlapping vertex. Let $N(v|C_Z)$ be the set of adjacent vertices of v belonging to at least one community in C_Z. Let $G_v = \{G_v^1, G_v^2, \ldots, G_v^l\}$ be the set of communities or overlapping zones containing the vertices in $N(v|C_Z)$. Let $N'(v|C_Z)$ be the set of adjacent vertices of v that belong to at most one community in C_Z.

A property we will expect an overlapping vertex like v satisfies is to have the vertices in $N(v|C_Z)$ equally distributed over the groups of G_v. The *uniformity* of v, denoted as $U(v)$, measures how much the distribution of vertices in $N(v|C_Z)$ deviates from the expected distribution of $N(v|C_Z)$ and it is computed as follows:

$$U(v) = 1 - \sum_{G_v^i \in G_v} abs\left(\frac{|N(v|C_Z) \cap G_v^i|}{|N(v|C_Z)|} - \frac{1}{|G_v|}\right), \qquad (4)$$

where $abs(\cdot)$ is the absolute value. $U(v)$ takes values in $[0,1]$ and the higher its value the better well-balanced v is.

Another property we would expect an overlapping vertex $v \in Z$ to fulfil is to be a connector between any pair of its adjacent vertices in $N'(v|C_Z)$; that is, we would expect that the shortest path connecting any pair of vertices $u, w \in N'(v|C_Z)$ should be the path made by the edges (u,v) and (v,w). The *simple betweenness* of v, denoted as $SB(v)$, measures how much connector v is and it is computed as follows:

$$SB(v) = \frac{2 \cdot \sum_{i=1}^{|C_Z|-1} \sum_{j>i}^{|C_Z|} \left(1 - \frac{|E(C_i, C_j)|}{|N'(v|C_Z) \cap C_i| \cdot |N'(v|C_Z) \cap C_j|}\right)}{|C_Z| \cdot (|C_Z| - 1)} \qquad (5)$$

where $E(C_i, C_j)$ is the set of edges with one vertex in C_i and the other one in C_j. $SB(v)$ takes values in $[0,1]$ and the higher its value the best connector v is.

Let $U_{ave}(Z)$ be the initial average uniformity of the vertices belonging to an overlapping zone Z. In order to improve the quality of Z we will analyse the addition or removal of one or mores vertices from Z. Thus, any vertex $v \in Z$ having $U(v) < U_{ave}(Z)$ is a candidate to be removed from Z, whilst any vertex $u \in N(v|C_Z), v \in Z$, such that $U(u) > U_{ave}(Z)$ is a candidate to be added to Z. Taking into account that both the uniformity and simple betweenness concepts can be straightforward generalised in order to be applied to Z, we employ such properties for measuring which changes in Z increase its quality as an overlapping zone and which do not.

Let T be an addition or removal which turns Z into Z'. T is considered as *viable* iff $(U(Z') + SB(Z')) - (U(Z) + SB(Z)) > 0$. The heuristic proposed for improving the set $O = \{Z_1, Z_2, \ldots, Z_j\}$ of overlapping zones detected by the expansion step is as follows: (1) computing $U_{ave}(Z_i)$ for each $Z_i \in O$, (2) detecting the set T of *viable* transformations to apply over O, (3) performing the transformation $t \in T$ which produces the higher improvement in its zone, and (4) repeat steps 2 and 3 while $T \neq \emptyset$.

3.4 Merging Step

Let $OC = \{C_1, C_2, \ldots, C_k\}$ be the set of overlapping communities detected after the improving step. Although it is allowable for communities to overlap, they should have a subset of vertices which makes them different from any other one.

The *distinctiveness* of a community C, denoted as D_C, is computed as the difference between the number of edges composed of vertices belonging only to C and the number of edges composed of at least one vertex community C shares with another community. Two communities C_i and C_j which overlap each other are candidate to be merged iff $D_{C_i} \leq 0$ or $D_{C_j} \leq 0$.

The strategy followed in this step in order to reduce the redundancy existing in the detected communities is as follows: (1) detecting the set PC of pair of communities that are candidate to be merged, (2) applying the roulette wheel selection method over the set PC, where the probability of selection of each pair is computed by using the highest absolute value of the distinctiveness of the two communities forming the pair, and (3) repeat steps 1 and 2 while $PC \neq \emptyset$.

4   Experimental Results

In this section, we conduct several experiments for evaluating the effectiveness of our proposal. With this aim, we apply it over two well known disjoint community detection algorithms, named MOCD [1] and MOGA-Net [12].

MOCD uses the locus-based adjacency graph encoding for representing each chromosome; the decoding of a chromosome requires the identification of all connected components, which in turn will be our seed clusters. This algorithm uses the PESA-II as the optimization mechanism and two objective functions proposed in [1]. The uniform two-point crossover operator is selected for crossover and for mutation, some genes are randomly selected and substituted by other randomly selected adjacent nodes. On the other hand, MOGA-Net uses the same representation as MOCD as well as the same evolutionary operator, but it employs the NSGA-II as its optimization framework. As objective function MOGA-Net uses the community score and community fitness [12]. Hereinafter, we will refer to as MOCD-OV and MOGA-OV, to the algorithms resulting from applying our proposal over MOCD and MOGA-Net, respectively.

The experiments were conducted over four real-life networks and they were focused on: (1) to compare the accuracy attained by MOCD-OV and MOGA-OV against the one attained by MEA_CDP [2], IMOQPSO [6], iMEA_CDP [5] and OMO [4] algorithms, (2) to compare the accuracy attained by MOCD-OV and MOGA-OV against the one attained by well known single-objective overlapping community detection algorithms, named CPM [3], OH [8] and COPRA [13] algorithms, (3) to evaluate the Pareto set, obtained by MOCD-OV and MOGA-OV in the first experiment for each network, (4) to evaluate the number of communities as well as the overlapping degree of these communities, obtained by MOCD-OV and MOGA-OV in the first experiment for each network, and (5) to evaluate the impact each proposed step has in the accuracy of MOCD-OV and MOGA-OV.

The networks used in our experiments were the American College Football network, the Zachary's Karate Club network, the Bottlenose Dolphins network, and the Krebs' books on American politics network; these networks can be downloaded from http://konect.uni-koblenz.de/networks. Table 1 shows the characteristics of these networks.

Table 1. Overview of the networks used in our experiments

Networks	# of Nodes	# of Edges	Ave. degree	# Communities
American Cool. Football	115	613	10.66	12
Zachary's Karate Club	34	78	4.58	2
Bottlenose Dolphins	62	159	5.129	2
Krebs' books	105	441	8.4	3

In the first experiment we used the NMI external evaluation measure [8], for evaluating the accuracy of each algorithm in the processing of each network. For computing the accuracy attained by MOCD-OV over a given network we executed it over each network and the highest NMI value attained by a solution of the Pareto set is selected. This execution is repeated twenty times the average of the highest NMI values attained is computed. For computing the accuracy attained by MOGA-OV the same above mentioned approach was used. Table 2 showed the average NMI value attained by each algorithm over each network; the average values for MEA_CDP, IMOQPSO, iMEA_CDP and OMO algorithms were taken from their original articles. The "X" in Table 2 means that IMOQPSO does not report any results on the Krebs' books network.

Table 2. Comparison of MOCD-OV and MOGA-OV againts Multi-objective algorithms, regarding the NMI value. Best values appears bold-faced

Networks	MEA_CDP	IMOQPSO	iMEA_CDP	OMO	MOCD-OV	MOGA-OV
Football	0.495	0.462	0.593	0.33	0.74	**0.75**
Zachary's	0.52	0.818	0.629	0.375	0.924	**0.97**
Dolphins	0.549	0.886	0.595	0.41	**0.944**	0.91
Krebs'	0.469	X	**0.549**	0.39	0.521	0.48
Ave. rank. pos.	4.5	4.25	3	5.75	**1.75**	**1.75**

As it can be seen from Table 2, both MOCD-OV and MOGA-OV outperforms the other methods in all the networks, excepting in Krebs' in which they attains the second and third best result, respectively. In the last row of Table 2 we also showed the average ranking position attained by each algorithm and as it can be observed, our proposals clearly outperforms the other methods. From the above experiments on real-life networks, we can see that both MOCD-OV and MOGA-OV are promising and effective for overlapping community detection in complex networks.

In the second experiment we compare the accuracy attained by MOCD-OV and MOGA-OV against that attained by CPM, OH and COPRA algorithms which follows a single-objective optimisation approach; the NMI values attained from the above mentioned algorithms were taken from [4] and [6]. This experiment were conducted only over Zachary's, Football and Dolphins networks. Table 3 showed the average NMI value attained by each algorithm over the selected networks.

Table 3. Comparison of MOCD-OV and MOGA-OV againts Single-objective algorithms, regarding the NMI value. Best values appears bold-faced

Networks	CPM	OH	COPRA	MOCD-OV	MOGA-OV
Football	0.697	**0.754**	0.33	0.74	0.75
Zachary's	0.170	0.690	0.37	0.924	**0.97**
Dolphins	0.254	0.781	0.41	**0.944**	0.91
Ave. rank. pos.	4.7	2.3	4.3	2	**1.7**

From Table 3 it can be observed, that our proposals clearly outperform the singe-objective algorithms in both Zachary's and Dolphins networks. In Football network, the OH algorithm obtained the best result although we can see that the result of our proposal is comparable with that of OH; moreover, it is almost identical. However, it can be said that MOGA-OV has a better performance than MOCD-OV.

In the third experiment, we evaluate the Pareto sets obtained by our proposals in the first experiment, in terms of the average number of solutions it contains, the modularity of the solution, measured using the overlapping Modularity [11], and the Pareto fronts quality, measured using the hypervolume [5]. Table 4 shows the results of this experiment.

Table 4. Evaluating the Pareto sets found by MOCD-OV and MOGA-OV for each network

Networks	MOCD-OV			MOGA-OV		
	#Solutions	HyperV	$Q_{overlapping}$	#Solutions	HyperV	$Q_{overlapping}$
Football	39.3	0.774	0.593	38.8	0.773	0.596
Zachary's	3.86	0.508	0.394	3.7	0.507	0.401
Dolphins	23.2	0.703	0.509	29	0.702	0.512
Krebs'	22.3	0.626	0.535	14.06	0.597	0.526

It can be seen from Table 4 that, in almost all cases, MOCD-OV explores more solutions than MOGA-OV, although the modularity (i.e., quality) of the communities detected by MOGA-OV is slightly better than those discovered by MOCD-OV, in almost all cases. We think that in the case of the Zachary's network, the low number of explored solutions is due to the size of the network which is very small. On the other hand, it can be conclude also from this table, that both algorithms produce Pareto fronts with high hypervolume values, showing a good convergence. As an example of the different granularity our proposal is able to detect, two of the solutions found by MOCD-OV and MOGA-OV over Zachary's network are showed in Fig. 1.

It can be concluded from Fig. 1 that our proposal is able to detect solutions with different number of communities and overlapping degree, each one with use-

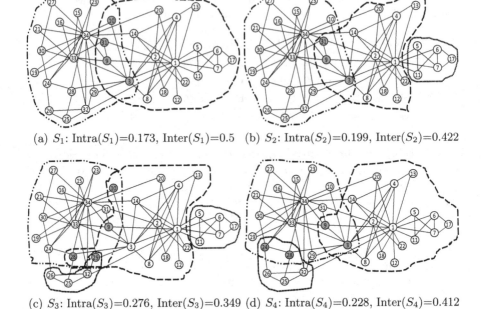

(a) S_1: Intra(S_1)=0.173, Inter(S_1)=0.5   (b) S_2: Intra(S_2)=0.199, Inter(S_2)=0.422

(c) S_3: Intra(S_3)=0.276, Inter(S_3)=0.349 (d) S_4: Intra(S_4)=0.228, Inter(S_4)=0.412

Fig. 1. Examples of the overlapping communities detected by MOCD (S_1 and S_2) and MOGA-OV (S_3 and S_4) over the Zachary's network.

ful information. These examples illustrate the advantages of the Multi-objective optimization approach over the single-objective approach.

In the third experiment, we compute the average number as well as the overlapping among the communities detected by MOCD-OV and MOGA-OV when they attained the highest NMI value showed in Table 2. The results of this experiment are shown in Table 5.

Table 5. Evaluating the average number of communities and their overlapp generated by MOCD-OV and MOGA-OV for each network

Networks	MOCD-OV		MOGA-OV	
	Ave # comm.	Ave. overlap. degree	Ave # comm.	Ave. overlap. degree
Football	11.26	1.07	10.86	1.04
Zachary's	2	1.02	2	1.008
Dolphins	2	1.01	2	1.005
Krebs'	2	1.01	2	1.01

As it can be seen from Table 5, our proposals detect a number of communities which, in the average case, is very close to the real number of communities existing in the networks. Moreover, our proposals do not produce solutions having high overlapping degree which means they are able to detect overlapping zones but they does not profit from this overlapping for boosting their accuracy.

Finally, in the fifth experiment, we evaluate the impact the *preprocessing*, *improving* and *merging* steps have over the performance of MOCD-OV and MOGA-OV over each network, considering two measures: the accuracy of the solutions and the hypervolume of the Pareto front of these solutions. With this aim, we compute for each network the average NMI attained by both algorithms without each above mentioned steps, and compare them against to the NMI of the algorithm when all steps are taken into account. This same procedure was followed but taking into account the hypervolume of the generated fronts instead of the accuracy of the solutions. Tables 6 and 7 show the results of this experiment for MOCD-OV and MOGA-OV, respectively.

Table 6. Evaluating the impact of each step in the performance of MOCD-OV over each network

Networks	NMI				Hypervolume			
	Zachary's	Dolphins	Football	Krebs'	Zachary's	Dolphins	Football	Krebs'
All steps	0.924	0.944	0.739	0.521	0.508	0.703	0.774	0.626
Not prep.	0.87	0.91	0.56	0.48	0.5	0.676	0.751	0.65
Not imp.	0.82	0.93	0.75	0.48	0.476	0.699	0.771	0.627
Not merg.	0.836	0.55	0.76	0.43	0.597	0.656	0.677	0.733

As it can be seen from Tables 6 and 7, excepting in one case, the inclusion of the *preprocessing* and *merging* steps allow to obtain higher NMI values for both MOCD-OV and MOGA-OV algorithms, whilst the inclusion of the *improving* step allows to obtain better solutions in most cases. On the other hand, the quality of the Pareto fronts obtained by MOGA-OV are better in almost cases, excepting when the *improving* and *merging* steps are excluded over the Zachary's network. MOCD-OV fails to build better Pareto fronts in the Krebs' network, when each evaluated step is independently excluded; in the Zachary's network, the inclusion of the *merging* step does not allow MOCD-OV to obtain better Pareto fronts.

Table 7. Evaluating the impact of each step in the performance of MOGA-OV over each network

Networks	NMI				Hypervolume			
	Zachary's	Dolphins	Football	Krebs'	Zachary's	Dolphins	Football	Krebs'
All steps	0.97	0.91	0.75	0.48	0.507	0.702	0.773	0.597
Not prep.	0.77	0.94	0.3	0.47	0.46	0.607	0.585	0.547
Not imp.	0.86	0.92	0.75	0.48	0.51	0.695	0.771	0.585
Not merg.	0.84	0.6	0.76	0.44	0.6	0.653	0.678	0.59

5   Conclusions

In this paper, we introduced four steps for extending the Pareto-dominance based MOEAs framework for discovering overlapping communities. These steps, named *preprocessing, expansion, improving* and *merging* allow to remove edges representing weak connections, as well as to detect overlapping zones existing in the network, to improve these zones and finally, to remove redundancy in the solutions by merging those overlapping communities having high overlapping.

Our proposal was applied over the MOEAs of two well known disjoint community detection algorithms: MOCD and MOGA-Net. The resulting algorithms, named MOCD-OV and MOGA-OV were evaluated over four real-life networks in terms of their accuracy and they were compared against four Multi-objective algorithms of the related work. These experiments showed that MOCD-OV and MOGA-OV outperform in almost all the networks the other algorithms. These experiments also showed the advantage of using a multi-objective approach over a single-objective approach. Another conclusion that can be drawn from the experimental evaluation is that the proposed steps allow to explore a large number of solutions, to detects a number of communities which is close to that existing in the networks, as well as to obtain Pareto fronts with high hypervolume values. Finally, these experiments showed that in almost all cases the introduced steps allow to obtain better solutions and Pareto fronts.

As future work, we would like to further evaluate our proposal over other MOEAs as well as to evaluate it over synthetical networks in order to have a better insight about its behaviour under different conditions.

References

1. Shi, C., Yan, Z., Cai, Y., Wu, B.: Multi-objective community detection in complex networks. Appl. Soft Comput. **12**(2), 850–859 (2012)
2. Liu, J., Zhong, W., Abbass, H., Green, D.G., et al.: Separated and overlapping community detection in complex networks using multiobjective evolutionary algorithms. In: IEEE Congress on Evolutionary Computation (CEC) (2010)
3. Palla, G., Dernyi, I., Farkas, I., Vicsek, T.: Uncovering the overlapping community structure of complex networks in nature and society. Nature **435**, 814–818 (2005)
4. Liu, B., Wang, C., Wang, C., Yuan, Y.: A new algorithm for overlapping community. In: Proceeding of the 2015 IEEE International Conference on Information and Automation Detection, pp. 813–816 (2015)
5. Liu, C., Liu, J., Jiang, Z.: An improved multi-objective evolutionary algorithm for simultaneously detecting separated and overlapping communities. Nat. Comput.: Int. J. **15**(4), 635–651 (2016)
6. Li, Y., Wang, Y., Chen, J., Jiao, L., Shang, R.: Overlapping community detection through an improved multi-objective quantum-behaved particle swarm optimization. J. Heuristics **21**(4), 549–575 (2015)
7. Wen, X., et al.: A maximal clique based multiobjective evolutionary algorithm for overlapping community detection. IEEE Trans. Evol. Comput. **21**, 363–377 (2016)
8. Lancichinetti, A., Fortunato, S., Kertesz, J.: Detecting the overlapping and hierarchical community structure of complex networks. New J. Phys. **11**(3), 033015 (2009)

9. Fortunato, S., Hric, D.: Community detection in networks: a user guide. Phys. Rep. **659**, 1–44 (2016)
10. Mukhopadhyay, A., Maulik, U., Bandyopadhyay, S.: A survey of multiobjective evolutionary clustering. ACM Comput. Surv. **47**(4), 1–46 (2015)
11. Shen, H., Cheng, X., Cai, K., Hu, M.B.: Detect overlapping and hierarchical community structure in networks. Phys. A: Stat. Mech. Its Appl. **388**(8), 1706–1712 (2009)
12. Pizzuti, C.: A multiobjective genetic algorithm to find communities in complex networks. IEEE Trans. Evol. Comput. **16**(3), 418–430 (2012)
13. Gregory, M.: Finding overlapping communities in networks by label propagation. New J. Phys. **12**(10), 103018 (2010)

New Advances in the Development of a Thermodynamic Equilibrium-Inspired Metaheuristic

Broderick Crawford[1], Ricardo Soto[1], and Enrique Cortés[1,2(✉)]

[1] Pontificia Universidad Católica de Valparaíso,
Avenida Brasil 2950, 2374631 Valparaíso, Chile
{broderick.crawford,ricardo.soto}@pucv.cl
[2] Universidad de Playa Ancha,
Leopoldo Carvallo 270, 2340000 Valparaíso, Chile
enrique.cortes@upla.cl

Abstract. In this paper, the new results obtained with the development of a novel thermodynamic equilibrium-inspired optimization algorithm are presented. This technique was developed in order to solve nonlinear optimization problems, with continuous domains. In our proposal, each variable is considered as the most volatile chemical component of a saturated binary liquid mixture, at a determined pressure and temperature. In the search process, the new value of each decision variable is obtained at some temperature of bubble or dew of the binary system. The search includes the random change of the chemical species and their compositions. The algorithm has being tested by using well-known mathematical functions as benchmark functions and has given competitive results in comparison with other metaheuristics.

Keywords: Metaheuristics · Stochastic search methods
Single-solution based metaheuristic · Combinatorial optimization

1 Introduction

In the field of science and engineering, the optimization problems are too complex. The exact optimization techniques do not provide suitable solutions due to that the optimization problems, in the reality, are very complex, i.e. they have highly non-linearity, many decision variables, differents domains of variables, and they are subject to many constraints. In addition to this, the time occuped to find the optimum is prohibitive in many cases [20]. So, in these cases, the use of these optimization techniques is not adequate. By fortune, the nature observation has allowed to the creation of auspicious and successful optimization algorithms in order to achieve good solutions for these problems.

The metaheuristics, which are approximate methods, do not guarantee that optimal solutions of these problems will be found, however, they provide good

© Springer Nature Switzerland AG 2018
F. Castro et al. (Eds.): MICAI 2017, LNAI 10632, pp. 142–153, 2018.
https://doi.org/10.1007/978-3-030-02837-4_12

solutions very quickly [17]. The use of metaheuristics has received increasingly attention in the last three decades. This is due to their success and also to that these optimization techniques are commonly easier to implement than exact techniques [3].

The metaheuristics are optimization algorithms whose search strategy is based in no more than a mimic of a natural process, as for example, in a biological process, a physical process or a chemical process. These techniques have been developed and improved by many researchers.

Several optimization algorithms of general application have been developed. Some of them are single-solution based algorithms, i.e. they begin the search starting from a single feasible solution. In the majority of metaheuristics, searching the optimum is based on multiple initial solutions, i.e. they search the solution starting from multiple initial feasible solutions, or a population of feasible solutions.

Examples of single solution-based metaheuristics, are the following: Simulated Annealing (SA), that it is based on the physical process of annealing of metals [13], Variable Neighborhood Search (VNS) [15], that done the search by changing systematically the search neighborhood, and Tabu Search (TS) [8] that increases the performance of local search by using memory structures. Some examples of population-based metaheuristics are: Gravitational Search Algorithm (GSA), that was built inspired on the law of gravity and the mass attractions [17], Black Hole (BH), where the best solution of a population is treated as a black hole which attract other solutions or normal stars around it during the search [10], Genetic Algorithms (GA), that are inspired on the theory of Darwin evolution [19], Ant Colony Optimization (ACO), that mimics an ant colony searching their food [6], Artificial Bee Colony (ABC), that is inspired on the behavior of honeybee swarms [12]. In population-based algorithms, also known as swarm algorithms, the results are surprising [6].

These methods have been applied in the solution of problems of diverses areas such as data mining [16], computer science [4,14], industry [7], and scheduling [9], however, none is able to solve all optimization problems [17]. Therefore, there is a big opportunity to propose and develop new optimization procedures in order to achieve better solutions for those problems.

This paper introduces the advances in the development of a new metaheuristic inspired on the thermodynamic equilibrium. This thermodynamic condition has been embedded in the optimization algorithm in order to be used to solve optimization problems. This new metaheuristic is being developed to solve nonlinear problems in continuous domains.

During the diversification stage, the search is based on the constructive application of two searching operators, this is, the dew point and the bubble point. Both operators, performs a local search in opposite directions in a parallel search space that represents the molar fraction of the more volatile chemical specie of a binary liquid mixture. A binary liquid mixture, also named here as binary system, is a mixture composed by two chemical species, one of them more volatile than the other. The molar fraction of anyone of this both chemical species vary between 0 and 1. The algorithm associates randomly one binary system to each decision variable of the real problem. By this way, the movement of a decision variable in the real domain it is determined applying the dew point operator and the bubble point operator for the binary system to a given pressure.

In the intensification stage, the search is performed using a third operator, that we have called bisection operator. The application of this operator permits a direct evaluation of the fitness for the intermediate thermodynamic state between the two best thermodynamic conditions reached for each binary system, i.e. between the last one and the actual.

The algorithm had been tested with six mathematical functions of benchmark demonstrating that this new method is a promising alternative, showing competitive results with other metaheuristics.

The paper is organized as follows: Sect. 2 provides the variable monemclature, the fundamental equations, and the mathematical models implemented. Section 3 describes the movement operators, the parameters required, the inputs and outputs of the optimization procedure, and the algorithm. Section 4 describes the benchmark functions used and presents the experimental results obtained. Finally, we present conclusions and future work.

2   The Thermodynamic Equilibrium as Inspiration Source

In the chemical process industry, the solution of many engineering problems requires the use of the equilibrium relationships between two phases in thermodynamic equilibrium, such as a vapours and liquids mixture in equilibrium. Under such conditions, each component of the mixture will be present in both phases and will have the same chemical potential between one phase and the other. The equilibrium state of a closed system like that, is that state for which the total Gibbs free energy is a minimum regarding all possible changes at a given temperature and pressure [11]. This thermodynamic condition of equilibrium was embedded in the optimization algorithm in order to be used in the solution of optimization problems.

In our proposal, each decision variable is treated as the most volatile chemical component of a binary liquid mixture in its bubble-point at a determined pressure.

Some algorithms perform the search assuming that there is a chemical change that transforms one solution in other, applying some particular type of chemical reaction [1,5]. In that cases, one solution is considered as an element, compound or chemical specie. Our algorithm simulate a physical change of a binary mixture of chemical species, where the variation of molar fraction of the more volatile chemical specie of the mixture, determines the change of the value of only one decision variable of a specific solution of the problem.

The optimization procedure is started with an initial solution randomly generated. In the diversification phase, the new value of each decision variable is obtained at the temperature of bubble or dew of the associated binary system that provides a better value of the objective function. In the intensification stage, the new value of a decision variable is obtained by averaging the two best values of it, determined by the two best thermodynamic equilibrium states for the corresponding chemical binary mixture, in the previous iteration. For all binary system, i.e for all decision variable, and for both phases of searching, the system pressure is the same and it remains constant. The search is carried out by repeating the corresponding calculations either during the diversification or the intensification stage. In the diversification stage, the search includes the random change of the chemical species and compositions of the binary mixtures assigned to the decision variables, and the acceptance of worse solutions to avoid being left trapped in local optimums.

In both stages of search, the objective function is evaluated by each time by using the values of the decision variables in $\mathbb{R}^n$ that corresponds to the current compositions of the saturated liquid phase, i.e. at their bubble point.

2.1   Variable Nomenclature

The variables used to model the thermodynamic equilibrium between a liquid phase and his vapour, in a binary mixture of chemical species, are: f_i, overall mole fraction of the chemical species i in the binary system; l_i and v_i, mole fractions of the chemical specie i in the liquid phase and the vapour phase; K_i, relationship of vapour-liquid equilibrium or K-value of chemical specie i; P_i^*, vapour pressure of chemical specie i; P, total system pressure; T, system temperature; and A_i, B_i and C_i, constants A, B and C of the Antoine equation [2] for vapour pressure calculation of the chemical specie i.

2.2   Fundamental Equations

Unitary Mass (Molar) Balance:

$$\Sigma v_i = 1 \qquad i \in \{1,2\} \tag{1}$$

$$\Sigma l_i = 1 \qquad i \in \{1,2\} \tag{2}$$

Phase Equilibrium Relationship:

$$v_i = K_i l_i \qquad i \in \{1,2\} \tag{3}$$

or

$$l_i = v_i/K_i \qquad i \in \{1,2\} \tag{4}$$

K-value:

$$K_i = P_i^*/P \qquad i \in \{1,2\} \tag{5}$$

Physical Properties: Vapour pressure of chemical specie i at a given temperature T:

$$P_i^* = \exp[A_i - B_i/(T + C_i)] \qquad i \in \{1,2\} \tag{6}$$

Equation (5) shows that we are assuming that the vapour-liquid equilibrium is defined by Raoult's law [11]. Combining these equations in a convenient way, permits to obtain the corresponding expressions that will serve to define the movement operators for the diversification stage of the algorithm.

2.3 Mathematical Models for the Bubble Point Calculation and the Dew Point Calculation

In the bubble point, the following condition must be satisfied in order to calculate the bubble point temperature T_{BP} and the composition (molar fraction) of the first vapour formed, i.e. v_i. Under these conditions, the vapour phase formed is in equilibrium with the liquid phase which has a molar fraction $l_i = f_i$. Combining the Eqs. (1), (3), (5) and (6) it can be obtained the Eq. (7).

$$\Sigma v_i = 1 = \Sigma(K_i l_i) \qquad i \in \{1, 2\} \qquad (7)$$

In the same way, in the dew point, the following condition must be satisfied in order to calculate the dew point temperature T_{DP} and the composition of the first drop of liquid formed, i.e. l_i. Under these conditions, the liquid phase formed is in equilibrium with the vapour phase which has a molar fraction $v_i = f_i$. Combining the Eqs. (2), (4), (5) and (6) it can be obtained the Eq. (8).

$$\Sigma l_i = 1 = \Sigma(v_i / K_i) \qquad i \in \{1, 2\} \qquad (8)$$

Equations (7) and (8) are solved for temperature T, of the bubble point or the dew point, using the bisection numerical method [18].

3   Algorithm

The algorithm consider a reliable strategy, with original movement operators, simple parameters, and the necessary inputs and outputs.

3.1   Movement Operators

In the diversification stage, our algorithm uses two search operators. These operators are the bubble point operator and the dew point operator. The operators are given by Eq. (9), for the bubble point, and the Eq. (11), for the dew point. Both operators "work" in the binary space $\mathbb{Z}^2$, were v_i and l_i are real numbers that vary between 0 and 1.

For the case of the bubble-point operator, from Eq. (3) we obtain Eq. (9):

$$l_i(t + 1) = v_i(t) = K_i l_i(t) \qquad i \in \{1, 2, 3, ..., n\} \qquad (9)$$

where $l_i(t)$ is equivalent to $x_i(t)$, but in the binary search space for the decision variable $x_i(t)$. The molar fraction of more volatile chemical specie of the liquid phase, i.e. $l_i(t)$, is calculated by the Eq. (10). This equation, is a transformation equation of variables from the real domain $[-100, +100]$ into variables of the real domain $[0, 1]$.

The real domain $[0, 1]$, is defined here as the search space for the decision variable $x_i(t)$, whose true value belongs to the domain in $\mathbb{R}$ determined by the range $[min, max]$. In the Eq. (10), $nmin = 0$ and $nmax = 1$ while $min = -100$ and $max = +100$. This two last limits values can be changed manually while $nmin$ and $nmax$ are fixed because they represent molar fractions, which has values between 0 and 1.

$$l_i(t) = \frac{nmax - nmin}{max - min}(x_i(t) - min) + nmin \qquad i \in \{1, 2, 3, ..., n\} \qquad (10)$$

For the case of the dew-point operator, from Eq. (4) we obtain Eq. (11):

$$l_i(t + 1) = v_i(t)/K_i \qquad i \in \{1, 2, 3, ..., n\} \qquad (11)$$

where $v_i(t)$ is equivalent to $x_i(t)$, but in the binary search space for the decision variable $x_i(t)$. The molar fraction of more volatile chemical specie in the vapour phase, is calculated by the Eq. (12).

$$v_i(t) = \frac{nmax - nmin}{max - min}(x_i(t) - min) + nmin \qquad i \in \{1, 2, 3, ..., n\} \qquad (12)$$

The Eq. (9) will be used to fill the rows 4 and 5 of the search table, and the Eq. (11) to fill the row 2 and 1 of the same search table. The current solution is located in the row 3 of the search table. The search table is a matrix used to perform a local search around the current solution, and select the more suitable movement for the decision variable in question, between the iteration t and the iteration $t + 1$, conserving the values of all the other variables.

The value of $x_i(t + 1)$, is determined by the composition of the liquid phase that providing the best value of the objective function among these five possible movements. This value, is calculated by the Eq. (13). This equation, that is the inverse transformation equation, takes the value of the molar fraction, and converts it into the corresponding value belonging to the search space true.

$$x_i(t + 1) = \frac{max - min}{nmax - nmin}(l_i(t + 1) - nmin) + min \qquad i \in \{1, 2, 3, ..., n\}(13)$$

In the intensification phase, the new values of the decision variables, are obtained calculating the average between the two last best values of each one of them, and using the bisection method in order to obtain a best approximation of the solution.

3.2 Parameters

Only three parameters are used. These are: P, the pressure for all binary systems, α, the autonomously adjustment parameter of subset of search space, and β, the acceptance probability of worse solutions during the exploration stage. The movement operators require that some pressure be specified. In this version, the pressure was fixed in 70 kPa.

3.3   Characterization of Chemical Especies

The chemical species are characterized here only by its vapour pressure, given by Antoine's Equation [2]. In this version, the chemical species are characterized dynamically and change by each restart until the search ends. The values for A_i, B_i and C_i are randomly generated using the general Eq. (14)

$$G_i = G^{il} + Random[0,1](G^{sl} - G^{il}) \quad i \in \{1,2,3,...,n\} \tag{14}$$

where, G is equal to A, B or C, G^{il} is the inferior limit of constant G, and G^{sl} the superior limit of constant G. The limit values of Antoine constants (for P, the system pressure, in kPa, and T, the system temperature, in °C) are: $[A^{il} = 15.7527, A^{sl} = 18.5875]$, $[B^{il} = 2132.50, B^{sl} = 3816.44]$ and $[C^{il} = -63.633, C^{sl} = -31.62]$.

3.4   Inputs and Outputs

Little input information are required. The input is restricted to the criteria of term and search parameters. The output information include the records of all iterations performed.

It is essential to specify three totalizers: the total number of movements to attempt (M), the total number of restarts to attempt (R), and the total number of decision variables (D) of the objective function.

By other side, it is required to start with an initial solution. The initial solution is also randomly generated. For each decision variable x_i, the initial value is randomly obtained accordingly Eq. (15):

$$x_i = x_i^{il} + Random[0,1](x_i^{sl} - x_i^{il}) \quad i \in \{1,2,3,...,n\} \tag{15}$$

In Eq. (15), x^{il} is the lower bound of decision variable x_i and x^{sl} is the upper bound of decision variable x_i. Usually, both of them are fixed in -100 and $+100$, respectively, but can be others values.

In addition to this, it is required to specify the autonomously adjustment parameter of subset of the search space, and the acceptance probability of worse solutions during the diversification stage.

Finally, all objective functions tested are embedded in the algorithm. If it is necessary to test any other function, this one can be added easily.

The output information include the minimum value reached, the location of the local optimum found, the convergence graph, and the records of all iterations. By each iteration, the best solution reached and its fitness is always shown. When a worse solution is accepted, the value of objective function is also showed.

3.5   Algorithm

The following algorithm describes the main procedure of our Thermodynamic Equilibrium-based metaheuristic:

```
read input data
initialize lists, search tables, accountants, totalizers
and indicators
generate an initial solution randomly
evaluate the fitness of the current solution
characterize the chemical species
create the search table for each decision variable
while m <= M-1 or r <= R-1
    if totvar < D /* (tot)alizer of (var)iables under exploration
        for d = 1 to D
            explore the search space
        end for
    else
        for d = 1 to D
            exploit the search space
        end for
    end if
    evaluate the fitness of the current solution
    evaluate the fitness change
    if fitcha < 0 /* (fit)ness (cha)nge
        make a downhill movement
        /* accepts the movement, and updates the records of the
        search table
    else
        make an uphill movement
        /* accepts the movement (a worse solution) with greater or
        equal probability than some acceptance probability,
        and updates the records of the search table
    end if
end while
write output data
```

4   Experimental Results

In this Section, the benchmark functions used are indicated, along with their reported minimum values and their corresponding location. Also, we present here the competitive results obtained along with the respective analysis.

4.1   Benchmark Functions

The mathematical functions of benchmark used in our experimental study were the Eqs. (16), (17), (18), (19), (20) and (21). Equations (16) and (17) are uni-modal test functions. Equations (18) and (19) are multimodal test functions. Equations (20) and (21) are multimodal test functions with fix dimensions. In Eqs. (16), (17), (18) and (19), the number of dimensions was $n = 30$.

The minimum value of benchmark functions (16), (17), (18) and (19), is zero. The optimal solution X_{opt} for functions (16), (18) and (19) are in $[0]^n$. For function (17) the optimal solution is in $[1]^n$. For Eq. (20), the minimum is 0.998

and the optimal solution is (-31.95). For Eq. (21), the minimum is 0.397887 and the optimal solution is $(9.42, 2.47)$ [21].

Schwefel's Function No. 1.2:

$$f_1(X) = \sum_{i=1}^{n} \left(\sum_{j=1}^{i} x_j \right)^2 \qquad i \in \{1, 2, 3, ..., n\} \tag{16}$$

Generalized Rosenbrock's Function:

$$f_2(X) = \sum_{i=1}^{n-1} [100(x_{i+1} - x_i^2)^2 + (x_i - 1)^2] \qquad i \in \{1, 2, 3, ..., n\} \tag{17}$$

Ackley's Function:

$$f_3(X) = -20 \exp \left(-0.2 \sqrt{\tfrac{1}{n} \sum_{i=1}^{n} x_i^2} \right) - \exp \left(\tfrac{1}{n} \sum_{i=1}^{n} \cos(2\pi x_i) \right) + 20 + e \tag{18}$$
$$i \in \{1, 2, 3, ..., n\}$$

Generalized Griewank's Function:

$$f_4(X) = \frac{1}{4000} \sum_{i=1}^{n} x_i^2 - \prod_{i=1}^{n} \cos \left(\frac{x_i}{\sqrt{i}} \right) + 1 \qquad i \in \{1, 2, 3, ..., n\} \tag{19}$$

Shekel's Foxholes Function:

$$f_5(X) = \left(\frac{1}{500} + \sum_{j=1}^{25} \frac{1}{j + \sum_{i=1}^{2} (x_i - a_{ij})^6} \right)^{-1} \tag{20}$$

where

$$a_{ij} = \begin{bmatrix} -32 & -16 & 0 & 16 & 32 & -32 & ... & 0 & 16 & 32 \\ -32 & -32 & -32 & -32 & -32 & -16 & ... & 32 & 32 & 32 \end{bmatrix}$$

Branin's Function:

$$f_6(X) = \left(x_2 - \frac{5.1}{4\pi^2} x_1^2 + \frac{5}{\pi} x_1 - 6 \right)^2 + 10 \left(1 - \frac{1}{8\pi} \right) \cos x_1 + 10 \tag{21}$$

4.2   Results

Our optimization algorithm was implemented in Visual Basic for Application (VBA) 7.0 of MS-Excel. All experiments were performed in a notebook Dell Inspiron N4010 Intel (R) Core (TM) i5 CPU M460 @ 2.53 GHz 4 GB RAM OS 64 bits Processor with MS Windows 10 Home.

Results are shown in Table 1 as follows: the benchmark function (BenFun), the average obtained with the benchmark function (Avg), the standard deviation (StdDev), the median (Med), the minimum value obtained with the benchmark function (Min), the optimal (Opt) value, the true percentage deviation (TPD, %) or the difference between the minimum value reached and the optimal value reported (DMO), the worst result obtained or maximum value reaced (Max), and the search subset (SeaSub) of $\mathbb{R}^n$ explored. All values were rounded to the last digit indicated. All experiments were repeated at least 31 times in order to guarantee a meaningful statistical analysis. After repetition 31, the experiment was repeated as many times as were necessary in order to eliminate all of atypical values. The elimination of all atypical values would reflect in a certain measure the computational effort of the search with respect to some determined functions and the effect of the random computational environment underlying. This aspect will be studied with posterity in a future work.

In all experiments, was considered a maximum of 1000 iterations or 100 restarts as criterion of stopping the search. In the 100.0% of the benchmark functions were obtained very good results.

We defined the True Percentage Deviation (TPD), given by Eq. (22), as measurement of success of search, in order to be used in some cases instead of the Relative Percentage Deviation (RPD), given by Eq. (23). This was done so, because we are using benchmark mathematical functions whose optimal are known. However, several of these functions have his optimal in zero, and it is not possible divide by zero. The true percentage deviation was used only for those functions whose optimals were different of zero. For the remainder of the functions, as success measurement, we calculated the difference between the minimum value reached with our algorithm and the optimal value reported for the benchmark function, or (DMO), as given by Eq. (24).

In Eq. (22), Min is the minimum value obtained for the benchmark function with our algorithm and Opt is the optimal value of the objective function. In Eq. (23), $Best$ is the best value known or reported of the benchmark function.

$$TPD = \left(\frac{Min - Opt}{Opt}\right) 100 \qquad (22)$$

$$RPD = \left(\frac{Min - Best}{Best}\right) 100 \qquad (23)$$

$$DMO = Min - Opt \qquad (24)$$

Table 1. Minimization result of benchmark functions used.

BenFun	Avg	StdDev	Med	Min	Opt	TPD/DMO	Max	SeaSub
$f_1(X)$	498.885	479.775	358.851	1.0241E−16	0	1.0241E−16	1800.98	$[-5,5]^n$
$f_2(X)$	24.8301	7.96295	28.6181	0.0212	0	0.0212	28.7514	$[-30,30]^n$
$f_3(X)$	0.07686	0.06904	0.06750	2.9310E−14	0	2.9310E−14	0.24111	$[-32,32]^n$
$f_4(X)$	0.10597	0.04369	0.12054	5.1446E−04	0	5.1446E−04	0.14524	$[-600,600]^n$
$f_5(X)$	0.99800	0	0.99800	0.99800	0.99800	0%	0.99800	$[-65.54,65.54]^2$
$f_6(X)$	0.39807	0.00030	0.39794	0.397887	0.397887	0%	0.398925	$[-5,15]^2$

5   Conclusions and Future Work

On the base of the results obtained in this work, we believe that the inspiration in the thermodynamic equilibrium is a promising idea to build a new and robust optimization algorithm.

The search of a local optimal can be performed in an efficient way using simple mathematical models to simulate really the physic or chemistry phenomenon. However, the use of this models may require the use of simple and efficient numeric techniques for the model resolution.

As a future work, we will extend our study including more mathematical benchmark functions of the three differents types considered in this paper. Furthermore, we will test the benchmark functions with several number of dimensions, in order to analyze the performance of our algorithm with the change of the dimensions number.

At present, we are working in the transformation of the current procedure based on a single starting solution, into a multi-start algorithm. Next, we will modify our algorithm in order to convert it in a populations-based procedure, and analysis the change in its performance.

By last, we will apply our algorithm in the resolution of a real optimization problem in the engineering area.

Acknowledgements. The authors would like to thank the grants given as follows: PhD. Broderick Crawford is supported by grant CONICYT/FONDECYT/ REGULAR/1171243. PhD. Ricardo Soto is supported by grant CONICYT/ FONDECYT/REGULAR/1160455. MSc. Enrique Cortés is supported by grant INF-PUCV 2015.

References

1. Astudillo, L., Melin, P., Castillo, O.: Introduction to an optimization algorithm based on the chemical reactions. Inf. Sci. **291**(C), 85–95 (2015)
2. Poling, B.E., Prausnitz, J.M., O'Connell, J.P.: The Properties of Gases and Liquids. McGraw-Hill, New York (2001)
3. Blum, C., Aguilera, M.J.B., Roli, A., Sampels, M. (eds.): Hybrid Metaheuristics: An Emerging Approach to Optimization. Studies in Computational Intelligence, vol. 114. Springer, Heidelberg (2008). https://doi.org/10.1007/978-3-540-78295-7
4. Crawford, B., Soto, R., Astorga, G., Garcia, J., Castro, C., Paredes, F.: Putting continuous metaheuristics to work in binary search spaces. Complexity **2017**, 8404231:1–8404231:19 (2017). https://doi.org/10.1155/2017/8404231
5. de la O, D., Castillo, O., Astudillo, L., Soria, J.: Fuzzy chemical reaction algorithm. In: Sidorov, G., Galicia-Haro, S.N. (eds.) MICAI 2015. LNCS (LNAI), vol. 9413, pp. 452–459. Springer, Cham (2015). https://doi.org/10.1007/978-3-319-27060-9_37
6. Dorigo, M., Maniezzo, V., Colorni, A.: Ant system optimization by a colony of cooperating agents. IEEE Trans. Syst., Man, Cybern., Part B **26**(1), 29–41 (1996)
7. Fox, B., Xiang, W., Lee, H.P.: Industrial applications of the ant colony optimization algorithm. Int. J. Adv. Manuf. Technol. **31**(7), 805–814 (2007)
8. Glover, F., Laguna, M.: General purpose heuristics for integer programming-part II. J. Heuristics **3**(2), 161–179 (1997)

9. Guo, Y., Li, W., Mileham, A., Owen, G.: Applications of particle swarm optimisation in integrated process planning and scheduling. Robot. Comput.-Integr. Manuf. **25**(2), 280–288 (2009)
10. Hatamlou, A.: Black hole: a new heuristic optimization approach for data clustering. Inf. Sci. **222**, 175–184 (2013)
11. Smith, J.M., Van Ness, H., Abbott, M.: Introduction to Chemical Engineering Thermodynamics. The McGraw-Hill Companies Inc., New York (2005)
12. Karaboga, D.: Artificial bee colony algorithm. Scholarpedia **5**(3), 6915 (2010)
13. Kirkpatrick, S., Gelatt Jr., C.D., Vecchi, M.P.: Optimization by simulated annealing. Science **220**(4598), 671–680 (1983)
14. Lanza-Gutierrez, J.M., Crawford, B., Soto, R., Berrios, N., Gomez-Pulido, J.A., Paredes, F.: Analyzing the effects of binarization techniques when solving the set covering problem through swarm optimization. Expert. Syst. Appl. **70**, 67–82 (2017)
15. Mladenovic, N., Hansen, P.: Variable neighborhood search. Comput. OR **24**(11), 1097–1100 (1997)
16. Rana, S., Jasola, S., Kumar, R.: A review on particle swarm optimization algorithms and their applications to data clustering. Artif. Intell. Rev. **35**(3), 211–222 (2011)
17. Rashedi, E., Nezamabadi-pour, H., Saryazdi, S.: GSA: a gravitational search algorithm. Inf. Sci. **179**(13), 2232–2248 (2009)
18. Chapra, S., Canale, R.: Numerical Methods for Engineers. McGraw-Hill Education, New York (2015)
19. Whitley, D.: An executable model of a simple genetic algorithm. In: Proceedings of the Second Workshop on Foundations of Genetic Algorithms, Vail, Colorado, USA, 26–29 July 1992, pp. 45–62 (1992)
20. Yaghini, M., Akhavan, R.: DIMMA: a design and implementation methodology for metaheuristic algorithms - a perspective from software development. Int. J. Appl. Metaheuristic Comput. **1**(4), 57–74 (2010)
21. Yao, X., Liu, Y., Lin, G.: Evolutionary programming made faster. IEEE Trans. Evol. Comput. **3**, 82–102 (1999)

Comparative Analysis of MOGBHS with Other State-of-the-Art Algorithms for Multi-objective Optimization Problems

Cristian Ordoñez[1,2], Edgar Ruano[1], Carlos Cobos[1(✉)],
Hugo Ordoñez[3], and Armando Ordoñez[2]

[1] Information Technology Research Group (GTI), Universidad del Cauca,
Popayán, Colombia
{cordonezq, eruano, ccobos}@unicauca.edu.co
[2] Intelligent Management Systems, University Foundation of Popayán,
Popayán, Colombia
jaordonez@unicauca.edu.co
[3] Research Laboratory in Development of Software Engineering,
Universidad San Buenaventura, Cali, Colombia
haordonez@usbcali.edu.co

Abstract. A multi-objective problem must simultaneously satisfy some conditions that may conflict with each other. Some examples of this problem are the design of machines with low power consumption and high power, or the development of software products in a short time and with high quality. Several algorithms have been proposed to solve this type of problems, such as NSGA-II, MOEA/D, SPEA2, and MSOPS. Each of these algorithms is based on different techniques such as the combination of objectives, Pareto efficiency, and prioritization. The selection of the best algorithm for a problem may become a cumbersome task. By its part, MOGBHS is a multi-objective algorithm based on the Global-Best Harmony Search, non-dominated sorting, and crowding distance that has shown great efficiency. This paper presents a comparative analysis of MOGBHS against other state-of-the-art algorithms. The analysis was performed over 21 multi-objective optimization problems from the IEEE CEC competition, 12 without restrictions and 9 with restrictions. The evaluation was performed using several evaluations of the objective function (2000, 5000, 10000 and 20000) and different metrics: Hypervolume, Epsilon, Generational Distance, Inverse Generational Distance, and Spacing. Finally, the analysis of the results was performed using non-parametric statistical tests (Wilcoxon and Friedman). MOGBHS obtained the best results according to the Inverse Generational Distance for 10000 and 20000 evaluations of the objective functions. Likewise, MOGBHS achieved competitive results for 2000 and 5000 evaluations. On the other hand, SPEA2 algorithm reached the best average results in all metrics.

Keywords: Multi-objective optimization · Comparative analysis
MOGBHS · NSGA-II · MOEA/D · SPEA2 · MSOPS

© Springer Nature Switzerland AG 2018
F. Castro et al. (Eds.): MICAI 2017, LNAI 10632, pp. 154–170, 2018.
https://doi.org/10.1007/978-3-030-02837-4_13

1   Introduction

Multi-objective optimization research area is responsible for studying and solving problems with multiple conflicting objectives. Problems of this kind are widespread nowadays in the different areas. For example, the design of machines with low energy consumption and high power, or high-quality software built in short time.

The multi-objective algorithms have been proposed to solve this type of problems. These algorithms are used when there is no evidence of an optimal solution, and obtaining this solution or a close one with deterministic algorithms can be time-consuming [1]. The result of these methods is not a single solution (as in the case of mono-objective optimization), but a set of the best possible solutions found [2].

Some existing approaches to the design of multi-objective algorithms have been gathered in Frameworks, such as paradisEO-MOEO and MOEA. These frameworks have emerged to make these algorithms accessible to the community so they can solve real problems. Among these frameworks, MOEA is one of the most outstanding. MOEA is a free, open-source, Java-based library that allows implementing new algorithms and experimenting with the problems from the IEEE CEC multi-objective optimization competition, and with other real problems documented in the framework. For the present research work, the Multi-Objective Global-Best Harmony Search (MOGBHS) was implemented [3] in MOEA Framework.

MOGBHS is a multi-objective algorithm based on Global-Best Harmony Search, non-dominated ordering, and crowding distance. MOGBHS has been used to solve routes and schedules problem in a massive transport system (Bus rapid system). In this problem, MOGBHS has been used to minimize the costs of the system and maximize the satisfaction of the users [3]. The implementation of MOGBHS in MOEA framework has allowed to carry out a comparative analysis of this algorithm with other widely used algorithms: SPEA2, MOEA/D, NSGA-II and MSOPS [4]. These algorithms are implemented in the MOEA framework.

The present analysis used twelve (12) multi-objective continuous problems without constraints and nine (9) with constraints. These problems were taken from the multi-purpose optimization competency repository of the IEEE Evolutionary Computing Congress [5, 6]. The study sought to determine the impact of the number (2000, 5000, 10000 and 20000) of evaluations of the objective function (EOF) on the algorithms with different types of problems (with and without constraints).

The comparative analysis used the following metrics commonly used in the multiobjective optimization field: Hypervolume, Epsilon, Generational Distance, Inverted Generational Distance, and Spacing [2]. Nonparametric statistical tests (Wilcoxon and Friedman) were also performed. The MOGHBS algorithm ranked fourth out of five compared algorithms when all the metrics were considered. Also, MOGHBS ranked first when only the inverted generational distance metric was considered (this algorithm generates very good solutions according to the accuracy and diversity). Finally, MOGHBS always ranked first on the CF7 problem for all the EOFs.

The rest of this paper is structured as follows. In Sect. 2, the related works are exposed. Then in Sect. 3 the characterization of the multi-objective algorithms to be compared is presented. Then, Sect. 4 the metrics used in the comparison are explained.

The results and their analysis are shown in Sect. 5. Finally, conclusions and future work are presented in Sect. 6.

2   Related Works

Algorithms that implement techniques based on stochastic optimization (meta-heuristics) are used to solve problems with n objectives. These algorithms use randomness to obtain optimal solutions to NP-hard problems (with a high degree of complexity). A detailed and updated survey of multi objective evolutionary algorithms is presented by Zhang and Xing in [7]. Likewise, another review of the related approaches in this field is presented by Vachhani et al. in [8]. A brief description of some approaches for multi-objective optimization is given below, as well as a discussion of the main differences of these approaches with the present work.

In 2017 [1] ε- MOABC was presented. ε- MOABC is an algorithm based on performance indicators to solve multi-objective and many objectives optimization problems. This algorithm creates an external file with non-dominated solutions produced in each generation based on the Pareto preference and dominance indicators. This algorithm has demonstrated to be competitive in multi-objective and many-objective optimization problems compared to other state-of-the-art algorithms such as NSGA-II SPEA2 and MOEA/D. The algorithm was analyzed in problems with constraints and more than one objective function like CEC09, LZ09, and DTLZ.

Trivedi et al. presented an exhaustive study of the MOEAs proposed over the last ten years [9]. This study is focused on the decomposition-based and hybrid (based on decomposition and dominance, etc.) MOEAs. This work includes the efforts made so far to expand the framework based on the decomposition of constrained multi-objective optimization and the many-objectives optimization. Authors conclude that there have been many attempts to create and apply decomposition-based MOEAs to solve complex real-world optimization problems.

In [10] multi-objective evolutionary algorithms are classified into set approximation methods and decomposition methods. In this work, a set approximation MOEA is combined with a sequential decomposition mechanism. Using this combination, a better running time is achieved on synthetic problems compared to the corresponding set approximation MOEAs by a factor n (problem size). Also, in recently (2017) published works, distributed parallel approaches [11, 12] are proposed for solving multi-objective problems of large-scale optimization.

In 2016 [13] a new selection scheme for multi-objective evolutionary algorithms based on the $\Delta\rho$ indicator was proposed. To solve the problem of the definition of the reference set in $\Delta\rho$ based approaches, a reference set is created at each generation using e-dominance. Besides, a set of non-dominated solutions is also created. The proposal outperforms MOEA/D using Penalty Boundary Intersection (decomposition approach), and SMS-EMOA-HYPE (a SMS-EMOA version that uses the hypervolume indicator) on standard test functions with 3–6 objective functions.

In 2014, a new approach that combines dominance and decomposition for multi-objective and many objectives optimization was presented in [14]. This approach takes advantage of both approaches (dominance and decomposition) to balance the convergence and diversity of the evolutionary process. The performance of the proposed algorithm was validated and compared with four state-of-the-art algorithms (unconstrained problems with up to fifteen objectives). The empirical results demonstrate the superiority of the proposed algorithm in the tests. Also, the proposed algorithm showed a highly competitive performance in all constrained optimization problems.

An improved version of the TAA algorithm (ITAA) was proposed in [15]. This algorithm incorporates a classification mechanism for updating the convergence file. The efficiency of ITAA was demonstrated with experimental studies on problems with up to 20 objectives. ITAA performance was assessed in 16 DTLZ test cases with 5–20 targets. The experimental results showed that ITAA exceeded TAA regarding the IGD convergence metric and the GSpread diversity metric.

A knee point-driven evolutionary algorithm for many-objective optimization KnEA is presented in [2]. KnEA significantly reduces computational complexity compared to other multi-objective algorithms. The experimental results show that KnEA is significantly superior to MOEA/D and hypo, and is comparable with GreA and NSGA-III in the optimization with more than three objectives. KnEA is computationally much more efficient compared to other Pareto-based MOEAs such as GREAT. Therefore, the overall performance of KnEA is highly competitive compared to the state-of-the-art MOEAs to solve problems with more than three objectives.

A new algorithm (MD-MOEA) was proposed in [16]. This algorithm is based on crossover and mutation operators of the NSGA-II algorithm. This algorithm includes a new selection mechanism based on the maximum fitness function, and a technique based on Euclidean distances between solutions to improve the diversity of the population in objective function space. This approach obtains good results in both low dimensionality and high dimensionality in objective function space when compared with MOEA/D using Penalty Boundary Intersection, and SMS-EMOA-HYPE.

Also in this year (2014), it was developed the algorithm proposed for the present analysis called multi-objective Global-Best Harmony Search (MOGBHS) [3]. This algorithm generates a set of harmonies and stores them in the harmonic memory (HM). Also, the algorithm evaluates all targets for each element of the HM and then orders them using the Pareto front. This algorithm was used to improve the definition of routes and schedules in a mass transit system (MEGABUS system in the city of Pereira, Colombia) using simulation based on discrete events. MOGBHS was compared to an NSGA-II implementation in the test case and showed better performance.

Finally, in 2009 [17], a comparative analysis of several multi-objective evolutionary algorithms was presented. The behavior of these algorithms with different complexities and problems (NP-hard) was observed. The compared algorithms were based on the Pareto front approach: NSGA-II, SPEA2, MOEA/D, GDE3, and POSDE. The results showed that GDE3 produces the best performances in these problems with the lowest time complexity.

Unlike the works mentioned in state of the art, the present work conducted four evaluations of the objective function per algorithm with different values (2000, 5000, 10000, and 20000 EOFs). Also, the non-parametric Friedman test was performed to observe the position or ranking of the evaluated algorithms. Then the Wilcoxon test was applied to observe the dominance relation between algorithms. Finally, a general performance analysis was done for each of the metrics mentioned above.

3 Compared Algorithms

NSGA-II: this genetic algorithm was proposed by Deb et al. in 2002 [18]. This algorithm generates an additional population from an original population by using the genetic operators of selection (binary tournament), crossover (SBX) and mutation (Polimonial). From here, the most promising individuals from both populations are selected for the next generation according to their rank (Pareto front number) and crowding distance. NSGA-II is used to solve continuous problems.

SPEA2: Is a genetic algorithm proposed by Zitler et al. 2001 in [19]. In this algorithm, a fitness value is assigned to each individual. This fitness is the sum of the strength raw fitness and a density estimation. SPEA2 applies selection, crossover and mutation operators to fill in a solution file (environmental selection, SBX, and polynomial mutation). Non-dominated solutions from the original population and the solution file are copied into a new population. If the number of solutions exceeds the maximum size of the population, a truncation operator is used based on the distance to the nearest kth neighbor.

MOEA/D: is a multi-objective optimization algorithm based on the decomposition of a problem. MOEA/D uses evolutionary operators to combine optimal solutions thus allowing high convergence. MOEA/D uses the differential evolution operator followed by a mutation of polynomials to create descendants, and the weighted Tchebycheff or boundary intersection as the decomposition method. Equally, a mechanism of diversity preservation, as proposed in the work of Zhang and Li [17].

MSOPS is a proposed multi-objective optimization algorithm proposed by He and Yen in 2014 [20]. MSOPS works in parallel to generate convergent systems of solutions. This algorithm is based on aggregate optimization that is driven by its weight or target vector. Thus, the algorithm uses an array of target vectors to find the best solutions in parallel. This algorithm does not rely on Pareto classification and provides better high-dimensional objective space pressure.

MOGBHS is the Multi-Objective Global-Best Harmony Search algorithm and was proposed in 2016 [3]. This algorithm randomly generates a set of harmonies and stores them in Harmonic Memory (HM). Then all objectives for each element in the HM are evaluated. From here, the ordering is carried out using the Pareto front based on non-dominated ordering and crowding distance. Afterward, a certain number of improvisations (evolutionary iterations) are performed. In each iteration: (A) a new harmony is generated applying the logic of the GBHS algorithm. (B) The new harmony is evaluated against all the objectives to optimize. (C) The new harmony is added to the existing HM. (D) The HM is ordered by Pareto front and crowding distance. (E) All elements that cause that the HM exceed the maximum size (defined by the Harmony Memory Size parameter of the algorithm) are removed (these are the worst elements in the HM).

4 Comparison Metrics

The following metrics were used to measure of performance and competitiveness of the algorithms: Hypervolume, Generational Distance, Inverted Generational Distance, Epsilon, and Spacing. These metrics are the most used to evaluate MOEAs [21] (Table 1).

Table 1. Metrics for evaluation of multi-objective algorithms

Ranking	Metrics	Classification	
		Aspects	Sets
1	Hypervolume (HV)	- Accuracy - Diversity	Unary
2	Epsilon family (EP)	- All	Binary
3	Generational distance (GD)	- Accuracy	Unary
4	Inverted generational distance (IGD)	- Accuracy - Diversity	Unary
5	Spacing (SP)	- Separability	Unary

These metrics make it possible to compare different algorithms. This comparison is based on the accuracy, diversity and separability of the solutions found by each algorithm. A description of these metrics is presented below [21]:

Hypervolume (HV) This metric calculates the volume (in objective space) covered by members of a given set, Q, of non-dominated solutions to problems where all objectives are to be minimized. Mathematically, for each $i \in Q$ an hypercube v_i is built with a reference point W an the solution i that represents the diagonal of the hypercube. The point W can be obtained with the worst values of the objective functions. The hypervolume (HV) is defined by the union of all the hypercubes [22] as is shown in Eq. 1.

$$HV = volume\left(\bigcup_{i=1}^{|Q|} v_i\right) \tag{1}$$

The algorithms that reach higher values of HV are better *(Maximize)*. Since HV depends on the values of the objective function it is necessary to normalize the non-dominated solutions.

Epsilon (EP) is a measure of the smallest distance required to translate each solution in A so that it dominates in the Optimal Pareto Front of the evaluated problem. More formally, given $\vec{z}^1 = \left(Z_1^1, ..., Z_n^1\right)$ and $\vec{z}^2 = \left(Z_1^2, ..., Z_n^2\right)$, where n is the number of objectives [23] *(Minimize)*.

$$I_{\epsilon+}^1(A) = \inf_{\epsilon \in R}\left(\forall \vec{z}^2 \in PF^* \exists \vec{z}^1 \in A : \vec{z}^1 \preccurlyeq_\epsilon \vec{z}^2\right)$$

Where $\vec{z}^1 \preccurlyeq_\epsilon \vec{z}^2$ if and only if $\forall 1 \le i \le n : Z_i^1 < \epsilon + Z_i^2$.

Generational distance (GD) and inverted generational distance (IGD) were proposed by Van Veldhuizen in 1999 [21]. GD calculates the average distance of a set of candidate solutions Z, with respect to a reference set p^* representing the Pareto front (PF). Formally, DG is defined by Eq. 2 (Minimize):

$$GD = \frac{\sqrt{\Sigma_{x \in z} d(x)^2}}{|z|} \tag{2}$$

Where $d(X)$ is the Euclidean distance between the solution X and the closest point p^* expressed by Eq. 3.

$$d(X) = \min_{X^* \in p^*} \sqrt{\sum_{m=1}^{M}(f_m(X) - f_m(X^*))^2} \tag{3}$$

Although GD is a metric for evaluating convergence, if we reverse the roles of Z and p^* in Eqs. 5 and 6, The generalized inverted distance (IGD) is obtained. It is also possible to consider the diversity of the whole set Z. Thus, A low value for IGD will indicate both good convergence and good distribution of the solutions *(Minimize)*. Formally, the IGD metric is defined by Eq. 4.

$$IGD = \frac{\sqrt{\Sigma_{x^* \in p^*} d(X^*)^2}}{|P^*|} \tag{4}$$

Where $d(X^*)$ Is the Euclidean distance between the reference point X^* and the closest solution Z (**Maximize**) expressed by Eq. 5.

$$d(X^*) = \min_{X \in Z} \sqrt{\sum_{m=1}^{M}(f_m(X) - f_m(X^*))^2} \tag{5}$$

Spacing (SP) Is a separation metric (SP) suggested by Schott [21]. Sp is calculated by measuring the relative distance between consecutive solutions in the non-dominated set obtained, as Eq. 6.

$$S = \sqrt{\frac{1}{|Q|} \sum_{i=1}^{|Q|}(d_i - \bar{d})^2} \tag{6}$$

Where $d_i = \min \min_{K \in Q \wedge K \neq i} \{\sum_{m=1}^{M} |f_m^i - f_m^k|\} and \bar{d}$ is the medium value of the above measures $\bar{d} = \sum_{i=1}^{|Q|} d_i/|Q|$. The distance measure is the minimum value of the absolute sum in the values of the objective function between the ith solution and any other solution of the non-dominated set. This distance is different from the minimum Euclidean distance between the two solutions. Therefore, a search algorithm for a set of non-dominated solutions that have smaller spacing (SP) is better (Minimize).

5   Results and Analysis

Here, the analysis of the metrics mentioned above for a different number of EOFs is presented. Also, the analysis of the nonparametric tests of Friedman and Wilcoxon is also included.

5.1   Analysis with 2000 EOFs

Regarding **Hypervolume** the Friedman Test was conducted according to a chi square distribution with 4 degrees of freedom: 7.12 and p = 0.12968. Results show that SPEA2 achieved better performance, followed by MOGBHS, Then NSGA-II sharing second place with MOEA/D and finally MSOPS. The result of the Wilcoxon showed that SPEA2 algorithm dominates NSGA-II, MOEA/D y MSOPS and MOGBHS algorithms with a significance level (SL) of 95%.

Regarding **Epsilon** Friedman test was conducted according to a chi square distribution with 4 degrees of freedom: 18.8 and p = 0.00119. Results indicate that SPEA2 achieved the best performance, followed by MOGBHS, NSGA-II in third place, followed by MOEA/D and MSOPS in the last place. Wilcoxon test shows that SPEA2 dominates NSGA-II, MOEA/D, and MSOPS with SL = 95%. Finally, MOGBHS dominates NSGA-II and MSOPS also with SL of 95%.

With regard to **Generational Distance**, the Friedman test was run according to a chi-square distribution with 4 degrees of freedom: 30.4 and p = 4.05733E−6, results show that SPEA2 achieved the best performance, followed by MOEA/D, MOGBHS, NSGA-II and finally MSOPS. Wilcoxon test showed that SPEA2, MOEA/D and, MOGBHS dominates MSOPS with an SL of 95%, besides MOEA/D, MOGBHS and SPEA2 dominate NSGA-II with the same SL.

With regard to **Inverted Generational Distance**, the Friedman test was run according to a chi-square distribution with 4 degrees of freedom: 24.28 and p = 7.01876E−5. Results show that MSOPS achieved the best performance, followed by MOEA/D, NSGA-II, MOGBHS and finally SPEA2. Wilcoxon test showed that MSOPS dominates NSGA-II, MOEA/D, MOGBHS and SPEA2 with an SL of 95% and that NSGA-II and MOEA/D dominate MOGBHS and SPEA2 with the same SL.

Regarding **Spacing**, the Friedman test was run according to a chi-square distribution with 4 degrees of freedom: 47.08 and p = 1.50153E−9. Results show that MOEA/D achieved the best performance, followed by SPEA2, MOGBHS, NSGA-II and finally MSOPS. Wilcoxon test showed that MOEA/D dominate NSGA-II, MSOPS y MOGBHS with an SL of 95%, Besides SPEA2 dominates NSGA-II and MSOPS with the same SL. Finally, MOGBHS dominates MSOPS y NSGA-II with SL of 90%.

In the present analysis, the ranking of 1 to 5 is created to determine the place occupied by each algorithm (see Table 2). The result is shown on the right side of the value obtained by each algorithm. Results indicate that the proposed algorithm MOGBHS is highly competitive with 2000 EOFs as it occupied the second place in the general ranking. Also, MOGBHS achieved the best solutions to problems such as CF4, CF5, CF6, CF7, UF1, UF6, UF8, and UF11 occupying the first place (according to the metrics HV, GD, IGD, EP, and SP) for each problem as observed in Table 2.

Table 2. MOGBHS with 2000 EOFs. Best results in bold.

Problem	Metric	NSGA-II	MOEA/D	MOGBHS	SPEA2	MSOPS
CF4	HV	0.0711 (4)	**0.1767 (1)**	0.1164 (3)	0.1527 (2)	0.0318 (5)
	GD	0.3709 (5)	0.1727 (2)	**0.1624 (1)**	0.2504 (3)	0.5963 (4)
	IGD	0.3762 (2)	0.3122 (3)	0.3076 (4)	0.2935 (5)	**0.4599 (1)**
	EP	0.5035 (3)	0.5586 (5)	**0.4468 (1)**	0.4479 (2)	0.5574 (4)
	SP	0.3227(4)	**0.1992 (1)**	0.2494 (3)	0.2430 (2)	0.5781 (5)
CF5	HV	0.0000 (1)	0.0000 (1)	0.0000 (1)	0.0000 (1)	0.0000 (1)
	GD	1.7486 (4)	1.2218 (3)	**0.9964 (1)**	1.1524 (2)	1.9755 (5)
	IGD	2.3312 (2)	1.8575 (3)	1.5526 (5)	1.6862 (4)	**3.1259 (1)**
	EP	2.2584 (4)	1.8425 (3)	**1.7386 (1)**	1.7547 (2)	2.8188 (5)
	SP	0.7376 (4)	0.6826 (2)	**0.3916 (1)**	0.7155 (3)	1.2206 (5)
CF6	HV	0.3823 (2)	0.3664 (4)	0.3717 (3)	**0.3905 (1)**	0.3134 (5)
	GD	0.0961 (3)	0.0952 (4)	**0.0416 (1)**	0.0666 (2)	0.1714 (5)
	IGD	0.2230 (4)	0.2489 (2)	0.2307 (3)	0.2012 (5)	**0.2608 (1)**
	EP	0.3589 (2)	0.4107 (5)	0.4045 (4)	**0.3419 (1)**	0.3731 (3)
	SP	0.1730 (4)	0.1062 (2)	**0.0776 (1)**	0.1330 (3)	0.2529 (5)
CF7	HV	0.0000 (1)	0.0000 (1)	0.0000 (1)	0.0000 (1)	0.0000 (1)
	GD	1.6733 (4)	**1.0617 (1)**	1.2454 (2)	1.5465 (3)	2.3646 (5)
	IGD	2.4812 (2)	1.7947 (5)	1.8725 (4)	1.9792 (3)	**3.3947 (1)**
	EP	2.3261 (4)	**1.7130 (1)**	1.8656 (2)	1.9484 (1)	2.9569 (5)
	SP	1.0644 (4)	0.6761 (2)	**0.6203 (1)**	0.9794 (3)	1.4939 (5)
UF1	HV	0.1504 (3)	0.0653 (5)	**0.1904 (1)**	0.1885 (2)	0.0695 (4)
	GD	0.1351 (3)	0.1398 (4)	0.1118 (2)	**0.1091 (1)**	0.1685 (5)
	IGD	0.4060 (3)	**0.5691 (1)**	0.3626 (4)	0.3464 (5)	0.5295 (2)
	EP	0.4611 (3)	0.6191 (5)	**0.4051 (1)**	0.4248 (2)	0.5383 (4)
	SP	0.0980 (3)	**0.0585 (1)**	0.1161 (4)	0.0655 (2)	0.1207 (5)
UF6	HV	0.0000 (1)	0.0000 (1)	0.0000 (1)	0.0000 (1)	0.0000 (1)
	GD	0.7761 (3)	0.8008 (4)	**0.6537 (1)**	0.6765 (2)	1.0286 (5)
	IGD	1.6501 (5)	**2.5656 (1)**	1.3081 (4)	1.3738 (3)	2.3684 (2)
	EP	1.5788 (3)	2.2508 (5)	**1.3317 (1)**	1.3844 (2)	2.0640 (4)
	SP	0.3763 (4)	**0.1759 (1)**	0.2863 (2)	0.3319 (3)	0.4203 (5)
UF8	HV	0.0000 (1)	0.0000 (1)	0.0000 (1)	0.0000 (1)	0.0000 (1)
	GD	0.2248 (4)	0.1826 (3)	**0.0986 (1)**	0.1126 (2)	0.3856 (5)
	IGD	0.8922 (2)	0.7733 (3)	0.4295 (5)	0.5364 (4)	**1.3364 (1)**
	EP	1.1697 (4)	1.0762 (3)	**1.0173 (1)**	1.0640 (2)	1.3802 (5)
	SP	0.2551 (4)	0.2183 (3)	0.2146 (2)	**0.1633 (1)**	0.4648 (5)
UF11	HV	0.0000 (1)	0.0000 (1)	0.0000 (1)	0.0000 (1)	0.0000 (1)
	GD	0.4074 (3)	0.5385 (4)	**0.2997 (1)**	0.3208 (2)	0.7757 (5)
	IGD	2.3042 (2)	1.8704 (3)	1.7243 (5)	1.7980 (4)	**2.7540 (1)**
	EP	2.0415 (4)	1.9562 (3)	**1.5253 (1)**	1.6883 (2)	2.5490 (5)
	SP	0.7446 (3)	0.7714 (4)	0.5340 (2)	**0.3504 (1)**	1.2797 (5)

5.2   Analysis with 5000 EOFs

Regarding **Hypervolume:** The Friedman test was run according to a chi-square distribution with 4 degrees of freedom: 6.84 and p = 0.14459. Results showed a ranking where SPEA2 achieved the best performance, followed by MOGBHS, MSOPS, MOEA/D y Finally NSGA-II. Wilcoxon test showed that SPEA2 dominates NSGA-II, MOEA/D with an SL of 95%.

With regard to **Epsilon:** The Friedman test was run according to a chi-square distribution with 4 degrees of freedom: 10.84 and p = 0.02842. Results showed a ranking where SPEA2 achieved the best performance, followed by MSOPS y NSGA-II, MOGBHS and finally MOEA/D. Wilcoxon test showed that SPEA2 dominates MOEA/D, MOGBHS, and NSGA-II with an SL of 95%.

With regard to **Generational Distance:** The Friedman test was run according to a chi-square distribution with 4 degrees of freedom: 29.2 and p = 7.11914E−6. Results showed a ranking where SPEA2 achieved the best performance, followed by MOEA/D MOGBHS, NSGA-II, and finally MSOPS. Wilcoxon test showed that SPEA2 MOEA/D and MOGBHS dominate NSGA-II and MSOPS with an SL of 95%, besides SPEA2 dominates MOGBHS with the same SL.

With regard to **Inverted Generational Distance:** The Friedman test was run according to a chi-square distribution with 4 degrees of freedom 5.96 and p = 0.20216. Results showed a ranking where NSGA-II achieved the best performance, followed by MOGBHS, MOEA/D, MSOPS, and finally SPEA2. Wilcoxon test showed that NSGA-II and MOGBHS dominate SPEA2 with an SL of 95%.

With respect to **Spacing:** The Friedman test was run according to a chi-square distribution with 4 degrees of freedom: 38.6 and p = 8.42835E−8. Results showed a ranking where SPEA2 achieved the best performance, followed by MOEA/D, NSGA-II and finally MOGBHS and MSOPS. Wilcoxon Test showed that SPEA2 dominate NSGA-II, MOEA/D, MOGBHS, and MSOPS with an SL of 95%, Besides MOGBHS dominates MOEA/D with the same SL. Finally, MOGBHS, MOEA/D, and NSGA-II dominate MSOPS with SL of 90%.

Results showed that MOGBHS is competitive with 5000 EOFs as it occupied the second place in the general ranking. Besides MOGBHS found the best solutions to problems with constraints such as CF4, CF5, CF7 and occupied the first place according to the metrics HV, SP, GD, and EP as can be seen in Table 3.

5.3   Analysis of the Algorithms with 10000 EOFs

Regarding **Hypervolume:** The Friedman test was run according to a chi-square distribution with 4 degrees of freedom: 11.47 and p = 0.02176. Results showed a ranking where MSOPS achieved the best performance, followed by SPEA2, MOEA/D, NSGA-II and finally MOGBHS. Wilcoxon test showed that MSOPS and SPEA2 dominate NSGA-II with an SL of 95%, besides MSOPS, SPEA2 and MOEA/D dominate MOHBGS with the same SL.

With respect to **Epsilon:** The Friedman test was run according to a chi-square distribution with 4 degrees of freedom: 23.36 and p = 1.07290E−4. Results showed a ranking where MSOPS achieved the best performance, followed by SPEA2, NSGA-II

Table 3. MOGBHS in 5000 EOFs. Best results in bold.

Problem	Metric	NSGA-II	MOEA/D	MOGBHS	SPEA2	MSOPS
CF4	HV	0.2538 (5)	0.2548 (4)	**0.3245 (1)**	0.2662 (3)	0.3190 (2)
	GD	0.0511 (5)	0.0302 (2)	**0.0296 (1)**	0.0345 (3)	0.0485 (4)
	IGD	0.1701 (2)	**0.2213 (1)**	0.1347 (4)	0.1623 (3)	0.1209 (5)
	EP	0.3400 (3)	0.4705 (5)	0.2513 (2)	0.3545 (4)	**0.2163 (1)**
	SP	0.0795 (5)	**0.0547 (1)**	0.0760 (4)	0.0683 (2)	0.0704 (3)
CF5	HV	0.0300 (3)	0.0123 (4)	**0.0358 (1)**	0.0347 (2)	0.0000 (5)
	GD	0.4589 (4)	0.3759 (3)	**0.1566 (1)**	0.3026 (2)	0.6135 (5)
	IGD	0.5141 (5)	0.5291 (4)	0.5807 (2)	0.5419 (3)	**0.7424 (1)**
	EP	**0.8460 (1)**	0.9060 (3)	0.9247 (4)	0.8532 (2)	0.9268 (5)
	SP	0.3153 (2)	0.5502 (5)	**0.0000 (1)**	0.3273 (3)	0.4278 (4)
CF7	HV	0.1035 (4)	0.1554 (3)	**0.2122 (1)**	0.1787 (2)	0.0000 (5)
	GD	0.4325 (4)	0.2581 (2)	**0.1348 (1)**	0.3558 (3)	0.5790 (5)
	IGD	0.4981 (2)	0.4765 (3)	0.3877 (5)	0.4082 (4)	**0.5386 (1)**
	EP	0.6907 (3)	0.7109 (4)	**0.5952 (1)**	0.6123 (2)	0.7498 (5)
	SP	0.1894 (2)	0.2043 (3)	0.2712 (4)	**0.1284 (1)**	0.3813 (5)

and MOEA/D in the fourth place, and finally MOGBHS. Wilcoxon test showed that MSOPS and SPEA2 dominate NSGA-II and MOGBHS with SL of 95%.

With regard to **Generational Distance:** The Friedman test was run according to a chi-square distribution with 4 degrees of freedom: 24.8 and $p = 5.51891E{-}5$. Results showed a ranking where SPEA2 achieved the best performance, followed by MOEA/D, NSGA-II, MOGBHS, and finally MSOPS. Wilcoxon test showed that SPEA2 and MOEA/D dominate NSGA-II, MSOPS, and MOGBHS with an SL of 95%.

With regard to **Inverted Generational Distance:** The Friedman test was run according to a chi-square distribution with 4 degrees of freedom 20.32 and $p = 4.31750E{-}4$. Results showed a ranking where MOGBHS achieved the best performance, followed by NSGA-II, MOEA/D, and finally SPEA2 and MSOPS sharing the third place. Wilcoxon test showed that MOGBHS and NSGA-II dominate SPEA2 and MSOPS with an SL of 95%.

Regarding **Spacing:** The Friedman test was run according to a chi-square distribution with 4 degrees of freedom: 37.16 and $p = 1.66982E{-}7$. Results showed a ranking where SPEA2 achieved the best performance, followed by NSGA-II, MOEA/D, MOGBHS and finally MSOPS. Wilcoxon test showed that SPEA2 dominates NSGA-II, MOEA/D, MOGBHS, and MSOPS with an SL of 95%. Besides MOGBHS dominates MSOPS with the same SL.

Results evidence that MOGBHS is competitive with 10000 EOFs in some problems achieving the best performance with constrained problems such as CF5, CF7. With these problems, MOGBHS occupied the first place according to the metrics GD, IGD and SP as can be seen in Table 4.

Table 4. MOGBHS with 10000 EOFs. Best results in bold.

Problem	Metric	NSGA-II	MOEA/D	MOGBHS	SPEA2	MSOPS
CF5	HV	0.1584 (4)	**0.1954 (1)**	0.1263 (5)	0.1774 (3)	0.1841 (2)
	GD	0.1741 (4)	0.1362 (3)	**0.0392 (1)**	0.0897 (2)	0.2517 (5)
	IGD	0.3331 (3)	0.3856 (2)	**0.5094 (1)**	0.3316 (4)	0.3216 (5)
	EP	0.6089 (2)	0.6809 (4)	0.8454 (5)	0.6458 (3)	**0.5758 (1)**
	SP	0.31470 (3)	0.3870 (5)	**0.0000 (1)**	0.2198 (2)	0.3373 (4)
CF7	HV	0.2872 (5)	0.3128 (3)	0.2962 (4)	0.3505 (2)	**0.3561 (1)**
	GD	0.1678 (5)	0.0770 (2)	**0.0528 (1)**	0.1488 (4)	0.1311 (3)
	IGD	0.3263 (3)	0.3522 (2)	**0.3977 (1)**	0.3028 (4)	0.2891 (5)
	EP	0.5366 (3)	0.6053 (5)	0.56520 (4)	0.4614 (2)	**0.4435 (1)**
	SP	0.3686 (5)	0.2227 (3)	**0.0000 (1)**	0.3008 (4)	0.1596 (2)

5.4 Analysis of Algorithms with 20000 EOFs

Regarding **Hypervolume:** The Friedman test was run according to a chi-square distribution with 4 degrees of freedom: 16.39 and p = 0.00254. Results showed a ranking where MSOPS achieved the best performance, followed by SPEA2, MOEA/D, NSGA-II, and finally MOGBHS. Wilcoxon test showed that MSOPS, MOEA/D, and SPEA2, dominate NSGA-II and MOGBHS with an SL of 95%.

With regard to **Epsilon:** The Friedman test was run according to a chi-square distribution with 4 degrees of freedom: 26.08 and p = 3.04907E−5. Results showed a ranking where MSOPS achieved the best performance, followed by SPEA2, NSGA-II, MOEA/D, and finally MOGBHS. The Wilcoxon test showed that MSOPS, and SPEA2 dominate MOEA/D, NSGA-II, and MOGBHS with an SL of 95%.

With regard to **Generational Distance**: The Friedman test was run according to a chi-square distribution with 4 degrees of freedom: 24.96 and p = 5.12501E−5. Results showed a ranking where SPEA2 achieved the best performance, followed by MOEA/D, NSGA-II, MSOPS and finally MOGBHS. Wilcoxon test showed that SPEA2 and MOEA/D dominate NSGA-II, MSOPS, and MOGBHS with an SL of 95%.

With regard to **Inverted Generational Distance**: The Friedman test was run according to a chi-square distribution with 4 degrees of freedom 17.48 and p = 0.00156. Results showed a ranking where MOGBHS achieved the best performance, followed by NSGA-II and MOEA/D with the same average value, the third place is occupied by SPEA2 and finally MSOPS. Wilcoxon test showed that MOGBHS and NSGA-II dominate SPEA2 y MSOPS with an SL of 95%.

Concerning **Spacing:** The Friedman test was run according to a chi-square distribution with 4 degrees of freedom: 38.2 and p = 1.01950E−7. Results showed a ranking where SPEA2 achieved the best performance, followed by NSGA-II, MOEA/D, MOGBHS, and finally MSOPS. Wilcoxon test showed that SPEA2 dominates MOEA/D, NSGA-II, MOGBHS, and MSOPS with an SL of 95%, besides MOEA/D dominates MOGBHS and MSOPS with the same SL.

Results evidence that MOGBHS achieved the best solutions over constrained problems such as CF7, occupying the first place according to 3 metrics (HV, EP, and SP) as can be seen in Table 5.

Table 5. MOGBHS en 20000 EOFs. Best results in bold.

Problem	Metric	NSGA-II	MOEA/D	MOGBHS	SPEA2	MSOPS
CF7	HV	0.3565 (4)	0.3250 (5)	**0.4353 (1)**	0.3691 (3)	0.3843 (2)
	GD	0.0443 (5)	**0.0052 (1)**	0.0183 (3)	0.0152 (2)	0.0277 (4)
	IGD	0.3003 (3)	**0.3570 (1)**	0.2131 (4)	0.3244 (2)	0.2020 (5)
	EP	0.4864 (4)	0.5593 (5)	**0.2863 (1)**	0.4801 (3)	0.3824 (2)
	SP	0.2425 (5)	0.0137 (2)	**0.0082 (1)**	0.1075 (4)	0.0643 (3)

5.5 Analysis of the Results Per Metric

The present analysis is based on the average of the best solutions found during the evaluations in the MOEA-Framework. The performance was measured according to the metrics. General results are shown in Table 6.

The overall ranking for **hypervolume** showed that **SPEA2** is the most competitive algorithm as its average ranking is 2.4, followed by MSOPS in the second place. The third position is occupied by MOEA/D followed by MOGBHS and NSGA-II in the last place. SPEA2 is better with 1000 and 2000 EOFs, and MSOPS is better with 10000 and 20000 EOFs. These results show that SPEA2 achieved the maximum value of hypervolume (accuracy and diversity of solutions) in the final set of solutions when EOFs is less than or equal to 20000.

The overall ranking for **Epsilon** showed that **SPEA2** is the most competitive algorithm as its average is 2.3, followed by MSOPS with 2.4. In the third place NSGA-II and finally MOGBHS and MOEA/D. SPEA2 is better with 2000 and 5000 EOFs and MSOPS is better with 10000 and 20000 EOFs. These results evidence that SPEA2 and MSOPS generated solutions closer to the optimal Pareto front (high level of accuracy, diversity, and separability). In other words, these solutions have a high level of similarity with the Pareto front solutions when EOFs is less than (or equal to) 20000.

The overall ranking for **Generational distance** showed that **SPEA2** is the most competitive algorithm with an average ranking of 1.9, followed by MOEA/D in the second place, MOBGHS in the third position followed by NSGA-II and MSOPS in the last place. SPEA2 is better with all EOFS values tested. SPEA2 achieved better performance (accuracy) as its solutions have short average distance from the Pareto front when EOFs is less than or equal to 20000.

The overall ranking for **Inverted Generational distance** showed that **MOGBHS** is the most competitive algorithm with an average ranking of 2.6 like NSGA-II, MOEA/D in the third place followed by MSOPS and SPEA2 in the last place. MSOPS is better with 2000 EOFs, and NSGA-II is better with 5000 EOFs. Finally, MOGBHS is better with 10000 and 20000 EOFs. These results allow evidence that solutions obtained with MOGBHS have a high level of convergence (accuracy and diversity) with respect to the distribution of solutions in the Pareto front. It is important to note the difference in

Table 6. Overall ranking of Friedman test by metrics. Best results in bold.

EOFs	MOGBHS	SPEA2	MSOPS	NSGA-II	MOEA/D	Chi^2	p-value
Hypervolume							
2000	2.95	**2.20**	3.35	3.25	3.25	7.12	0.1297
5000	3.00	**2.25**	3.05	3.50	3.20	6.84	0.1446
10000	3.75	2.55	**2.53**	3.55	2.63	11.47	0.0218
20000	3.78	2.60	**2.08**	3.65	2.90	16.39	0.0025
Avg.	3.4 (4)	**2.4 (1)**	2.8 (2)	3.5 (5)	3.0 (3)		
Epsilon							
2000	2.65	**1.85**	3.55	3.30	3.65	18.08	0.0012
5000	3.25	**2.30**	2.60	3.05	3.80	10.84	0.0284
10000	3.95	2.35	**1.95**	3.05	3.70	23.36	0.0001
20000	3.85	2.75	**1.55**	3.35	3.50	26.08	3.0491
Avg.	3.4 (4)	**2.3 (1)**	2.4 (2)	3.2 (3)	3.7 (5)		
Generational distance							
2000	2.55	**1.95**	4.35	3.65	2.50	30.40	4.E+00
5000	2.85	**1.75**	4.20	3.65	2.55	29.20	7.1191
10000	3.55	**1.95**	3.85	3.50	2.15	24.80	5.5189
20000	3.85	**1.90**	3.75	3.25	2.25	24.96	0.0001
Avg.	3.2 (3)	**1.9 (1)**	4.0 (5)	3.5 (4)	2.4 (2)		
Inverted generational distance							
2000	3.60	4.20	**2.10**	2.45	2.65	24.28	7.E+00
5000	2.80	3.75	2.90	**2.65**	2.90	5.96	0.2022
10000	**2.00**	3.80	3.80	2.50	2.90	20.32	4.3175
20000	**2.00**	3.45	3.95	2.80	2.80	17.48	0.0016
Avg.	**2.6 (1)**	3.8 (5)	3.2 (4)	**2.6 (1)**	2.8 (3)		
Spacing							
2000	3.10	1.95	4.65	3.60	**1.70**	47.08	2.E+06
5000	3.55	**1.60**	4.50	2.90	2.45	38.60	0.0000
10000	3.80	**1.55**	4.30	2.65	2.70	37.16	1.6698
20000	3.90	**1.70**	4.30	2.25	2.85	38.20	1.0195
Avg.	3.6 (4)	**1.7 (1)**	4.4 (5)	2.9 (3)	2.4 (2)		

the results of this metric compared to the results of the Hypervolume metric. Although both metrics evaluate accuracy and diversity, the results are opposite.

The overall ranking for **Spacing** showed that **SPEA2** is the most competitive algorithm with an average ranking of 1.7 followed by MOEA/D in the second place, NSGA-II in the third place and MOGBHS in the fourth place, finally MSOPS in the last place. MOEA/D is better with 2000 EOFs, and SPEA2 is better with 5000, 10000, and 20000 EOFs.

By analyzing all the metrics, it can be said that SPEA2 is the most competitive with different EOFs. MOGBHS is closer to the best solutions with few EOFs (2000 and 5000) but does not get good results when the number of EOFs grows. However, when considering the metric of inverted generational distance, MOGBHS gets the best results with 10000 and 20000 EOFs. A detailed review of the MOEA Framework and the metrics of hypervolume and inverted generational distance is necessary to find the explanation of these opposite results.

5.6   Overall Analysis

After observing the overall rankings, it can be stated that SPEA2 is the most competitive algorithm according to all the metrics (HV, EP, GD, IGD, and SP) with 2000, 5000, 10000, and 20000 EOFs. The second place is occupied by MOEA/D, NSGA-II in the third place, MOGBHS in the fourth and MSOPS in the last place (see Table 7).

Table 7. Average results using all metrics

Metric	Average				
Algorithm	MOGBHS	SPEA2	MSOPS	NSGA-II	MOEA/D
2000	3.0 (3)	**2.4 (1)**	3.6 (5)	3.3 (4)	2.8 (2)
5000	3.0 (2)	**2.3 (1)**	3.6 (5)	3.1 (3)	3.1 (3)
10000	3.4 (5)	**2.4 (1)**	3.3 (4)	3.1 (3)	2.8 (2)
20000	3.5 (5)	**2.5 (1)**	3.1 (3)	3.1 (3)	2.9 (2)
Avg.	3.2 (4)	**2.4 (1)**	3.4 (5)	3.1 (3)	2.9 (2)

In Table 7, SPEA2 showed a consistent performance in the test carried out. Equally, it can be observed that MOGBHS is competitive with 2000 and 5000 EOFs occupying the first place according to the metrics IGD and EP which are commonly used for testing MOEAs [17].

6   Conclusions and Future Work

In this paper, a comparative analysis of the MOGBHS algorithm with other four state-of-the-art algorithms is presented. Results showed that the most competitive algorithm for the families of problems UF1–UF12 and CF1–CF9 is SPEA2. The analysis used the metrics Hypervolume, Epsilon, generational distance, Inverted generational distance, and Spacing. SPEA2 remained constant in the best rankings positions generated during the tests (with 2000, 5000, 10000 and 20000 EOFs).

It was observed that the MOGBHS algorithm obtained the best solutions according to the metric inverted generational distance. Equally, the results of the overall analysis showed that as the number of evaluations of EOFs increased the performance of MOGBHS decreased. The opposite happens with the MSOPS algorithm, which obtained better performance as the number of EOFs increased. Therefore, MOGBHS should be used to solve problems when there exist time restrictions or the number of EOFs is established.

It was observed that MOGBHS is very competitive in constrained problems, because this algorithm was designed to solve transportation problems with several constrains. Also, MOGBHS was designed to solve problems in which the fitness calculation is time-consuming (the simulation of buses was done in a tool based on discrete events) and some restrictions in the number of EOFs were defined. For all the EOFs MOGBHS obtained the best solutions for the CF7 problem.

As future work, it is expected to incorporate covering arrays and tournament objectives to MOGBHS in order to tackle many-objectives optimization problems. Likewise, it is planned to experiment with problems of much more than two goals (objectives) such as the DTLZ and WFG family of problems.

References

1. Luo, J., Liu, Q., Yang, Y., Li, X., Chen, M.R., Cao, W.: An artificial bee colony algorithm for multi-objective optimisation. Appl. Soft Comput. J. **50**, 235–251 (2017)
2. Li, B., Li, J., Tang, K., Yao, X.: Many-objective evolutionary algorithms. ACM Comput. Surv. **48**, 1–35 (2015)
3. Ruano, E., Cobos, C., Torres-Jimenez, J.: Transit network frequencies-setting problem solved using a new multi-objective global-best harmony search algorithm and discrete event simulation. In: Pichardo-Lagunas, O., Miranda-Jiménez, S. (eds.) MICAI 2016. LNCS (LNAI), vol. 10062, pp. 341–352. Springer, Cham (2017). https://doi.org/10.1007/978-3-319-62428-0_27
4. Von Lücken, C., Barán, B., Brizuela, C.: A survey on multi-objective evolutionary algorithms for many-objective problems. Comput. Optim. Appl. **58**, 707–756 (2014)
5. Bechikh, S., Elarbi, M., Ben Said, L.: Many-objective optimization using evolutionary algorithms: a survey. In: Bechikh, S., Datta, R., Gupta, A. (eds.) Recent Advances in Evolutionary Multi-objective Optimization. ALO, vol. 20, pp. 105–137. Springer, Cham (2017). https://doi.org/10.1007/978-3-319-42978-6_4
6. Zhang, X., Tian, Y., Jin, Y.: Approximate non-dominated sorting for evolutionary many-objective optimization. Inf. Sci. (NY). **369**, 14–33 (2016)
7. Zhang, J., Xing, L.: A survey of multiobjective evolutionary algorithms. In: 2017 IEEE International Conference on Computational Science and Engineering (CSE) and IEEE International Conference on Embedded and Ubiquitous Computing (EUC), pp. 93–100. IEEE (2017)
8. Vachhani, V.L., Dabhi, V.K., Prajapati, H.B.: Survey of multi objective evolutionary algorithms. In: 2015 International Conference on Circuits, Power and Computing Technologies, ICCPCT 2015, pp. 1–9. IEEE (2015)
9. Trivedi, A., Srinivasan, D., Sanyal, K., Ghosh, A.: A survey of multiobjective evolutionary algorithms based on decomposition. IEEE Trans. Evol. Comput. **21**, 1 (2016)
10. Shi, J.-C., Qian, C., Yu, Y.: Evolutionary multi-objective optimization made faster by sequential decomposition. In: 2017 IEEE Congress on Evolutionary Computation (CEC), pp. 2488–2493. IEEE (2017)
11. Cao, B., et al.: Distributed parallel particle swarm optimization for multi-objective and many-objective large-scale optimization. IEEE Access **5**, 8214–8221 (2017)
12. Cao, B., Zhao, J., Lv, Z., Liu, X.: A distributed parallel cooperative coevolutionary multiobjective evolutionary algorithm for large-scale optimization. IEEE Trans. Ind. Inform. **13**, 2030–2038 (2017)
13. Menchaca-Mendez, A., Hernandez, C., Coello, C.A.C.: Δp-MOEA: a new multi-objective evolutionary algorithm based on the Δp indicator. In: 2016 IEEE Congress on Evolutionary Computation, CEC 2016, pp. 3753–3760. IEEE (2016)

14. Li, K., Deb, K., Zhang, Q., Kwong, S.: An evolutionary many-objective optimization algorithm based on dominance and decomposition. IEEE Trans. Evol. Comput. **19**, 694–716 (2015)
15. Wang, H., Jiao, L., Yao, X.: Two Arch2: an improved two-archive algorithm for many-objective optimization. IEEE Trans. Evol. Comput. **19**, 524–541 (2015)
16. Menchaca-Mendez, A., Coello, C.A.C.: MD-MOEA: a new MOEA based on the maximin fitness function and Euclidean distances between solutions. In: Proceedings of the 2014 IEEE Congress on Evolutionary Computation, CEC 2014, pp. 2148–2155 (2014)
17. Cremene, M., Suciu, M., Pallez, D., Dumitrescu, D.: Comparative analysis of multi-objective evolutionary algorithms for QoS-aware web service composition. Appl. Soft Comput. **39**(C), 124—139 (2016). https://doi.org/10.1016/j.asoc.2015.11.012. ISSN 1568-4946
18. Deb, K., Pratab, S., Agarwal, S., Meyarivan, T.: A fast and elitist multiobjective genetic algorithm: NGSA-II. IEEE Trans. Evol. Comput. **6**, 182–197 (2002)
19. Zitzler, E., Laumanns, M., Thiele, L.: SPEA2: Improving the Strength Pareto Evolutionary Algorithm. Swiss Federal Institute of Technology (ETH) Zurich (2001). http://citeseerx.ist.psu.edu/viewdoc/summary?doi=10.1.1.22.4617
20. He, Z., Yen, G.G.: Diversity improvement in decomposition-based multi-objective evolutionary algorithm for many-objective optimization problems. In: Conference Proceedings - IEEE International Conference on Systems, Man and Cybernetics, pp. 2409–2414 (2014)
21. Mirjalili, S., Lewis, A.: Novel performance metrics for robust multi-objective optimization algorithms. Swarm Evol. Comput. **21**, 1–23 (2015)
22. Rostami, S., Neri, F.: A fast hypervolume driven selection mechanism for many-objective optimisation problems. Swarm Evol. Comput. **34**, 50–67 (2017)
23. Durillo, J.J., Nebro, A.J.: JMetal: a Java framework for multi-objective optimization. Adv. Eng. Softw. **42**, 760–771 (2011)

Hybrid Intelligent Systems and Fuzzy Logic

Global Maximum Power Point Tracking Based on Intelligent Approach for Photovoltaic System Under Partial Shading Conditions

Moulay Rachid Douiri[1]($\boxtimes$) and Sidi Mohamed Douiri[2]

[1] Department of Electrical Engineering, Higher School of Technology,
Cadi Ayyad University, Essaouira, Morocco
douirirachid@hotmail.com
[2] Laboratory of Mathematic Informatics and Applications,
Faculty of Sciences, University Mohammed V-Agdal, Rabat, Morocco

Abstract. This paper presents the design of a controller for Maximum Power Point Tracking (MPPT) of a photovoltaic system. The proposed controller relies upon a Recurrent Neuro-Fuzzy (RNF) which is designed as a combination of the concepts of Sugeno fuzzy model and neural network. The controller employs the RNF of four-layer with sixty-four fuzzy rules. Moreover, for the proposed RNF an improved self-tuning method is developed based on the photovoltaic system and its high performance requirements. The principal task of the tuning method is to adjust the parameters of the Fuzzy Logic (FL) in order to minimize the square of the error between actual and reference output. Simulations with practical parameters show that our proposed MPPT using RNF outperform the conventional MPPT controller terms of tracking speed and accuracy.

Keywords: Maximum power point tracking · Photovoltaic system
Recurrent Neuro-Fuzzy

1 Introduction

The cost of electricity from the solar array system is generally more expensive compared to electricity from the utility grid [1, 2]. For this reason, it is necessary to study carefully the efficiency of the entire solar system to design an efficient system that meets the load demands with lower cost. Solar irradiance, ambient temperature and speed of the wind are the main external influences that affect the maximum power that can be generated from a PV panel. These external influences also change the position of the maximum power point on the *I-V* curve. Furthermore, in direct coupled systems, load is the main internal factor that can drive PV panels to operate at a strict point on *I-V* curve. If there is any small change in external influences, the position of maximum power point changes. Operating faraway from maximum power point decreases the output power of PV system. Therefore, it is necessary to continually track the maximum power point of a PV solar array. However, with huge changes in external influences the electrical parameters of PV panels are modified continuously and thus there is a difficulty in measuring these parameters. Accordingly, it is difficult to locate

F. Castro et al. (Eds.): MICAI 2017, LNAI 10632, pp. 173–184, 2018.
https://doi.org/10.1007/978-3-030-02837-4_14

the maximum power point mathematically as a function of the internal and external influences. Many control techniques have been proposed to track the maximum power point of a PV system with traditional and artificial intelligence techniques. Several methods are referred in the bibliography: the P&O method is the most commonly used in practice due to its simplicity and ease of implementation [3], however, this algorithm can fail or oscillate around the Maximum Power Point (MPP) under sudden sunlight changes [4]. Incremental conductance is also commonly used as it can overcome some aspects of the P&O algorithm instabilities. Nevertheless this method involves current and voltage differentiation which requires a relatively complex decision making process and therefore needs more complex calculation capacity and memory [5]. The use of Artificial Intelligence (AI) methods to improve the performance P&O based MPPT technique is well reviewed in [6]. ANN was used to improve the performance of P&O technique in [7]. Besides conventional MPPT techniques, Artificial Intelligence-based MPPT methods are efficient and can get better performances [8–10]. Fuzzy logic is used to improve the performance of perturb and observe in [11] and increment of conductance in [12]. Proportional-Integral-Derivate (PID) controller is widely used in control systems due to its simplicity, performance and stability in the steady state regime. An MPPT control using a fuzzy PID controller is proposed in [13]. The hybrid controller combines the advantages of fuzzy logic and conventional PID control. Since the relation between the extracted power and the output voltage (P-V) is a highly non linear, FL and ANN are a suitable solutions for the MPPT problem. The digital implementation of the fuzzy controller has been carried out in [14, 15]. The fuzzy controller was improved by selecting the best membership functions using genetic algorithms in [16] and particle swarm optimization in [17]. ANN approach is proposed and investigated in several works in the literature [18, 19]. The requirement of a large database for training the ANN model is the main constraint of such controller. In work [20], the database was established from measurements of irradiance, temperature and the corresponding optimal duty cycle. In [21], the fuzzy controller is used to generate the database for training the neural network. Authors in [22, 23] proposed an optimization of the ANN structure using genetic algorithms. A complex approach is proposed in [24] where a fuzzy controller is used to perform the choice between many ANN models, the choice of the local model is based on the optimal performance in the operating range of temperature and irradiance.

This paper proposes a novel approach to tracking the maximum power point of solar cells by using a RNF. The proposed method has several advantages over [27] and [28]. That is the controller: (*i*) determines the maximum power point faster; (*ii*) gives smoother output power at steady state; and (*iii*) requires no external sensors for solar intensity and temperature measurements. In this research work, we propose a structure for the MPPT controller based upon RNF technique and derive its associated adaptation. Simulations are presented to confirm superiority of the proposed method. In addition to the simulations, preliminary experimental results are presented.

2 PV Cell Modeling

Solar cell is made up of semiconductor material with doping of *p-n* junction, to absorb the irradiance and temperature of the solar energy with non linear characteristics and converts into the *DC* current [25]. Most commonly, single diode model is considered because of its simple and accurate. The cells are connected in series and/or parallel to achieve the corresponding voltage and current. If the cells are connected in series then it obtains the large output voltage whereas, if the connection is in parallel it produces large output current. The modeling of the solar cell is defined by voltage–current relationship of PV system as follows [25]:

$$I = I_{pv} - I_s \left(\exp\left[\frac{q(V + R_s I)}{N_s k T_a}\right] - 1 \right) - \frac{V + R_s I}{R_p} \tag{1}$$

$$I_{pv} = \left(I_{pv,n} + K_I \Delta T \right) \frac{G}{G_n} \tag{2}$$

$$I_s = \frac{I_{sc,n} + K_I \Delta T}{\exp\left(V_{oc,n} + K_V \Delta T\right)/a(N_s k T/q) - 1} \tag{3}$$

where I_{pv} is the PV current, $I_{pv,\,n}$ is nominal PV current, I_s is the saturation current, q is the electron charge (1.60217×10^{-19} C), k is the *Boltzmann* constant (1.38065×10^{-23} J/K), a is the diode ideality constant, R_s and R_p is the series and parallel resistance of cell, N_s is the number of cells connected in series, T is the absolute temperature, T_n is the nominal temperature, G is the irradiance and G_n is nominal irradiance from solar energy. $\Delta T = T - T_n$ is the deviation from operating temperature. $I_{sc,\,n}$ and $V_{oc,\,n}$ are the short circuit current and open circuit voltage based on nominal condition ($T_n = 25\ °\mathrm{C}$ and $G_n = 1000\ \mathrm{W/m^2}$). K_I is the ratio of short circuit current variation with temperature in standard condition; K_V is the ratio of open circuit voltage with respect to temperature.

3 Detailed Design of Proposed TSK-Type RNF

Feed-Forward Algorithm

Figure 1 depicts the structure of our proposed MPPT controller using RNF. The main purpose of the controller is to move an operation point of the solar array as close to the maximum power point or knee of the *I-V* curve as possible. In our design, the adjustment of the operating point is achieved by modifying a duty ratio D of a switch S_1 in the boost converter.

The RNF is organized using an input layer (2 variables), a membership layer (10 term nodes), a rule layer (50 nodes), and an output layer (1 node). Layer 1, the input layer, accepts the input signals into the RNF. The nodes at layer 1 represent linguistic variables. Layer 2, the membership layer, calculates the *Gaussian* membership variables to form the membership function. Layer 3, the rule layer, indicates the fuzzy rule

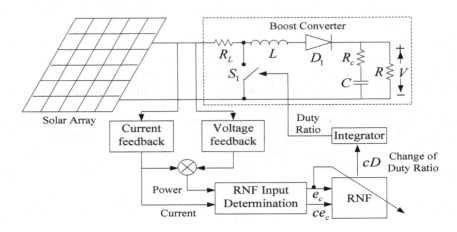

Fig. 1. The proposed MPPT controller using RNF

base. Every node at layer 3 stands for one fuzzy rule. Layer 4 is the output layer (change of duty ratio), where the nodes are represented by an RNF individual output. The function of each layer of the proposed RNF is briefly described as follows:

Layer 1 (Input Layer): The nodes transmit the input signal values x_i to the next layer linearly. Thus, the both current and voltage of a solar array are measured to form the error function and its associated change of error, which are given by:

$$x_e^{(1)} = y_{e,i}^{(1)} = e_c(k) = \frac{P(k) - P(k-1)}{I(k) - I(k-1)}, \ 1 \le i \le 5. \tag{4}$$

$$x_{\dot{e}}^{(1)} = y_{\dot{e},i}^{(1)} = ce_c(k) = e_c(k) - e_c(k-1), \ 1 \le j \le 5. \tag{5}$$

Layer 2 (Membership Layer): This is the fuzzification layer. Each crisp input value is fuzzified by using its membership functions. In the proposed controller strategically the *Gaussian* membership functions are selected for both the inputs. Thus, the outputs $y_{e,i}^{(2)}, y_{\dot{e},j}^{(2)}$ in layer 2 can be expressed as:

$$x_{e,i}^{(2)} = y_{e,i}^{(1)}, y_{e,i}^{(2)} = \exp\left[-\left(\frac{x_{e,i}^{(2)} - m_{e,i}}{\gamma_{e,i}}\right)^2\right], \ 1 \le i \le 5. \tag{6}$$

$$x_{\dot{e},j}^{(2)} = y_{\dot{e},j}^{(1)}, y_{\dot{e},j}^{(2)} = \exp\left[-\left(\frac{x_{\dot{e},j}^{(2)} - m_{\dot{e},j}}{\gamma_{\dot{e},j}}\right)^2\right], \ 1 \le j \le 5. \tag{7}$$

where $m_{i,j}$ and $\gamma_{i,j}$ are the center and the standard deviation of the *Gaussian* function respectively. If $x_{\dot{e},j}^{(2)}, x_{e,j}^{(2)}$ represents the layer 1 input to the node of layer 2, the inputs of this layer for discrete time n can be represented by:

$$x_{e,i}^{(2)}(n) = y_{e,i}^{(1)}(n) + r_i y_{e,i}^{(2)}(n-1), \ 1 \le i \le 5. \tag{8}$$

$$x_{\grave{e},j}^{(2)}(n) = y_{\grave{e},j}^{(1)}(n) + r_j y_{\grave{e},j}^{(2)}(n-1), \ 1 \le j \le 5. \tag{9}$$

where r_i, r_j represent the link weight of the feedback unit. It is obvious that the input of this layer contains the memory terms $y_{e,i}^{(2)}(n-1), y_{\grave{e},j}^{(2)}(n-1)$ which store the past information of the network. Every node in this layer has three adjustable parameters: m, γ and r. By assigning different value, they can express the different membership functions of function of the different fuzzy set.

Layer 3 (Rule Layer): Each node in this layer represents the precondition part of one fuzzy rule. Therefore, each node of this layer is denoted by Π which multiplies the incoming signals and outputs the product result, i.e., the firing strength of a rule. For the kth rule node:

$$x_k^{(3)} = x_{e,i}^{(3)} \times x_{\grave{e},j}^{(3)}, \ y_k^{(3)} = y_{e,i}^{(2)} \times y_{\grave{e},j}^{(2)}, \ \begin{cases} 1 \le k \le 50 \\ 1 \le i \le 5 \\ 1 \le j \le 5 \end{cases}. \tag{10}$$

where $x_{e,i}^{(3)}, x_{\grave{e},j}^{(3)}$ is the layer 3 element output to the node of layer 2. $y_{e,i}^{(2)}, y_{\grave{e},j}^{(2)}$ is the layer 2 element input to the node of layer 3. The value of $y_k^{(3)}$ is always positive.

Layer 4 (Output Layer): This layer acts a defuzzifier. The single node in this layer is labeled Σ and it sums all incoming signals to obtain the final inferred result:

$$x^{(4)} = w_k^{(4)} y_k^{(3)}, \ y^{(4)} = \sum_{k=1}^{50} w_k^{(4)} y_k^{(3)}. \tag{11}$$

where the link weight $w_k^{(4)}$ is the output action strength associated with the kth rule and $y_o^{(4)}$ is the output of the RNF. The consequent part of one fuzzy rule is implicitly contained in $w_k^{(4)}$. In this study, the output is $y_o^{(4)} = i_{qs}^*$.

Therefore, this RNF structure possesses the features of FL control due to the operation of linguistic variables, characteristic functions and FL control rules, as well as the symptoms if ANNs control due to the structure involving nodes, layers, and weights.

3.1 On-Line Learning Algorithm

The parameters of the RNF will affect the system output performance. The goal of the RNF controller is to adjust the controller parameters to the optimal values for reducing tracking error, resisting system parameter variations and rejecting outside disturbances. To describe the on-line learning algorithm of the RNF using the supervised gradient decent method, first the energy function E is defined as:

$$E = \frac{1}{2}\varepsilon^2. \tag{12}$$

Then, the learning algorithm based on back-propagation method is described below.

Using the gradient method, the related weights for the RNF are calculated, i.e., the update rule of the weights becomes:

$$w_k^{(4)}(n+1) = w_k^{(4)}(n) + \eta_w \Delta w_k^{(4)}. \tag{13}$$

$$x_{i,j}(n+1) = x_{i,j}(n) + \eta_m \Delta x_{i,j}. \tag{14}$$

$$\gamma_{i,j}(n+1) = \gamma_{i,j}(n) + \eta_\gamma \Delta \gamma_{i,j}. \tag{15}$$

where η_w, η_m, η_γ are the learning-rate parameters referring to the connecting weights, the mean of the *Gaussian* function, and the standard deviation of *Gaussian* function, respectively.

Applying the chain rule for (13)–(15), the weight increments between layers 4 and 3 are given by:

$$\Delta w_k^{(4)} = -\frac{\partial E}{\partial \Delta w_k^{(4)}} = -\frac{\partial E}{\partial y^{(4)}}\frac{\partial y^{(4)}}{\partial \Delta w_k^{(4)}} = \delta^{(4)} y_k^{(3)}. \tag{16}$$

Because the weights in layer 3 are unity, we can pass on calculating the mean and standard deviation update law for the *Gaussian* function in layer 2.

$$\Delta m_{e,i} = -\frac{\partial E}{\partial m_{e,i}} = -\frac{\partial E}{\partial y^{(4)}}\frac{\partial y^{(4)}}{\partial x^{(4)}}\frac{\partial x^{(4)}}{\partial y_k^{(3)}}\frac{\partial y_k^{(3)}}{\partial x_k^{(3)}}\frac{\partial x_k^{(3)}}{\partial y_{e,i}^{(2)}}\frac{\partial y_{e,i}^{(2)}}{\partial m_{e,i}}. \tag{17}$$

$$\Delta m_{e,i} = \sum_k^{25} \delta^{(4)} w_k^{(4)} y_k^{(3)} \frac{2\left(x_{e,i}^{(2)} - m_{e,i}\right)}{\left(\gamma_{e,i}\right)^2}. \tag{18}$$

$$\Delta m_{\dot{e},j} = -\frac{\partial E}{\partial m_{\dot{e},j}} = -\frac{\partial E}{\partial y^{(4)}}\frac{\partial y^{(4)}}{\partial x^{(4)}}\frac{\partial x^{(4)}}{\partial y_k^{(3)}}\frac{\partial y_k^{(3)}}{\partial x_k^{(3)}}\frac{\partial x_k^{(3)}}{\partial y_{\dot{e},j}^{(2)}}\frac{\partial y_{\dot{e},j}^{(2)}}{\partial m_{\dot{e},j}}. \tag{19}$$

$$\Delta m_{\dot{e},j} = \sum_k^{25} \delta^{(4)} w_k^{(4)} y_k^{(3)} \frac{2\left(x_{\dot{e},j}^{(2)} - m_{\dot{e},j}\right)}{\left(\gamma_{\dot{e},j}\right)^2}. \tag{20}$$

and

$$\Delta\gamma_{e,i} = -\frac{\partial E}{\partial\gamma_{e,i}} = -\frac{\partial E}{\partial y^{(4)}}\frac{\partial y^{(4)}}{\partial x^{(4)}}\frac{\partial x^{(4)}}{\partial y_k^{(3)}}\frac{\partial y_k^{(3)}}{\partial x_k^{(3)}}\frac{\partial x_k^{(3)}}{\partial y_{e,i}^{(2)}}\frac{\partial y_{e,i}^{(2)}}{\partial\gamma_{e,i}}. \tag{21}$$

$$\Delta\gamma_{e,i} = \sum_k^{25}\delta^{(4)}w_k^{(4)}y_k^{(3)}\frac{2\left(x_{e,i}^{(2)} - m_{e,i}\right)^2}{\left(\gamma_{e,i}\right)^3}. \tag{22}$$

$$\Delta\gamma_{\dot{e},j} = -\frac{\partial E}{\partial\gamma_{\dot{e},j}} = -\frac{\partial E}{\partial y^{(4)}}\frac{\partial y^{(4)}}{\partial x^{(4)}}\frac{\partial x^{(4)}}{\partial y_k^{(3)}}\frac{\partial y_k^{(3)}}{\partial x_k^{(3)}}\frac{\partial x_k^{(3)}}{\partial y_{\dot{e},j}^{(2)}}\frac{\partial y_{\dot{e},j}^{(2)}}{\partial\gamma_{\dot{e},j}}. \tag{23}$$

$$\Delta\gamma_{\dot{e},j} = \sum_k^{25}\delta^{(4)}w_k^{(4)}y_k^{(3)}\frac{2\left(x_{\dot{e},j}^{(2)} - m_{\dot{e},j}\right)^2}{\left(\gamma_{\dot{e},j}\right)^3}. \tag{24}$$

The mean and the standard deviation of the *Gaussian* function in layer 2 are updated from (6)–(12). The learning algorithm based on back-propagation method is used to train RNF structure. However, it is necessary to use some prior knowledge, such as the sensitivity derivative or *Jacobian* of the system, in order to apply the back-propagation algorithm to the RNF. Although an addition ANN or NF can be incorporated to estimate the *Jacobian*, it requires heavy computational effort and suffers from difficulty in implementation. In order to solve the problem due to the unknown *Jacobian*, an approximation of $\delta^{(4)}$ can be employed [26] as given by:

$$\delta^{(4)} = \frac{\partial E}{\partial y^{(4)}} = \frac{\partial E}{\partial\omega_r}\frac{\partial\omega_r}{\partial y^{(4)}} \approx -\varepsilon\mathrm{sgn}\left(\frac{\partial\omega_r}{\partial y^{(4)}}\right). \tag{25}$$

$\mathrm{sgn}\left(\frac{\partial\omega_r}{\partial y^{(4)}}\right)$ is generally known during operation.

4 Results and Discussion

A SPM085P-BP PV polycrystalline silicon solar cells is used in this study. The electrical characteristics of PV module at STC are shown in Table 1. Simulations were conducted to evaluate the performance of the proposed MPPT controller using RNF in comparison with [27] and [28] methods. We employ the solar cell model described in Sect. 2. Note that five hundred cells are used to form a solar array.

Neuro-Fuzzy based model properties are indicated in Table 2. The model training was set as 2000 epochs. The computation time for running the NF model was less than 1 min. The training data error declined for the primary epochs of the training data. Generally, the test error is used as an authentic evaluation of model's prediction. The result suggests that the good model is considered as the main one with the lowest test error. At the initial part, a hybrid learning employed for predicting the parameters.

Table 1. Specification of SPM085P-BP PV module.

Electrical specifications	Manufacturer data	Measured data
Maximum power (P_{mp}) (W)	85	83
Open circuit voltage (V_{oc}) (V)	65	63.6
Short circuit current (I_{sc}) (A)	6.4	5.76
Operating voltage at maximum power (V_{mp}) (V)	17.2	15.8
Operating current at maximum power (I_{mp}) (A)	4.95	5.04

AM 1.5, 1000 W/m^2, 25 °C.

For this simulation studies three different shading patterns are selected.

In the Case-1: According to the shading pattern 0.5 kW/m^2, 0.5 kW/m^2 and 0.9 kW/m^2. There are two MPP regions on the *P-V* curve. It is clearly observed in Fig. 2a that global MPP is tracked in shorter time compared with other approaches proposed in [27] and [28]. Tracking efficiency is 98.12% within a period of 5 s when the proposed algorithm is used. The approach used in [28] employs wide voltage search range, increasing convergence time and decreasing tracking efficiency. In this approach, tracking efficiency is calculated as 92.31%. In another approach [27], since the first MPP is tracked by Incremental Conductance algorithm, convergence time increases.

Table 2. Details of the RNF.

Parameter	Description/value
Fuzzy structure	Sugeno-type
Initial FIS for training	Genfis3
MF type	Gaussian
Output MF	Linear
Number of clusters	Auto (default)
Number of inputs	2
Number of outputs	1
Optimization method	Hybrid (least square and back-propagation techniques)
Number of fuzzy rules	64
Training maximum epoch number	2000
Initial step size	0.01
Step size decrease rate	0.9
Step size increase rate	1.1
Computation time	Less than 1 min

Consequently, tracking efficiency is small compared with the proposed algorithm. Simulation results of proposed method and algorithm used in [27] and [28] are seen in Fig. 2a–c.

In the Case-2: values of the solar insolation are 0.3 kW/m^2, 0.4 kW/m^2 and 1 kW/m^2. Proposed algorithm performs better than the other two methods considered.

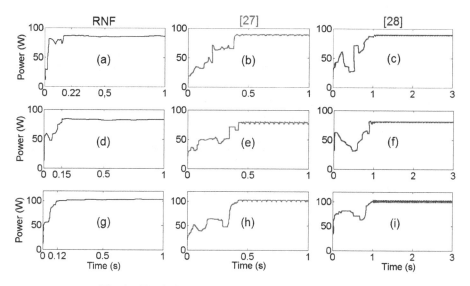

Fig. 2. Simulation results of Case-1, Case-2 and Case-3.

While tracking efficiency is 98.94% in proposed algorithm, the other algorithms employed in [28] and [27] have smaller efficiency by 5.09% and 6.67%, respectively. Power variations of this simulation are shown in Fig. 2d–f.

The global MPP exists in the middle MPP region in the Case-3. The method in [15] tracks the global MPP in a big convergence time with respect to the proposed algorithm, since the first MPP is tracked by Incremental Conductance algorithm. Surely,

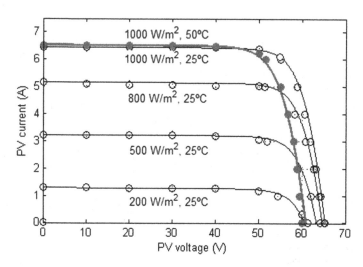

Fig. 3. Predicted *I-V* curves (the solid lines) and experimental points (the circle markers) for different values of solar irradiance and $T = 25\ °C$, in addition to the case that $T = 50\ °C$ (the thicker line and the solid circle markers).

tracking efficiency is always small in the method proposed by [28], since voltage of PV module is scanned in a large voltage range as can be seen in Fig. 2c, f, i. In this case, tracking efficiency of the proposed algorithm is 98.51%.

From Figs. 3 and 4, it can be seen that the proposed method extracts a PV model that predicts accurately matched *I-V* curves to experimental measurements, provided by manufacturers. In order to indicate improved accuracy of the proposed method, the measured identification error, as the sum of STC identification errors, is also compared with the corresponding values introduced by the methods in [27] and [28]. It is observed that the identified model by the proposed full method generates the least overall error among all methods.

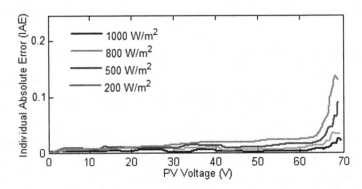

Fig. 4. Absolute normalized curve errors between the experimental and predicted *I-V* curves different amounts of solar irradiance.

5 Summary

A novel RNF controller based MPPT controlled photovoltaic system has been presented in this paper. The proposed method has several advantages over a [27] and [28]. That is the controller: (*i*) determines the maximum power point faster; (*ii*) gives smoother output power at steady state; and (*iii*) requires no external sensors for solar intensity and temperature measurements. It does require on-line tuning of its parameters: scaling factors, membership functions and rules during drive operation to form an adaptive RNF to improve its steady-state performance. This will increase the scheme complexity and computational effort. Results obtained from RNF look promising.

References

1. Luque, A., Hegedus, S.: Handbook of Photovoltaic Science and Engineering, 2nd edn. Wiley, Hoboken (2010)
2. Sick, F., Erge, T.: Photovoltaic in Building. International Energy Agency, Paris (1996)

3. Enrique, J.M., Andujar, J.M., Bohorquez, M.A.: A reliable, fast and low cost maximum power point tracker for photovoltaic applications. Sol. Energy **84**, 79–89 (2010). https://doi. org/10.1016/j.solener.2009.10.011
4. Hohm, D.P., Ropp, M.E.: Comparative study of maximum power point tracking algorithms. Prog. Photovolt. Res. Appl. **11**(1), 47–62 (2003). https://doi.org/10.1002/pip.459
5. Esram, T., Chapman, P.L.: Comparison of photovoltaic array maximum power point tracking techniques. IEEE Trans. Energy Convers. **22**(2), 439–449 (2007)
6. Dileep, G., Singh, S.: Maximum power point tracking of solar photovoltaic system using modified perturbation and observation method. Renew. Sustain. Energy Rev. **50**, 109–129 (2015). https://doi.org/10.1016/j.rser.2015.04.072
7. Messalti, S., Harrag, A., Loukriz, A.: A new neural networks MPPT controller for PV systems. In: Proceedings of the Renewable Energy Congress (IREC) (2015). https://doi.org/ 10.1109/irec.2015.7110907
8. Chekired, F., Mellit, A., Kalogirou, S., Larbes, C.: Intelligent maximum power point trackers for photovoltaic applications using {FPGA} chip: a comparative study. Sol. Energy **101**, 83–99 (2014). https://doi.org/10.1016/j.solener.2013.12.026
9. Lyden, S., Haque, M.: Maximum power point tracking techniques for photovoltaic systems: a comprehensive review and comparative analysis. Renew. Sustain. Energy Rev. **52**, 1504–1518 (2015). https://doi.org/10.1016/j.rser.2015.07.172
10. Bendib, B., Belmili, H., Krim, F.: A survey of the most used {MPPT} methods: conventional and advanced algorithms applied for photovoltaic systems. Renew. Sustain. Energy Rev. **45**, 637–648 (2015). https://doi.org/10.1016/j.rser.2015.02.009
11. Radjai, T., Gaubert, J.P., Rahmani, L., Mekhilef, S.: Experimental verification of po MPPT algorithm with direct control based on fuzzy logic control using CUK converter. Int. Trans. Electr. Energy Syst. **25**(12), 3492–3508 (2015). https://doi.org/10.1002/etep.2047
12. Radjai, T., Rahmani, L., Mekhilef, S., Gaubert, J.P.: Implementation of a modified incremental conductance {MPPT} algorithm with direct control based on a fuzzy duty cycle change estimator using dspace. Sol. Energy **110**, 325–337 (2014). https://doi.org/10.1016/j. solener.2014.09.014
13. Dounis, A.I., Kofinas, P., Alafodimos, C., Tseles, D.: Adaptive fuzzy gain scheduling PID controller for maximum power point tracking of photovoltaic system. Renew. Energy **60**, 202–214 (2013). https://doi.org/10.1016/j.renene.2013.04.014Technicalnote
14. Chekired, F., Larbes, C., Rekioua, D., Haddad, F.: Implementation of a {MPPT} fuzzy controller for photovoltaic systems on FPGA circuit. Energy Proc. **6**, 541–549 (2011). https://doi.org/10.1016/j.egypro.2011.05.062
15. Messai, A., Mellit, A., Pavan, A.M., Guessoum, A., Mekki, H.: FPGA-based implementation of a fuzzy controller (MPPT) for photovoltaic module. Energy Convers. Manag. **52**(7), 2695–2704 (2011). https://doi.org/10.1016/j.enconman.2011.01.021
16. Larbes, C., Cheikh, S.A., Obeidi, T., Zerguerras, A.: Genetic algorithms optimized fuzzy logic control for the maximum power point tracking in photovoltaic system. Renew. Energy **34**(10), 2093–2100 (2009). https://doi.org/10.1016/j.renene.2009.01.006
17. Cheng, P.-C., Peng, B.-R., Liu, Y.-H., Cheng, Y.-S., Huang, J.-W.: Optimization of a fuzzy logic-control-based MPPT algorithm using the particle swarm optimization technique. Energies **8**(6), 5338–5360 (2015). https://doi.org/10.3390/en8065338
18. Lin, W.-M., Hong, C.-M., Chen, C.-H.: Neural-network-based MPPT control of a standalone hybrid power generation system. IEEE Trans. Power Electron. **26**(12), 3571–3581 (2011). https://doi.org/10.1109/TPEL.2011.2161775
19. Liu, Y.-H., Liu, C.-L., Huang, J.-W., Chen, J.-H.: Neural-network-based maximum power point tracking methods for photovoltaic systems operating under fast changing environments. Sol. Energy **89**, 42–53 (2013). https://doi.org/10.1016/j.solener.2012.11.017

20. Hatti, M., Meharrar, A., Tioursi, M.: Power management strategy in the alternative energy photovoltaic/PEM fuel cell hybrid system. Renew. Sustain. Energy Rev. 15(9), 5104–5110 (2011). https://doi.org/10.1016/j.rser.2011.07.046

21. Boumaaraf, H., Talha, A., Bouhali, O.: A three-phase {NPC} grid-connected inverter for photovoltaic applications using neural network {MPPT}. Renew. Sustain. Energy Rev. 49, 1171–1179 (2015). https://doi.org/10.1016/j.rser.2015.04.066

22. Kulaksız, A.A., Akkaya, R.: A genetic algorithm optimized ANN-based {MPPT} algorithm for a stand-alone {PV} system with induction motor drive. Sol. Energy 86(9), 2366–2375 (2012). https://doi.org/10.1016/j.solener.2012.05.006

23. Ramaprabha, R., Gothandaraman, V., Kanimozhi, K., Divya, R., Mathur, B.: Maximum power point tracking using GA-optimized artificial neural network for solar PV system. In: Proceedings of the Electrical Energy Systems (ICEES), pp. 264–268 (2011). https://doi.org/10.1109/icees.2011.5725340

24. Chaouachi, A., Kamel, R.M., Nagasaka, K.: A novel multi-model neuro-fuzzy-based {MPPT} for three-phase grid-connected photovoltaic system. Sol. Energy 84(12), 2219–2229 (2010). https://doi.org/10.1016/j.solener.2010.08.004

25. Villalva, M.G., Gazoli, G.R., Filho, E.R.: Comprehensive approach to modeling and simulation of photovoltaic arrays. IEEE Trans. Power Electron. 24(5), 1198–1208 (2009). https://doi.org/10.1109/TPEL.2009.2013862

26. Zhang, Y., Sen, P., Hearn, G.E.: On-line trained adaptive neural controller. IEEE Control Syst. 15(5), 67–75 (1995). https://doi.org/10.1109/37.466260

27. Tey, K.S., Mekhilef, S.: Modified incremental conductance algorithm for photovoltaic system under partial shading conditions and load variation. IEEE Trans. Ind. Electron. 61 (10), 5384–5391 (2014). https://doi.org/10.1109/TIE.2014.2304921

28. Koutroulis, E., Blaabjerg, F.: A new technique for tracking the global maximum power point of PV arrays operating under partial shading conditions. IEEE J. Photovolt. 2(2), 184–190 (2012). https://doi.org/10.1109/JPHOTOV.2012.2183578

Automatic Closed Modeling of Multiple Variable Systems Using Soft Computation

Angel Kuri-Morales[(⊠)] and Alejandro Cartas-Ayala

Instituto Tecnológico Autónomo de México, Río Hondo No. 1, 01000 Mexico,
D.F., Mexico
akuri@itam.mx, alejandro.cartas@gmail.com

Abstract. One of the most interesting goals in engineering and the sciences is the mathematical representation of physical, social and other kind of complex phenomena. This goal has been attempted and, lately, achieved with different machine learning (ML) tools. ML owes much of its present appeal to the fact that it allows to model complex phenomena without the explicit definition of the form of the model. Neural networks and support vector machines exemplify such methods. However, in most of the cases, these methods yield "black box" models, i.e. input and output correspond to the phenomena under scrutiny but it is very difficult (or outright impossible) to discern the interrelation of the input variables involved. In this paper we address this problem with the explicit aim of targeting on models which are closed in nature, i.e. the aforementioned relation between variables is explicit. In order to do this, in general, the only assumption regarding the data is that they be approximately continuous. In such cases it is possible to represent the system with polynomial expressions. To be able to do so one must define the number of monomials, the degree of every variable in every monomial and the coefficients associated. We model sparse data systems with an algorithm minimizing the min-max norm. From mathematical and experimental evidence we are able to set a bound on the number of terms and degrees of the approximating polynomials. Thereafter, a genetic algorithm (GA) identifies the coefficients which correspond to the terms and degrees defined as above.

Keywords: Mathematical modeling · Machine learning
Multivariate regression · Genetic algorithms

1 Introduction

The problem of finding a synthetic expression from an experimental set of data for a variable of interest given a matching set of independent variables has repeatedly received attention because of its inherent importance. If we were able to find a method of general application, in principle, any system susceptible to data representation would be amenable to automatic modeling. It may be called multivariate regression or supervised training (ST) depending on the approach taken. ST has given rise to a wide sub-area within the realm of artificial neural networks (NN). Some approaches include

© Springer Nature Switzerland AG 2018
F. Castro et al. (Eds.): MICAI 2017, LNAI 10632, pp. 185–196, 2018.
https://doi.org/10.1007/978-3-030-02837-4_15

multi-layer perceptron networks [1, 2], radial basis function networks [3, 4] and support vector machines [5, 6]. In all of these cases a main concern has been the fact that the architecture of the model yields little information of the inter-relations between the variables of the system. On the other hand, if seen as a multivariate regression problem, where, conceivably, such inter-relation is explicit, the following issues arise: (a) How to determine the form of the model [7], (b) How to calculate the free parameters of such model when one is selected [8] and, (c) How to handle the complexity of its equations and the numerical instability they frequently convey [9]. The last issue has to do with the fact that a closed model of a system of multiple variables frequently leads to complex expressions whose determination depends on solving large sets of simultaneous linear or non-linear equations. These sets of equations are prone to result in ill-conditioned matrices [10]. It is common, as discussed in [21], to attempt polynomial approximations from pre-defined mathematical models. The case here is essentially different as the form of the model is left for the method to determine. The use of NNs, for instance, has opened a way out of the numerical limitations. NNs represent the embodiment of an alternative approach which replaces one complex expression by sets (networks) of simpler ones. The free parameters and architecture of the NN, when adequately determined, yield the desired results [11]. It is interesting to point out that categorical variable encoding is a subject, in itself, of particular difficulty, as discussed in [24]. In any case, the explicit relations between the independent variables remain unknown. In the present work we explore an alternative which allows us to keep the closed nature of an algebraic model (along with its inherent explanatory properties) while avoiding the pitfalls of numerical instability and leaving the task of determining the mathematical model that is best suited for the problem at hand to the method itself. This work is an extension of ideas presented in [21]. Here we expand several details regarding the general methodology.

In Sect. 2, we show that it is possible to work backwards from the Universal Approximation Theorem (UAT) [12] in the sense that we may derive an algebraic expression starting from a NN architectural approach. Hence, we know that a logistic function $(1/(1 + e^{-x}))$ may be used as the nonlinearity in the UAT. An approximation of the *logistic* may be gotten from a Chebyshev polynomial basis [15]. We generalize the UAT by using the explicit algebraic approximation of the *logistic* and calculate the number of elements in the explicit polynomial representation for an arbitrary function. In Sect. 3 we discuss a method which allows us to express any polynomial selecting only the most relevant monomials by using a genetic algorithm (GA). In Sect. 4 we obtain the polynomial expressions for two problem cases. Finally, in Sect. 5 we offer our conclusions.

2   Universal Approximation Theorem for Polynomials

We start by enunciating the Universal Approximation Theorem. The UAT relies on the properties of a well-defined non-linear function [12].

Theorem 1. Let $\varphi(\cdot)$ be a nonconstant, bounded, and monotonically-increasing continuous function. Let I_{mO} denote the m_O-dimensional unit hypercube $[0, 1]$. The space of continuous functions on I_{m_O} is denoted by $C(I_{mO})$. Then, given any function $f \in C(I_{mO})$ and $\varepsilon > 0$, there exist an integer M and sets of real constants α_i, b_i and w_{ij}, where $i = 1, 2, ..., m_I$ and $j = 1, 2, ..., m_O$ such that we may define:

$$F(x_1,...,x_{mO}) = \sum_{i=1}^{mI} \left[\alpha_i \cdot \varphi \left(\sum_{j=1}^{mO} w_{ij}x_j + b_i \right) \right] \qquad (1)$$

as an approximate realization of the function $f(\ )$, that is,

$$|F(x_1,...,x_{mO}) - f(x_1,...,x_{mO})| < \varepsilon \qquad (2)$$

for all $x_1,...,x_{m_O}$ in the input space.

The universal approximation theorem is directly applicable to multilayer perceptrons. Perceptrons are computational units which generally include an extra constant valued input called the *bias*. When including the bias of the output neuron into (1) we get

$$F(x_1,...,x_{m_0}) = \alpha_0 + \sum_{i=1}^{m_I} \left[\alpha_i \cdot \varphi \left(\sum_{j=1}^{m_0} w_{ij}x_j + b_i \right) \right] \qquad (3)$$

Now, the equation for the perceptron is given by $y_i = \varphi[\sum_{i=0}^{mO} w_{ij}x_j]$, where, for convenience, we have made $x_0 = 1$, $w_0 = b_0$. We can select $\varphi(x) = logistic(x)$ as the nonlinearity in a neuronal model for the construction of a multi-layer perceptron (MLP) network. We note that (1) represents the output of a MLP described as follows: (a) The network has m_O input nodes and a single hidden layer consisting of m_I neurons; the inputs are denoted by $x_1, ..., x_{mO}$, (b) Hidden neuron i has synaptic weights w_{i1}, w_{i2}, ..., w_{imO}, (c) The network output is a linear combination of the outputs of the hidden neurons, with $\alpha_1, ..., \alpha_{mI}$ defining the synaptic weights of the output layer.

The UAT states that *a single hidden layer is sufficient for a multilayer perceptron to compute a uniform ε approximation to a given training set represented by the set of inputs $x_1, ..., x_{mO}$ and a desired (target) output $f(x_1, ..., x_{mO})$.*

We know [13, 20] that the *logistic* function $1/(1 + e^{-x})$ may be approximated by a polynomial $P_n(x)$ of degree n with an error $\varepsilon = |P_n(x) - logistic(x)|$ where $\varepsilon \to 0$ as $n \to \infty$, i.e. $logistic(x) \approx P_n(x) = \varsigma_0 + \sum_{i=1}^{n} \varsigma_i x^i$. Likewise, we know [14, 15] that a function $y = f(x)$ in $[0, +1)$ may be approximated by a polynomial based on a set of Chebyshev polynomials which achieves the minimization of the least squared error norm and simultaneously approaches the minimum largest absolute error. Finally, an application of the previous concepts allows us to find that the polynomial $P_n(x)$ of theorem (2) may be approximated by a polynomial $Q_l(x) = \beta_0 + \sum_{l=1}^{n} \beta_l x^{2l-1}$ with an error $\varepsilon \to 0$.

The logistic function may be approximated by the polynomial $P_{11}(x) \sim \beta_0 + \sum_{i=1}^{6} \beta_i x^{2i-1}$ with an RMS error $\varepsilon_2 \sim 0.000781$ and a min-max error $\varepsilon_\infty \sim 0.001340$, where $\beta_0 \sim 0.5000$, $\beta_1 \sim 0.2468$, $\beta_2 \sim -0.01769$, $\beta_3 \sim 0.001085$, $\beta_4 \sim -0.0000$ 40960, $\beta_5 \sim 0.0000008215$, $\beta_6 \sim -0.00000000664712$. Therefore, we find that any function as in (3) may be approximately realized with a linear combination of monomials which has a constant plus terms of odd degree.

Theorem. Any function of m_O variables may be approximated with a polynomial whose terms are of degree 2^{k-1}.

Proof. (1) Directly from the UAT we derive the expression of a universal approximating polynomial. (2) The undefined function is chosen to be a logistic $1/(1 + e^{-x})$ whose argument x is replaced by the output of the neuron (generally called the induced local field) $\sum_{k=0}^{m_O} w_{ik} x_k$. (3) Such function may be replaced by its infinite series expansion. (4) Next, this infinite expansion is replaced by the approximation derived from Chebyshev polynomials. This is also an infinite expansion of a constant plus terms of odd powers of the argument. (5) However experimentally determined that no more than 6 terms are needed to achieve a close approximation. Following these steps we may write,

$$
\begin{aligned}
F(x_1,\ldots,x_{m_O}) &= \alpha_0 + \sum_{i=1}^{m_I} \alpha_i \cdot \varphi \left(\sum_{k=0}^{m_O} w_{ik} x_k \right) \\
&= \alpha_0 + \sum_{i=1}^{m_I} \alpha_i \cdot logistic \left(\sum_{k=0}^{m_O} w_{ik} x_k \right) \\
&= \alpha_0 + \sum_{i=1}^{m_I} \alpha_i \cdot \sum_{j=0}^{\infty} \lambda_j \cdot \left(\sum_{k=0}^{m_O} w_{ik} x_k \right)^j \\
&= \alpha_0 + \sum_{i=1}^{m_I} \alpha_i \cdot \left[\beta_0 + \sum_{j=1}^{\infty} \beta_j \cdot \left(\sum_{k=0}^{m_O} w_{ik} x_k \right)^{2j-1} \right] \\
&\approx \alpha_0 + \sum_{i=1}^{m_I} \alpha_i \cdot \left[\frac{1}{2} + \sum_{j=1}^{6} \beta_j \cdot \left(\sum_{k=0}^{m_O} w_{ik} x_k \right)^{2j-1} \right]
\end{aligned}
\tag{4}
$$

3 Approximation Using Genetic Algorithms

The number of terms of (4) is very large, in general. However, the terms corresponding to the hidden neurons may be lumped into terms of degree 0, 1, 3, ..., 11 and, subsequently, those at the output neuron will consist of those resulting from the power

Table 1. Combinations of odd powers for the expansion of logistic(x)

1	11	33	63
3	15	35	77
5	21	45	81
7	25	49	99
9	27	55	121

combinations of degree $(0, 1, 3, ..., 11)^1$, $(0, 1, 3, ..., 11)^3$, ..., $(0, 1, 3, ..., 11)^{11}$. A simple analysis shows that only 20 of the possible power combinations are possible. These combinations are shown in Table 1.

We can make a list (say L) of these possible powers. In other words, the polynomial at the output neuron will be of the form $P_O = k + \sum_{i=1}^{20} T(i)$, where $T(i) \equiv$ *terms of degree $L(i)$; $L(i)$* denoting the i-th element in L. For instance, $T(5) = 9$; $T(12) = 35$; $T(19) = 99$ and so on. Notice, however, that even if the powers of the monomials are all odd the powers of the variables in the i-th monomial may take any possible combination of the factors of $L(i)$. There remains the problem of determining the coefficients associated to every term.

One way to circumvent this problem is to define a priori the number (say M) of desired monomials of the approximant and then to properly select which of the p possible ones these will be. There are $C(p, M)$ combinations of monomials and even for modest values of p and M an exhaustive search is out of the question. This is an optimization problem which we tackled using the genetic algorithm (EGA) discussed in [16, 17], as follows.

The chromosome is a binary string of size p. Every bit in it represents a monomial ordered as per the sequence of the consecutive powers of the variables. If the bit is '1' it means that the corresponding monomial is retained while if it is a '0' it is discarded. One has to ensure that the number of 1's is equal to M. Assume, for example, that $y = f(v_1, v_2, v_3)$ and that $d_1 = 1$, $d_2 = d_3 = 2$. In such case the powers assigned to the $2 \times 3 \times 3 = 18$ positions of the genome are 000, 001, 002, 010, 011, 012, 020, 021, 022, 100, 101, 102, 110, 111, 112, 120, 121, 122. If $M = 6$ the chromosome 110000101010000001 corresponds to the polynomial $P(v_1, v_2, v_3) = c_{000} + c_{001}v_3 + c_{020}v_2^2 + c_{022}v_2^2v_3^2 + c_{101}v_1v_3 + c_{122}v_1v_2^2v_3^2$. The population of the EGA consists of a set of binary strings of length p in which there are only M 1's. That is, for every genome the monomials (corresponding to the 1's) are determined by EGA. Then the Ascent Algorithm (AA) (to be discussed in the sequel) is applied to obtain the set of M coefficients minimizing $\varepsilon_{MAX} = max(|f_i - y_i|) \; \forall i$. Next, for this set of coefficients ε_{RMS} is calculated. This is the fitness function of EGA. The EGA's individuals are selected, crossed over and mutated for a number of generations. In the end, we retain the individual whose coefficients minimize ε_{RMS} out of those which best minimize ε_{MAX} (from the AA). We refer to this as the L_∞-L_2 error measure.

3.1   The Ascent Algorithm

The purpose of this algorithm is to express the behavior of a dependent variable (y) as a function of a set of m_O independent variables (v). $y = f(v_1, v_2, ..., v_{mO})$ and $y = f(v)$. The form of the approximant is $y = c_1X_1 + c_2X_2 + ... + c_mX_m$; X_i denotes a combination of the independent variables. That is, $X_i = f_i(v)$. The method assumes that there is a sample of size N such that for every set of the independent variables v there is a known value of the dependent variable f, as illustrated in Table 2. By convention N stands for the number of objects in the sample and $M = m + 1$ (m = number of desired terms of the approximant). The AA has the distinct advantage that the X_i may be arbitrarily defined. This allows us to find the approximation coefficients for different combinations of the powers of the variables.

The goal of the AA is to find the values of the coefficients such that the approximated values minimize the difference between the known values of the dependent variable f in the sample and those calculated (say y) for all the objects in it. We define the approximation error as $\varepsilon_{MAX} = max(| f_i - y_i|)$. The AA is based on a two-phase iterative methodology. First, a subset of the sample (of size M) is randomly selected (this is called the inner set) and the best approximant (a set of coefficients) in the minimax sense is found. Second, the approximant is tested to see whether $y = f(X)$ satisfies the minimax norm for the remaining $N-M$ objects (this set of cardinality $N-M$ is called the outer set) of the sample. If the minimax condition is attained by all the objects the algorithm ends: the coefficients are those of the best possible approximant. If at least one of the objects in the outer set does not comply with the minimax condition then appropriately selected objects of the inner and outer sets are swapped and the process is repeated. It is easy to prove that the AA will always converge to the best absolute error [18]. Therefore, another distinct advantage of the AA is that, regardless of the value of N, only an $M \times M$ set of equations is solved in every step. This is a clear advantage over alternative algorithms relying on the L_2 norm, such as the Levenberg-Marquardt [22] or Powell algorithms [23] which require the computer's memory to hold matrices of size $N \times N$.

Table 2. A data sample.

v_1	v_2	v_3	v_4	v_5	f
0.2786	0.2319	0.5074	0.9714	0.5584	0.4938
0.4929	0.9710	0.8676	1.0000	0.7411	0.9135
...	...	...	...	...	...
0.4357	0.9130	0.8309	0.6500	0.8579	0.7037

3.2 Implementation of the Ascent Algorithm

1. Input the data vectors (call them **D**).
2. Input the degrees of each of the variables of the approximating polynomial.
3. Map the original data vectors into the powers of the selected monomials (call them **P**).
4. Select a subset of size M from **D**. Call it **I**. Call the remaining vectors **E**.

BOOTSTRAP
(Execute steps 5,6 only once)

5. Obtain the minimax signs (σ) (**A** is the matrix incorporating such signs).
6. Obtain the inverse of **A** (call it **B**).

LOOP
(Execute steps 7-14 iteratively until convergence is reached)

7. Calculate the coefficients **C** = **f B**. The maximum absolute internal ε_θ error is also calculated.

8. Get the maximum absolute external error ε_ϕ from **C** and **E**. Call its index I_E

9. $\varepsilon_\theta \geq \varepsilon_\phi$? YES: Stop. The coefficients of **C** are those of the minimax polynomial for the **D** vectors.

10. Calculate the λ vector from $\lambda = A^{I_E} B$
11. Calculate the ξ vector which maximizes $\sigma_{I_E} \lambda_j / B_j$. Call its index I_I.

12. Interchange vectors I_E and I_I.

13. Calculate the new inverse $\overline{B}$. Make $B \leftarrow \overline{B}$.

14. Go to step 7.

The implementation above is a very fast one. Every iteration of the AA requires only $O(M^2)$ flops.

4 Case Studies

To illustrate our method we present two case studies, both taken from the UCI repository [19]. All combination of degrees was allowed. The data set was split in a training subset (80%) and a test subset (20%). The algorithm was trained from the first subset; the results shown correspond to the test subset.

4.1 CPU Performance

Case 1 is related to the relative CPU performance of a set of selected ones. There are 209 instances of the following attributes: (1) Vendor name, (2) Model Name, (3) MYCT: machine cycle time in nanoseconds, (4) MMIN: minimum main memory in kilobytes, (5) MMAX: maximum main memory in kilobytes, (6) CACH: cache memory in kilobytes, (7) CHMIN and (8) CHMAX: minimum and maximum channels, (9) PRP: published relative performance, (10) ERP: estimated relative performance.

We used variables 3, 4, 5, 6, 7, 8 as input and variable 10 as the dependent variable. In our nomenclature the independent variables 1, 2, 3, 4, 5 and 6 correspond to MYCT, MMIN, MMAX, CACH, CHMIN and CHMAX. We found the approximating L_∞-L_2 polynomials of 4, 8, 12 and 20 terms. The EGA ran for only 50 generations and yielded errors smaller than 5% in all cases. Figure 1 illustrates these results.

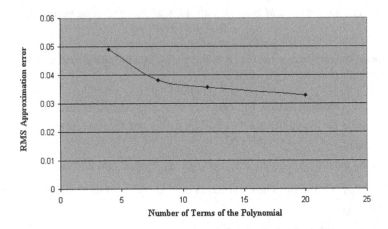

Fig. 1. Approximation error for different number of terms

A graph comparing the behavior of the original and the approximated data for 8 terms is shown in Fig. 2. Data were scaled to the [0, 1) interval.

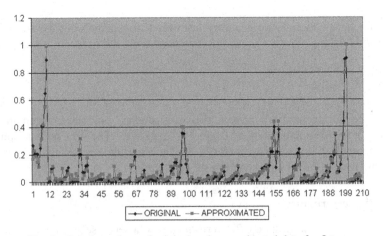

Fig. 2. Relative values of original and approximated data for 8 terms

The approximation coefficients are shown in Table 3.

Table 3. Coefficients for the 8 term polynomial

C000020	0.980773369
C000100	0.290797966
C001001	0.711390467
C002100	−0.450999443
C011000	0.805336608
C101120	−292.8313131
C110122	1397.763302
C121121	−594.6122132

The indices of the coefficients denote the degree of the associated monomial. For instance, the first coefficient corresponds to variable CHMIN squared; the other variables not appearing. Likewise, coefficient C002100 corresponds to variable MMAX squared and CACH to the first power.

4.2   Wine Classification

The second case corresponds to a wine recognition data base. In the UCI documentation we may find *"The classes are separable, though only RDA has achieved 100% correct classification."* These data are the results of a chemical analysis of wines grown in the same region in Italy but derived from three different cultivars. The analysis determined the quantities of 13 constituents found in each of the three types of wines. The 13 considered variables are: (1) Alcohol, (2) Malic acid, (3) Ash, (4) Alcalinity of ash, (5) Magnesium, (6) Total phenols, (7) Flavanoids, (8) Nonflavanoid phenols, (9) Proanthocyanins, (10) Color intensity, (11) Hue, (12) OD280/OD315 of diluted

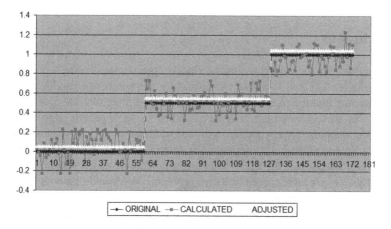

Fig. 3. Classification results for a 20 term polynomial

Table 4. Results for regression case study (CPU)

Data base	Variables	Instances	Terms	Max degree	% Classification
CPU	7	209	20	10	3.28%
CPU	7	209	12	9	3.57%
CPU	7	209	8	8	3.81%
CPU	7	209	4	11	4.89%

Table 5. Results for classification case study (wines)

Data base	Variables	Instances	Terms	Max degree	% Classification
Wines	13 (3 classes)	178	20	11	96.63%
Wines	13 (3 classes)	178	12	13	92.70%
Wines	13 (3 classes)	178	8	9	89.33%
Wines	13 (3 classes)	178	4	5	70.79%

wines, (13) Proline. There are 178 instances of the attributes. 3 classes are identified. In this case EGA was run for 100 generations. Classification is harder than regression for a polynomial because it has to approximate integer values (1, 2, 3 for the corresponding classes). As before, we found the approximating L_∞-L_2 polynomials of 4, 8, 12 and 20 terms. In Fig. 3 we show the best classification results corresponding to 20 terms. The wiggly values correspond to the actual ones gotten from the polynomial. However, since the achieved maximum difference is smaller than the threshold between the classes it is simple to obtain the integer values for all non-integer ones, thus yielding the number of the class. The line is denoted as "adjusted" in the graph. Since the approximation and original values were so similar, we offset the results by 0.05 so as to make the two lines original/adjusted discernible.

Basic results for case study 1 are shown in Table 4; those for case study 2 are shown in Table 5.

5   Conclusions

We have shown that any function may be closely approximated using a polynomial of maximum degree 121 and found an expression for the number of resulting terms. We have also shown that the terms may be lumped into no more than 20 monomials. The coefficients of these monomials may be searched using a genetic algorithm whose individuals correspond to polynomials with a predefined number of monomials. Every individual suggests a particular combination of terms whose coefficients may be found using the AA, whereupon the EGA finds the combination which optimizes the RMS error. To illustrate we have solved two case problems. We found that both a regression and classification problems may be satisfactorily tackled. One unsolved issue is how to determine the number and maximum degree of the lumped polynomial. To this effect we conducted a Monte Carlo experiment where we simulated 300,000 functions and analyzed the contribution of each of the 20 monomials. Space does not allow us to discuss this issue in length. But we may report that we have experimentally bounded the maximum relative importance of the terms to degree 35. If we accept the Monte Carlo results, the only matter that remains is to determine the number of terms in the approximation. Immediate future research will focus on these last two issues.

References

1. Rumelhart, D.E., Hinton, G.E., Williams, R.J.: Learning internal representations by error propagation. In: Rumelhart, D., McClelland, J., The PDP Research Group (eds.) Parallel Distributed Processing: Explorations in the Microstructure of Cognition. Volume 1: Foundations. MIT Press, Cambridge (1986)
2. Haykin, S.: Neural Networks and Learning Machines, 3rd edn. Prentice Hall, Upper Saddle River (2009). ISBN-13: 978-0-13-147139-9. Chap. 4, Multilayer Perceptrons
3. Powell, M.J.D.: The theory of radial basis functions. In: Light, W. (ed.) Advances in Numerical Analysis II: Wavelets, Subdivision, and Radial Basis Functions. King Fahd University of Petroleum & Minerals, Dhahran (1992)
4. Haykin, S.: op. cit, Chap. 5, Kernel Methods and Radial Basis Functions (2009)
5. Cortes, C., Vapnik, V.: Support-vector networks. Mach. Learn. 20 (1995). http://www.springerlink.com/content/k238jx04hm87j80g/
6. Haykin, S.: op. cit, Chap. 6, Support Vector Machines (2009)
7. MacKay, D.: Information Theory, Inference, and Learning Algorithms. Cambridge University Press, Cambridge (2004). ISBN 0-521-64298-1
8. Ratkowsky, D.: Handbook of Nonlinear Regression Models. Marcel Dekker, Inc., New York (1990). Library of Congress QA278.2 .R369
9. Beckermann, B.: The condition number of real Vandermonde, Krylov and positive definite Hankel matrices. Numer. Math. 85(4), 553–577 (2000). https://doi.org/10.1007/PL00005392
10. Meyer, C.: Matrix Analysis and Applied Linear Algebra. Society for Industrial and Applied Mathematics (SIAM), Philadelphia (2001). ISBN 978-0-89871-454-8
11. Kuri Morales, A.: Training neural networks using non-standard norms – preliminary results. In: Cairó, O., Sucar, L.E., Cantu, F.J. (eds.) MICAI 2000. LNCS (LNAI), vol. 1793, pp. 350–364. Springer, Heidelberg (2000). https://doi.org/10.1007/10720076_32
12. Cybenko, G.: Approximation by superpositions of a sigmoidal function. Math. Control Signals Syst. 2, 303–314 (1989)
13. Bishop, E.: A generalization of the Stone-Weierstrass theorem. Pac. J. Math. 11(3), 777–783 (1961)
14. Koornwinder, T., Wong, R., Koekoek, R., Swarttouw, R.: Orthogonal polynomials. In: Olver, F., Lozier, D., Boisvert, R., et al. (eds.) NIST Handbook of Mathematical Functions. Cambridge University Press, Cambridge (2010). ISBN 978-0521192255
15. Scheid, F.: Schaum's Outline of Numerical Analysis (1968). ISBN 07-055197-9. Chap. 21, Least Squares Polynomial Approximation
16. Kuri-Morales, A., Aldana-Bobadilla, E.: The best genetic algorithm I. In: Castro, F., Gelbukh, A., González, M. (eds.) MICAI 2013. LNCS (LNAI), vol. 8266, pp. 1–15. Springer, Heidelberg (2013). https://doi.org/10.1007/978-3-642-45111-9_1
17. Kuri-Morales, A.F., Aldana-Bobadilla, E., López-Peña, I.: The best genetic algorithm II. In: Castro, F., Gelbukh, A., González, M. (eds.) MICAI 2013. LNCS (LNAI), vol. 8266, pp. 16–29. Springer, Heidelberg (2013). https://doi.org/10.1007/978-3-642-45111-9_2

18. Cheney, E.W.: Introduction to Approximation Theory, pp. 34–45. McGraw-Hill Book Company (1966)
19. Bache, K., Lichman, M.: UCI Machine Learning Repository. University of California, School of Information and Computer Science, Irvine (2013). http://archive.ics.uci.edu/ml
20. http://www.math.nus.edu.sg/~matngtb/Calculus/MA3110/Chapter10WeierstrassApprox-imation.pdf
21. Kuri-Morales, A., Cartas-Ayala, A.: Polynomial multivariate approximation with genetic algorithms. In: Sokolova, M., van Beek, P. (eds.) AI 2014. LNCS (LNAI), vol. 8436, pp. 307–312. Springer, Cham (2014). https://doi.org/10.1007/978-3-319-06483-3_30
22. Moré, J.J.: The Levenberg-Marquardt algorithm: implementation and theory. In: Watson, G. A. (ed.) Numerical Analysis. LNM, vol. 630, pp. 105–116. Springer, Heidelberg (1978). https://doi.org/10.1007/BFb0067700
23. Powell, M.J.D.: A fast algorithm for nonlinearly constrained optimization calculations. In: Watson, G.A. (ed.) Numerical Analysis. LNM, vol. 630, pp. 144–157. Springer, Heidelberg (1978). https://doi.org/10.1007/BFb0067703
24. Liang, K.-Y., Zeger, S.L., Qaqish, B.: Multivariate regression analyses for categorical data. J. R. Stat. Soc. Ser. B (Methodol.) **54**, 3–40 (1992)

Fuzzy Cognitive Maps Reasoning with Words Based on Triangular Fuzzy Numbers

Mabel Frias[1]([⊠]), Yaima Filiberto[1], Gonzalo Nápoles[2],
Yadira García-Socarrás[4], Koen Vanhoof[2], and Rafael Bello[3]

[1] Universidad de Camagüey, Carretera de Circunvalación Norte entre Camino Viejo
de Nuevitas y Ave Ignacio Agramonte, Camagüey, Cuba
{mabel.frias,yaima.filiberto}@reduc.edu.cu
[2] Hasselt Universiteit, Agoralaan gebouw D, Diepenbeek, Belgium
{gonzalo.napoles,koen.vanhoof}@uhasselt.be
[3] Central University of Las Villas, Carretera Camajuaní km 5.5, Santa Clara, Cuba
rbellop@uclv.edu.cu
[4] Universidad de Ciencias Médicas de Camagüey,
Carretera Central Oeste km 4.5 s/n., Camagüey, Cuba
yadipavel@nauta.cu

Abstract. A pivotal difference between Artificial Neural Networks and
Fuzzy Cognitive Maps (FCMs) is that the latter allow modeling a physical system in terms of concepts and causal relations, thus equipping the
network with interpretability features. However, such components are
normally described by quantitative terms, which may be difficult to handle by domain experts. In this paper, we explore a reasoning mechanism
for FCMs based on the Computing with Words paradigm where numerical concepts and relations are replaced with linguistic terms. More explicitly, we include triangular fuzzy numbers into the qualitative reasoning
process attached to our model, thus proving further interpretability and
transparency. The simulations show the potential behind the symbolic
reasoning mechanism proposed in this study.

Keywords: Fuzzy cognitive maps · Computing with Words
Triangular fuzzy number · Chondromalacia

1 Introduction

The reasoning mechanism behind *Fuzzy Cognitive Maps* (FCMs) [12] combines
elements of fuzzy logic, neural networks and causal modeling. Fuzzy cognitive mapping allows modeling a real world system as a collection of concepts
and causal relations [2]. One of the most attractive features attached to these
knowledge-based networks lies in their graphical nature, their transparency and
adaptability and their ability to perform WHAT-IF simulations.

These advantages have motivated the scientific community to use fuzzy cognitive mapping in a wide spectrum of application domains including: social and

© Springer Nature Switzerland AG 2018
F. Castro et al. (Eds.): MICAI 2017, LNAI 10632, pp. 197–207, 2018.
https://doi.org/10.1007/978-3-030-02837-4_16

political sciences, engineering, information technology, robotics, expert systems, education, prediction, environment, medicine, etc. Most of these solutions have a strong social and interdisciplinary scientific value as the study carried out by Nápoles et al. [15], who proposed an FCM-based representation of proteins for modeling the resistance of HIV mutations to existing drugs.

In an FCM, the knowledge is usually expressed by means of numerical values. However, in day-to-day activities, there are situations with imprecise information comprising qualitative aspects that are difficult to evaluate by the use of exact values [11]. Therefore, aiming at expanding the action field of fuzzy cognitive mapping, we combine its graphical nature with natural language techniques to describe both the concepts' activation values and the causal relations between them. In that way, we obtain a qualitative reasoning model.

In the FCM literature, some attempts to accomplish that can be found. For example, in [20] the authors proposed an FCM-model based on Computing with Words (CWW) [25] to improve the interpretability of diagnostic models of cardiovascular diseases. Gónzalez et al. [10] employed a representation model based on linguistic 2-tuple for modeling project portfolio interdependencies. Likewise, Rickard et al. [17] introduced another symbolic model based on interval type-2 fuzzy membership functions and the weighted power mean operator, [7,8,18,19], while Dodurka et al. [9] analyzed the causal effect for fuzzy cognitive maps designed with non-singleton fuzzy numbers.

The use of linguistics terms to describe the whole network moves beyond the knowledge representation; preserving the semantics during the neural inference rule is pivotal towards developing an accurate linguistic model. In this paper, we further explore the hybridization between FCMs and the CWW paradigm where the activation vectors and the weight matrix are described using words. More precisely, we use triangular fuzzy numbers to describe the linguist terms. The numerical simulations using two case studies evidence the potentialities attached to our proposal when operating in qualitative scenarios.

The paper is organized as follows. Section 2 goes over some important concepts concerning to fuzzy cognitive mapping. In the Sect. 3, we provide a brief introduction to Computing with Words, whereas Sect. 4 describes the reasoning model for linguistic FCMs. The simulations are presented in the Sect. 5, while Sect. 6 provides concluding remarks.

2   Fuzzy Cognitive Maps

Fuzzy Cognitive Maps (FCMs) are a kind of recurrent artificial neural networks introduced by Kosko in 1986 [12]. These knowledge-based networks combine elements of fuzzy logic in their representation scheme and elements of neural networks to perform the inference process. Unlike classic neural networks that often operate like black-boxes, both concepts and relations in an FCM network have a precise meaning for the problem being modeled.

The relationship between two concepts are characterized by a signed weight $w_{ij} \in [-1, 1]$ that encloses a causal relationship [13]. The sign of w_{ij} indicates whether the relationship between two concepts C_i and C_j is direct or inverse. These relationships have three possible states: (i) if $w_{ij} > 0$ then there is a *positive causal relationship*, thus suggesting that the first concept positively causes the second one; (ii) if $w_{ij} < 0$ then there is a *negative causal relationship*, which means that the first concept negatively causes the second one; and (iii) if $w_{ij} = 0$ then there is no causal relation between such concepts.

During the reasoning stage, an FCM-based model uses a neural reasoning rule to update the activation values of concepts given a certain activation vector. Equation 1 shows a widely used reasoning rule, where N denotes the number of concepts comprised into the causal network, $A_j^{(t)}$ denotes the activation value of the C_j concept at the current iteration step, w_{ji} is the causal weight to which C_j causes C_i and $f(.)$ is a transfer function that maps the inner product into the activation interval e.g., $f(x) = 1/(1 + e^{-\lambda x})$.

$$A_i^{(t+1)} = f\left(\sum_{j=1}^{N} A_j^{(t)} w_{ji}\right), i \neq j \qquad (1)$$

The above reasoning rule is repeated until either the network converges to a fixed-point attractor or a maximal number of cycles is reached. The former scenario implies that a hidden pattern was discovered [14] whereas the latter suggests that the system outputs are cyclic or chaotic. This iterative reasoning process allows performing WHAT-IF simulations through the modification of the activation values of meaningful processing entities.

3   Computing with Words

The introduction of the *linguistic variable* notion in 1973 by Zadeh opened new research horizons in the field of symbolic reasoning. This notion allows computing words instead of numbers [25] as an alternative to quantitative reasoning models. In general terms, the concept of linguistic variable is used to describe situations that are complex or are not clearly defined in quantitative terms. Moreover, the linguistic variables allow translating natural language into logical or numerical statements that can be effectively computed.

Long story short, *Computing with Words* (CWW) refers to the paradigm devoted to operating words or linguistic terms in order to build reasoning modules with high interpretability. The flexibility of CWW for modeling decision-making situations has boosted the emergence of several linguistic computational models. Some of these models are briefly described next.

– *Linguistic Computational Model based on membership functions.* The linguistic terms are expressed by fuzzy numbers, which are usually described by membership functions. This computational model makes the computations directly on the membership functions of the linguistic terms by using the Extension Principle [6].

$$S^n \xrightarrow{\tilde{F}} F(R) \xrightarrow{app_1(.)} S$$

where S^n symbolizes the n-Cartesian Product, $\tilde{F}$ is an aggregation operator based on the extension principle, $F(R)$ is the set of fuzzy sets over the set of real numbers and $app_1(.)$ is an approximation function that returns a label from the linguistic term set S.

- Linguistic Computational Symbolic Model [5]. This model performs the computation of indexes attached to linguistic terms. Usually, it imposes a linear order to the set of linguistic terms $S = \{S_0, \ldots, S_g\}$ where $S_i < S_j$ if and only if $i < j$. Formally, it can be expressed as:

$$S^n \xrightarrow{R} [0, g] \xrightarrow{app_2(.)} \{0, \ldots, g\} \to S$$

where R is a symbolic linguistic aggregation operator, $app_2(.)$ is an approximation function used to obtain an index $\{0, \ldots, g\}$ associated to a term in $S = \{S_0, \ldots, S_g\}$ from a value in the $[0, g]$ interval.

- The 2-tuple Fuzzy Linguistic Representation Model [11]. The above models perform simple operations with high transparency, but they have a common drawback: the loss of information caused by the need of expressing results in a discrete domain. The 2-tuple model is based on the notion of symbolic translation that allows expressing a domain of linguistic expressions as a continuous universe. This can be formalized as follows:

$$S \xrightarrow{\Delta} (S_i, a_i) \xrightarrow{app_3(.)} (S_i, \alpha_i) \xrightarrow{\Delta^{-1}} S$$

where $S_i \in S$ and $\alpha_i \in [-0.5, 0.5)$, $app_3(.)$ is the aggregation operator for 2-tuples, whereas the functions Δ and Δ^{-1} transform numerical values into a 2-tuples and vice-versa, without losing information.

4   FCM Reasoning Using Triangular Fuzzy Numbers

In this section, we propose a linguistic FCM model that replaces the numerical components of the FCM reasoning (i.e., the concepts' activation values and the causal weights) with linguistic terms. In order to develop an effective linguistic FCM model, two key problems arise: (i) how to multiply two linguistic terms or words, and (ii) how to add the result of this product.

Let us consider the following set of linguistic terms: $S = \{VL/ - VL$ (Very Low), $L/ - L$ (Low), $ML/ - ML$ (Moderate Low), $M/ - M$ (Moderate), $MH/ - MH$ (Moderate High), $H/ - H$ (High), $VH/ - VH$ (Very High), NA (No Activated)$\}$. The negative terms in S will be used only to describe a negative causal weights w_{ij} between two concepts since we are assuming that concept's activation values $C = \{C_1, C_2, \ldots, C_N\}$ are always positive. Figure 1 illustrates the membership functions associated with these terms.

Let us consider a set of linguistic terms S attached to C_i and w_{ji}. Aiming at mapping the product $A_j^{(t)} w_{ji}$ into the CWW model, we consider the operator described in Eq. 2, where $\tau(w_{ji})$ and $\tau(A_i^{(t)})$ are the triangular fuzzy numbers (TFN) [23] for w_{ij} and $A_i^{(t)}$, respectively.

$$I(w_{ji}, A_j^{(t)}) = \tau(w_{ji})\tau(A_j^{(t)}) \tag{2}$$

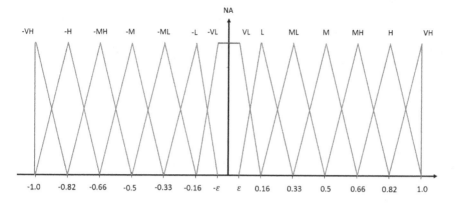

Fig. 1. Linguistic terms and their membership functions.

A triangular fuzzy number may be expressed as follows. Let $\hat{a} = [a^L, a^M, a^U]$, where $a^L \leq a^M \leq a^U$, then $\hat{a}$ is called a TFN, where a^L and a^U stand for the lower and upper values of $\hat{a}$, and a^M is the modal value. There are many papers related to the fuzzy number arithmetic (e.g., [1, 22–24]). In this paper, we adopted the notation introduced by [23] that defines the multiplication between two TFNs $\hat{a} = [a^L, a^M, a^U]$ and $\hat{b} = [b^L, b^M, b^U]$ as follows: $\hat{a} \times \hat{b} = [min(a^L \times b^L, a^L \times b^U, a^U \times b^L, a^U \times b^U), a^M \times b^M, max(a^L \times b^L, a^L \times b^U, a^U \times b^L, a^U \times b^U)]$. Equation 3 displays the aggregation of the N_i linguistic terms impacting the ith concept, which produces a TFN codifying a linguistic term.

$$\tau(C_i^{(t+1)}) = \sum_{j=1}^{N_i} I_j(w_{ji}, A_j^{(t)}) \tag{3}$$

The next step of the proposed symbolic reasoning model for linguistic FCM-based systems is devoted to recovering the linguistic term attached to $\tau(C_i^{(t+1)})$. With this goal in mind, we use the deviation between two TFNs as a distance function [4], which can be defined as follows:

$$\delta(\hat{a}, \hat{b}) = \sqrt{\frac{1}{3}\left[(a^L - b^L)^2 + (a^M - b^M)^2 + (a^U - b^U)^2\right]} \tag{4}$$

Equation 5 displays the reasoning rule for this configuration, which computes the corresponding linguistic term for the ith linguistic concept. This function determines the linguistic term reporting the minimal distance between its TFN and the one resulting from Eq. 3. However, the linguistic term computed in this steps could be defined by a TFN comprising negative values, which is not allowed in our activation model. Aiming at overcoming this issue, we rely on a transfer function for symbolic domains.

$$A_i^{(t+1)} = \arg \min_{S_k \in S}\{\delta(\tau(C_i^{(t+1)}), \tau(S_k))\} \tag{5}$$

Figure 2 shows the transfer function adopted in this paper, which is inspired on the sigmoid function. It should be highlighted that this function ensures computing positive linguistic values for concepts, while causal relations could be described using either positive or negative terms.

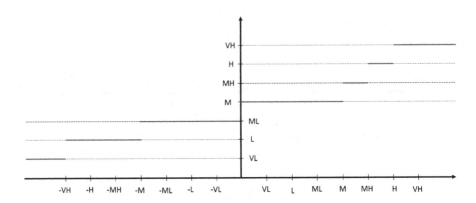

Fig. 2. Transfer function for symbolic domains

In order to show how the model operates, let us consider the FCM displayed in Fig. 3. The activation values of concepts are fixed as follows: $C_1 \leftarrow High(H)$, $C_2 \leftarrow High(H)$, $C_3 \leftarrow Medium(M)$, $C_4 \leftarrow Low(L)$. The goal of this example is to compute the linguistic activation term for the C_5 concept.

Once the concepts have been activated, we can perform the reasoning process as explained above. This implies computing the linguistic activation value A_5 as the result of aggregating the linguistic activation terms attached to concepts C_1–C_4 and their corresponding linguistic weights. Next we illustrate the operations related to one iteration in the symbolic reasoning process:

$$I_1 = \tau(H)\tau(-H) = [0.66, 0.82, 1] * [-1, -0.82, -0.66] = [-1, -0.67, -0.44]$$

$$I_2 = \tau(H)\tau(M) = [0.66, 0.82, 1] * [0.33, 0.5, 0.67] = [0.22, 0.42, 0.66]$$

$$I_3 = \tau(M)\tau(-M) = [0.33, 0.5, 0.67] * [-0.66, -0.5, -0.33] = [-0.44, -0.25, -0.11]$$

$$I_4 = \tau(L)\tau(L) = [0.01, 0.16, 0.33] * [0.01, 0.16, 0.33] = [0.0001, 0.03, 0.003]$$

then,

$$\tau(C_5) = (I_1 + I_2 + I_3 + I_4) = (-1, -0.48, 0.11)$$

$$\delta(\tau(C_5), S_1) = \sqrt{\tfrac{1}{3}\left[(-1+1)^2 + (-0.48+1)^2 + (0.11+0.82)^2\right]} = 0.62$$

$$\vdots$$

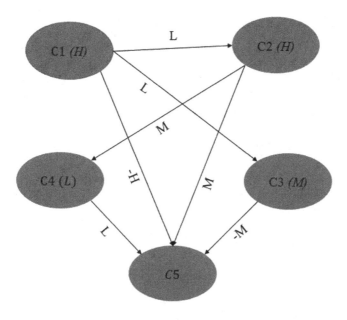

Fig. 3. Linguistic FCM-based system.

$$\delta(\tau(C_5), S_4) = \sqrt{\tfrac{1}{3}\left[(-1+0.66)^2 + (-0.48+0.5)^2 + (0.11+0.33)^2\right]} = 0.32$$

$$\vdots$$

$$\delta(\tau(C_5), S_{15}) = \sqrt{\tfrac{1}{3}\left[(-1+0.82)^2 + (-0.48+1)^2 + (0.11+1)^2\right]} = 1.45$$

$$A_5 = \min\{0.62, 0.49, 0.38, 0.32, 0.34, 0.56, 0.64, 0.64, 0.65,$$

$$0.70, 0.85, 1.01, 1.16, 1.32, 1.45\} = 0.32$$

$$A_5 = \arg\min_{S_k \in S}\{\delta(\tau(C_i^{(t+1)}, \tau(S_k))\} = S_4 = f(-M) = ML.$$

It is worth mentioning that our symbolic FCM-based model preserves its recurrent nature. This implies that the FCM will produce a state vector comprised of linguistic terms at each iteration-step until either a fixed-point is discovered or a maximal number of iterations is reached.

5 Numerical Simulations

In this section, we present two case studies in order to asses the reliability of the proposed symbolic model for FCM-based systems.

5.1   Crime and Punishment

Figure 4 displays the "crime and punishment" case study employed by Cavalho in [3] and Rickard in [17]. This FCM model attempts simulating the effects of various coupled social attributes on the prevalence of theft in a community. Aiming at illustrating how our model works for this case study, we need to transform the numerical weights into linguistic terms. Figure 1 portrays the triangular membership functions associated with the seven linguistic terms defined in S. These functions are regularly used in fuzzy cognitive modeling.

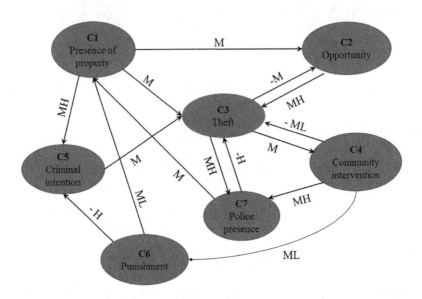

Fig. 4. Crime and punishment FCM model.

The experiments are oriented to calculating the linguistic activation values of each concept according to the proposed model using three simulation scenarios. These simulation scenarios are described as follow:

1. The concepts *Community Intervention* and *Police Presence* are set to VH, while the others are set to VL. For this scenario, the symbolic FCM model converges in three iterations to the state vector:

$$A = [M, M, ML, M, M, L, MH]$$

whereas the linguistic FCM model proposed by Rickard in [17] converges in six iterations to a final state given by:

$$B = [VH, MH, ML, VH, M, VH, VH].$$

2. The concept *Police Presence* is set to VH, whereas the other map concepts are set to VL. For this second simulation scenario, the proposed linguistic FCM converges in three iteration-steps as well:

$$A = [M, M, ML, M, M, L, MH]$$

whereas Rickard's model converges in four iterations to the state:

$$B = [H, M, MH, VL, H, VL, VH].$$

Notice that vectors are similar for key concepts. For example, the proposed linguistic FCM approach frequently converges to states where the activation value of *Theft* is lower than the activation value of *Police Presence*.

5.2 Chondromalacia Presence

The second case study refers to a medical problem that analyzes the effects of different variables (i.e., concepts) leading to the presence of Chondromalacia in a patient. *Chondromalacia patellae* is a medical condition that affects the articular cartilage of the patella. It encompasses a spectrum of clinical severity, ranging from mild fissuring of the articular cartilage to complete cartilage loss and erosion of the underlying subchondral bone. Chondromalacia patellae can be considered a medical condition contained within the patellofemoral pain syndrome [16]. This medical condition has become an active research field for practitioners. For example, Santiago-Santos et al. [21] evaluated the efficacy of hylan GF 20 administered immediately after arthroscopy.

Using the opinion of three experts, we establish the causal relations between variables. Furthermore, we use two scenarios to analyze the activation values of concepts and validate the incidence of a concept to another. Figure 5 shows the linguistic FCM resulting from the experts' consensus.

1. The concepts *Extracellular matrix* and *Weight* are set to M, while *Chondromalacia* is MH, *Cell* is L and *Physical exercises* is H. For this scenario, the linguistic FCM converges to the following state vector:

$$A = [M, L, L, H, L]$$

2. The concept *Chondromalacia* is set to M, whereas the other concepts are set to H. For this second simulation scenario, the proposed linguistic model converges to the following state vector:

$$A = [M, L, L, H, L]$$

The results obtained are compatible with the observations made by experts who indicate that patients with low fissure of the articular cartilage, the presence of chondromalacia is medium. The criterion of experts referred to the need to carry out the study separately of each variable, was corroborated.

We have illustrated the practical advantages of using symbolic expressions to describe the FCM components and its reasoning mechanism, specially when performing WATH-IF simulations. As a result, we obtained a symbolic inference model with improved interpretability features, which is appreciated by users with no background in Mathematics or Computer Science.

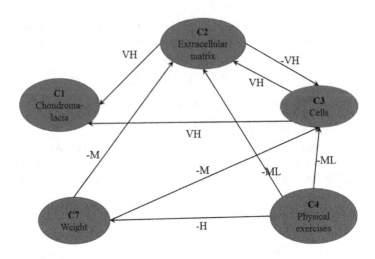

Fig. 5. Chondromalacia FCM model.

6   Conclusions

In this paper, we presented a symbolic reasoning mechanism for linguistic FCM models. In such systems, both the concepts' activation values and the causal weights are described by linguistic terms. In the proposed model, we referred to these terms as the *linguistic activation values* and the *linguistic causal weights*. Aiming at implementing this symbolic approach, we explored the use of triangular fuzzy numbers because of their simple interpretation.

The simulations have shown that our approach is able to computing consistent results. In spite of that, we observed differences on results when compared with the model proposed by Rickard et al. [17]. We could conjecture that these differences may be a result of losing relevant information when processing information on such qualitative models. The lack of flexibility on the definition of triangular fuzzy numbers may also affect the model's accuracy. These issues, however, become a strong motivation towards exploring other alternatives to improve the performance of our model as a future research work.

Acknowledgment. The authors would like to thank Isel Grau (Vrije Universiteit Brussel, Belgium) for her valuable suggestions on the transfer function design.

References

1. Akther, T., Ahmad, S.U.: A computational method for fuzzy arithmetic operations. Daffodil Int. Univ. J. Sci. Technol. **4**(1), 18–22 (2009)
2. Bourgani, E., Stylios, C.D., Georgopoulos, V.C., Manis, G.: A study on fuzzy cognitive map structures for medical decision support systems. In: 8th Conference of the European Society for Fuzzy Logic and Technology (EUSFLAT 2013) (2013)
3. Carvalho, J.: On the semantics and the use of fuzzy cognitive maps and dynamic cognitive maps in social sciences. Fuzzy Sets Syst. **214**, 6–19 (2013)

4. Chen, C.: Extension of the topsis for group decision-making under fuzzy environment. Fuzzy Sets Syst. **114**, 1–9 (2000)
5. Delgado, M., Verdegay, J.L., Vila, M.A.: On aggregation operations of linguistic labels. Int. J. Intell. Syst. **8**, 351–370 (1993)
6. Dubois, D., Prade, H.: Fuzzy Sets and Systems: Theory and Applications. Academic, New York (1980)
7. Dujmovic, J.: Continuous preference logic for system evaluation. IEEE Trans. Fuzzy Syst. **15**(6), 1082–1099 (2007)
8. Dujmovic, J., Larsen, H.: Generalized conjunction/disjunction. Int. J. Approx. Reason. **46**, 423–446 (2007)
9. Dodurka, M.F., Yesil, E., Urbas, L.: Causal effect analysis for fuzzy cognitive maps designed with non-singleton fuzzy numbers. Neurocomputing **232**, 122–132 (2017)
10. Gónzalez, M.P., Rosa, C.G.B.D.L., Moran, F.J.C.: Fuzzy cognitive maps and computing with words for modeling project portfolio risks interdependencies. Int. J. Innov. Appl. Stud. **15**(4), 737–742 (2016)
11. Herrera, F., Martínez, L.: A 2-tuple fuzzy linguistic representation model for computing with words. IEEE Trans. Fuzzy Syst. **8**(6), 746–752 (2000)
12. Kosko, B.: Fuzzy cognitive maps. Int. J. Man-Mach. Stud. **24**, 65–75 (1986)
13. Kosko, B.: Neural Networks and Fuzzy Systems, a Dynamic System Approach to Machine Intelligence. Prentice Hall, Englewood Cliffs (1992)
14. Kosko, B.: Hidden patterns in combined and adaptive knowledge networks. Int. J. Approx. Reason. **2**(4), 377–393 (1988)
15. Nápoles, G., Grau, I., Bello, R., Grau, R.: Two-steps learning of fuzzy cognitive maps for prediction and knowledge discovery on the HIV-1 drug resistance. Expert Syst. Appl. **41**(3), 821–830 (2014)
16. Ramírez Sánchez, K.T.: Condromalacia rutinaria. Revista Médica de Costa Rica y Centroamerica LXXI, pp. 551–553 (2014)
17. Rickard, J.T., Aisbett, J., Yager, R.R.: Computing with words in fuzzy cognitive maps. In: Proceedings of the World Conference on Soft Computing, pp. 1–6 (2015)
18. Rickard, J., Aisbett, J., Yager, R., Gibbon, G.: Fuzzy weighted power means in evaluation decisions. In: 1st World Symposium on Soft Computing (2010)
19. Rickard, J., Aisbett, J., Yager, R., Gibbon, G.: Linguistic weighted power means: comparison with the linguistic weighted average. In: IEEE International Conference on Fuzzy Systems (FUZZ-IEEE 2011), pp. 2185–2192 (2011)
20. Saleh, S.H., Rivas, S.D.L., Gomez, A.M.M., Mohsen, F.S., Vzquez, M.L.: Representación del conocimiento mediante mapas cognitivos difusos y conjuntos de términos lingüisticos difusos dudosos en la biomedicina. Int. J. Innov. Appl. Stud. **17**(1), 312–319 (2016)
21. Santiago-Santos, A., Blancas-Vargas, M.E., Silva-Escobedo, J.G.: Eficacia del hilano g-f 20 aplicado en dosis única intraarticular posterior a artroscopia en el tratamiento del sndrome de dolor patelo-femoral. Rev Sanid Milit Mex **69**, 301–308 (2015)
22. Su, W., Peng, W., Zeng, S., Pen, B., Pand, T.: A method for fuzzy group decision making based on induced aggregation operators and euclidean distance. Int. Trans. Oper. Res. **20**, 579–594 (2013)
23. Van, L., Pedrycz, W.: A fuzzy extension of Saaty's priority theory. Fuzzy Sets Syst. **11**, 229–241 (1983)
24. Xu, Z.: Fuzzy harmonic mean operators. Int. J. Intell. Syst. **24**, 152–172 (2009)
25. Zadeh, L.A.: Outline of a new approach to the analysis of complex systems ad decision processes. IEEE Trans. Syst. Man Cybern. SMC **3**(1), 28–44 (1973)

A Fuzzy Approach for Recommending Problems to Solve in Programming Online Judges

Raciel Yera[1]([⊠]) and Yailé Caballero[2]

[1] University of Ciego de Ávila, Ciego de Ávila, Cuba
yeratoledo@gmail.com
[2] University of Camagüey, Camagüey, Cuba

Abstract. Programming online judges are e-learning tools usually used in programming practices for the automatic evaluation of source code developed by students, for solving programming problems. Specifically, they contain a large collection of such problems where the students, at their own personalized pace, have to select and try to solve. Therefore, the increasing of the number of problems makes difficult the selection of the right problem to solve according to the previous users performance, causing information overload and a widespread discouragement. The current contribution proposes a recommendation approach to mitigate this issue by suggesting problems to solve in programming online judges, through the use of fuzzy tools which manage the uncertainty related to this scenario. The proposal evaluation, using real data obtained from a programming online judge, shows that the new approach improves previous recommendation strategies which do not consider uncertainty management in the programming online judge scenarios.

Keywords: Programming online judges · Fuzzy logic
Problems recommendation

1 Introduction

Programming online judges (POJs) are currently popular software tools in computer science careers and in the students' training for ACM-ICPC-like programming contests [3,4,11]. Specifically, they contain a large collection of programming problems to be solved, and their main feature is that POJs automate the evaluation process of the solutions. Such motivating feature has attracted a worldwide attention in POJs, having as some successful examples of the development and use of this kind of applications, the Peking University Online Judge (600000+ users, 3000+ problems), the University of Valladolid Online Judge (210000+ users, 1700+ problems), and the Caribbean Online Judge (3000+ users, 3400+ problems).

Basically, POJs continuously present to the users a sequential list of programming problems to be solved [3]. The individuals have then to choose and

© Springer Nature Switzerland AG 2018
F. Castro et al. (Eds.): MICAI 2017, LNAI 10632, pp. 208–220, 2018.
https://doi.org/10.1007/978-3-030-02837-4_17

try to solve at their personalized pace the problems they consider. Once some problem's solution is completed, the POJ allows the uploading of the associated source code, which is automatically evaluated as correct or incorrect. Afterwards, the POJ arranges users according to the amount of solved problems, being the top ranked users those with the bigger amount of solved problems. It has been demonstrated by several authors such as Regueras [9] that this competitive nature has a positive influence in the students motivation in programming subjects, in contrast to the typical programming practices that do not contain a well-defined incentive mechanism.

The increasing popularity of POJs has caused that many users are strongly interested in performing an active participation in POJs in order to evaluate and prove their programming skills [11]. In addition, this acceptance has also implied an increment in the number of available problems to be solved. Therefore, it is becoming to be difficult, both for the novice and the expert users, the identification of the appropriate problems where they have more opportunities to solve them, according to their knowledge levels. This issue implies a high discouragement and frustration in the users, missing in several cases the initial interest on the POJ.

In the context of e-learning tools, such kind of problems related to the users guiding through the learning content, is typically faced with very traditional approaches such as Intelligent Tutoring Systems (ITSs) [8] or ontologies-supported solutions [7]. However, these approaches require structured and detailed information related to the corresponding application domain, in order to build a precise user model, which is used for the further guiding across content. Such information is missing in the case of the context of POJs, regarding that they are only available the users attempts when they try to solve the proposed problems [3]. Therefore, in this context it is necessary to use more general-purposed tools, beyond the specific ITSs or ontologies.

In this way, recommender systems have been converting in the last few years in a typical tool for providing users with the information items that best match their preferences and needs in a search space composed of possible options [6]. Such solutions have been successfully employed in diverse context such as e-commerce, e-learning, e-services, or social networks [6]. Therefore, the current research work will make use of several principles taken for the recommender systems research field, to propose an uncertainty-aware framework for suggesting problems to solve in POJs, supporting students in the identification of those problems they are able to solve according to their knowledge level, avoiding failures and frustration.

The contribution of the paper is twofold:

- A fuzzy logic-based framework for suggesting problems to solve in Programming Online Judges.
- The proposal of a data preprocessing method to be applied over the POJ data as a previous step, for improving the recommendation accuracy associated to the fuzzy logic-based framework.

A key feature of this framework is the management of fuzzy information in a recommender system scenario. The use of fuzzy tools in recommender systems has been recently identified as a hot research area that needs further development [14]. Therefore, the current contribution shows how a flexible management of the vague information associated to POJs, leads to the improvement of the recommendation generation in this scenario.

The contribution is structured as follows. Section 2 presents the necessary background for the current research, including programming online judges, recommender systems, and recommender systems in POJs scenarios. Section 3 presents the new proposal, using fuzzy logic, for problems recommendation in POJs. Furthermore, it proposes its integration with a data preprocessing approach for removing anomalous behaviors in the users' data. Section 4 develops the experimental evaluation of the proposal. Finally, Sect. 5 concludes the contribution.

2   Background

This section provides the required background for the posterior proposal presentation. It is composed of brief references to programming online judges, recommender systems, and the application of recommender systems in POJ scenarios.

2.1   Programming Online Judges

POJs are typically web applications that contain a large list of programming problems to be solved. Usually, any user can enter to the system and try to solve the problem he/she consider. Once the source code needed to solve the selected problem is completed, it is uploaded to the POJ. Immediately, this code is evaluated through previously predefined input-output data. If the code retrieves the required output for all cases, then the solution is *accepted* and the problem is considered as solved. Otherwise, if the output was not the expected one, then the POJ could give different judgments according to the kind of failure (e.g. Time Limit Exceeded, Runtime Error, or Wrong Answer). Finally, if the problem was not successfully solved, it can be attempted again as many times as the user considers it.

Several authors have reported their experiences with online judges for supporting programming subjects. One of the first references to POJs was performed by Kurnia et al. [3], where they are presented as useful tools for the evaluation of source codes written by the students. Beyond this pioneer work, the development of such kind of applications has been subsequently continued, reaching more portable solutions that could be also used on-the-fly in programming contests [4], and more recently with the addition of new administration facilities [5]. In parallel, it has been documented the integration of a POJ with the Moodle learning management system [10], and recently it has been proposed and evaluated the direct incorporation of a POJ inside a course of Foundations of Programming [11].

The previous developments suggest the interest of several researchers in the expansion of POJs as a relevant e-learning tool. As it was pointed out in the previous section, the aim of the current proposal is the development of an approach to suggest problems to solve in programming online judges, through the use of fuzzy tools, and assuming that the users' goal in POJs is to solve the larger amount of problems.

2.2 Recommender Systems

Recommender systems are software tools focused on providing users the information that best fits their preferences and needs, in a search space overloaded with possible options. According to their working principle, they can be grouped in two big families: the content-based recommendation approaches, and the collaborative filtering-based recommendation approaches [6].

Content-based approaches [6] typically manage big volumes of information, and they are basically focused on the use of such information for composing items profiles, for building the users profiles, and finally generating the recommendations according to the matching degree between the users' and items' profiles.

In contrast, collaborative filtering (CF) [6] is able to generate recommendations even in the presence of a small information source, basically regarding that the recommendations are generated by exploring the profile of the current user, together with the profile of the top similar users. Specifically, there are two groups of CF approaches: the memory-based, explicitly focused on the similarity between users for the recommendation generation, and the model-based, focused on learning a predictive model using all the available data, being used later in the recommendation generation task.

Although the memory-based collaborative filtering approaches have been used since several years ago, currently they are the basis of several new recommendation algorithms, because of their simplicity, justifiability, efficiency, and stability [6]. For such reasons, the proposal developed at the current contribution will follow this recommendation paradigm.

2.3 Recommender Systems in POJs Scenarios

In the last few years, they have been developed some previous efforts focused on incorporating recommender systems in a POJ scenario.

An early documented experience on the use of a recommendation approach in POJs was presented by Yera and Caballero [12], where they use a basic user-based collaborative filtering approach for suggesting problems to solve considering binary information. Specifically, they perform this task by considering the problems solved and not solved by those users which are similar to the current one. This proposal is evaluated through the use of real data associated to a POJ, proving its effectiveness in the recommendation of problems that were, at last, finally solved by the users.

Recently, Yera and Martínez [15] presented a new approach focused on a deeper characterization of the user profiles by considering, in addition to the solved or not solved problems, also the number of previous failed attempts needed for the final successful or unsuccessful problem solution. Therefore, it considers that each problem could be solved with more or less user's effort, and also that each unsolved problem can have previously attracted more or less effort, by the corresponding user. Such information is included as a component of the user profile, leading to an improvement in the final recommendation generation. Additionally, this approach also includes a data preprocessing step to remove anomalous users behaviors that could affect the recommendation accuracy.

Although the mentioned research works present an incipient but successful framework for the recommendation of problems to solve in Programming Online Judges, they suffer as a major issue the lack of reliability and flexibility of the user profiling, regarding that it is based on crisp models. Therefore, the current contribution presents a new approach focused on a more flexible and precise management of the user profile, through the use of fuzzy logic tools for supporting the recommendation tasks [14]. Additionally, it is proposed a new data preprocessing approach for this scenario, which fits well with the new fuzzy logic-based approach.

The performance of these new approaches is compared with previous proposals already mentioned in this section, and focused on the same research task.

3   Problems Recommendation in Programming Online Judges Using Fuzzy Tools

This section presents the fuzzy logic-based recommendation framework for programming online judges. At first, Sect. 3.1 presents the core approach for the problems recommendation generation. Complementary, Sect. 3.2 presents a data preprocessing strategy to be integrated with such approach, for removing inconsistent users' behavior.

3.1   A Fuzzy Approach for Recommendation in Programming Online Judges

In a similar way to previous recommendation approaches in POJs, the current proposal receives as input the past performances of all the registered users, i.e. a set of triplets $<u, p, j>$, each one representing an attempt of the user u for solving the problem p, receiving as verdict the judgment j, which could be *accepted* if the problem was successfully solved, or *not accepted*, if not. In the current work it will not be considered the several kinds of failures mentioned in Sect. 2.

In order to transform these initial data in a suitable format for the proposal presentation, they are converted in two matrices M and F with dimensions n_u x n_p, being n_u and n_p the number of users and problems. These matrices respectively represent the judgments and the number of failures of each user, trying to solve each problem. Specifically, $M[u, p] = 1$ if the user u has successfully solved the problem p, and $M[u, p] = 0$ otherwise. For the F matrix, $F[u, p]$ will represent the amount of solution attempts the user u has tried over the problem p, disregarding if it was finally solved or not.

Considering these two matrix, it is proposed a memory-based collaborative filtering approach to suggest problems to solve. The approach is composed by the following steps, which will be subsequently detailed.

- Matrix F fuzzy transformation
- Neighborhood calculation for the current user
- Top n recommendation generation.

Matrix F Fuzzy Transformation. In order to provide flexibility to the representation of the interaction between any user u and problem p, it is considered the fuzzy set *many attempts* (*many* in the following), which is represented through the membership function presented in Fig. 1. As it is typically considered in this kind of fuzzy modeling, it is very difficult the predefined initialization for the parameter t in the figure; therefore, its optimal values will be analyzed as part of the experimental section.   Considering this fuzzy set, the matrix F containing

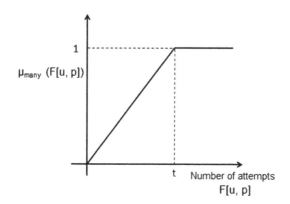

Fig. 1. Membership function for the fuzzy set *many*.

the number of failures for each user, is transformed into a new matrix F^* which contains the membership values of such kind of failures, according to the fuzzy set many. (Equation 1)

$$F^*[u, p] = \mu_{many}(F[u, p]) \tag{1}$$

This transformed matrix F^* will be actively used in the next step of the proposal.

Neighborhood Calculation for the Current User. In order to obtain such neighborhood for a current user, at first it is necessary to consider the set $C_{u,v}$ of problems which solutions have been attempted (successfully or unsuccessfully), by each pair of users u and v. (Equation 2).

$$C_{u,v} = \{set\ of\ problems\ where\ F^*[u, p] > 0\ and\ F^*[v, p] > 0\} \tag{2}$$

Afterwards, it is defined the similarity $SimProb_p(u, v)$ between the users u and v according to a specific problem p, taking as basis the absolute difference between the membership values in the F^* matrix, for both users at the problem p. Specifically, it will be considered for those problems located in the set $C_{u,v}$, and which have the same final verdict for both users ($M[u, p] = M[v, p]$). In other cases, the value of $SimProb_p(u, v)$ will be zero. Equation 3 formalizes this similarity function.

$$SimProb_p(u, v) = \begin{cases} 1 - abs(F^*[u, p] - F^*[v, p]), if \ M[u, p] = M[v, p] \\ \qquad\qquad\qquad and \text{ problem } p \text{ is in } C_{u,v} \\ 0, \text{otherwise} \end{cases} \quad (3)$$

Finally, the global similarity between two users u and v is calculated as the average value for all the $SimProb_p(u, v)$ values, considering all the problems p in the set $C_{u,v}$ (Eq. 4).

$$Sim(u, v) = \frac{\sum_{p \in C_{u,v}} SimProb_p(u, v)}{|C_{u,v}|} \quad (4)$$

This similarity function will be used by the current proposal, for finding the top k nearest neighbors for a current user u, to suggest him/her problems to solve.

Top n Recommendation Generation. Once the similarity values between certain user u and the remaining users are calculated, the users with the top k higher values are employed to calculate a score w_p for each problem p not solved by u, as the sum of the similarities of u with the neighbors that solve p (Eq. 5). At last, the top n problems p with the highest scores w_p are recommended to the active user u.

$$w_p = \sum_{v \in \ top\_k(u)} Sim(u, v) \quad (5)$$

In the experimental section it will be considered the behavior of this approach across several sizes of the recommendation list.

3.2 Integrating the Fuzzy Approach with a Data Preprocessing Method

This section proposes the application of a simple but effective data preprocessing approach, to be used over the users' data as a previous step before the execution of the fuzzy approach presented in the previous section.

It is worthy to note that the previous antecedents to this approach, also focused on preprocessing programming online judge's data [15], cannot be applied in the proposal presented in the previous section because such previous contributions, work on discrete categories that characterize users' interactions in relation to problems. In contrast, the current proposal does not include any discretization process on such interactions (users' attempts). Instead, it uses fuzzy tools for dealing with the original POJ data. Therefore, it is necessary to consider other data preprocessing strategies that could be coupled to this new approach presented in the previous section.

With this purpose in mind, as a traditional data preprocessing approach, in this work it will be considered the outliers detection over the amount of users attempts, trying to solve a specific problem. Specifically, for each user, it will be identified those problems where the amount of attempts is out of the range $[\alpha * (x_u - dev_u); \alpha * (x_u + dev_u)]$, being x_u the average number of attempts for user u and dev_u the average deviation of such attempts. In addition, it is considered the coefficient α for adding some flexibility to the definition of the range.

For the problems that fall out of this range, their associated amount of attempts is replaced by x_u (Eq. 9). We name this strategy as the *global* data preprocessing approach:

$$Attempted_u = \{set\ of\ problems\ p\ attempted\ by\ user\ u,\ i.e.,\ verifying\ F[u,p] > 0\}$$
$$(6)$$

$$x_u = \frac{\sum_{p \in Attempted_u} F[u,p]}{|Attempted_u|}$$
$$(7)$$

$$dev_u = \frac{\sum_{p \in Attempted_u} abs(F[u,p] - x_u)}{|Attempted_u|}$$
$$(8)$$

$$p \in Attempted_u\ and\ F[u,p] \notin [\alpha * (x_u - dev_u); \alpha * (x_u + dev_u)] \quad \rightarrow \quad F[u,p] = x_u$$
$$(9)$$

As second, it will be considered an *evaluation-based* data preprocessing strategy, where the outliers detection is performed independently at first for the set of accepted problems, and at second for the set of problems attempted but finally not solved. Here, for each user two pairs are defined: 1) a pair $[\alpha * (x_u^s - dev_u^s); \alpha * (x_u^s + dev_u^s)]$ characterizing accepted problems, and a pair $[\alpha * (x_u^f - dev_u^f); \alpha * (x_u^f + dev_u^f)]$ characterizing problems attempted but failed. Here the parameter α is also used with the same purpose in relation to the previous strategy:

$$Solved_u = \{problems\ p\ solved\ by\ user\ u,\ i.e., verifying\ M[u,p] = 1\} \quad (10)$$

$$Failed_u = \{problems\ p\ failed\ by\ user\ u,\ i.e., verifying\ M[u,p] = 0\ and\ F[u,p] > 0\}$$
$$(11)$$

$$x_u^s = \frac{\sum_{p \in Solved_u} F[u,p]}{|Solved_u|}$$
$$(12)$$

$$dev_u^s = \frac{\sum_{p \in Solved_u} abs(F[u,p] - x_u^s)}{|Solved_u|}$$
$$(13)$$

$$x_u^f = \frac{\sum_{p \in Failed_u} F[u,p]}{|Failed_u|} \qquad (14)$$

$$dev_u^f = \frac{\sum_{p \in Failed_u} abs(F[u,p] - x_u^f)}{|Failed_u|} \qquad (15)$$

Afterwards, if an accepted problem p falls out of the range $[\alpha * (x_u^s - dev_u^s); \alpha * (x_u^s + dev_u^s)]$, for recommendation purposes, its amount of previous failures is replaced by x_u^s (Eq. 16). On the other hand, if the problem was attempted but failed, and its amount of failures is out of the range $[\alpha * (x_u^f - dev_u^f); \alpha * (x_u^f + dev_u^f)]$, then it is replaced by x_u^f, for recommendation purposes (Eq. 17). Both conditions are checked for all the users in the POJ dataset.

$$p \in Solved_u \text{ and } F[u,p] \notin [\alpha * (x_u^s - dev_u^s); \alpha * (x_u^s + dev_u^s)] \quad \rightarrow \quad F[u,p] = x_u^s$$
$$(16)$$

$$p \in Failed_u \text{ and } F[u,p] \notin [\alpha * (x_u^f - dev_u^f); \alpha * (x_u^f + dev_u^f)] \quad \rightarrow \quad F[u,p] = x_u^f$$
$$(17)$$

4   Experimental Study

In a similar way to previous works focused on recommending problems to solve in programming online judges [12,15], the evaluation of the current proposal is performed by using a dataset obtained from the Caribbean Online Judge, composed of 1910 users, 584 problems, and around 148000 user attempts.

Considering this dataset, the training and test sets were created according to Gunawardana and Shani [2] by randomly splitting all the solved problems for each user, in two sets adding one of them to the training set and the other one to the test set. The current proposal also needs the information related with the unsuccessful attempts, consequently such information is stored independently and used as input for each evaluation.

The current experimental study will use F1 for evaluating the generated recommendations, being a popular evaluation criteria for the top n recommendation generation task [2]. F1 is calculated in terms of Precision (based on the amount of recommended problems that were solved), and Recall (based on the amount of solved problems that were recommended).

Specifically, the evaluation protocol is developed by generating a list of recommended problems for each user, considering the data in the training set. This list, together with the solved problems at the test set, are used for getting the F1 value for each user. At last, the global F1 value is calculated by averaging the F1 values obtained for each user. This procedure is repeated ten times, obtaining the definitive F1 values presented later in this section, as the average of the ten obtained F1 values.

The current proposal depends on three main parameters:

- The amount of k nearest neighbors: Here it will be used $k = 80$, considering that it is a value previously used in related works such as [12]. As a further work beyond the current contribution, it would be worthy to explore the behavior of the proposal for other values of k.
- The value of t, in the fuzzy membership function presented in Fig. 1. Here it will be considered $t = 4$, $t = 5$, and $t = 6$. Further experiments were developed considering other values, but their performances were under the associated to the mentioned ones.
- The value of α in the data preprocessing strategy. In order to verify if the flexibility in the definition of the interval for the outliers characterization brings positive results, it will be considered $\alpha = 1$ (no flexibility), and $\alpha = 0.8$ (a small flexibility, considering correct values to some small amounts of attempts treated as outliers by $\alpha = 1$).

The current experiments have two main objectives: **(1)** Determine whether the fuzzy recommendation approach outperforms previous approaches that do not consider the management of the uncertainty associated to POJ data, and **(2)** Determine the effect of proposed data preprocessing strategy, in contrast to previous approaches that also consider data preprocessing in this scenario. For both cases, it will considered as size of the recommendation list, the values n in the range [5, 30] with step 5.

Objective 1. In order to accomplish this objective, we compare the accuracy (F1) of the current proposal, in relation to the proposals presented by Yera and Caballero [12], and Yera and Martínez [15], in the last case without considering the data preprocessing step. As it was explained before, for the current proposal it was considered $t = 4$, $t = 5$, and $t = 6$ as possible values of the parameter t. Table 1 shows the results of this comparison. As it was expected the performance associated to the new proposal is similar or better than the related to the previous approaches. Specifically, the more notable improvements were obtained for $n = 5$. However, for larger values of n the improvement becomes modest in relation to Yera and Martínez [15]. Furthermore, the best results of the proposal were obtained for $t = 6$ and $t = 5$, leaving for $t = 4$ a lower accuracy value.

Table 1. Comparison between the current proposal and previous approaches, without considering data preprocessing

	5	10	15	20	25	30
Yera and Caballero [12]	0.3568	0.3694	0.3555	0.3389	0.3237	0.3073
Yera and Martínez [15], no preproc	0.3613	0.3738	0.3610	0.3449	0.3277	0.3121
Current (t = 6)	**0.3663**	0.3738	0.3600	0.3448	0.3281	**0.3122**
Current (t = 5)	0.3640	**0.3741**	**0.3613**	**0.3452**	**0.3286**	0.3121
Current (t = 4)	0.3625	0.3727	0.3607	0.3446	0.3279	0.3114

Objective 2. To accomplish this objective it will be considered the use of the data preprocessing strategy previously presented in the current scenario, in order

to clean the original data and therefore improve the recommendation accuracy. With this aim in mind, it will be considered the values of t and α previously mentioned in this section, together with the two data preprocessing schemes explained in the previous section (global and evaluation-based). The analysis of the presented results (Table 2), at first concludes that for small sizes of the recommendation list the proposal introduces an improvement in the recommendation accuracy (e.g., for $n = 5$, the F1 value for the proposal was 0.3667, while for the previous work was 0.3615). However, for larger sizes ($n > 20$) the improvements become more modest. An exception for this behavior was for $n = 10$, where the current proposal does not outperform Yera and Martínez [15]. However, the associated behavior keeps close to such previous work.

Table 2. Comparison between the current proposal and previous approaches, considering data preprocessing

	5	10	15	20	25	30
Yera and Martínez [15]	0.3615	**0.3758**	0.3619	0.3438	0.3280	0.3120
Current ($t = 6$, $\alpha = 1$, global)	0.3652	0.3745	0.3607	0.3449	0.3288	0.3124
Current ($t = 5$, $\alpha = 1$, global)	0.3652	0.3744	0.3604	0.3446	0.3285	0.3121
Current ($t = 4$, $\alpha = 1$, global)	0.3643	0.3742	0.3612	0.3444	0.3288	0.3116
Current ($t = 6$, $\alpha = 0.8$, global)	0.3649	0.3754	0.3624	0.3450	**0.3291**	**0.3126**
Current ($t = 5$, $\alpha = 0.8$, global)	0.3649	0.3750	0.3614	**0.3453**	0.3289	0.3123
Current($t = 4$, $\alpha = 0.8$, global)	0.3640	0.3738	0.3606	0.3448	0.3288	0.3123
Current($t = 6$, $\alpha = 1$, eval-based)	0.3633	0.3744	**0.3626**	0.3451	0.3280	0.3123
Current ($t = 5$, $\alpha = 1$, eval-based)	0.3649	0.3753	0.3609	0.3442	0.3273	0.3122
Current($t = 4$, $\alpha = 1$, eval-based)	0.3662	0.3739	0.3611	0.3446	0.3275	0.3121
Current ($t = 6$, $\alpha = 0.8$, eval-based)	0.3659	0.3751	0.3620	0.3446	0.3279	0.3120
Current ($t = 5$, $\alpha = 0.8$, eval-based)	0.3644	0.3735	0.3601	0.3436	0.3274	0.3115
Current ($t = 4$, $\alpha = 0.8$, eval-based)	**0.3667**	0.3747	0.3605	0.3433	0.3268	0.3115

Additionally, it is worthy to note that although for higher values of n the best performance was obtained for the global strategy for $t = 6$ and $\alpha = 0.8$; for smaller values (where the improvement is more relevant), it is not a specific execution scenario that leads to the achievement of the best F1 values. Here, the best performance was obtained for the evaluation-based strategy with $t = 4$ and $\alpha = 0.8$ (in $n = 5$), with $t = 6$ and $\alpha = 1$ (in $n = 15$), and for the global strategy with $t = 5$ and $\alpha = 0.8$ in $n = 20$.

Globally, as an unexpected finding, it was detected that the most sophisticated data preprocessing strategy (the evaluation-based), does not necessarily lead to the reaching of a best recommendation accuracy. In fact, only for two of the six sizes considered for the recommendation list (values of n), the evaluation-based strategy outperforms the global strategy. Further works are needed in the next future to identify the reasons of this behavior.

Beyond such findings, Table 2 suggests that the use of techniques for preprocessing the data in the current POJ scenario, could improve the recommendation accuracy in a similar way to the improvement associated to other preprocessing approaches for recommendation scenarios [1,13].

5 Conclusions

This contribution exploits fuzzy logic tools for proposing an approach to recommend problems to solve in programming online judges. This approach is complemented with a data preprocessing strategy to correct anomalous users' behavior. The experimental results show that both the fuzzy approach and the data preprocessing strategy lead to improvements in the recommendation accuracy, in relation to previous works. A relevant advantage of the contribution is the management of the uncertainty associated to the POJ scenario, not performed previously as far as we know. However, it could be still identified some shortcomings related to the computational complexity of the nearest neighbors algorithms. Therefore, future works will be focused on exploring the use of alternative recommendation techniques in the POJs scenario, such as rule-based recommendation, that would allow a balance between recommendation accuracy, efficiency, diversity, and transparency.

References

1. Castro, J., Yera, R., Martínez, L.: An empirical study of natural noise management in group recommendation systems. Decis. Support Syst. **94**, 1–11 (2017)
2. Gunawardana, A., Shani, G.: A survey of accuracy evaluation metrics of recommendation tasks. J. Mach. Learn. Res. **10**, 2935–2962 (2009)
3. Kurnia, A., Lim, A., Cheang, B.: Online judge. Comput. Educ. **36**(4), 299–315 (2001)
4. Leal, J.P. and Silva, F.: Mooshak: a web-based multi-site programming contest system. Softw.: Pract. Exp. **33**(6), 567–581 (2003)
5. Llana, L., Martin-Martin, E., Pareja-Flores, C., Velázquez-Iturbide, J.: FLOP: a user-friendly system for automated program assessment. J. Univ. Comput. Sci. **20**(9), 1304–1326 (2014)
6. Jie, L., Dianshuang, W., Mao, M., Wang, W., Zhang, G.: Recommender system application developments: a survey. Decis. Support Syst. **74**, 12–32 (2015)
7. Miranda, S., Orciuoli, F., Sampson, D.G.: A SKOS-based framework for subject ontologies to improve learning experiences. Comput. Hum. Behav. **61**, 609–621 (2016)
8. Polson, M.C., Richardson, J.J. Foundations of Intelligent Tutoring Systems. Psychology Press (2013)
9. Regueras, L.M., et al.: Effects of competitive e-learning tools on higher education students: a case study. IEEE Trans. Educ. **52**(2), 279–285 (2009)
10. Verdú, E., Regueras, L.M., Verdú, M.J., Leal, J.P., de Castro, J.P., Queirós, R.: A distributed system for learning programming on-line. Comput. Educ. **58**(1), 1–10 (2012)
11. Wang, G.P., Chen, S.Y., Yang, X., Feng, R.: OJPOT: online judge & practice oriented teaching idea in programming courses. Eur. J. Eng. Educ. **41**(3), 304–319 (2016)

12. Toledo, R.Y., Mota, Y.C.: An e-learning collaborative filtering approach to suggest problems to solve in programming online judges. Int. J. Distance Educ. Technol. **12**(2), 51–65 (2014)
13. Toledo, R.Y., Mota, Y.C., Borroto, M.G.: A regularity-based preprocessing method for collaborative recommender systems. J. Inf. Process. Syst. **9**(3), 435–460 (2013)
14. Yera, R., Martínez, L.: Fuzzy tools in recommender systems: a survey. Int. J. Comput. Intell. Syst. **10**(1), 776–803 (2017)
15. Yera, R., Martínez, L.: A recommendation approach for programming online judges supported by data preprocessing techniques. Appl. Intell. **47**(2), 277–290 (2017)

A Fuzzy-Based Approach for Selecting Technically Qualified Distributed Software Development Teams

Vinicius Souza and Gledson Elias$^{(\boxtimes)}$

Informatics Center, Federal University of Paraíba, João Pessoa, Paraíba, Brazil
vinicius@compose.ufpb.br, gledson@ci.ufpb.br

Abstract. In Distributed Software Development, the cooperation among globally distributed development teams can reduce development cost and time. However, such benefits can only be achieved with teams that hold the specific technical background required to implement software modules. As a consequence, it is a key task to contrast technical background possessed by development teams against specified technical requirements expected to implement the various software project modules, making possible to identify the more skilled teams to develop each software module. In such a context, this paper proposes, implements and evaluates a fuzzy-based approach to support selection processes of distributed development teams, which are technically skilled to implement software modules in distributed software projects. As the main contribution, experimental results show that the proposed approach represents and formalizes an extremely complex problem in a systematic and structured way, allowing its direct or customized adoption in selection processes of globally distributed development teams.

Keywords: Fuzzy logic · Global software development · Selection process

1 Introduction

The software engineering field has accumulated a great body of knowledge over the last decades concerning methods, techniques, processes and tools, which improves productivity and software quality. In such a direction, several software development approaches have been proposed by academia and industry. As one of the most promising approaches, *Distributed Software Development* (DSD) promotes the adoption of globally distributed teams for the development of different software product modules, reducing the development cost and time, favored by the option of hiring cheaper staff in different locations, the faster formation of development teams and the adoption of the follow-the-sun development strategy [1, 2]. In addition, DSD enables to find qualified workforces and domain experts in outsourced teams or even teams in global coverage companies, in which there can be subsidiaries spread worldwide [3–5].

Consequently, in order to achieve the DSD benefits, it is a key task to identify development teams with specific skills and technical knowledge required to develop the various software modules that constitute the software products. In such a context, it is

F. Castro et al. (Eds.): MICAI 2017, LNAI 10632, pp. 221–235, 2018.
https://doi.org/10.1007/978-3-030-02837-4_18

of fundamental importance to contrast the skills and technical knowledge of the candidate development teams against the technical requirements specified to implement each module of the software product, making possible to identify those that are more qualified to implement each module.

However, regarding the geographic dispersion involved in DSD projects, it becomes quite difficult for the project manager to assess the skills and technical knowledge of the candidate development teams, since in most cases the project manager does not develop face-to-face activities with such teams, without neither direct personal contact nor informal talks [6]. It is therefore difficult for the project manager to get accurate and up-to-date information about the skills and technical knowledge of the members of such remote teams, since formal communication mechanisms based on documents or data repositories do not react as quickly as informal ones.

In addition, even in cases where the project manager has a bit of information regarding the skills and technical knowledge of the candidate teams, in large software projects, the task of selecting teams is quite complex and subject to evaluation errors, given that candidate teams may adopt different ambiguous vocabularies and incompatible methods to identify and evaluate their skills and technical knowledge.

In such a context, this paper proposes, implements and evaluates, a fuzzy-based approach for supporting selection processes of distributed development teams, which are technically skilled to implement software modules in DSD projects. As the main contribution, experimental results show that the proposed approach represents and formalizes an extremely complex problem in a systematic and structured way, allowing its direct or customized adoption in selection processes of globally distributed development teams.

The remainder of this paper is organized as follows. Section 2 discusses related work, evincing the main contributions of the proposed approach. Then, Sect. 3 presents the proposed approach, detailing how to extract and evaluate the skills and technical knowledge of the candidate teams in order to identify those that are more qualified to implement each software module. As a mean to assess the applicability and usability of the proposed approach, Sect. 4 presents a use case. In conclusion, Sect. 5 presents final remarks and future work.

2   Related Work

This section discusses related proposals, evincing the main contributions of the proposed approach. Although the present proposal selects qualified development teams in DSD projects, this section discusses proposals related to evaluation and allocation of personnel to software projects, given that some aspects have direct relation with the proposed approach, and, more importantly, to the best of our knowledge, this is the first time an automated approach for selecting qualified distributed developments teams is proposed. Based on varied techniques, many approaches have been proposed in the literature, such as constraint satisfaction [7, 8], metaheuristics [9, 10], linear and dynamic programming [11, 12], and fuzzy theory [13–18].

For instance, Barreto et al. propose a support approach for staffing a software project as a constraint satisfaction problem [7]. As such, the approach regards attributes related to skills required by development tasks, capabilities possessed by members of the development team, and constraints on cost, experience and team size. Based on such attributes, for each task, the approach suggests the set of members that satisfy as many constraints as possible, eventually prioritizing a given selected factor. Unlike the proposed approach, which adopts configurable policies, the Barreto's proposal supports only a set of preconfigured selection policies, and besides, does not discriminate capabilities levels according to skills required by different development tasks.

Like the Barreto's proposal, Dugan *et al.* propose a tool for allocating members of the development team to implement software packages [11]. To do that, it characterizes the required complexity to implement packages and the competency owned by candidate developers, indicating how reliable and fast are them. Besides, the proposal has two preconfigured selection policies based on partial and full team allocation. However, unlike the proposed approach that adopts a weighted single-objective formulation, the Dugan's proposal explores a multi-objective formulation based on evolutionary algorithms, which can be considered a more valuable approach given that an experienced decision-maker can analyze recommended solutions and select the most suitable one in relation to conflicting objectives.

Like the proposed approach, Dugan's and Barreto's proposals adopt discrete terms such as *novice, average, good* and *expert* to define the developers' skills. Despite that, unlike the proposed approach that adopts fuzzy terms, such discrete terms always associate the developers' experience to a single term without a membership degree. Thus, the adoption of fuzzy sets in the proposed approach allows to deal with subjectivity and uncertainty in a better way, since the developers' skills can be associated to multiple terms with different membership degrees.

Based on dynamic programming, Silva and Costa [10] present a framework for assigning human resources to software development projects. The framework determines the fit between the capabilities available in the existing staff and the skills required by the software project. Besides, it regards personality factors related to capabilities possessed by the staff and required by the software project. However, it also fails in addressing subjectivity and uncertainty related to capabilities and skills.

In the relevant literature, we have found some proposals based on fuzzy theory. As one representative proposal, Ruskova [13] proposes a fuzzy-based model for human resource evaluation and selection. The model is structured in three modules. The first describes job positions, creating a list of requirements for each one. The second describes candidates, generating a list of characteristics for each candidate based on certificates, tests and self-assessment. Then, in the third module, the previous two modules are combined to suggest a list of selected candidates that better satisfy the requirements for each job position. Although based on fuzzy logic as the one proposed herein, Ruskova [13] does not address configurable selection policies.

As another fuzzy-based proposal, in [14], Shen *et al.* propose a decision-making support tool for allocating developers to roles associated to tasks of a workflow-based software project. Like the proposed approach and the Ruskova's model [13], the Shen's proposal also characterizes skills expected by tasks and possessed by developers using fuzzy sets. However, as a weakness, unlike the proposed approach, it also does not mention the possibility of configuring selection policies.

In a similar way, MRES [15] is a fuzzy-based tool for allocating developers to development tasks. Like the proposed approach, MRES characterizes skills expected by tasks and possessed by developers using fuzzy sets. Besides, similarly, it also adopts fuzzy rules for inferring suitable allocations, allowing the project manager to specify configurable selection policies. Unlike all other proposals, as a mean to represent the skill evolution of the developers, MRES and the proposed approach allow the project manager to provide a feedback at the end of the software project, making possible to adjust the skills of the developers based on their performance or productivity. However, as a weakness, MRES represents each skill possessed by candidate developers as a single fuzzy term directly informed as input. Differently, as a strength, the proposed approach defines a form-based scheme for estimating the skills possessed by developers, expressed as crisp values that can be fuzzified into membership functions.

Another fuzzy-based approach is proposed in [16]. In such an approach, the researchers propose a rule-based expert architecture for capability assessments in skill-based environments, in which fuzzy sets represent personnel capabilities as imprecise parameters, fuzzy rules describe relationships between required expertise and possessed skills, and fuzzy reasoning performs capability assessments. However, unlike the approach proposed herein that defines configurable fuzzy rules as selection policies, in [16], such rules are internally codified in the knowledge base, making difficult to adapt them to different software projects and development organization needs.

A different fuzzy-based approach is taken in the decision-making methodology proposed by Dodangeh *et al.* [17], which integrates group decision-making and fuzzy linguistic reasoning. In such a methodology, decision makers can assess candidates using linguistic variables, enabling the aggregation of subjective evaluations provided by them, which favors more robust human resource selection processes.

Also based on group decision-making and fuzzy linguistic reasoning, Gerogiannis *et al.* [18] introduce an approach to evaluate the suitability of candidate developers, considering skills possessed by developers and required by development tasks. It is based on qualitative evaluations, derived in the form of fuzzy linguistic 2-tuples composed of a linguistic term and a number. By applying a group, multi-criteria, similarity degree-based algorithm, the approach obtains an objective aggregation of the ratings of skills related to tasks and developers. As an innovation, which is not present in neither the approach proposed herein nor the Dodangeh's proposal [17], the Gerogiannis's approach deals with skill relationships and dependencies, reflecting how prior knowledge in various skills can contribute to the learning of other skills.

3 Proposed Approach

The main goal of the proposed approach is to support the selection of technically qualified distributed software development teams for implementing software modules in a DSD project. Thus, in the proposed approach, a distributed software project is composed of a set of software modules that can be implemented by a set of globally distributed development teams. As illustrated in Fig. 1, the approach is structured in four interrelated stages.

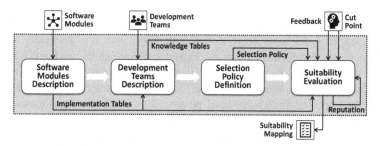

Fig. 1. Stages of the proposed approach.

The first stage, called **Software Modules Description**, is responsible for gathering the technical requirements expected to implement each software module. This stage receives as input the set of *software modules* that compose the architecture of the software project under consideration. As output, this stage produces *implementation tables*, being one table per software module, which characterizes the technical requirements in terms of technologies (operating systems, platforms, tools, programming languages, development processes, etc.) expected to implement each module.

Upon characterizing the expected technical requirements, the second stage, called **Development Teams Description**, is responsible for gathering the skills and technical knowledge of the candidate development teams in relation to the identified technical requirements. This stage takes as input the *implementation tables*, characterizing the technical requirements for each software module, together with the set of candidate *development teams*. As output, this stage produces *knowledge tables*, being one per development team, which characterizes the skill levels possessed by each development team in each expected technical requirement.

At this point, based on implementation and knowledge tables, the suitability of the teams can be evaluated in relation to a given configurable selection policy. Thus, the third stage, called **Selection Policy Definition**, has the goal of customizing the set of selection rules that composes the adopted selection policy, for instance, favoring development teams more qualified to implement software modules, or development teams with skills closer to expected technical requirements. Note that, as output, this stage produces the *selection policy*.

Now, taking as input *implementation tables*, *knowledge tables*, as well as the *selection policy*, the fourth stage, called **Suitability Evaluation** has the goal of assessing the suitability of teams for implementing each software module. The evaluation process crosses all teams with all modules and, following the adopted selection policy, determines which teams are the most appropriate for the development of each identified software module, generating as output the *suitability mapping*, which recommends an ordered list of the most technically qualified development teams to implement each module.

Upon presenting the stages of the proposed approach, the remainder of this section describes in more depth the following concepts and procedures: how to characterize software modules and development teams; how to customize selection policies; and how to evaluate teams' suitability.

3.1   Software Modules Description

As mentioned, in order to evaluate teams' suitability, first, it is necessary to gather information about technical requirements expected to implement each software module. In the proposed approach, for each software module, such technical requirements are represented as an *implementation table,* which associates each technical requirement with the expected knowledge level possessed by candidate development teams.

Table 1 presents an example of an implementation table, in which each column is associated with a given *knowledge level* and cells represent *technical requirements.* For instance, on the one hand, it is expected a *low* knowledge level for the technical requirement *SQL.* On the other hand, it is expected a *high* knowledge level for the technical requirement *Android.*

Table 1. Implementation table.

Knowledge level	Low	Medium	High
Technical requirements	SQL	Java	Android
	Reflexive programming	Communication paradigms	Network protocols Sockets

As can be noticed, the approach adopts fuzzy sets for representing the different terms assigned to knowledge levels. By default, the predefined terms are *low, medium* and *high,* which are given by a fuzzy singleton as shown in Fig. 2. In other words, the adopted terms define a fuzzy set with a membership function that is unity at a one particular point and zero everywhere else. Note that, crisp values assigned to terms *low, medium* and *high* are *0.2, 0.5* and *0.8,* respectively. Nevertheless, the number of fuzzy-terms and their values can be customized by project managers, if at all needed.

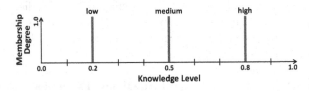

Fig. 2. Fuzzy set for knowledge levels in technical requirements.

Note that the project manager, possibly together with software architects, identifies the required technical requirements and estimates the expected knowledge levels on the basis of their own experience and expertise, some heuristic knowledge or method, subjective perceptions or even intuition, which are out of the scope of this paper.

3.2   Development Teams Description

After characterizing the technical requirements expected for software modules, it is necessary to gather information from the development teams, characterizing their skills and technical knowledge on such technical requirements, called *skill level* in the proposed approach. Here, a form-based scheme is adopted as a basis for estimating the possessed skill level of the teams, in which three pieces of data are collected: *years of experience*; *number of developed projects*; and *number of degrees*. In the literature [11, 13, 15, 19, 20], an interested reader can find the rationale that justifies the usage of such pieces of data to estimate the teams' skill levels.

Regarding that each development team is composed of a set of developers, each one has to answer a form for each technical requirement related to software modules. For instance, Fig. 3 illustrates the form for the technical requirement *Java*. As can be seen in the form, as default, the approach suggests the adoption of the following options for years of experience: *none*; *1–3*; *3–5*; *5–7*; *7–9* and *+9*. Besides, for the number of developed projects, the suggested options are: *none*; *1–5*; *5–10*; *10–15*; *15–20*; and *+20*. Note that the adopted intervals and number of options can be customized by project managers, if at all needed. Differently, instead of a predefined set of options, for the number of degrees, the form can simply enumerate the names of related certification programs and courses, or even a blank space that can be filled by developers.

Technical Requirement: JAVA

How many years have you been developing JAVA projects?
( ) none   ( ) 1-3   ( ) 3-5   ( ) 5-7   (•) 7-9   ( ) +9

How many projects have you been developed using JAVA?
( ) none   ( ) 1-5   ( ) 5-10   (•) 10-15   ( ) 15-20   ( ) +20

Which certifications do you have in JAVA?
(•) SCJA   ( ) SCJP   ( ) SCJD   ( ) SCWCD
( ) SCBCD   ( ) SCDWJC   ( ) SCEA   ( ) SMAD

Fig. 3. Form for technical requirement.

It can sound strange to adopt a coarse-grained scale based on intervals for years of experience and number of developed projects, instead of a fine-grained scale based on units of years/projects, or even months/tasks. The rationale behind the adopted strategy is to accommodate in some degree the variations related to the learning capabilities for different developers. For instance, a developer with three years of experience is not necessarily more expert than another one with two years of experience, and vice-versa. Thus, by using a coarse-grained scale, the proposed approach tries to reduce discrepancies in relation to learning capabilities, correlating skills with less distortion than a fine-grained scale.

Upon gathering such information, it is required to process forms in order to estimate the possessed skill level for each individual developer. To do that, first, based on the filled forms, the answers are mapped in real values in the interval [0, 1].

For years of experience and number of developed projects, let be n the number of options related to a question. In such questions, the mapped value for the option in position i is given by the expression $(i-1)/(n-1)$. For instance, considering the number of years, which has six options, the mapped values are $\{0.0, 0.2, 0.4, 0.6, 0.8, 1.0\}$. For number of degrees, let be n the number of options and i the number of selected or informed options. Then, in such a case, the mapped value is simply calculated by the expression i/n. For instance, considering the option indicated for Java in Fig. 3, the mapped value is *0.125*.

Thereafter, the mapped values, represented by $Y_{dv,tr}$, $P_{dv,tr}$ and $D_{dv,tr}$, are weighted in (1), deriving the skill level $SK_{dv,tr}$ for developer dv in technical requirement tr, whose value is also in the interval [0, 1]. In (1), the terms w_Y, w_P and w_D represent the weights associated to years of experience, number of developed projects and number of degrees, which by default has the values 4, 4 and 2, respectively.

$$SK_{dv,tr} = (Y_{dv,tr} \cdot w_Y + P_{dv,tr} \cdot w_P + D_{dv,tr} \cdot w_D)/(w_Y + w_P + w_D) \qquad (1)$$

Next, based on the skill level $SK_{dv,tr}$ for each developer of a team in a given technical requirement, the approach can derive the skill level $SK_{tm,tr}$ of team tm in technical requirement tr, as defined in (2). The term $N_{tm,tr}$ denotes the number of developers in team tm that has knowledge in technical requirement tr, and the term $\mu_{tm,tr}$ represents the mean value of the skill level for such developers. As stated, it is assumed that the more developers exist in a team, the more people share knowledge, raising the teams' skill level at a rate that decreases as the number of developers increases.

$$SK_{tm,tr} = \mu_{tm,tr}^{(N_{tm,tr}+1)/(2 \cdot N_{tm,tr})} \qquad (2)$$

Then, in order to better deal with subjectivity and uncertainty, the estimated skill level for each team is fuzzified to fuzzy sets, in which linguistic terms have membership degrees mapped by membership functions. By default, as illustrated in Fig. 4, the adopted fuzzy sets have the corresponding linguistic terms: *none*, *low*, *medium*, and *high*. Note that the project manager can customize the fuzzy sets, redefining the number of linguistic terms and their membership functions, which may have different shapes like triangular, trapezoidal, Gaussian, bell-shaped and sigmoidal waveforms.

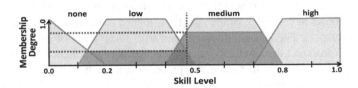

Fig. 4. Fuzzy set for skill levels of development teams

As shown in Fig. 4, by default, the proposed approach adopts triangular and trapezoidal waveforms. The rationale for adopting such waveforms is directly related to the coarse-grained scale based on predefined intervals, which does not impose high precision as a mean to deal with variability in learning capabilities. Thus, on the one hand, in overlapped points of neighbor fuzzy sets, skills levels can be categorized in such fuzzy sets with different membership degrees. However, on the other hand, in non-overlapped points of a given fuzzy set, skills levels have equal membership degrees.

Upon estimating the skill level for each development team in each expected technical requirement, the output of this stage is generated, called *knowledge tables*, being one table for each pair of development team and technical requirement.

3.3   Selection Policy Definition

Before evaluating the technical suitability of development teams, it is needed to define the selection policy adopted for contrasting knowledge levels expected by technical requirements and skill levels possessed by candidate development teams.

Considering the needs of the software project, different policies may be adopted, changing the way the teams can be selected. For instance, if a project is late, selecting more qualified teams to implement modules may be the best option, making easier to perform tasks in a shorter time. Nevertheless, the choice of the most qualified teams may cause workforce waste, leading to higher costs, given that their skill levels are much higher than the knowledge levels expected by technical requirements. Hence, it can be interesting to define a policy that tries to choose teams with skill levels as close as possible to knowledge levels expected by technical requirements, avoiding work-force waste and so minimizing project costs.

In such a direction, a selection policy can be understood as a table of rules, defined by *if-then* expressions, which correlate the fuzzy terms in rows with the ones in columns, defining rules that generate the desired results, represented by cells in their intersections. Table 2 shows a possible example of selection policy, in which one can understand the rule composition with the following example: *IF Skill Level is "none" AND Knowledge Level is "medium" THEN Suitability Level is "low"*.

Table 2. Selection policy

			Technical requirements		
			Knowledge level		
			Low	Medium	High
Teams	Skill level	None	Medium	Low	None
		Low	High	Medium	Low
		Medium	Medium	High	Medium
		High	Low	Medium	High

The customization of selection rules is determined by the specific needs of the software project and by the organizational context in which the software project is immersed. As a mean to facilitate the project manager role, grounded on observations and analysis in other proposals [7, 15, 21], the approach predefine four distinct policies:

equivalent qualification – selects teams that have skill levels closer to expected knowledge levels; *most skilled teams* – selects teams that have the highest skill levels above expected knowledge levels; *minimum qualification* – selects equally all teams that possess skill levels above expected knowledge levels; and *training provision* – selects teams that have skill levels below expected knowledge levels.

Despite the four suggested policies, project managers have autonomy to create new policies or refine existing policies. In this way, policies not foreseen in the approach, but adopted by project managers, can be easily configured and adopted. Besides, as exemplified in Table 2, proposed selection policies adopt three and four fuzzy terms for representing knowledge levels and skill levels, respectively. However, as already mentioned, project managers can also change the number and the value of such terms.

3.4 Suitability Evaluation

At this point, regarding *implementation tables, knowledge tables* and *selection policy*, the approach adopts a fuzzy-based reasoning engine for inferring the *suitability level* for each development team in each technical requirement expected by each software module, according to the selection policy.

In the fuzzy-based reasoning engine, depending on the crisp values associated to skill levels, more than one fuzzy term with different membership degrees can be identified, given that membership functions have intersections (Fig. 4). As a result, more than one selection rule can be applied, leading to more than one fuzzy term with different membership degrees for the suitability level of a given team and a given technical requirement. Now, considering such terms and membership degrees, the approach adopts the well-known defuzzification method, called *Center of Sums* [22], in order to calculate the crisp value associated to the suitability level, represented by $SL_{tm,tr}$, which can assume a real value on the interval $[0, 1]$. In the proposed approach, the rationale for choosing the *Center of Sums* method is that it is computationally faster and more efficient than many currently in use, it is applicable to symmetric and non-symmetric membership functions and, in addition, it allows the participation of several fuzzy sets in the reasoning process.

At this point, it is possible to estimate the technical *suitability level* for each development team *tm* in each software module *sm*, represented by $SL_{tm,sm}$, as defined in (3). Note that the approach adopts the mean value of the suitability level for the development team *tm* in relation to all technical requirements *tr* in the implementation table of the software module *sm*, which is defined by $IT_{sm} = \{tr_1, tr_2, \cdots, tr_x\}$. As such, the suitability level $SL_{tm,sm}$ can assume a real value in the interval $[0, 1]$.

$$SL_{tm,sm} = \sum\nolimits_{tr \in IT_{sm}} SL_{tm,tr} / |IT_{sm}| \tag{3}$$

After estimating the suitability level for all development teams in all software modules, the initial version of the *suitability mapping* is produced, in which columns represent software modules and rows represents the ordered suitability level for all development teams, as illustrated in Table 3.

Table 3. Suitability mapping.

Module M1		Module M2		Module M3	
Team T5	0.8379	Team T2	0.8366	Team T5	0.8619
Team T2	0.7817	Team T5	0.7690	Team T3	0.7943
Team T3	0.7401	Team T3	0.6852	Team T3	0.7524
Team T1	0.6915	Team T7	0.6723	Team T7	0.7354
Team T7	0.6794	Team T6	0.6688	Team T6	0.7083
Team T6	0.6385	Team T1	0.5215	Team T1	0.6040
Team T4	0.4140	Team T4	0.3680	Team T4	0.4706

Now, the initial suitability mapping ought to be reordered based on the impact of the *reputation* (Fig. 1) of the teams on their suitability level. The reputation of a team R_{tm} is estimated based on the historical performance or productivity of the team in previous projects, which is updated by the *feedback* (Fig. 1), informed by the project manager about teams. The rationale for balancing suitability levels and reputations is to regard a trade-off among subjective concerns and real-world observations.

The feedback of a team F_{tm} also adopts fuzzy terms, which by default are: *unsatisfied*, *weak unsatisfied*, *indifferent*, *weak satisfied*, and *satisfied*. The positive and negative terms are indicated when the team performance is better or worse than expected, respectively. The crisp values associated to feedback terms are $\{0.0, 0.25, 0.5, 0.75, 1.0\}$. Based on informed feedback, the reputation is recalculated as indicated in (4), where the terms w_R and w_F represent the weights associated to reputation and feedback, respectively. Notice that the default values for w_R and w_F are 2 and 1, respectively, allowing a gradual updating of teams' reputation.

$$R_{tm} = (R_{tm} \cdot w_R + F_{tm} \cdot w_F)/(w_R + w_F) \qquad (4)$$

In order to produce the final version of the suitability mapping, the suitability level is updated as defined in (5). Considering that the team reputation R_{tm} can assume real values in the interval $(0, 1]$, observe that: *(i)* a value above *0.5* represents strong reputation and so the final suitability is increased; *(ii)* a value equal to *0.5* represents normal reputation and so the final suitability keeps stable; and *(iii)* a value below *0.5* represents weak reputation and so the final suitability is reduced. Note that the initial reputation for all teams is *0.5*.

$$SL_{tm,sm} = SL_{tm,sm}^{0.5/R_{tm}} \qquad (5)$$

As the final point, the project manager defines a *cut-point* (Fig. 1) for the software project under development, establishing a suitability level that is the minimum for development teams to be considered adequate to implement software modules. Thus, considering the defined cut-point, the final version of the suitability mapping is produced by rejecting all teams with suitability level below the cut point, as illustrated in Table 3, in which the default value of the cut point is *0.7*.

In conclusion, based on the suitability mapping recommended by the proposed approach and considering project constraints and organizational context, the project manager can choose and then allocate qualified distributed development teams to implement software modules.

4   Use Case

The proposed approach was evaluated in three use cases as a mean to assess its applicability and usability, regarding two software product lines, two groups of development teams, and four selection policies, which together lead to 24 experiments. The two first cases regarded a synthetic e-commerce project, evaluated in two development iterations, contemplating domain and application engineering. The third use case regards a real-world project for mobile middleware. Both groups of development teams are composed of professionals and graduate students in computer science. The former has 56 developers that define 7 teams, varying from 2 to 18 members. The latter has 123 developers that define 15 teams, varying from 3 to 15 members. In respect to teams' reputation, values were randomly picked. On all cases, default configurations for weights, fuzzy sets, membership functions, and cut-points were adopted.

Due to space limit, this section details the use case based on the *mobile middleware project*, which is packaged in *5 software modules* (*M1* to *M5*). The case considers the group composed of *7 development teams* (*T1* to *T7*), each one assembled of *9, 5, 18, 8, 9, 2* and *5* developers, respectively. Also, the case adopts the *equivalent qualification policy*, which selects teams that have skill levels closer to expected knowledge levels, as shown in Table 2. Note that, due to space limit, knowledge levels expected by technical requirements, and skill levels possessed by developers and teams are not shown. Instead, only single examples are presented for facilitating the understanding.

In the use case, the *implementation tables* were defined by the software architect responsible for the architectural design of the mobile middleware, indicating the set of technical requirements expected for each software module. For instance, Table 1 represents the implementation table for module *M2*.

Next, all participating developers answered web-based forms, contemplating all technical requirements expected by all software modules to be implemented in the mobile middleware project. An example of the form for *Java* is illustrated in Fig. 3.

In order to define the *knowledge tables*, the answered forms were processed for estimating the skill level possessed by each developer in each technical requirement. For instance, considering the form presented in Fig. 3, it is possible to estimate the crisp value for years of experience ($Y_{dv,java} = 0.8$), number of developed project ($P_{dv,java} = 0.6$), and number of degrees ($D_{dv,java} = 0.125$). Then, based on (1), the skill level of the developer in Java is estimated ($SK_{dv,java} = 0.5850$).

Next, based on the skill level for each developer in each technical requirement, it is possible to estimate the skill level for each development team in each technical requirement. As an example, based on (2), the skill level in *Java* for team *T1*, composed of *9* developers and to which the previously exemplified developer belongs, is estimated ($SK_{T1,java} = 0.7107$).

At this time, the suitability level for each team in each technical requirement can be inferred by the fuzzy-based reasoning engine based on the adopted selection policy, which in this case is the equivalent qualification policy (Table 2). Thereafter, based on (3), the suitability level for each team in each software module can be estimated. For instance, considering team $T1$, its suitability level in relation to module $M2$ that has *Java* as technical requirement (Table 1) is estimated ($SL_{T1,M2} = 0.6401$).

Lastly, based on (5), the suitability level for each team in each software module is updated based on their reputations, producing the recommended *suitability mapping*. For instance, the suitability level $SL_{T1,M2} = 0.6401$ is now reduced to $SL_{T1,M2} = 0.5215$, given that its reputation is below *0.5*.

Remember that, considering a defined cut-point, teams with suitability level below the cut-point value are rejected. For instance, in this case, a partial view of the recommended suitability mapping is shown in Table 3, where teams with suitability above *0.7* are technically qualified for implementing software modules. After applying the cut-point, for 7 candidate teams in 5 software modules, the approach recommends *3, 2, 5, 5* and *5* teams to implement modules $M1$ to $M5$, respectively.

Concluding, experimental results show that, as the main contribution, the proposed approach represents and formalizes an extremely complex problem in a systematic and structured way, allowing its direct or customized adoption in selection processes of globally distributed development teams. More importantly, to the best of our knowledge and belief in the related research field, this is the first time an automated approach for supporting the allocation of qualified distributed development teams is proposed in the literature. Besides, the approach provides a scheme for estimating the skills and technical knowledge of developers and development teams.

5 Concluding Remarks

This paper has presented a fuzzy-based approach for supporting project managers in the process of allocating technically qualified distributed development teams to implementation tasks of software modules in DSD projects. The approach has four related concept blocks that allow to perform the characterization of the following elements in a software project: *(i)* technical requirements expected to implement software modules; *(ii)* skills and technical knowledge possessed by development teams in such technical requirements; *(iii)* selection policies adopted for inferring technically qualified teams; and *(iv)* technical suitability of development teams to software modules.

By adopting the strategy *divide and conquer*, the main innovation of the proposed approach is the analytical, fuzzy-based model and formalization of an extremely complex problem in a systematic and structured way, allowing its direct or customized adoption in selection processes of technically qualified teams in DSD projects.

Despite cited contributions, an instantiation of the approach for a DSD project may require a considerable effort for handling forms and tables. However, the approach has potential to be reused in different scenarios. For instance, once a DSD project is instantiated, with its modules, technologies, teams and policies, the evaluation of another policy may easily reuse all forms and tables produced in the first instantiation. In a most significant way, if one adopts a repository of previous software projects, including most technical requirements usually expected to implement software modules, a large number of teams and the main selection policies, the evaluation of a new project may also reuse all forms and tables already available from previous projects.

As future work, it is under laboratory work the refinement of the prototype implementation into a user-friendly web-based tool, in which the main objectives are ease of understanding and usability. Upon releasing the tool, the intention is to apply the approach in a real-world company with DSD projects developed by globally or at least nationally distributed teams, bringing up the opportunity for contrasting allocations recommended by the approach against those enacted by project managers.

References

1. Martignoni, R.: Global sourcing of software development: a review of tools and services. In: 4th International Conference on Global Software Engineering, Ireland, pp. 303–308. IEEE (2009)
2. Carmel, E., Dubinsky, Y., Espinosa, A.: Follow the sun software development: new perspectives, conceptual foundation, and exploratory field study. In: 42nd Hawaii International Conference on System Sciences, USA, pp. 1–9. IEEE (2009)
3. Herbsleb, J., Moitra, D.: Global software development. IEEE Softw. 18(2), 16–20 (2001)
4. Ovaska, P., Rossi, M., Marttiin, P.: Architecture as a coordination tool in multi-site soft-ware development. Softw. Process Improv. Pract. 8(4), 233–247 (2003)
5. Prikladnicki, R., Audy, J.L.N., Evaristo, R.: Global software development in practice: lessons learned. Softw. Process Improv. Pract. 8(4), 267–281 (2003)
6. Mockus, A., Herbsleb, J.: Challenges of global software development. In: 7th International Symposium on Software Metrics, UK, pp. 182–184. IEEE (2001)
7. Barreto, A., Barros, M.O., Werner, C.M.L.: Staffing a software project: a constraint satisfaction and optimization-based approach. Comput. Oper. Res. 35(10), 3073–3089 (2008)
8. Kang, D., Jung, J., Bae, D.H.: Constraint-based human resource allocation in software projects. Softw. Pract. Exp. 41(5), 551–577 (2011)
9. Otero, L.D., Centano, G., Torres, A.J.R., Otero, C.E.: A systematic approach for resource allocation in software projects. Comput. Ind. Eng. 56(4), 1333–1339 (2009)
10. Silva, L.C., Costa, A.P.C.S.: Decision model for allocating human resources in information system projects. Int. J. Proj. Manag. 31(1), 100–108 (2013)
11. Duggan, J., Byrne, J., Lyons, G.J.: A task allocation optimizer for software construction. IEEE Softw. 21(3), 76–82 (2004)
12. Kurien, V., Nair, R.S.: Software project planning and resource allocation using ant colony optimization with uncertainty handling. Int. J. Innov. Res. Sci. Eng. Technol. 3(5), 355–361 (2014)
13. Ruskova, N.A.: Decision support system for human resources appraisal and selection. In: 1st International Symposium on Intelligent Systems, Bulgaria, vol. 1, pp. 354–357. IEEE (2002)
14. Shen, M., Tzeng, G.H., Liu, D.R.: Multi-criteria task assignment in workflow management systems. In: 36th Hawaii International Conference on System Sciences, USA, pp. 1–9. IEEE (2003)
15. Callegari, D.A., Bastos, R.M.: A multi-criteria resource selection method for software projects using fuzzy logic. In: Filipe, J., Cordeiro, J. (eds.) ICEIS 2009. LNBIP, vol. 24, pp. 376–388. Springer, Heidelberg (2009). https://doi.org/10.1007/978-3-642-01347-8_32

16. Otero, L.D., Otero, C.E.: A Fuzzy expert system architecture for capability assessments in skill-based environments. Expert Syst. Appl. **39**(1), 654–662 (2012)
17. Dodangeh, J., Sorooshian, S., Afshari, A.R.: Linguistic extension for group multicriteria project manager selection. J. Appl. Math. **2014**, 8 p. (2014)
18. Gerogiannis, V., Rapti, E., Karageorgos, A., Fitsilis, P.: On using fuzzy linguistic 2-tuples for the evaluation of human resource suitability in software development tasks. Adv. Softw. Eng. **2015**, 15 p. (2015)
19. Shanteau, J., Weiss, D.J., Thomas, R.P., Pounds, J.C.: Performance-based assessment of expertise: how to decide if someone is an expert or not. Eur. J. Oper. Res. **136**(2), 253–263 (2002)
20. Weiss, D.J., Shanteau, J., Harries, P.: People who judge people. J. Behav. Decis. Mak. **19**(5), 441–454 (2006)
21. Collofello, J., Houston, D., Rus, I., Chauhan, A., Sycamore, D.M., Daniels, D.S.: A system dynamics software process simulator for staffing policies decision support. In: 31st Hawaii International Conference on System Sciences, USA, pp. 103–111. IEEE (1998)
22. Ross, T.J.: Fuzzy Logic with Engineering Applications, 3rd edn. Wiley, Hoboken (2010)

Smart Selection of Materials for Product Prototype Fabrication

Francisco Torres, Leticia Neira, and Luis M. Torres-Treviño(✉)

CIIDIT-FIME, Universidad Autónoma de Nuevo León,
San Nicolás de los Garza, Mexico
luis.torres.ciidit@gmail.com

Abstract. A fuzzy expert system is proposed for a smart selection of materials for fabrication of specific parts for products. Knowledge of expert used for selection materials is encapsulated in a fuzzy rule base, using a hierarchical form. As a case of study, a selection of materials is made for case fabrication where durability, low price, and resistance is considered as criteria selection. The fuzzy system for smart selection can be used in a variety of materials.

Keywords: Selection of materials · Fuzzy knowledge based systems
Fuzzy systems

1 Introduction

Design and production involves several decisions usually to cover the requirements of the final product satisfying several criteria of quality robustness, resistance, color, appearance,. etc. This paper present an expert system based on fuzzy systems that generates recommendations about the use of specific materials considering several criteria given by human experts and fitting client/users requirements. Knowledge for material selection given by human experts is linguistic in majority of times and involves several variables usually with a high component of uncertain. However, generation of an expert system that involves many inputs could be prohibitive to maintain considering a high number of rules required. A factible expert system can be build using hierarchies. Language that we use in every day situations can be hierarchized easily because we can generate complex abstraction using language so using this mental capability, a set of sub-fuzzy systems are build, then all sub-systems are joined to form an hierarchical fuzzy system.

In the work of Sancin et al. [4], an intelligent decision system is proposed where expert knowledge about material properties, production process, and design guidelines are used to generate as outputs proposal materials, manufacture parameters, tooling recommendation and design guidelines.

In the work of Ipek [1], an expert system is proposed for material selection considering a set of if-then rules proposed by experts and processed by a

© Springer Nature Switzerland AG 2018
F. Castro et al. (Eds.): MICAI 2017, LNAI 10632, pp. 236–242, 2018.
https://doi.org/10.1007/978-3-030-02837-4_19

backward-forward chaining inference mechanism to generate appropriate qual-
ifications. Knowledge involves impact resistance, density, formability, corrosion
resistance price index, loss coefficient, middle strength, elastic module all related
with a specific product.

Wilk et al. [5] propose an integrated system of a knowledge base with a Logic
of Pausible Reasoning (LPR) where LPR generates proper queries for specific
search on database for material selection based on diagnosis. Knowledge is represented in hierarchies of qualification, hierarchies of measures and hierarchies
of schemes.

Penciuc et al. [3] propose a platform that integrate several approaches to
improve product life cycle management used for material selection to production,
determine recycled phases and calculating its impact on the environment. Our
principal motivation is the use of fuzzy systems to represent knowledge from
expert in material selection, form an hierarchical structure an use it for smart
selection of materials.

2   Fuzzy Logic and Fuzzy Systems

Architecture of a fuzzy system is shown in Fig. 1. Following equation are derived
from the work of Mendel [2]. A fuzzy system is used to represent linguistic
knowledge to make a relationship between linguistics inputs to linguistic outputs
making inference of knowledge represented in form of if- then rules. These fuzzy
rules can be represented using a matrix DB where every element represent a
fuzzy set considering five linguistic values of Very Low (1), Low (2), regular or
medium (3), High (4) and very high (5). The fuzzy rule base is a matrix (which
we shall denote by DB) where every row is a rule and every column is an integer
that represents the linguistic value associated with that rule from antecedents to
consequents. In the case of three variables and five linguistic values, a maximum
of $5^3 = 125$ rules or rows and 4 columns (three inputs and one output) build up
the matrix.

We define a type1 function where it is considered five linguistic values per
input variable (Eq. 1), inference max-min is used by means of Eq. 2

$$type1(x,n) = \begin{cases} trapezoidal(x,0,0,0.1666,0.3333) & \text{if } n = 1 \\ triangular(x,0.1666,0.3333,0.5) & \text{if } n = 2 \\ triangular(x,0.3333,0.5,0.6666) & \text{if } n = 3 \\ triangular(x,0.5,0.6666,0.8333) & \text{if } n = 4 \\ trapezoidal(x,0.6666,0.8333,1,1) & \text{if } n = 5, \end{cases} \quad (1)$$

where x is an input value and n corresponds to a specific membership function
of a linguistic variable. Considering a fuzzy system of three inputs, a *max-min*
inference engine is defined as follows:

$$I(r) = \min(type1(x_1, DB(r,1)), type1(x_2, DB(r,2)), type1(x_3, DB(r,3))) \quad (2)$$

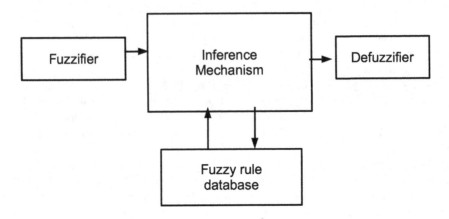

Fig. 1. Components of a fuzzy system.

where r is the fuzzy rule number, DB is the fuzzy rule base, and I is the inference calculated. Finally, output can be determined using centroid defuzzification and height defuzzification, this one shown below:

$$yh = \sum_{r=1}^{R}(I(r) * y_m(DB(r,4)))/\sum_{r=1}^{R}I(r) \qquad (3)$$

where y_m is a pre-calculated center of mass of every membership function of the output (the predefined values could be $y_m = [\ 0\ 0.25\ 0.5\ 0.75\ 1]$) and R is the number of rules. DB establishes correct output linguistic value depending of the fuzzy rule, i.e. fourth column.

3   Hierarchical Fuzzy System for Material Qualifications

First sub-system establishes the Heat resistance of material proposed based on Thermic expansion of the material and its Thermic capacity (Fig. 2b). Second sub-system determines cost production considering density of the material, its size and cost. A heavy and with high volumen is expected a high cost of production including its unitary cost (Fig. 2b).

Third sub-system determines the capacity of portability of the material, this means when a container is made from a specific material is under a tension resistance and a specific strength. A light material with low density is more easy to transport from one place to another (Fig. 3a). Fourth sub-system determines usability considering elasticity module, impact resistance and fracture resistance (Fig. 3b).

Finally, all sub-systems forms a system for material qualification considering heat resistance of proposed material, production cost, and functionality determined with portability and usability of the material proposed (Fig. 4).

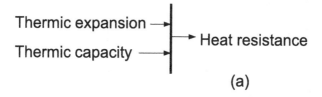

(a)

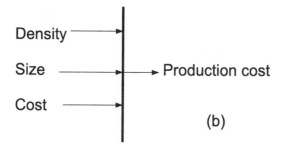

(b)

Fig. 2. Sub-systems for Heat resistance (a) and Cost production (b).

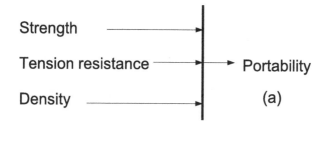

(a)

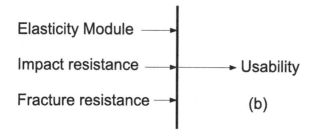

(b)

Fig. 3. Sub-systems for Portability (a) and Usability (b).

4 Application of Hierarchical Fuzzy System

Construction of a case that contains electronic components imply the use of several parts; however the external cover of the case id the most important part because the protection of the case is the first criteria that must be satisfied.

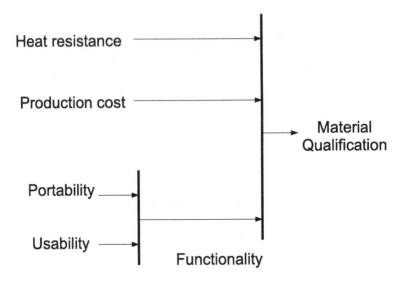

Fig. 4. Sub-systems for Portability (a) and Usability (b).

Portability is required so a metal case has a strong resistance but could be too heavy or to expensive. Other materials like polymers, nylon or polyester could be portable but usually cases made by these materials could be to lights and tend to deform or generate bumps. This condition is undesirable for the electronic instruments that the case must contains. Rigid polymers are desirable and they are usually used for containers of electronics instruments. We have consider three materials (i) Acrilotrilo Butadeno Estireno (ABS), polipropileno (PP) and policarbonate (PC). It is necessary to make a comparison of every material by means of mechanical, thermic, electric, physical and chemical test to establish the best materials; however, in majority of cases the tests have been made; considering this situation, only a criterium of selection can be established depending of functionality of the case (conditions of exterior cover) and characteristics of its contains. It is desirable a rigid structure, that isolate internal components from exterior, with high heat resistance, hit resistance and it must prevent humidity. It must be portable either a low weigh and finally, it must be inexpensive.

Selection using tables could be very hard to make inclusive considering only three materials (Fig. 5). Usually, selection is made using formulation with credit assignment to establish influence factors depending of the property that it is required to maximize or minimize the performance of the case.

It is necessary to make a comparison of every material by means of mechanical, thermic, electrical, physical and chemical tests to establish the best material; however, in majority of cases, these test have been made, then only criteria of selection can be established depending of functionality of the case (conditions of exterior cover) and characteristics of its contains criteria.

It is desirable a rigid structure that isolate internal componente from exterior, with high heat resistance, and it must prevent humidity, it must be portable,

Material	Thermic expansion (1e-6/k)	Thermic capacity (J/g-K)	density (g/cc)	size	cost material (%Us/Lb)
ABS	107	2	1.115	x	11.3
PC	77	1.1	1.31	x	7.47
PP	51	2	1.18	x	2.58

Hardiness (Brinell)	tension resistance (Mpa)	elastic module (Gpa)	Impact resistance IZOD (J)	fracture resistance (Mpa) (m)^0.5
103	47	2.4	3.2	2.4
70	65	2.3	4.78	3.1
110	36	3.75	1.12	3.7

Fig. 5. Materials under test.

with a low weight and finally it must be inexpensive. Selection using tables could be very hard to made inclusive considering three materials. Usually selection is made using formulation with credit assignment to establish influence factors that depends of the property that it is required to maximize or minimize. A hierarchical fuzzy expert system is used to simplify the selection considering more appropriate criteria that a desirable for the cover of the case. Considering the properties of material under test as inputs, every fuzzy system is executed. First subsystems are executed and finally system of qualification. Results indicate that ABS has a qualification of 0.33, polipropileno has a qualification of 0.5 and policarbonate has a qualification of 0.42. In this situation, the use of polipropileno is the best option to build the case.

5   Conclusion

Material selection involves knowledge of several experts in different areas like chemistry, metallurgy, design, engineering, etc. Tradicional expert systems involves several rules and usually is a challenging task maintaining these systems. Using hierarchical fuzzy systems is possible to reduce the number of rules because every subsystem uses a very low number of inputs, consequently the number of rules is reduced and second advantage is the fusion of knowledge that comes from several experts. As future work, more cases could be considered and the integration of these systems as a tool in normal processes of product design made in industry.

References

1. Ipek, M., Selvi, I.H., Findik, F., Torkul, O., Cedimoğlu, I.: An expert system based material selection approach to manufacturing. Mater. Des. **47**, 331–340 (2013). http://www.sciencedirect.com/science/article/pii/S0261306912008187
2. Mendel, J., Hagras, H., Tan, W.W., Melek, W.W., Ying, H.: Introduction To Type-2 Fuzzy Logic Control: Theory and Applications, 1st edn. Wiley, Hoboken (2014)
3. Penciuc, D., Duigou, J.L., Daaboul, J., Vallet, F., Eynard, B.: Product life cycle management approach for integration of engineering design and life cycle engineering. Artif. Intell. Eng. Des. Anal. Manuf. **30**(4), 379–389 (2016)
4. Sancin, U., Dobravc, M., Dolšak, B.: Human cognition as an intelligent decision support system for plastic products design. Expert Syst. Appl. **37**(10), 7227–7233 (2010). http://www.sciencedirect.com/science/article/pii/S0957417410002769
5. Wilk-Kolodziejczyk, D.: Supporting the manufacturing process of metal products with the methods of artificial intelligence. Arch. Metall. Mater. **61**(4), 1995–1998 (2017)

Machine Learning and Data Mining

A Comparative Study of Harmony Search Algorithms for Improving the Training Process of Extreme Learning Machines

Daniel Pusil, Carlos Cobos$^{(\boxtimes)}$, and Martha Mendoza

Information Technology Research Group (GTI), Universidad del Cauca,
Popayán, Colombia
{danielpusil,ccobos,mmendoza}@unicauca.edu.co

Abstract. Extreme Learning Machine (ELM) is a model for the training of single-hidden feedforward networks and is used extensively in problems of classification and regression for its good results and reduced training time compared to backpropagation. Previous work has shown that to define randomly the input weights and biases of the hidden layer reduces quality (accuracy) of ELM. This paper makes a comparative study of three variants of harmony search (the original Harmony Search, Global-best Harmony Search, and New Global Harmony Search), a memetic algorithm from the state of the art denominated M-ELM and a random walk algorithm named RW-ELM on 20 classical classification datasets available in the UCI repository. The results show that the best algorithm for training ELMs is Harmony Search and that the other two variants of this algorithm are better than M-ELM and RW-ELM when cross-validation is used. The experiments were performed at first using separate archives for training and testing, then using cross-validation with 5 folders. Based on literature, authors recommend the use of cross-validation technique because more realistic accuracy results can be obtained.

Keywords: Extreme learning machine · Harmony search
Global-best harmony search · Hill climbing · Memetic algorithm
Simulated annealing

1 Introduction

Feedforward Neural Networks (FNN) are a type of neural network characterized by connecting neurons in one layer with only neurons in the next layer. The information is processed in a unidirectional way that makes the training process faster, easy to implement and requiring only minimal human intervention. A FNN with a single hidden layer is known as a Single Layer Feed-forward Network (SLFN) and as with FNNs they are generally trained using the Back-propagation algorithm, which is time-consuming especially in large-scale problems [1].

An Extreme Learning Machine (ELM) is a specific architecture of SLFN where the transfer function in the hidden layer is infinitely differentiable and the one of the output layer is linear, the weights that connect the nodes of the hidden layer and the output layer are calculated analytically using the inverse generalized by Moore–Penrose by

F. Castro et al. (Eds.): MICAI 2017, LNAI 10632, pp. 245–256, 2018.
https://doi.org/10.1007/978-3-030-02837-4_20

previously defining in a random and one-off manner the weights that connect the input layer and the hidden layer, as well as the biases of the hidden layer [2, 3]. These networks produce good results in classification and regression problems and are trained much faster than networks that use Back-propagation algorithm. However, the parameters chosen in their design remain unchanged during the training phase. Many random weights and biases that are defined between the input and hidden layer are not optimal and decrease the power of generalization of the network. As a result, several studies have been carried out to better define these weights and biases. Within these, there are several that approach this problem as an optimization problem. These can be divided mainly into 3 groups:

A. Evolutionary: such as E-ELM (Evolutionary Extreme Learning Machine) [4] proposed in 2005, PSO-ELM (Particle swarm optimization for ELM) [5] proposed in 2006, ICGA-PSO-ELM (combines genetic algorithms with Particle swarm optimization to classify cancer) [6] and GSO-ELM (an evolutionary algorithm based on group search optimization) [7] proposed in 2011, SaE-ELM (self-adaptive evolutionary Extreme Learning machine) [8] and HS-ELM (Harmony Search for Hydrologic Time Series Forecasting) [9] proposed in 2012, Evo-ELM (evolving Extreme Learning) [10] and CPSOS-ELM (Particle Swarm Optimization and Clustering Strategies) [11] proposed in 2013, and DE-ELM (Differential Evolution Extreme Learning Machine for the Classification of Hyperspectral Images) [12] and SADHS-OELM (A self-adaptive differential harmony search-based optimized extreme learning machine for financial time series prediction) [13] proposed in 2014, which use methods based on global optimization to calculate weights of input for the network and use ELM to calculate the output weights.

B. Non-evolutionary: such as EN-ELM (Ensemble Extreme Learning Machine) [14] proposed in 2010 and V-ELM (Voting Extreme Learning Machine) [15] proposed in 2012, both of which perform well in special domains, but in general they obtain a classification rate inferior to the evolutionary approaches due, among other factors, to the conservation of randomness in input weights.

C. Memetic: where the only exponent to date is M-ELM (Memetic Extreme Learning machine) [16] proposed in 2016. M-ELM uses an algorithm that combines a global optimizer (Differential Evolution) with a local optimizer (Simulated Annealing, SA) and obtains better results than the evolutionary approaches.

It should be noted that (1) in the M-ELM proposal the authors compare their work against a simple ELM, non-evolutionary EN-ELM and V-ELM, evolutionary SaE-ELM and Evo-ELM and show that its results in classification problems are better in terms of accuracy with competitive run time and computational complexity, (2) based on the Non-Free Lunch Theorem [17] it can be said that, given a specific optimization-type problem, the best metaheuristic for solving it is not known until they are evaluated and compared experimentally, and that (3) Harmony Search was used to optimize the parameters of an ELM neural network in a regression problem with good results [9, 13, 18].

In this work, a comparison was made of M-ELM against an adaptation of the original Harmony Search (HS-ELM), Global-Best Harmony Search (GHS-ELM) and Novel Global Harmony Search (NGHS-ELM) algorithms for the classification problem using ELMs through datasets divided into two (training and testing) files and using cross-validation with 5 folders. The results show that variants of the harmony search algorithm for training ELM are better than the state-of-the-art algorithm M-ELM when cross-validation technique is used, Also, HS-ELM obtains the best results using separate archives for training and testing, and using cross-validation. A non-parametric Friedman test supports these results.

In the following, Sect. 2 describes Extreme Learning Machines and the harmony search algorithms used in this work. Section 3 then presents how the algorithms were adapted to solve the problem of training the input weights in the ELM. Section 4 describes the experiments performed and analyzes the results. Finally, Sect. 5 presents the conclusions of the work carried out as well as future work planned by the research team.

2   Theoretical Context

2.1   Extreme Learning Machines

ELM [19] is a novel training model for a specific SFLN network. The training strategy of an ELM is very simple. Unlike conventional neural networks whose weights need to be adjusted using the Back-propagation algorithm, in ELM the network input weights and hidden layer biases are generated randomly and the activation function is infinitely differentiable. The weights between the hidden layer and the output layer are calculated analytically using the Moore–Penrose (MP) generalized inverse.

Mathematically, let $\{x_i, t_i\}$ be a training set, $i = \{1, 2, 3, \ldots, N\}$ where $x_i = \{x_{i1}, x_{i2}, \ldots, x_{in}\}^T \in R^n$ has n input attributes and $t_i = \{t_{i1}, t_{i2}, \ldots, t_{im}\}^T \in R^m$ contains m outputs or classes, assuming that SLFNs have l nodes (neurons) in the hidden layer and an activation function $g(x)$, we can define the structure of an ELM as $t_i = \sum_j^l \beta_j g(\omega_j x_i + b_j)$, where $j = 1, 2, 3, \ldots, l$; $\omega_j x_i$ indicates the internal product of the input weights ω_j for the input values x_i. Since the input layer and the hidden layer are connected by the input weight matrix $\varpi_{l \times n}$ with dimensions $l \times n$ where $\varpi_j = \{\omega_{j1}, \omega_{j2}, \ldots, \omega_{jn}\}^T$ is the vector that connects the i-th hidden node to the input nodes. In addition, b is the bias vector of each node of the hidden layer, $\beta_j = \{\beta_{j1}, \beta_{j2}, \beta_{j3}, \ldots, \beta_{jm}\}$ is the vector of weights that connects the j-th hidden node with the output nodes.

According to the universal approximation theorems of ELM [20], several activation functions can be used. This work uses the sigmoid function described as $g(x) = \frac{1}{1 + e^{(-\varpi x + b)}}$. When the activation function is infinitely differentiable it can be shown that a number of hidden nodes $l < N$ are needed [2]. Hence, the N equations can be written as $H\beta = T$ where:

$$H = \begin{bmatrix} g(\omega_1 x_1 + b_1) & \ldots & g(\omega_l x_1 + b_l) \\ \ldots & \ldots & \ldots \\ g(\omega_1 x_N + b_1) & \ldots & g(\omega_l x_N + b_l) \end{bmatrix}_{N*l} \quad Hidden\ layer\ output$$

$$\beta = \begin{bmatrix} \beta_1^T \\ \cdot \\ \vdots \\ \beta_l^T \end{bmatrix}_{l*m} \quad Output\ weights;\ and\ T = \begin{bmatrix} t_1^T \\ \cdot \\ \vdots \\ t_N^T \end{bmatrix}_{N*m} \quad Output\ matrix$$

To determine the β output weights between the nodes of the hidden layer and the output layer it is necessary to find the solution of least squares for the given linear system. The minimum norm for this linear system is $\hat{\beta} = H^\dagger T$, where $H^\dagger$ is the Moore–Penrose generalized inverse of matrix H.

2.2 Harmony Search

Harmony Search (HS) was proposed in 2001 by Geem and Leen [21]. It is a metaphor of the process of musical improvisation that occurs when a jazz musician seeks the optimal harmony and is useful as a meta-heuristic of optimization. When a musician is improvising, he performs one of the following three actions: (1) Plays a known melody he has learned, (2) Plays something like the previous melody by adapting it slightly to the desired tone and (3) Composes a new melody based on his knowledge using random notes. These three operations formalized in [21] correspond to the components of the algorithm: (1) Use of harmony memory, (2) pitch adjustment and (3) randomness.

HS has several advantages, namely: it uses few configuration parameters [22], it is fast [23], it is easy to implement and it has a search process with a lot of diversity since it uses random data (similar to the mutation in a genetic algorithm) and any of the values available in the solutions that are in the harmony memory (population in the genetic algorithm) to generate new solutions (children in a genetic algorithm).

HS has been extensively studied and applied in different areas [9, 13, 24, 25] and to date there are a number of variants in the literature. These include Improved Harmony Search (IHS) [22], Global-best Harmony Search (GHS) [26], Novel Global Harmony Search (NGHS) [27] and Global-best Harmony Search using learnable evolution models (GHS + LEM) [28].

GHS [26] combines HS with the Particle Swarm Optimization (PSO) concept proposed in [29] where the position of a particle is influenced by the best position visited by itself (its own experience) and the position of the best particle in the swarm (swarm experience). GBHS modifies from HS the tone adjustment of the new harmony toward the best harmony found in the harmony memory, reducing a parameter, and adding a social component to HS. This modification allows it to work with ease and efficiency in a wide range of optimization problems [26].

NGHS [27] proposed in 2010 uses the concept of swarm intelligence and genetic mutation for the process of creating new solutions. NGHS eliminates the use of two parameters of the original HS algorithm and includes a new one related to a probability of mutation. Swarm intelligence is included ensuring that the dimensions of the new solutions are created with parameters that vary in a range defined by the best and worst solution present in the harmony memory without leaving the search space.

3   Adaptation of HS Variants for ELM

The representation of the solution (harmony) in the ELM problem is composed of a vector of real values that represent the input weights (connections between the input layer and the hidden layer) and the biases of the hidden layer; in addition to a real value that represents the Fitness of the solution and that corresponds to the accuracy achieved by the ELM in the classification problem that is being solved (see Fig. 1).

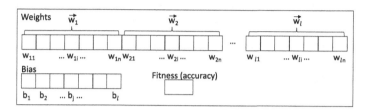

Fig. 1.   Representation of a harmony in all algorithms.

The general steps of each of the adaptations, HS-ELM, GHS-ELM, and NGHS-ELM are as follows:

Step 1: Initialize Parameters. The HS parameters are specified in this step. These parameters are Harmony Memory Size (HMS), Harmony Memory Consideration Rate (HMCR), Pitch Adjustment Rate (PAR), Bandwidth (BW) and Number of Improvisations (NI). Usually HMCR is between 0.6 and 0.9, PAR between 0.1 and 0.5, and HMS between 5 and 20.

In the case of GHS, the PAR parameter is removed and two other parameters included: Minimum Pitch Adjustment Rate (PARmin) and Maximum Pitch Adjustment Rate (PARmax) with which the value of PAR depending on the number of improvisations that were carried out is calculated. The BW parameter is also removed.

NGHS removes the PAR, HMCR and BW parameters of the original HS algorithm and includes a probability of mutation (Pm).

Step 2: Randomly Create the Harmonic Memory. In this step, a set of HMS solutions or harmonies is created. Each harmony $x' = \{x_1, x_2, x_3 \ldots x_p\}$ is a p-dimensional vector containing the values of the parameters to be optimized, for this study $p = l * (n + 1)$ where l corresponds to the number of hidden nodes and n to the number of inputs to the ELM. The parameters are determined randomly between the lower LB and upper UB limits. For this study $LB = -1 \ and \ UB = 1$. These parameters correspond to the hidden weights and biases required to construct the ELM.

Step 3: Calculate the Fitness of the Harmonic Memory. For each x_i; $i = 1, 2, \ldots, HMS$ harmony of the harmony memory the output weights and the corresponding accuracy of the ELM must be calculated. The latter value is assigned as the fitness of each harmony. The accuracy calculation involves training the ELM with the random weights and biases stored inside the harmony. Using the training data from the classification problem, the value of the ELM output weights β is calculated. The structure defined for the ELM is then used on test data and the accuracy of the model is calculated on this data. In the case that cross-validation of F folders is used, F models of ELM are created with different training and test data and thus the result is less optimistic or pessimistic depending on the case, although it implies a higher computational cost, since F ELMs are made to calculate the accuracy. In counting Fitness Function Evaluations (FFEs) the first training/test option adds one (1) time while the second of cross-validation adds F times. In the experiments, F = 5 was used, which is why the cost is five times higher than the first option, which implies that in this second option fewer solutions are generated than in the first one to be able to compare the two options.

Step 4: Improvisation of New Harmonies. The objective of this step is to generate a new harmony based on the available harmonies in the harmony memory. The new harmony $x' = \{x_1, x_2, x_3 \ldots \ldots x_n\}$ is generated based on the specific rules of each algorithm.

Figure 2 presents the HS improvisation process. Line 01 shows that each parameter of the solution must be generated, in this case the $l * n$ input weights and the l biases of the hidden layer, in total $l * (n + 1)$ parameters. For each parameter p, a random number between 0 and 1 is generated and if it is smaller than HMCR (line 02) the value is taken from the harmony memory. Otherwise it is generated randomly in the defined ranges (line 10). Now, if the value was taken from the harmony memory it may or not be adjusted, so in line 05 a random number between 0 and 1 is generated and if that value is less than PAR the adjustment shown in line 06 is made.

```
01    for each p = {1, 2, ..., l * (n + 1)} do
02        if U(0,1) < HMCR then /*consideration of memory*/
03            begin
04                x'_p = x^j_p, where j ~ U(1, ..., HMS)
05                if U(0,1) ≤ PAR then /*tone adjustment*/
06                    x'_p = x'_p ± U(0,1) × bw
07                end_if
08            end
09        unless /*random selection*/
10            x'_p = LB + (UB - LB) × U(0,1)
11        end_if
12    end_for
```

Fig. 2. Improvisation step in HS-ELM.

Figure 3 presents the GHS improvisation process. Line 00 shows the dynamic calculation of PAR based on the current improvisation number (t) and the minimum and maximum pitch adjustment parameters. The algorithm changes against HS between lines 05 and 07, first because the value of PAR is not static but dynamic and because in line 06 the parameter setting is not done with a BW parameter but the value of one of the values of the best of the harmony memory is selected, thereby achieving swarm behavior.

```
00   PAR(t) = PAR_min + ((PAR_max - PAR_min)/(NI-1)) × (t - 1)
01   for each p = {1, 2, ..., l * (n + 1)} do
02       if U(0,1) < HMCR then /*memory consideration*/
03           begin
04               x'_p = x^j_p, where j ~ U(1, ..., HMS)
05               if U(0,1) ≤ PAR(t) then /*tone adjustment*/
06                   x'_p = x^best_p, where best is the index of the best
                                      harmony in the HM
07               end_if
08           end
09       unless /*random selection*/
10           x'_p = LB + (UB - LB) × U(0,1)
11       end_if
12   end_for
```

$$00 \quad PAR(t) = PAR_{min} + \frac{(PAR_{max} - PAR_{min})}{(NI-1)} \times (t - 1)$$

Fig. 3. Improvisation step in GHS-ELM.

Figure 4 presents the NGHS improvisation process. First, the algorithm generates an x_R value (line 02), that is a value defined by the value of the best and the worst in the harmony memory. Then this value is controlled within the limits of the search space (lines 03 and 04). The value of the parameter is randomly generated (line 05) between the position of the worst and x_R. This is where the concept of PSO is applied. Then, if this value requires a mutation (line 06) this is applied by generating the value at random from the entire search range.

```
01   for each p = {1, 2, ..., l * (n + 1)} do
02       x_R = 2 × x^best_p - x^worst_p
03       if x_R > UB then x_R = UB
04       if x_R < LB then x_R = LB
05       x'_p = x^worst_p + U(0,1) × (x_R - x^worst_p) /*position updating as PSO*/
06       if U(0,1) ≤ Pm then /*genetic mutation*/
07           x'_p = LB + (UB - LB) × U(0,1)
08       end_if
09   end_for
```

Fig. 4. Improvisation step in NGHS-ELM.

Step 5: Calculate the Fitness of the New Harmony. Like Step 3, in this step the accuracy of the new harmony generated in the previous step is calculated.

Step 6: Replacement of the Worst Solution. If the new harmony is better (has greater accuracy) than the worst harmony in the harmony memory, the new harmony is included in the harmony memory and the worst harmony is removed.

Step 7: Check the Stop Criterion: Finish when the maximum number of improvisations is reached.

Step 8: Return the Best Solution: The best solution or harmony of the harmony memory is returned (including the best input weights and biases of the ELM) for the specific classification problem that is being solved.

4   Experiments and Results

4.1   Configuration of the Experiments

The algorithms were implemented in JAVA and run on a computer with an AMD a-10 processor, 3.2 GHz, 8 GB RAM, Windows 10 and the validation was made using 20 traditional datasets available at the UCI (University of California Irvine) repository. In the experiments, the attributes of each data set are normalized in a range of $[-1,1]$ as suggested in [8, 16]. Table 1 describes the datasets used for experimentation with the training instance number, the number of test instances, the number of attributes or variables, and the number of classes in the target variable. As can be seen, the training instances correspond to approximately 70% of the total data.

Table 1. Description of the datasets

Data set	#Train	#Test	#Attributes	#Class
Blood	500	248	4	2
Car	1152	576	6	4
Connectionist sonar	138	70	60	2
Contraceptive	1000	473	9	3
Control Chart	400	200	60	6
E coli	224	112	7	8
Fertility	70	30	9	2
Glass	154	60	10	8
Haberman	204	102	3	3
Indian	393	190	10	3
Ionosphere	234	117	34	2
Iris	100	50	4	3
Leaf	230	110	14	36
Vertebral (2c)	210	100	6	2
Vertebral (3c)	210	100	6	3
Vowel	365	163	10	11
Wdbc	379	190	30	2
Wine	118	60	13	3
Years	989	495	8	10
Zoo	70	31	16	7

Algorithm Parameters: The results of the experiments are obtained as the average of 30 executions of each algorithm in each dataset, showing also the standard deviation of the results. In the process of initialization of the harmonies these were initialized randomly between −1 and 1 and the ELM had 50 nodes in the hidden layer, while the activation function is the Sigmoidal.

The parameters used for all algorithms are summarized in Table 2. It is necessary to carry out a detailed parameter tuning process for all the algorithms since at the time the most recommended in the literature were used.

Table 2. Algorithm parameters

Parameter	HMS-ELM	GHS-ELM	NGHS-ELM
HMS	10	10	10
HMCR	0.9	0.9	–
PAR	0.4	–	–
BW	0.2	–	–
PARmin	–	0.1	–
PARmax	–	0.5	–
Pm	–	–	0.2
NI	3000	3000	3000

The comparison included an algorithm that randomly generated 3000 ELMs for each problem and selected the best from all of them (Random Walk algorithm, RW-ELM). It was also run 30 times for each problem and its mean and standard deviation were calculated. Finally, the M-ELM algorithm was included as it represents the current state of the art in ELM training. The parameters of M-ELM were: population size NP = 50, maximum of generations maxGen = 50, probability of mutation Pm = 0.4; for the local optimizer 10 optimizations were performed per individual in each generation and the stop criterion was also of 3000 evaluations of ELM.

Table 3 shows the results of running the algorithms using the two training and test stages with separate data and in Table 4 the results are presented with cross-validation. In general, accuracy results are a bit better when algorithms use separate archives for training and testing (Table 3), but according to the literature the use of cross-validation is a best choice because a more realistic (less optimistic or pessimistic) calculations of accuracy is executed.

Taking the results of Table 4, the non-parametric Friedman test was carried out, obtaining the ranking in Table 5. It is thereby evident that in the task of classification on the datasets evaluated using cross-validation or separate archives for training and testing, HS-ELM performs better than M-ELM (state of the art) and the rest of the algorithms. Also, the harmony search algorithms obtain better results than M-ELM and RW-ELM when the comparison is based on cross-validation technique.

Furthermore, the Wilcoxon non-parametric test show that with a 95% of confidence the HS algorithm dominates GHS-ELM when separate archives for training and testing are used. In cross-validation, no dominance relationship could be established.

Table 3. Results using separate training and testing data (partial results to stay within the size limits of the paper). The best test results are shown in bold

Data set	RW-ELM	M-ELM	HS-ELM	GBHS-ELM	NGHS_ELM
Blood	**79.2070 ± 0.2482**	78.9651 ± 0.3306	79.2070 ± 0.2692	79.1667 ± 0.3005	79.1532 ± 0.2582
Car	84.4271 ± 1.8860	83.2986 ± 1.6989	84.7106 ± 1.9621	84.1204 ± 2.2223	**85.0405 ± 2.0978**
Contraceptive	55.3347 ± 1.3820	54.7921 ± 1.2976	55.2008 ± 1.0922	54.9471 ± 1.4913	**55.6801 ± 1.5435**
Control Chart	52.6667 ± 1.9762	52.8333 ± 2.6936	**54.3833 ± 2.0884**	52.9833 ± 2.6220	54.3667 ± 2.7566
Fertility	77.3333 ± 7.0132	75.6667 ± 7.9884	**79.4444 ± 6.7266**	77.1111 ± 7.9225	77.6667 ± 7.6085
Glass	87.6667 ± 2.9690	87.8333 ± 2.6926	87.8333 ± 3.0777	87.2222 ± 2.8974	**88.1667 ± 2.6300**
Haberman	**69.9673 ± 1.2267**	69.7059 ± 1.2491	69.8039 ± 1.5889	69.7059 ± 1.3478	69.8693 ± 1.1582
Leaf	74.0000 ± 2.3891	75.2121 ± 2.5598	**75.2121 ± 2.4045**	74.5455 ± 2.4167	74.7879 ± 2.5274
Vowel	84.0082 ± 1.8195	83.1902 ± 2.2658	**85.4192 ± 2.4778**	84.6421 ± 1.8094	84.8057 ± 2.2496
Zoo	92.3656 ± 3.5808	92.3656 ± 3.5808	92.3656 ± 3.5808	92.3656 ± 3.5808	92.3656 ± 3.5808

Table 4. Results using cross-validation. The best test results are shown in bold

Data set	RW-ELM	M_ELM	HS-ELM	GBHS-ELM	NHS-ELM
Blood	78.3602 ± 0.5136	78.3602 ± 0.4335	**78.6156 ± 0.5556**	78.1720 ± 0.3566	78.2661 ± 0.4460
Car	84.2882 ± 1.7946	83.3044 ± 2.1554	84.4444 ± 1.8366	**84.5544 ± 2.2718**	83.9236 ± 2.0642
Connectionist sonar	75.7143 ± 4.6217	74.2857 ± 5.2424	**76.0000 ± 3.6589**	75.3810 ± 4.4521	74.7619 ± 5.1684
Contraceptive	54.9894 ± 1.8897	55.2079 ± 1.3256	55.2290 ± 1.6042	**55.5814 ± 1.5701**	54.8978 ± 1.3082
Control Chart	52.7500 ± 2.6887	52.6833 ± 2.6504	53.3833 ± 3.3731	53.7333 ± 2.5289	**54.1667 ± 2.0262**
E coli	86.4583 ± 1.4412	85.6250 ± 1.5002	86.1310 ± 1.2571	85.9524 ± 1.4199	**86.5476 ± 1.3626**
Fertility	75.8889 ± 5.6884	75.7778 ± 5.8962	**76.8889 ± 7.2996**	75.4444 ± 6.9646	73.6667 ± 7.8575
Glass	88.7778 ± 3.2184	89.2222 ± 2.7465	**89.3333 ± 2.8087**	89.2222 ± 2.2662	88.1667 ± 3.0837
Haberman	69.0196 ± 1.0314	**69.2810 ± 1.2487**	69.2484 ± 1.0883	68.9542 ± 1.1130	69.2157 ± 1.2034
Indian	70.4211 ± 1.6555	70.2281 ± 1.9251	70.3333 ± 1.3824	**71.0702 ± 1.4089**	70.8421 ± 1.3698
Ionosphere	88.9744 ± 2.8718	**89.7436 ± 1.8064**	88.3476 ± 1.8917	89.2877 ± 1.8691	89.6866 ± 2.4168
Iris	93.3333 ± 0.9428	**93.2667 ± 0.9638**	92.6000 ± 1.2806	**93.2667 ± 0.9638**	93.0000 ± 1.0000
Leaf	74.4545 ± 2.1558	74.7879 ± 1.9908	**75.1818 ± 2.6983**	74.8485 ± 2.3394	74.7273 ± 2.4326
Vertebral (2c)	**81.6667 ± 2.1029**	81.6333 ± 1.9746	81.4333 ± 2.0279	81.1000 ± 1.5567	81.1000 ± 1.9382
Vertebral (3c)	**82.2333 ± 1.7065**	81.9333 ± 1.3646	81.9000 ± 1.5780	81.6667 ± 1.6600	82.1000 ± 1.5351
Vowel	84.0082 ± 1.7987	83.1697 ± 2.1701	84.4376 ± 2.0067	84.7853 ± 1.4203	**84.8671 ± 1.6334**
Wdbc	95.6316 ± 1.0183	96.0702 ± 1.0326	95.7719 ± 0.8320	95.9123 ± 0.8561	**96.1053 ± 0.9474**
Wine	94.4444 ± 2.3701	**95.8333 ± 2.0526**	94.3889 ± 2.7717	94.8889 ± 2.6851	94.6111 ± 2.2229
Years	57.4815 ± 0.9283	57.4545 ± 0.6507	57.0370 ± 0.6563	**57.6566 ± 0.8420**	57.5286 ± 0.6187
Zoo	92.3656 ± 2.8225	91.8280 ± 3.1970	92.4731 ± 2.9250	92.3656 ± 2.5649	**92.6882 ± 3.1090**

Table 5. Ranking of algorithms based on the Friedman test

Algorithm	Ranking cross-validation	Ranking training/testing
HS-ELM	**2.850 (1)**	**2.300 (1)**
NGHS-ELM	2.875 (2)	3.025 (3)
GHS-ELM	2.900 (3)	3.400 (5)
RW-ELM	3.050 (4)	3.000 (2)
M-ELM	3.325 (5)	3.275 (4)
p-value	0.870 (chi-square with 4 degrees of freedom: 1.25)	0.214 (chi-square with 4 degrees of freedom: 5.81)

5   Conclusions and Future Work

In the present work, the Harmony Search, Global-best Harmony Search, and Novel Global Harmony Search algorithms were adapted to the problem of training Extreme Learning Machines using datasets divided into separate archives for training and testing and using cross-validation to evaluate the ELM classifier.

Harmony Search adaptation is a better alternative for ELM training in the datasets used for testing than the state-of-the-art algorithm, M-ELM, and the use of multiple random searches, RW-ELM. Finally, the harmony search algorithms obtain better results than M-ELM and RW-ELM when cross-validation is used.

The research group hopes to expand the number of test datasets, include regression problems, configure ELM for each dataset, and evaluate a wider set of meta-heuristics including those available in jMetal and the winners of the large scale continuous optimization competition in the Congress of Evolutionary Computation of the IEEE.

References

1. Rumelhart, D.E., Hinton, G.E., Williams, R.J.: Learning representations by back-propagating errors. Nature **323**, 533–536 (1986)
2. Huang, G.B., Zhu, Q.Y., Siew, C.K.: Extreme learning machine: theory and applications. Neurocomputing **70**, 489–501 (2006)
3. van Heeswijk, M.: Advances in Extreme Learning Machines (2015). http://urn.fi/URN: ISBN:978-952-60-6149-8
4. Zhu, Q.Y., Qin, A.K., Suganthan, P.N., Huang, G.: Bin: evolutionary extreme learning machine. Pattern Recognit. **38**, 1759–1763 (2005)
5. Han, F., Yao, H.F., Ling, Q.H.: An improved evolutionary extreme learning machine based on particle swarm optimization. Neurocomputing **116**, 87–93 (2013)
6. Saraswathi, S., Sundaram, S., Sundararajan, N., Zimmermann, M., Nilsen-Hamilton, M.: ICGA-PSO-ELM approach for accurate multiclass cancer classification resulting in reduced gene sets in which genes encoding secreted proteins are highly represented. IEEE/ACM Trans. Comput. Biol. Bioinform. **8**, 452–463 (2011)
7. Silva, D.N.G., Pacifico, L.D.S., Ludermir, T.B.: An evolutionary extreme learning machine based on group search optimization. In: 2011 IEEE Congress of Evolutionary Computation (CEC), pp. 574–580 (2011)
8. Cao, J., Lin, Z., Huang, G.: Bin: self-adaptive evolutionary extreme learning machine. Neural Process. Lett. **36**, 285–305 (2012)
9. Valença, I., Valença, M.: Optimizing the extreme learning machine using harmony search for hydrologic time series forecasting. Intell. Data Eng. Autom. Learn. IDEAL **2012**, 261–269 (2012)
10. Kong, H.: Evolving extreme learning machine paradigm with adaptive operator selection and parameter control. Int. J. Uncertain. Fuzziness Knowl. Base Syst. **21**, 143–154 (2013)
11. Learning, A.E., Elm, M.: Evolutionary extreme learning machine based on particle swarm optimization and clustering strategies. In: Proceedings of the 2013 International Joint Conference Neural Networks, vol. 560, pp. 305–310 (2013)
12. Bazi, Y., Alajlan, N., Melgani, F., AlHichri, H., Malek, S., Yager, R.R.: Differential evolution extreme learning machine for the classification of hyperspectral images. IEEE Geosci. Remote Sens. Lett. **11**, 1066–1070 (2014)

13. Dash, R., Dash, P.K., Bisoi, R.: A self adaptive differential harmony search based optimized extreme learning machine for financial time series prediction. Swarm Evol. Comput. **19**, 25–42 (2014)

14. Liu, N., Wang, H., Member, S.: Ensemble based extreme learning machine. IEEE Sig. Process. Lett. **17**, 754–757 (2010)

15. Cao, J., Lin, Z., Huang, G., Liu, N.: Voting based extreme learning machine. Inf. Sci. (Ny) **185**, 66–77 (2012)

16. Zhang, Y., Wu, J., Cai, Z., Zhang, P., Chen, L.: Memetic extreme learning machine. Pattern Recogn. **58**, 135–148 (2016)

17. Wolpert, D.H., Macready, W.G.: No free lunch theorems for optimization. IEEE Trans. Evol. Comput. **1**, 67–82 (1997)

18. Wong, W.K., Guo, Z.X.: A hybrid intelligent model for medium-term sales forecasting in fashion retail supply chains using extreme learning machine and harmony search algorithm. Int. J. Prod. Econ. **128**, 614–624 (2010)

19. Huang, G., Zhu, Q., Siew, C.: Extreme learning machine: a new learning scheme of feedforward neural networks. Neurocomputing **70**, 489–501 (2006)

20. Huang, G.B., Chen, L., Siew, C.K.: Universal approximation using incremental constructive feedforward networks with random hidden nodes. IEEE Trans. Neural Netw. **17**, 879–892 (2006)

21. Geem, Z.W., Kim, J.H., Loganathan, G.V.: A new heuristic optimization algorithm: harmony search. Simulation **76**, 60–68 (2001)

22. Mahdavia, M., Fesangharyb, M., Damangirb, E.: An improved harmony search algorithm for solving optimization problems. Appl. Math. Comput. **188**, 1567–1579 (2007)

23. Lee, K.S., Geem, Z.W.: A new meta-heuristic algorithm for continuous engineering optimization: harmony search theory and practice. Comput. Methods Appl. Mech. Eng. **194**, 3902–3933 (2005)

24. Manjarres, D., et al.: A survey on applications of the harmony search algorithm. Eng. Appl. Artif. Intell. **26**, 1818–1831 (2013)

25. Cobos, C., Pérez, J., Estupiñan, D.: A survey of harmony search. Av. en Sist. e Inform. **8**, 67–80 (2011)

26. Omran, M.G.H., Mahdavi, M.: Global-best harmony search. Appl. Math. Comput. **198**, 643–656 (2008)

27. Zou, D., Gao, L., Wu, J., Li, S., Li, Y.: A novel global harmony search algorithm for reliability problems. Comput. Ind. Eng. **58**, 307–316 (2010)

28. Cobos, C., Estupiñán, D., Pérez, J.: GHS + LEM: global-best harmony search using learnable evolution models. Appl. Math. Comput. **218**, 2558–2578 (2011)

29. Eberhart, R., Kennedy, J.: A new optimizer using particle swarm theory. In: Proceedings of the Sixth International Symposium Micro Machine and Human Science, pp. 39–43 (1995)

A Survey of Machine Learning Approaches for Age Related Macular Degeneration Diagnosis and Prediction

Antonieta Martínez-Velasco$^{(\boxtimes)}$ [ID]
and Lourdes Martínez-Villaseñor$^{(\boxtimes)}$ [ID]

Facultad de Ingeniería, Universidad Panamericana,
Augusto Rodin 498, 03920 Ciudad de México, Mexico
{amartinezv,lmartine}@up.edu.mx

Abstract. Age Related Macular Degeneration (AMD) is a complex disease caused by the interaction of multiple genes and environmental factors. AMD is the leading cause of visual dysfunction and blindness in developed countries, and a rising cause in underdeveloped countries. Currently, retinal images are studied in order to identify drusen in the retina. The classification of these images allows to support the medical diagnosis. Likewise, genetic variants and risk factors are studied in order to make predictive studies of the disease, which are carried out with the support of statistical tools and, recently, with Machine Learning (ML) methods. In this paper, we present a survey of studies performed in complex diseases under both approaches, especially for the case of AMD. We emphasize the approach based on the genetic variants of individuals, as it is a support tool for the prevention of AMD. According to the vision of personalized medicine, disease prevention is a priority to improve the quality of life of people and their families, as well as to avoid the inherent health burden.

Keywords: AMD · Machine Learning · Automated diagnosis
Classification · Pattern recognition · Predictive diagnosis

1 Introduction

A complex disease is caused by the interaction of multiple genes and environmental factors; they are also called multifactorial diseases. Complex diseases are caused by a complex system of interactions between genetic changes in more than one gene [1]. Epidemiological studies have demonstrated the importance of the hereditary component in some disorders such as diabetes, hypertension, and age-related macular degeneration (AMD), among others. AMD is the leading cause of visual dysfunction and blindness in developed countries, and a rising cause in underdeveloped countries [2]. In the United States, its prevalence in the population over the age of 65 years is 9% and increases to 28% in those over 75 years. AMD is characterized by progressive degeneration of the macula, causing central field vision loss. A characteristic feature of AMD is the formation of deposits in the macula, called drusen, which may progress to either geographic atrophy or subretinal neovascularization, indicators of late AMD [3].

F. Castro et al. (Eds.): MICAI 2017, LNAI 10632, pp. 257–266, 2018.
https://doi.org/10.1007/978-3-030-02837-4_21

The AMD risk models can be grouped into two categories: prediction, and inference. In the first category, the interest is to develop models that provide the best performance for risk assessment. AMD predictive models contains a combination of genetic, non-genetic and clinical risk factors which could be used to predict an individual's risk level. Predictive models are not fully accepted by a part of the medical community. The American Academy of Ophthalmology (AAO) has stated that genetic testing for multifactorial diseases will not be a routine practice until "clinical trials can demonstrate that patients with specific genotypes benefit from specific types of therapy or surveillance" [4]. The main difficulty of developing a predictive test is based on the complexity of the disease; the various clinical phenotypes and other confounding factors that may limit its usefulness. Until now, the classical statistical models have been the main method to model AMD. Nowadays we are in an era where diagnosis of AMD is most commonly pursued by image analysis [5].

We present a review of articles that have been developed based on ML. The first approach is based on retinal images and the second one in the study of risk factors. It is worth mentioning that the studies based on images are numerous and have developed since drusen have been identified as symptoms of AMD. Studies based on risk factors, especially genetic variants, have been recently developed because of the exploration of the genome. Some previous surveys have been made by Caixinha et al. [6] addressing both approaches, and Dasgupta [7] takes the approach of genetic variations.

In retinal image studies, the aim is to identify AMD-related lesions to improve AMD diagnosis. Traditionally, the AMD-related lesions are detected by physicians, being time-consuming and susceptible to variability. This paper presents the most recent studies under both approaches. Bellow, we will present the most recent and representative work done using methods of ML in the study of retinal images. Afterwards, we present works focused in the study of risk factors including genetic variants. There are fewer publications on this address, so we take the latest ones.

2   Machine Learning Approaches

The purpose of ML techniques is to automatically recognize complex patters in a given data set, allowing therefore for inference or prediction in new data sets [8]. The ML process to study retinal diseases is illustrated in Fig. 1. Those techniques are frequently used in clinical vision sciences. Studies done using ML have addressed the problem of retinal diseases under two approaches: the study of retinal images and the association with risk factors. In general, imaging studies are used as support in the diagnosis of retinal diseases such as AMD. Studies of the association with genetic and environmental risk factors have as their main objective the prognosis of diseases.

2.1   Retinal Image Analysis Approach

One of the first symptoms of AMD is presence of drusen on the retina. They may be identified through manual inspection/screening of retinal images or by automatized detection. Based on the performance of the used algorithms, the computational complexity and the obtained clinical results, the researcher may select the method that best

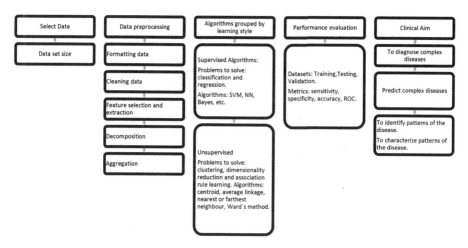

Fig. 1. ML process to study retinal diseases

fits the dataset used and the purpose of the work. Several problems still need to be solved to obtain unbiased predictive models in clinical vision sciences. In this sense, Hijazi et al. [9] presented two approaches to classify retinal images. First mentioned spatial histograms using Case Base generation and image classification using Case Based Reasoning (CBR) and Dynamic Time Warping (DTW). The process started with an image pre-processing in two stages. The second approach presents AMD screening using Hierarchical Decomposition (HD). It is a partitioning technique interlining images in angular and circular manner. Trees obtained as result are processed with SVM for feature selection. The hierarchical decomposition based approach produced much better results than the spatial histogram based approach with an accuracy of 100%. They report the problem of insufficient number of samples proposing to investigate ways to increase the size of the available data set.

Priya [10] used retinal fundus images to report an automated approach to help in the early detection of AMD using three models. They compare probabilistic neural network (PNN), Bayesian classification and support vector machine (SVM) performance to classify preprocessed retinal images. The extent of the disease spread can be identified by extracting the features of the retina. In the feature extraction process authors proposed to use dilation after thresholding to detect the drusen as the best proposed method applied in the dataset studied. SVM achieves higher performance than Bayes and PNN with 100% of accuracy. In order to identify neovascularization (CNV) in retinal images, which is one of the complications of AMD. Tsai et al. [11] analyses fluorescein angiography (FA) image sequences to segment choroidal CNV. Some kinds of CNV produce blood leakage. Authors determined the fluorescence intensity variation to determine the extent of CNV. They used AdaBoost algorithm to summarize the variation in fluorescence intensity. A severity map and segmentation of CNV were generated using the contribution scores of the classifiers. The average accuracy of CNV delineation obtained was 83.26%.

The presence of drusen and CNV is studied in Acharya et al. [12]. Their work is focused in AMD fundus images. Images have higher contrast than normal images in the green channel due to the presence of drusen and CNV. The appearance of normal fundus image is affected due to the presence of abnormal features. Authors present a Radon Transform (RT), Discrete Wavelet Transform (DWT) based method to extract these features which are useful to discriminate to normal and AMD classes. Feature dimension are reduced using Locality Sensitive Discriminant Analysis (LSDA) and ranked using t-test. The highest classification accuracy of 99.49%, 96.89% and 100% are reported for private, ARIA and STARE datasets. Results were presented an AMD index obtained by trial and error using LSDA components to discriminate AMD or not AMD images. This method limitation is to identify the early stage of AMD.

Mookiah [13] proposed a AMD classification method using statistical moments, energy, entropy, and Gini index extracted from wavelet coefficients without previous drusen segmentation. They formulated an AMD Risk Index based on the combination of the ranked features. It classifies images in normal and dry AMD classes. The Risk index can help the clinicians in faster and accurate screening of disease and could be used to assist the clinicians for mass AMD screening programs.

In the task of AMD grading, drusen segmentation is important given that appearance of drusen is the main symptom of AMD. In this way, Liu et al. [14] described a method to localize drusen even if they do not have rigid shape or size, and healthy structures of the fundus may be confused with drusen. In severe conditions, the drusen may clump together increasing the difficulty of drusen segmentation. After support vector machine (SVM) classification they obtained drusen locations. Afterwards, they used Growcut to track drusen boundaries with the aim of AMD grading by their classification. Continuing with AMD grading work, Liu [15] proposed a method to track the drusen localization from weakly labeled images. They considered drusen sparsity when the existence of them is known but not the exact locations or boundaries, by employing Multiple Instance Learning (MIL). This method is compared with reported works, achieving performance comparable with them on the task of AMD detection. They obtained comparable performance compared with fully supervised SVM. Authors considered to reduce the need for manual labeling of training data to improve classification results.

The early AMD detection was studied by Cheng et al. [16] using biologically inspired features (BIF). It imitates the process of human visual perception. The proposed focus scene is the macula. The differentiated images with drusen from those images without drusen was based on the extracted features. This method does not segment the drusen, it looks for intrinsic feature that differentiates retinal images with drusen from those images without drusen. The comparison of BIF with conventional methods based on interest points showing that BIF outperforms them. In the same way, including a high number of features does not help much as it might lead to slight overfitting. The results show that focal BIF from macula has a sensitivity of 86.3% and specificity of 91.9% and variable accuracy.

The diagnosis of AMD can also be based on the presence and quantity of drusen in the retina. With this approach Garg et al. [17] reported two methods to detect and count them based in their texture and the 3D profile of drusen. In first approach drusen texture is characterized in terms of the local energy, considering that energy is maximum at the locations of drusen. The energy maximum is computed with Garbor function. In the second approach, as drusen have a hilly profile, the Surface Tangent Derivative (STD) is used to detect hill-like features in the images. Those have high values of STD. They used a hill detection algorithm. In Acharya et al. [18], Pyramid of Histograms of Orientation Gradients (PHOG) technique was implemented to capture changes in pixels of fundus images. Various nonlinear features are extracted from the PHOG descriptor. To balance the number of images in three classes, an adaptive synthetic sampling (ADASYN) approach is used. Two feature selection techniques namely ant colony optimization genetic algorithm (ACO-GA) which imitates the behavior of social ants to search for the optimal features in a feature space, and particle swarm optimization (PSO) is used to select the best method. The selected features were subjected to an analysis of variance (ANOVA) to determine significant features for classification. The system has not been tested on enough wet AMD images so, its accuracy remains pending.

Studies in retinal images provide valuable support in the diagnosis of visual conditions as shown by some studies listed in Table 1. In case where the disease is to be prevented rather than diagnosed, the genetics and risk factors of individuals should be studied.

Table 1. Relevant studies of image analysis approach

	Data	Task	Method	Results
Hijazi et al. [9]	Retinal images	To classify images as either AMD or non-AMD	CB, HD. HD, SVM	Best accuracy 100%
Priya et al. [10]	Retinal images	To diagnose early AMD. Classifying wet, dry and normal classes	SVM, PNN, Bayesian Classification	Best accuracy 100%
Tsai et al. [11]	Image frames of FA sequences	To diagnose and quantify CNV by generating a CNV severity map	AdaBoost	Average accuracy 83.26%
Acharya et al. [12]	Retinal images	To classify AMD or no AMD images, AMD index	RT, DWT, LSDA	Best accuracy 100%
Mookiah et al. [13]	Retinal images	To classify dry AMD or normal images and AMD index	DWT, KLD, SVM	Best accuracy 93.7%, sensitivity 91.11%, specificity 96.30%
Liu et al. [14]	Retinal images	AMD grading by drusen segmentation	SVM, Growcut	Sensitivity 68%, specificity 94%
Liu et al. [15]	Retinal images	AMD detection and grading by drusen localization	MIL	Average precision 96%, p value <0.01
Cheng et al. [16]	Retinal images	Early AMD detection by determining presence of drusen	BIF, SVM	Sensitivity 86.3%, Specificity 91.9%
Garg et al. [17]	Retinal images	To grading drusen by counting and segmentation	STD	No assessment of the accuracy reported
Acharya et al. [18]	Retinal images	To identify normal, dry, and wet AMD images	PHOG, ACO-GA	Best accuracy 85.12%, Sensitivity 87.2%, Specificity 80%

2.2   Genetic Variations Analysis Approach

Since the importance of hereditary component in complex illnesses, scientists have sought to identify the genes and polymorphisms involved in diseases. In Genome Wide Association Studies (GWAS), a gene considered as a risk factor is chosen [19]. Some of its polymorphisms are identified and analyzed to determine the association between their alleles and a particular phenotype or the association with the frequency of a disease. Each year, GWAS are published with a growing number of associations of SNPs with diseases or phenotypic [20]. Further statistical analysis must be done in order to find a polymorphism or variant of a gene associated with a disease in a specific population. First, family aggregation is studied to determine if the disease is genetically determined. Second, it is necessary to locate genes of interest for the disease. In the identified areas there may be thousands of polymorphisms of interest [21].

Traditionally, probability and statistical techniques have been used to understand complex diseases. The difficulty of handling large amounts of data due to their volume, speed and variability makes the current methods computationally unfeasible, but the possibility of finding predictors related to the onset of the disease is a key reason to use ML techniques [22].

A major goal of personalized medicine is to pre-symptomatically identify individuals at high risk for disease using knowledge of individual´s genetic profile and their environmental risk factors. Larrañaga [23] mentioned ML as an important tool to solve the problem to transform the huge volume of complex data into knowledge. This article presents some of the most useful techniques for modelling and optimization for bioinformatics and emphasizes in the application of ML methods in genetics. Spencer [24] proposes to increase accuracy datasets by using multifactor dimensionality reduction (MDR) and grammatical evolution of neural networks (GENN), in addition to logistic regression (LR) approach. Combining the results from LR and GENN models, the algorithm achieves sensitivity of 77.0%, specificity 74.1%. Jiang [25] proposed a Random forest (RF) adaptation for epistatic interactions. The main contributions of epiForest (detection of epistatic interactions using sliding window sequential forward feature selection and RF) algorithm presented are the incorporation of the RF into case-control studies and the automated screening of the candidate SNPs for further statistical analysis. ML approaches are presented as a complement statistical methods to facilitate the exploration of interactions between multiple SNPs, because epistasis plays such an important role in the pathogenesis of AMD. Author proposed the gini importance, obtained from ML classification methods, may complement the p-value from the statistics studies, to measure for the associations between SNPs and AMD. To identify the possible combinations genetic variants that are protective for AMD, Gold et al. [26] analyzed an AMD risk factors dataset with an statistical model and then with a ML model using software based in Genetic Algorithms (GA). The benefit of GA models over traditional approaches is their ability to incorporate multiple loci from across the genome in making a prediction. This enables models to identify a complex interaction of polymorphisms that correlate with outcomes.

Chen et al. [27] proposed a forest-based method to identify gene–gene and gene–environment interactions. This method is proposed as a treatment of missing data, to reach variable selection, and model selection simultaneously. This approach avoids collinearity problem for genome wide data, and it does not require any a priori assumption. Forests based algorithms are a popular ML tool that are data adaptive, applies to large and small problems, and is able to consider correlation and interactions among features. False discovery is a major concern in disease gene identification. Authors demonstrated that the false-positive rate of the method can successfully distinguish disease-associated regions from neutral regions with a false – positive rate (FPR) less than 5%. Çelebiler [28] studied the relationship between the presence of multiple gene polymorphisms, risk factors, and dry and wet AMD. Three types of Bayesian Networks (BN) were constructed to investigate the relationship between the presence of multiple gene polymorphisms and AMD. Receiver Operating Characteristic (ROC) was selected to determine the optimum models. BN improves the learning process by attaching prior knowledge and causes less noise and overfitting than other methods. Its models flexibility allows to reach accurate decisions from uncertain data.

Fraccaro [5] compared "white-box" (WB) (including LR and decision trees), as the more interpretable of them, and "black-box" (BB) (support vector machine (SVM), Random forests and AdaBoost) methods. Both methods identified soft drusen and age as the most important features to diagnose AMD. Author emphasizes on interpretability and the limitation of the number of samples needed to obtain reliable results to make early diagnoses. A graphical user interface is proposed showing the diagnostic pathway or variable importance to provide to specialist decision paths to make early diagnoses feasible and better differentiating ambiguous subsets of patients. Krishnaiah et al. [29] presents the predictive performance of ANN model compared to the predictive ability of the LR model, it is shown that ANN performs better due to the relationship between variables. They obtained a risk score models. Studies under the generic variant approach offer a powerful tool for disease prognosis. In Table 2, we present the most representative works in the genetic approach of AMD.

Table 2. Relevant studies of genetic variations approach

	Data	Task	Method	Results
Spencer et al. [24]	Genetic variants and risk factor dataset	To identify individuals at high risk for AMD	MDR, GENN, LR	Sensitivity 77.0%, Specificity 74.1%
Jiang et al. [25]	SNPs dataset	Contribution of each SNP to the classification performance	EpiForest	8.5% classification error rate
Gold et al. [26]	SNPs and risk factors dataset	To identify risk and protective AMD haplotypes	GA	Sensitivity 58.37% Specificity 77.13%
Chen et al. [27]	Genetic variants dataset	To identify disease related haplotypes	Forest Algorithms	FPR <5%
Çelebiler et al. [28]	Clinical signs and genetic variants dataset	Relationship between SNPs and AMD	BN	Accuracy 83.3% (±4.7)
Fraccaro et al. [5]	Clinical signs dataset	To obtain a interpretable system to AMD diagnosis	WB: LR, DT BB: SVM, RF and AdaBoost	Mean performance WB 92%, BB: 90%
Krishnaiah et al. [29]	Risk factors dataset	To develop prediction models for AMD	LR, ANN	Sensitivity 79% Specificity 69%

3   Discussion

ML techniques are powerful tools to support the clinical decisions for AMD prevention and treatment. Image analysis support the diagnosis using segmentation and classification techniques. On the other hand, genetic variants and risk factors allows also the prognosis of AMD. Personalized medicine seeks to prevent illnesses instead of curing them.

Images of the retina are easy to obtain in the ophthalmology clinic. Their interpretation is based on the data present in the image, which can be refined and automated through ML techniques. The results obtained allow the diagnosis of AMD in order to give treatment indicated by the physician. Dataset of risk factors is generated from information of the patient and healthy persons, coming from the medical history. DNA samples usually come from blood samples. This should be genotyped, the process requires expensive inputs and the use of specialized laboratory equipment. The results of the studies can be diagnostic and preventive. Prognosis of AMD prevents people from getting sick by making changes in lifestyle and environment as directed by the physician. This avoids the high costs inherent to the disease, as well as the deterioration in the quality of life of the patients and their relatives. The study of genetic variants is recommended when data from close relatives who have suffered AMD are available. In both cases established ethical codes must be fulfilled. The general population is more likely to undergo an ophthalmologic study because of problems of reduced visibility. A study of genetic variants associated with a disease, is very seldom performed unless it is indicated because a close relative has had the disease. The study approach of the images is considered more accessible.

Regarding the methods applied for each approach, Support Vector Machines (SVM) are one of the techniques best evaluated in studies presented for retinal image approach. Despite its simplicity, it has proven to be a robust algorithm, and generalizes well in typical problems. It can be used in both classification and regression problems. SVM is robust for generalization, makes a good separation between classes. This allows a correct classification. For genetic variants and risk factors dataset analysis, the most commonly used algorithm that delivers better results is Random Forest. Adaptations such as epi-forest have been made on the basis of random forest principles, this is due to their advantages. Forest based techniques are precise classifiers, work efficiently on large databases, can handle hundreds of input variables without excluding any. It can also estimate which features are important in classification, has an efficient method to estimate missing data and maintain accuracy when missing a large proportion of the data, offers an experimental method to detect the interactions of the variables. It has some disadvantages, for example, classification made with Random Forest techniques is difficult to interpret by a specialist. If data contains groups of correlated attributes with performance similarity, then smaller groups are favored over the larger groups [7].

False discovery is the most important concern in the identification of AMD, so accuracy metric is always relevant for this problem. Other metrics generally used are sensitivity, which is the proportion of people with the disease that will have a positive result, specificity that is the proportion of people without the disease that will have a negative result, and accuracy is the ability to differentiate the patient and healthy correctly [27].

One of the problems that must be solved to improve the performance of both approaches is insufficiency in number of samples. Given the difficulty of obtaining samples, it is desirable to have public data sets. To the extent that methods are applied to a greater number of samples, their results will be more reliable, and valid comparisons can be made between them. Another important problem, as mentioned above, is interpretability. Specialist do not use automated systems because they do not trust them. This is because the method of decision-making is unknown by the specialist. Therefore, it is proposed that the path that is followed in ML to draw conclusions is revealed to specialists [27]. A friendly way to do that can be through decision trees.

It is important to consider that results of the studies will be different according to the origin of the samples. This means that they may vary according to the ethnicity being analyzed. Related works presented in this review were designed each based on different group of people, all with the common aim of looking elements to support the diagnosis and prognosis of AMD. The majority of the populations studied are Caucasian. By extending the ethnic groups studied, it was proved that AMD is not prevalent in groups with white skin and light-colored eyes [30]. Hence, more studies should be done in different ethnic groups.

References

1. Nitsch, D., Gonçalves, J.P., Ojeda, F., de Moor, B., Moreau, Y.: Candidate gene prioritization by network analysis of differential expression using machine learning approaches. BMC Bioinform. **11**, 460 (2010)
2. Wong, W.L., et al.: Global prevalence of age-related macular degeneration and disease burden projection for 2020 and 2040: a systematic review and meta-analysis. Lancet Glob. Health **2**, e106–e116 (2014)
3. Sivakumaran, T.A., et al.: A 32 kb critical region excluding Y402H in CFH mediates risk for age-related macular degeneration. PLoS ONE **6**, e25598 (2011)
4. Stone, E.M., et al.: Recommendations for genetic testing of inherited eye diseases: report of the American academy of ophthalmology task force on genetic testing. Ophthalmology **119**, 2408–2410 (2012)
5. Fraccaro, P., et al.: Combining macula clinical signs and patient characteristics for age-related macular degeneration diagnosis: a machine learning approach. BMC Ophthalmol. **15**, 10 (2015)
6. Caixinha, M., Nunes, S.: Machine learning techniques in clinical vision sciences. Curr. Eye Res. **42**, 1–15 (2016)
7. Dasgupta, A., Sun, Y.: Brief review of regression-based and machine learning methods in genetic epidemiology: the Genetic Analysis Workshop 17 experience. Genet. Epidemiol. **35**, 1–13 (2011)
8. Duda, R.O., Hart, P.E., Stork, D.G.: Pattern Classification, 2nd edn., p. 654. Wiley (2001)
9. Hijazi, M.H.A., Coenen, F., Zheng, Y.: Data mining techniques for the screening of age-related macular degeneration. Knowledge-Based Syst. **29**, 83–92 (2012)
10. Priya, R., Aruna, P.: Automated diagnosis of age-related macular degeneration using machine learning techniques. Int. J. Comput. Appl. Technol. **49**, 157 (2014)

11. Tsai, C.-L., Yang, Y.-L., Chen, S.-J., Lin, K.-S., Chan, C.-H., Lin, W.-Y.: Automatic characterization of classic choroidal neovascularization by using adaboost for supervised learning. Investig. Opthalmol. Vis. Sci. **52**, 2767 (2011)

12. Acharya, U.R., et al.: Novel risk index for the identification of age-related macular degeneration using radon transform and DWT features. Comput. Biol. Med. **73**, 131–140 (2016)

13. Mookiah, M.R., et al.: Decision support system for age-related macular degeneration using discrete wavelet transform. Med. Biol. Eng. Comput. **52**, 781–796 (2014)

14. Liu, H., Xu, Y., Wong, D.W.K., Liu, J.: Growcut-based drusen segmentation for age-related macular degeneration detection. In: 2014 IEEE Visual Communications and Image Processing Conference, VCIP 2014, pp. 161–164 (2015)

15. Liu, H., Xu, Y., Wong, D.W.K., Liu, J.: Effective drusen localization for early AMD screening using sparse multiple instance learning. In: Effective Drusen Localization for Early AMD Screening Using Sparse Multiple Instance Learning, pp. 73–80 (2015)

16. Cheng, J., et al.: Early age-related macular degeneration detection by focal biologically inspired feature. In: Proceedings of International Conference on Image Processing, pp. 2805–2808. ICIP (2012)

17. Garg, S., Sivaswamy, J., Datt Joshi, G.: Automatic drusen detection from colour retinal images. In: Conference on Computational Intelligence and Multimedia Applications, pp. 377–381. IEEE (2007)

18. Acharya, U.R., et al.: Automated screening tool for dry and wet age-related macular degeneration (ARMD) using pyramid of histogram of oriented gradients (PHOG) and nonlinear features. J. Comput. Sci. **20**, 41–51 (2017)

19. Cacheiro Martínez, P., Ordovás, J.M., Corella, D.: Métodos de selección de variables en estudios de asociación genética. Aplicación a un estudio de genes candidatos en Enfermedad de Parkinson, Coruña, España (2011)

20. Hindorff, L.A., et al.: Potential etiologic and functional implications of genome-wide association loci for human diseases and traits. Proc. Natl. Acad. Sci. **106**, 9362–9367 (2009)

21. Iniesta, R.: Análisis estadístico de polimorfismos genéticos en estudios epidemiológicos. Gac. Sanit. **19**, 333–341 (2005)

22. Zhang, M., Baird, P.N.: A decade of age-related macular degeneration risk models: what have we learned from them and where are we going? Ophthalmic Genet. **38**, 1–7 (2016)

23. Larrañaga, P., et al.: Machine learning in bioinformatics. Brief. Bioinform. **7**, 86–112 (2006)

24. Spencer, K.L., et al.: Using genetic variation and environmental risk factor data to identify individuals at high risk for age-related macular degeneration. PLoS ONE **6**, e17784 (2011)

25. Jiang, R., Tang, W., Wu, X., Fu, W.: A random forest approach to the detection of epistatic interactions in case-control studies. BMC Bioinform. **10**(Suppl 1), S65 (2009)

26. Gold, B., et al.: Variation in factor B (BF) and complement component 2 (C2) genes is associated with age-related macular degeneration. Nat. Genet. **38**, 458–462 (2006)

27. Chen, X., Liu, C.-T., Zhang, M., Zhang, H.: A forest-based approach to identifying gene and gene–gene interactions. Proc. Natl. Acad. Sci. U. S. A. **104**, 19199–19203 (2007)

28. Çelebiler, A., Şeker, H., Yüksel, B., Oruns, A., Karaca, M.B.: Discovery of the connection among age-related macular degeneration, MTHFR C677T and PAI 1 4G/5G gene polymorphisms, and body mass index by means of Bayesian inference methods. Turk. J. Electr. Eng. Comput. Sci. **21**, 2062–2078 (2013)

29. Krishnaiah, S., Surampudi, B., Keeffe, J.: Modeling the risk of age-related macular degeneration and its predictive comparisons in a population in South India. Int. J. Community Med. Public Health **2**, 137 (2015)

30. Swaroop, A., Branham, K.E.H., Chen, W., Abecasis, G.: Genetic susceptibility to age-related macular degeneration: a paradigm for dissecting complex disease traits. Hum. Mol. Genet. **16**, 174–182 (2007)

Outliers and the Simpson's Paradox

Eduarda Portela[1], Rita P. Ribeiro[1,3], and João Gama[1,2(✉)]

[1] LIAAD-INESC TEC, University of Porto, Porto, Portugal
eduarda.portela@gmail.com, rpribeiro@dcc.fc.up.pt, jgama@fep.up.pt
[2] Faculty of Economics, University Porto, Porto, Portugal
[3] Faculty of Sciences, University Porto, Porto, Portugal

Abstract. There is no standard definition of outliers, but most authors agree that outliers are points far from other data points. Several outlier detection techniques have been developed mainly with two different purposes. On one hand, outliers are the interesting observations, like in fraud detection, on the other side, outliers are considered measurement observations that should be removed from the analysis, e.g. robust statistics. In this work, we start from the observation that outliers are effected by the so called Simpson paradox: a trend that appears in different groups of data but disappears or reverses when these groups are combined. Given a dataset, we learn a regression tree. The tree grows by partitioning the data into groups more and more homogeneous of the target variable. At each partition defined by the tree, we apply a box plot on the target variable to detect outliers. We would expected that deeper nodes of the tree contain less and less outliers. We observe that some points previously signaled as outliers are no more signaled as such, but new outliers appear. The identification of outliers depends on the context considered. Based on this observation, we propose a new method to quantify the level of outlierness of data points.

1 Introduction

Data science is a field in constant and rapid evolution. More than ever before we understand that due to the knowledge acquired from data regarding any kind of population we can identify features that allow us not only to understand but also to predict their behaviors. Normally we aim to identify relevant patterns among populations, but sometimes the most valuable information is not in the general pattern but in the deviant behaviors. Such uncommon observations, outliers, may be mere errors in measurement or may represent very important individuals with very particular features of interest. Sometimes this kind of observation may not be so obvious as they are being purposely disguised, for example, when trying to cover fraud. Geology studies or public health services are other fields which make the study of methods for outlier detection a matter of interest. It may seem pretty simple, but in fact it is a difficult task to uncover some outliers. There are different kinds of outliers and the technique we choose to use will depend on it. In this paper we propose a method to uncover and score extreme outliers regarding

F. Castro et al. (Eds.): MICAI 2017, LNAI 10632, pp. 267–278, 2018.
https://doi.org/10.1007/978-3-030-02837-4_22

one specific numerical variable of interest - target variable, using other known variables as contextualizing factors to divide the data in groups as homogeneous as possible. Using these results we point out that outlier detection is an example of Simpsons Paradox: a trend that appears in divided sets of data and reverses or disappears when combining them. The paper is organized as follows: Sect. 2 introduces some important definitions and refers to some of the related work regarding outlier detection; Sect. 3 presents our method for outlier detection and scoring. Section 4 shows some preliminary results of the application of this method to in two known datasets; finally, Sect. 5 presents the conclusions.

2   Related Work

2.1   Outlier Definition

Outliers are observations that are considered abnormal. Formally defined in 1980 by Hawkins [1], *"An outlier is an observation which deviates so much from the other observations as to arouse suspicions that it was generated by a different mechanism."*. However, depending on the nature of the outlier, Singh [2] classified them as:

Point Outliers: The simplest type of outliers, a mere observation that falls away from the other observations. It may be a measurement error or an abnormal behavior/feature of the individual. For instance, a high quantity of water consumed in a month in a house may suggest a broken pipe or other problem in the infrastructure.

Contextual Outliers: Sometimes outliers are not obvious because of the context they are in. For instance, if we observe a very low usage of electricity in a family house in August we do not think of it as an outlier: besides being normal lower consumption in the summer, the house was probably empty for a couple of weeks as the family went on vacations. But if it happened in January we would consider it an abnormal observation.

Collective outliers: Outliers may not be only one value but a collection of values in a certain order. For example, if we consider a person's daily travel distance and assume this individual travels a longer path on working days than in the weekends. If for seven consecutive days this person shows a short travel distance and after that returns to the usual distance, we may assume that, for some reason, this person did not go to work that week. So the distance values were not considered outliers as they were normal for the weekends but the fact that they appear for 7 consecutive observations is considered abnormal.

When looking for outliers, we must be aware of two possible situations: Masking effect and Swamping effect. These situations may disguise some outliers [3]. Both occur when deviant observations skew the mean and the covariance estimated towards it. The masking effect occurs when a deviant observation *a* is not considered as outlier because other abnormal observation *b* is influencing the mean and covariance in the direction of observation *a*. In other words, if the observation

b is removed, observation a will be considered an outlier. In this case, outlier a is masked by outlier b. The swamping effect occurs when a deviant observation a, is considered an outlier only in the presence of other abnormal observation or observations. The influence of these may skew the mean and covariance towards it and make observation a seem like an outlier when in fact it is not.

2.2   Outlier Detection

Different kinds of outliers require different detection methods. We can find in the literature many outlier detection techniques. Hodge and Austin [4] and Chandola, Banerjee and Kumar [5] summarize some outlier detection techniques of which we refer the most important. These techniques can be divided into statistic based and distance based techniques.

Statistical-Based Techniques. These techniques are divided in **parametric** if it is assumed a known distribution of the population in study and **non-parametric** when there is no assumption of this kind.

Depending on the number of variables one may divide these techniques in **univariate** (if search is done in only one variable) or **multivariate**, otherwise. Two simple methods of univariate outlier detection techniques are described next.

- **Boxplot Analysis.** Point Outliers, as mentioned before, are abnormal observations. In case of numeric variables, these observations have values that are much lower or much higher than most of the others. The most common way to identify them is by boxplot analysis. We take the interquartile range, ($IQR = Q_3 - Q_1$) and consider as outliers the observations that fall farther than $1.5 * IQR$ up the third quartile or down the first quartile. If this distance is $3 * IQR$, the outliers are considered extreme.
- **Detecting Outliers using Standard Deviation.** When data are normally distributed they present an empirical behavior where 99.7% of the observations fall within a distance of three standard deviations ($3\,\sigma$) from the mean (μ), 95% within a distance of 2σ and 68% within a distance of σ. When it is possible to assume the data are normally distributed, the standard deviation can be use as an outlier detection measure. Choosing a ($a \in \Re$, $a \geq 1$), according to nature of the data and the goal of the analysis, observations that fall $a\sigma$ away from the mean are considered outliers [6].

Proximity-Based Techniques. Two of the most known types of outlier detection techniques are distance based and density based which are succinctly described next.

- **Distance-based Analysis.** General distance-based techniques define outliers according to the distance to the k nearest neighbor. There is no need to have previous knowledge about the data distribution model. These methods assume the k nearest neighbor distance is much larger in outliers than in normal data. Usually, Euclidean distance or Mahalanobis distance are used. These techniques have simple implementations but show an exponential computational growth with the increasing of dimensionality and number of records as the number of distances to be computed increases exponentially.

- **Density-Based Analysis.** Distance-based techniques may be sensitive to data locality. If we divide a dataset in clusters, being some of them much sparser then the others, depending on the distance defined, observations may be wrongly considered as outliers or outliers may go unnoticed. If the distance is too small, many points in the sparser cluster may be considered outliers; if it is too large, an observation that is faraway from a denser cluster, comparing to the observations within that cluster, will not be considered abnormal. To overcome this problem, density based algorithms started to appear. One example is LOF - Local Outlier Factor, Breunig, [7], which assigns to each observation a score. This score is the average of the density of the instance and its k neighbors. The density of an instance is calculated by dividing k for the volume of the hyper-sphere centered in the instance and with the smallest radius possible to contain the k neighbors.

Clustering Techniques. Assuming that a normal observation is in a cluster, close to the centroid of the cluster or belong to a large and dense cluster, we may define as outlier any observation that lies otherwise. Depending on the situation three types of anomaly detection techniques are defined. Papers [5] and [4] summarize the techniques mentioned as well as many others in the literature.

In this paper we propose a method that aims to detect outliers in a target numeric variable and considers the other available variables to group (contextualize) the individuals of the population.

3   Methodology

Let us assume a variable of interest Y whose domain is $\Re$. Our goal is to analyze this variable, and one direction is outlier identification. For this purpose, several well known techniques are available in the literature. We represent the "outlierness" of an individual, Y as $Out(Y)$. If we want to go deep in the analysis, we might be interested in understanding *why* a given $y_i \in Y$ value is an outlier. We can collect other variables that provide contextual information about the y_i. Assume we can measure a contextual variable X_k taking values in a discrete or continuous domain $\{x_{k1}, x_{k2}, \ldots, x_{kn}\}$. Given the contextual variable X_k, we can analyze the distribution of the target variable Y given the values of X_k. For example, if Y is Customer satisfaction and X_k represents regions with domain $\{North, South, East, West\}$, we can analyze the "outlierness" of Customer satisfaction per region: $Out(Customer\ Satisfaction|Region)$ or $Out(Y|X_k)$, obtaining this way a finer granularity analysis of the "outlierness" of a given y_i value. Assume two contextual variables X_1, X_2 with a domain of cardinality k and j respectively. Now, we can analyze $Out(Y|X_1)$, $Out(Y|X_2)$ or $Out(Y|X_1, X_2)$. The number of subsets we obtain is k, j and $k \times j$, respectively. Given several contextual variables, we can extend our analysis to the subsets of Y given by all possible combinations of the contextual variables. Of course, this is problematic due to the exponential number of possible combinations. To avoid the exponential growth of subsets, we grow a **regression tree** for the target variable using as explanatory variables the contextual ones [8]. A regression tree grows by selecting the explanatory variables that presents the higher reduction of the variance in the target variable. This way, we obtain subsets of growing homogeneity in terms of variance of Y. Breiman [9] in 1984, defined the CART (classification and regression trees) algorithm. This is a simple non-linear method that offers very good results and consists in the recursive partitioning of the heterogeneous initial dataset (root), dividing it in subsets for which the target variable partition is as homogeneous as possible. In order for that to happen, the algorithm aims to decrease the variance of the target variable. It starts by computing the sum of squares in the root, $SS_N = (y_i - \bar{y})^2$ being y_i the value that the target variable takes for individual i and $\bar{y}$ the mean value in the node. This value is then compared to the sum of squares of the two child nodes (Left and Right), $SS_L + SS_R$. The partition that minimize this sum is chosen (maximizing the difference SS_N-$(SS_L + SS_R)$ thus minimizing the global variance of the tree). The process is repeated for each new node until they no longer can be divided or the variance does not show a significant improvement. Both criteria can be a user defined parameter. The user can also define a maximum depth of the tree, so it will not get to long or create a node for each observation.

3.1   Detecting and Scoring Outliers

In this paper, we propose a method to detect outliers and assign score values to them. This aims to measure the "outlierness" $Out(y_i | x_{i1}, ..., x_{ic})$ of an observation i in the target variable Y considering the contextual variables $X_1, ..., X_c$, $c \in \{1, ..., C\}$, being C the total number of variables used in the regression tree learned. First, we take all the observations, I_i, $i \in \{1, ..., J\}$ where J is the total number of individuals. From those we will consider only the ones that are extreme outliers by the boxplot analysis at any node of the tree. Remember that an observation may be considered an outlier in some nodes but not in others. At each node n, $n \in \{1, ..., N\}$, where N represents the maximum number of possible nodes in the learned tree, we consider the median of the target variable, $MED(Y)_n$, and the standard deviation, $SD(Y)_n$. For each observation I_i in each node n, if I_i is considered an extreme outlier regarding the target variable y_i, we compute it's distance to the median and normalize it dividing it by the standard deviation of the correspondent node (Eq. 1):

$$Dist(y_i)_n = \frac{y_i - MED(Y)_n}{SD(Y)_n} \tag{1}$$

We then weight these distances using the fraction of individuals in the correspondent node in comparison to the total number of individuals (Eq. 2),

$$WDist(y_i)_n = \frac{W_n * Dist(y_i)_n}{J} \tag{2}$$

where W_n is the number of individuals in node n and J is the total number of individuals. The score assigned to each individual I_i is the sum of their correspondent $WDist(y_i)_n$ divided by the number of times the observation was consider as an extreme outlier, $EO(i)$, along the regression tree, as showed on Eq. 3:

$$Score(i) = \frac{\sum_n WDist_i(n)}{EO(i)} \tag{3}$$

In the next section we show some results of the application of this method to two public available datasets.

4   Experimental Work

In this section, we present an illustrative example of the proposed method using a very well known regression dataset: **Housing**. The regression problem consists of predicting the house value in the suburbs of Boston. We use the version of the dataset available at the UCI repository [10]. It consists of 506 instances evaluated in 14 variables, 12 of them continuous, 1 binary and the target variable which is the house value. Table 1 explains each variable.

Table 1. Housing - variables discription

Variable	Discription
CRIM	Per capita crime rate by town
ZN	Proportion of residential land zoned for lots over 25,000 sq.ft
INDUS	Proportion of non-retail business acres per town
CHAS	Charles River dummy variable ($=1$ if tract bounds river; 0 otherwise)
NOX	Nitric oxides concentration (parts per 10 million)
RM	Average number of rooms per dwelling
AGE	Proportion of owner-occupied units built prior to 1940
DIS	Weighted distances to five Boston employment centres
RAD	Index of accessibility to radial highways
TAX	Full-value property-tax rate per \$10,000
PTRATIO	Pupil-teacher ratio by town
B	1000(Bk - 0.63)^2 where Bk is the proportion of blacks by town
LSTAT	% lower status of the population
MEDV	Median value of owner-occupied homes in \$1000's

We start this analysis with the primary statistic measures from the target variable - MEDV. On Table 2 we see the range is 45 thousand dollars, the interquartile range (IQR) is 7.98 which is low compared to the range: at least 50% of the houses show a price between 17.02 and 25 thousand dollars (1st and

Table 2. Basic statistics measures from MEDV

Min	1st Qu	Median	Mean	3rd Qu	Max	SD	IQR	Outlier count
5	17,02	21,20	22,53	25	50	9,20	7,98	16

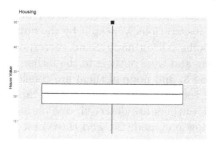

Fig. 1. Boxplot analysis of the target variable MEDV from Housing dataset

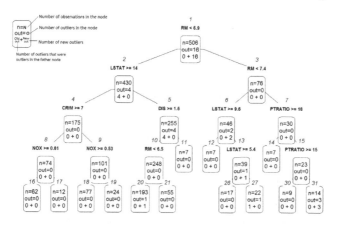

Fig. 2. Regression tree until level 4 - Housing dataset

3rd Quartiles). The standard deviation value is 9.20, a little higher than the IQR. As for the centrality measures, mean and median show values of 21.20 and 22.53, respectively. The mean value is greater than the median which suggests a right skewed distribution. These deviant observations may explain the higher values of mean and standard deviation when comparing to median and IQR values. The firsts are more sensitive to outliers than the seconds. The boxplot analysis detects 16 outliers and, as we can see on Fig. 1, all the abnormal observations (which present the same value - 50 thousand dollars) are represented by one point that falls farther than three times the IQR above the third quartile. The box is divided into two sections with similar size, but the upper whisker is longer which suggests (once again) a right skewed distribution.

We learn a regression tree for the Housing dataset in order to get a division of subsets of houses as homogeneous as possible regarding variance of the target variable (MEDV). We choose the CART algorithm [9], which is one of the best known algorithms and it is implemented on rpart package [11] from R software [12]. We use the default rpart parameters, and the result is an unbalanced tree with depth 11 and 83 nodes. The first leafs appear at level 3. For illustration purposes, we will analyze Fig. 2, that shows the first four levels of the boxplot tree. As expected in the root node there are 506 observations, and 16 of them are outliers. On level 1 the observations were split by the number of rooms. The ones with less than seven rooms fall on node 2 and correspond to 430 observations. Four of those are outliers and were outliers in the father node. The remaining 76 observations fall on node 3, and none of them are consider extreme outliers. As the analysis goes down the tree we can see outliers "appear" and "disappear". Focusing at level 4, five outliers are detected: one on node 27 (that was outlier in the father node), a new one, node 20, and three new ones on node 31.

Table 3. Housing - outliers scores and ranks

Obs	369	370	372	373	162	163
Score	3.2776 (1)	3.2776 (1)	3.2776 (1)	3.2776 (1)	3.1314 (2)	3.1314 (2)
Obs	164	167	187	196	205	226
Score	3.1314 (2)	3.1314 (2)	3.1314 (2)	3.1314 (2)	3.1314 (2)	3.1314 (2)
Obs	258	268	284	182	371	381
Score	3.1314 (2)	3.1314 (2)	3.1314 (2)	1.7843 (3)	1.1882 (4)	0.319 (5)
Obs	376	203	262	269	490	218
Score	0.2547 (6)	0.0725 (7)	0.0649 (8)	0.0612 (9)	0.0518 (10)	0.0481 (11)
Obs	433	473	231	157	311	343
Score	0.0381 (12)	0.0371 (13)	0.0298 (14)	0.0284 (15)	0.0283 (16)	0.0278 (17)

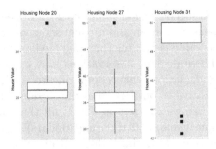

Fig. 3. Boxplot analysis of the target variable MEDV from Housing dataset on nodes 20, 27 and 31

Figure 3 shows the resultant boxplots of the mentioned nodes. Both outliers on nodes 20 and 27 show a very high value comparing to the observations that fall in the same node. On node 31 the three outliers values are much lower than the others. We identify these individuals (203, 262 and 269) and deepen the analysis of this node. This analysis show that they do not present big deviations in other variables other than the target variable. In fact, 9 of the 16 extreme outliers detected at the first boxplot analysis, fall on node 31 where are a total of 14 observations. In this context, these observations are considered normal. None of these outliers would be uncovered without the contextualization provide by the learned regression tree. After detecting the outliers along the tree, we score them according to their distance to the median value of the target variable in the nodes they were considered as outliers. In order to differentiate the outliers in nodes with bigger population as stronger than the ones in nodes with less individuals, we weight the distances by the fraction of individuals in the correspondent node according to Eq. 3. Table 3 shows the results. Outliers assigned with the higher score are observations 369, 370, 372 and 373. This observations were detected as outliers with the boxplot analysis and with the boxplot tree analysis at levels 1 and 2. They are followed by all the observations that were detected with the boxplot analysis but not with the boxplot tree analysis. Observation 371 was considered outlier three times (boxplot analysis and boxplot tree analysis at levels 3 and 4) but is below individual 182. This last was considered as an outlier only two times (levels 4 and 5). Part of it is explained by the higher distance to the mean presented by this observation than observation 371 and the other part relays on the fact that observation 182 is considered outlier on nodes 20 and 40 with 193 and 150 observation respectively while observation 371 is considered outlier at the root, where the weight for score calculation purpose is one, but also falls on nodes 13 and 27 with 39 and 22 observations respectively. For this reason this median distances are less influent. Observations 203, 262 and 269, the ones that fall on node 31, are ranked at 20th, 21st and 22nd places. We expected that they would be assigned with a low score value given there are only 14 observations on this node. In general, the outliers scored with the lower values are the ones that were uncovered at higher levels. At all we uncover 30 extreme outliers. Only sixteen of them where detected with the boxplot analysis. Our boxplot tree analysis not only suggests contextual outliers but also suggests some of the detected extreme outliers may, in the right context, be considered as normal observations.

The proposed method detects, scores and ranks individuals that at some level were considered abnormal. To understand the nature of the observations and take any real conclusions about it, a deeper inspection is required.

Another Example - Energy Efficiency. The Energy Efficiency dataset was created by Angeliki Xifara and processed at University of Oxford, UK [13]. It consists of 768 instances (buildings) characterized by eight real or integer variables. There are two target variables - Heating Load and Cooling Load. Due to redundant results it what comes to outliers detection in both target variables we chose to show the Cooling Load results. The variable description is seen on Table 4.

Table 4. Energy Efficiency - variables description

Variable	Description
X1	Relative compactness
X2	Surface area
X3	Wall area
X4	Roof area
X5	Overall height
X6	Orientation
X7	Glazing area
X8	Glazing area distribution
y1	Heating Load
y2	Cooling Load

Table 5. Basic statistic measures from Cooling Load

Min	1st Qu	Median	Mean	3rd Qu	Max	SD	Range	IQR	Outlier count
10,90	15,62	22,08	24,59	33,13	48,03	9,51	37.04	17,51	0

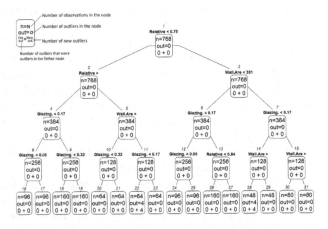

Fig. 4. Boxplot tree analysis of the target variable Cooling Load from Energy Efficiency dataset

Table 6. Energy Efficiency - outliers scores and ranks

Obs	750	24	44	48	45	43	47
Score	0.284 (1)	0.084 (2)	0.084 (2)	0.082 (3)	0.081 (4)	0.081 (4)	0.081 (4)
Obs	41	42	22	21	23	46	291
Score	0.08 (5)	0.079 (6)	0.079 (6)	0.077 (7)	0.077 (7)	0.076 (8)	0.033 (9)

Once again we will start with a univariate analysis of the "Cooling Load" variable. Table 5 summarizes the statistics. Notice the range is 37.4 and the Interquartile range is 17.51 which is almost half of the range. Mean and median values are close but the mean value being higher suggests a right skewed distribution. The box is not evenly divided: the distances between 1st Quartile and the Median is lower than the Median and 3rd Quartile. There are no outliers detected in this boxplot analysis. In order to analyze the contextual outliers, we learned a regression tree. As in the previous case, we did not limit the rpart algorithm in any of the parameters. The result, showed at Fig. 4 is an unbalanced tree with depth 9 and 141 nodes. The analysis of the boxplot tree shows that in this case the first outliers were detected at level 4 on nodes 22 and 28 as Fig. 4 illustrates. Deeper inspection showed that at level 5 were detected 5 extreme outliers and finally, at level 8 individual 291 appears as an outlier too. None of these observations are considered abnormal more than once. At all we detected fourteen extreme outliers when preforming the boxplot tree analysis. The simple boxplot analysis did not detect any of them. Individual 750 stands out with a higher score value as we can see at Table 6. A deeper inspection revealed that observation 750 was uncovered as an extreme outlier at level 5. With the exception of this individual and individual 291, detected as extreme outlier at level 8, all the other observations, uncovered as outliers at levels 4 and 5 are scored with near values. We considered that the results obtained by the boxplot tree method are not comparable with other methods, e.g. LOF, because of the different nature of the measurements.

5 Conclusions

Outlier detection is not as simple as one may think. In order to understand if an observation could be considered an outlier or not according to one target variable, we should contextualize it considering the other available variables. By combining the boxplot analysis with regression trees, we were able to uncover outliers in different datasets as well as score and rank them. Learning a decision tree using CART algorithm provided different contexts at each node, grouping individuals in a way that the variance of the target variable decreased. As expected, some extreme outliers "disappear" but some "appear". These last cases are of special importance, as we would expect that individuals with similar characteristics would show similar values in the target variable. The appearance and disappearance of outliers seems to be an instance of the Simpsons Paradox [14]: *a trend that appears in different groups of data but disappears or reverses when these groups are combined.* Different outliers are detected depending if we take partitions of a dataset or if we use the dataset as a whole. Outliers change when context changes. In [8] we observe this effect in a fraud detection case study. The score value assigned to an individual is based on the distance to the median of the target variable normalized by its standard deviation along the nodes of the tree. The higher scores may not be assigned to the most persistent outliers in terms of times they are considered as such. The number of individuals at the respective nodes influences the score values, the higher the number the higher the importance. Our method suggests possible contextual outliers, but only deeper investigations can show the meaning or reason for such deviant observations. This outlier detection and scoring method may be a robust tool in many applications such as fraud detection, medical diagnosis or earth science.

Ackowledgements. This work is financed by the European Regional Development Fund through the COMPETE 2020 Programme within project POCI-01-0145-FEDER-006961, and by National Funds through the FCT - Fundaao para a Cincia e a Tecnologia as part of project UID/EEA/50014/2013.

References

1. Hawkins, D.M.: Identification of Outliers, vol. 11. Springer, Dordrecht (1980). https://doi.org/10.1007/978-94-015-3994-4
2. Singh, K., Upadhyaya, S.: Outlier detection: applications and techniques. Int. J. Comput. Sci. Issues **9**(1), 307–323 (2012)
3. Acuna, E., Rodriguez, C.: A meta analysis study of outlier detection methods in classification. Technical paper, Department of Mathematics, University of Puerto Rico at Mayaguez (2004)
4. Hodge, V.J., Austin, J.: A survey of outlier detection methodologies. Artif. Intell. Rev. **22**(2), 85–126 (2004)
5. Chandola, V., Banerjee, A., Kumar, V.: Anomaly detection: a survey. ACM Comput. Surv. (CSUR) **41**(3), 15 (2009)
6. Shewhart, W.A.: Economic Control of Quality of Manufactured Product. ASQ Quality Press, Milwaukee (1931)
7. Breunig, M.M., Kriegel, H.-P., Ng, R.T., Sander, J.: LOF: identifying density-based local outliers. In: ACM SIGMOD record, vol. 29, pp. 93–104. ACM (2000)
8. Ribeiro, R.P., Oliveira, R., Gama, J.: Detection of fraud symptoms in the retail industry. In: Montes-y-Gómez, M., Escalante, H.J., Segura, A., Murillo, J.D. (eds.) IBERAMIA 2016. LNCS (LNAI), vol. 10022, pp. 189–200. Springer, Cham (2016). https://doi.org/10.1007/978-3-319-47955-2_16
9. Breiman, L., Friedman, J., Olshen, R., Stone, C.: Classification and Regression Trees. Wadsworth and Brooks, Monterey (1984)
10. Lichman, M.: UCI machine learning repository (2013)
11. Therneau, T., Atkinson, B., Ripley, B.: rpart: Recursive Partitioning and Regression Trees. R package version 4.1-10 (2015)
12. R Development Core Team: R: a language and environment for statistical computing. R Foundation for Statistical Computing, Vienna, Austria (2008). ISBN 3-900051-07-0
13. Tsanas, A., Xifara, A.: Accurate quantitative estimation of energy performance of residential buildings using statistical machine learning tools. Energy Build. **49**, 560–567 (2012)
14. Blyth, C.R.: On Simpson's paradox and the sure-thing principle. J. Am. Statist. Assoc. **67**(338), 364–366 (1972)

Full Model Selection in Big Data

Angel Díaz-Pacheco[(⊠)] [iD], Jesús A. Gonzalez-Bernal,
Carlos Alberto Reyes-García, and Hugo Jair Escalante-Balderas

Computer Science Department,
Instituto Nacional de Astrofísica, Óptica y Electrónica (INAOE),
Luis Enrique Erro No. 1, Santa Mara Tonantzintla, 72840 Puebla, Mexico
diazpacheco@inaoep.mx

Abstract. The increasingly larger quantities of information generated
in the world over the last few years, has led to the emergence of the
paradigm known as Big Data. The analysis of those vast quantities of
data has become an important task in science and business in order
to turn that information into a valuable asset. Many data analysis tasks
involves the use of machine learning techniques during the model creation
step and the goal of these predictive models consists on achieving the
highest possible accuracy to predict new samples, and for this reason
there is high interest in selecting the most suitable algorithm for a specific
dataset. This trend is known as model selection and it has been widely
studied in datasets of common size, but poorly explored in the Big Data
context. As an effort to explore in this direction this work propose an
algorithm for model selection in Big Data.

Keywords: Big Data · Model selection · Machine learning

1 Introduction

The lowering costs and the emergence of new technologies has favoured the generation and storing of massive quantities of information, which can be turned
into a valuable asset through its analysis. With the advent of new technologies
such as social networks, the quantity and variety of data has grown to unprece-
dented scales. In 2014, 2.5 quintillions of Bytes of information were daily created
[18]. Big Data became popular due to this phenomenon. A widespread definition
of Big Data describes this concept in terms of three characteristics of information in this field: Volume, Velocity and Variety (delrio2014). Subsequently
other Vs have been added: Veracity and Value [17]. In this regard, turning the
information into a valuable asset is carried out through machine learning techniques and choosing an appropriate learning algorithm is not a trivial task. This
process requires finding the combination of learning algorithms together with
their hyper-parameters to achieve the lowest misclassification rate in a wide

Supported by CONACyT.

F. Castro et al. (Eds.): MICAI 2017, LNAI 10632, pp. 279–289, 2018.
https://doi.org/10.1007/978-3-030-02837-4_23

search space [16]. In that same spirit, the Full Model Selection (FMS) paradigm proposed by Escalante et al. [9] considers also the data preparation as the discretization or data normalization and the dimensionality reduction through a feature selection algorithm. FMS has been addressed as an optimization problem varying the search technique employed. As an example, in [10] was proposed a hybrid method based on grid search and the theoretic hyper-parameter decision technique (ThD) of Cherkassy and Ma for the algorithm SVR (Support Vector Regression). In [3] evidence was obtained that random search can get similar or even better models than grid search in a fraction of the computing time. In [11] a genetic algorithm was employed for the hyper-parameter tuning of the SVM algorithm. [6] tackled and defined the full model selection problem with the use of a particle swarm optimization algorithm (PSO), in [9] a PSO algorithm was also used but just for hyper-parameter optimization for the ls-SVM algorithm meanwhile in [2]was proposed the use of the bat algorithm for solving FMS. In [5] was presented a method for model selection, based on a multi-objective genetic algorithm where the evaluation function takes into account sensitivity as well as specificity. [14] Also tackled the search phase with a multi-objective genetic algorithm. They take into account the misclassification rate and the complexity of the models computed through the Vapnik-Chervonenkis dimension (VC). In 2015 [13] proposed the inclusion of surrogate functions in order to decrease the use of expensive fitness functions. All of the previous approaches for the model selection problem work with datasets that can be loaded in main memory, but if the amount of data is larger than a conventional personal computer can store, the model exhibiting the lowest error will not be found. This paper has the following organization. Section 2 provides a definition of the FMS problem. In Sect. 3 we present some background on Big Data and MapReduce. Section 4 describes our proposed algorithm. Section 5 shows the experiments performed to test the validity of our proposal. Finally, Sect. 6 presents conclusions and future work.

2   Full Model Selection (FMS)

As mentioned in the previous section, full model selection is the combination of several factors in order to obtain the lowest misclassification rate in the dataset under analysis. These factors are feature selection, data preparation, and the selection of a learning algorithm with its hyper-parameters tuned [6]. Equation 1 is given as formal definition. Given a set of learning algorithms A, data preparation techniques P and feature selection algorithms F, the goal of the FMS is to determine the combination of algorithms: $a_{wA}^* \in A$ (a machine learning algorithm with an specific configuration in its hyper-parameter values), $p^* \in P$ and $f^* \in F$ with the lowest misclassification rate. The misclassification rate is estimated over the dataset D and this dataset is splitted in two disjoint partitions ($D_{train}^{(i)}$ and $D_{validation}^{(i)}$ for $i = 1, 2, \ldots, k$). The misclassification rate is calculated with the loss function $\frac{1}{k}\sum_{i=1}^{k} \mathcal{L}(a_{wA}, p^j, f, D_{train}, D_{validation}^{(i)})$, training the algorithm a_{wA} in the partition $D_{train}^{(i)}$, and evaluated in the partition $D_{validation}^{(i)}$. The data partitions are previously transformed by p and f.

$$a^*_{wA}, p^*, f^* \in argmin \frac{1}{k} \sum_{i=1}^{k} \mathcal{L}(a_{wA}, p, f, D^{(i)}_{train}, D^{(i)}_{validation})$$

$$a^{(i)} \in A, p^{(i)} \in P, f^{(i)} \in F, w_A \in W_A \tag{1}$$

Where:

A	= Set of available learning algorithms
P	= Set of available data-preparation algorithms including $\varnothing$
F	= Set of available feature selection algorithms including $\varnothing$
W_A	= Set of hyperparameters of a learning algorithm a
D_{train}, D_{val}	= Disjoint partitions of the dataset under analysis
$\mathcal{L}$	= Loss function calculated on the validation set (misclassification rate)
$argmin$	= Values that obtains the lowest misclassification rate on the loss function $\mathcal{L}$.

3   Big Data and the MapReduce Programming Model

In this section we present some antecedents about the MapReduce programming model, the standard framework for the development of Big Data analysis applications. MapReduce was introduced by Dean and Ghemawat in 2004 with the goal of enabling the parallelization and distribution of big scale computation required to analyse the large datasets. This programming model was designed to work over computing clusters and it works under the master-slave communication model. The master is responsible for scheduling the jobs on the worker nodes and the worker nodes execute the tasks as directed by the master. The design of MapReduce considers the following fundamental principles: (1) Low-Cost Unreliable Commodity Hardware. (2) Extremely Scalable Cluster. The nodes can be taken out of service with almost no impact to keep the MapReduce jobs running. (3) Fault tolerant. The MapReduce framework applies straightforward mechanisms to replicate data and keep processes running in case of failures. In the MapReduce programming model a computing task is specified as a sequence of stages: map, shuffle and reduce that works on a dataset $X = \{x_1, x_2, \ldots, x_n\}$. The map step applies a function μ to each value x_i to produce a finite set of key-value pairs (k, v). To allow for parallel execution, the computation of function $\mu(x_i)$, must depend only on x_i. The shuffle step collects all the key-value pairs produced in the previous map step, and produces a set of lists, $L_k = (k; v_1, v_2, \ldots, v_n)$ where each of such lists consists of all values v_i, such that $k_i = k$ for a key k assigned in the map step. The reduce stage applies a function ρ to each list $L_k = (k; v_1, v_2, \ldots, v_n)$, created during the shuffle step, to produce a set of values $y_1, y_2, \ldots, y_n$. The reduce function ρ is defined to work sequentially on L_k but should be independent of other lists L_k, where $k' \neq k$ [7]. Despite being an extended definition, the 5 V's of Big Data are little ambiguous and do not provides rules to identify a huge dataset. Therefore in this work we propose an alternative definition but related to the model selection problem. For our definition we propose that a huge dataset for the model selection problem must accomplish two rules: (1) The dataset size is big enough that at least one of the considered classification algorithms in their sequential version cannot process it. (2) The dataset size is defined by their file size considering the number of instances (I) and features (F) as long as $I \gg F$.

4 A MapReduce Based Particle Swarm Model Selection (PSMS) Algorithm

As previously mentioned one of the most popular and successful algorithm to perform the FMS analysis is the PSMS algorithm proposed by [6]. This algorithm is based on the PSO algorithm which is a population-based search algorithm inspired by the behavior of biological communities that exhibit both individual and social behavior [6]. PSMS is faster and easy to implement because relies in just one operator unlike the evolutionary algorithms. Those algorithms requires different types of operators for crossover and mutation depending on the type of codification employed in the several parts that form an individual. Due to the aforementioned reasons the PSMS algorithm was chosen and adapted to the MapReduce paradigm in order to deal with the datasets that belongs to Big Data. In the following subsections the proposed algorithm will be explained.

4.1 Codification and Functioning

The solutions encoded in PSMS needs to be codified in a vector called particle. Each particle $x_i^t = [x_{i,1}^t, x_{i,2}^t, \ldots, x_{i,16}^t,]$ is encoded as follows: In position 1 the fitness of the potential models is stored. Position 2 allows to determine which operation will be done first: data-preparation or feature selection. Position 3 indicates if the data-preparation step will be done. Positions 4 to 6 are parameters for the data-preparation step (method identifier, parameter 1 and parameter 2). Position 7 determines if the feature selection step will be done. Positions 8 and 9 are for the feature selection step (Method identifier and number of features to be selected respectively). Positions 10 to 16 are for the machine learning algorithm construction. The range of values that every element in the vector can take is as follows: [0–100]; [0, 1], [0, 1], [1, 30], [1, NF], [1, 50], [0, 1], [1, 5], [1, NF], [1, 6], [1, 2], [1, 4], [1, 100], [1, 60], [1, 400], [−20, 20] with NF = Number of Features. At each time t, each particle, i, has a position in the search space. A set of particles $S = \{x_1^t, x_2^t, \ldots, x_m^t\}$ is called a swarm. Every particle has a related velocity value that is used to explore the search space and the velocity of such particle at time t is as follows $V_i^t = [v_{i,1}^t, v_{i,2}^t, \ldots, v_{i,16}^t]$ where $v_{i,k}^t$ is the velocity for dimension k of the particle i at time t. The search trajectories are adjusted employing the following equations:

$$v_{i,j}^{t+1} = W \times v_{i,j}^t + c1 \times r1 \times (p_{i,j} - x_{i,j}^t) + c2 \times r2 \times (p_{g,j} - x_{i,j}^t) \qquad (2)$$

$$x_{i,j}^{t+1} = x_{i,j}^t + v_{i,j}^{t+1} \tag{3}$$

from the previous equations $p_{i,j}$ is the value in dimension j of the best solution found so far, also called personal best. $p_{g,j}$ is the value in dimension j of the best particle found so far in the swarm. Regarding to $c1, c2 \in \mathbb{R}$, are constants weighting the influence of local and global best solutions, and $r1, r2 \sim U[0,1]$ are values that introduce randomness into the search process. The inertia weight W controls the impact of the past velocity of a particle over the current one, influencing the local and global exploration. As in the original paper, the inertia weight is adaptive and specified by the triplet $W = (w_{start}, w_f, w_{end})$; where w_{start} and w_{end} are the initial values of W, w_f indicates the fraction of iterations in which W is decreased. W is decreased by $W = W - w_{dec}$ from the first iteration where $W = W_{start}$ to the last iteration where $W = w_{end}$ and $w_{dec} = \frac{w_{start} - w_{end}}{Number\_of\_iterations}$ [6].

4.2   Models Evaluation

This version of PSMS was developed under Apache Spark 1.6.0, that is based on MapReduce. Apache Spark was selected because of its enhanced capacity to deal with iterative algorithms and the possibility to perform data processing in main memory (if memory capacity allows it). An analysis of the advantages of Spark over traditional MapReduce is out of the scope of this work, but we refer to [20]. The cornerstone of Apache Spark is the RDD or Resilient Distributed Dataset which is a collection of partitioned data elements that can be processed in parallel [8]. In Algorithm 1 a procedure to obtain an RDD from a plain text file is shown.

Algorithm 1. Get the RDD

1: **procedure** GETRDD(PathDataset,numparts)
2:     RowRDD = Load(PathDataset,numparts)
3:     ▷ Obtains RDD[String] and divide it among each node
4:     RDDcol = RowRDD.map(row → row.split(","))
5:     ▷ The split function is applied to every row in the RDD[String] and then it is transformed into RDD[Array[String]] (separated by columns)
6:     RDDVect = RDDcol.map(row → Vector(row.map(ColInR → ColInR.toDouble)))
7:     ▷ Every column is transformed to Double type and RDD[Vector[Double]] is obtained
8:     Return(RDDvVect)
9: **end procedure**

As described above, the models evaluation stage is comprised of data preparation, feature selection, and training of a classification algorithm, in the following algorithms this process is described.

Algorithm 2. Fitness calculation

1: **procedure** MRFITNESS(Swarm,TrainSet)
2:     fitness = Array[Double](Population.length)
3:     **for** i = 0; i < Swarm.length; i++ **do**
4:         particle = Swarm(i)
5:         precedence = particle(2)
6:         **if** precedence == 0 **then**
7:             RDDPrep = DataPrep(TrainSet,particle)   ▷ Performs data preparation
8:             RDDFS = FeatSelection(RDDPrep,particle)   ▷ Performs feature selection
9:             fitness(i) = Classification(RDDFS,particle)   ▷ Performs classification
10:        **else**
11:            RDDFS = FeatSelection(TrainSet,particle)   ▷ Performs feature selection
12:            RDDPrep = DataPrep(RDDFS,particle)   ▷ Performs data preparation
13:            fitness(i) = Classification(RDDPrep,particle) ▷ Performs classification
14:        **end if**
15:    **end for**
16:    Return(fitness)
17: **end procedure**

The constitutive parts of Algorithm 2 are shown in the following algorithms for data preparation, feature selection and classification under the MapReduce paradigm.

Algorithm 3. Data preparation

1: **procedure** DATAPREP(DataSet,particle)
2:     Return(DataSet.map(row → row.toArray.map(col → Transform(col,particle))))
3:     ▷ The Transform function is applied to every column of each row in the RDD according to the parameters encoded in the particle
4: **end procedure**

Algorithm 4. Feature Selection

1: **procedure** FEATSELECTION(DataSet,particle)
2:     numFeat = particle(9)
3:     rankRDD = DataSet.map(row → RankingCalculation(row))
4:     ▷ The RankingCalculation function obtains the ranking of the features of the dataset
5:     reducedRDD = rankRDD.map(row → getF(row,numFeat))
6:     ▷ The function getF is applied to every row in rankRDD and returns a reduced dataset
7:     Return(reducedRDD)
8: **end procedure**

Algorithm 5. Classification

1: **procedure** CLASSIFICATION(DataSet,particle)
2:     NumFolds = 2
3:     kFolds = createFold(DataSet,NumFolds)
4:     ▷ The createFold function creates an RDD for k-Fold Cross validation
5:     error=kFolds.map {
6:         **case**(Training,Validation)
7:     ▷ The dataset is separated in Training and Validation partitions
8:         model = createModel(Training, particle)
9:     ▷ The createModel function create a model using the parameters codified in the particle
10:        PredictedTargets = Validation.map(Instance → model.predict(Instance.features))
11:    ▷ Performs the predictions in the validation set
12:        accuracy= getAcc(PredictedTargets,Validation.targets)
13:    ▷ Obtains the accuracy in each fold
14:        error = 100-accuracy
15:        Return(error)
16:    }
17:    meanError=error.sum/error.length
18:    Return(meanError)
19: **end procedure**

In the proposed version of PSMS, the mean error over the 2-fold cross validation is used in order to evaluate the performance of every potential model. During the test stage in the development of the algorithm, different number of folds were evaluated (2, ..., 10) without significant differences, but adding to the computing time factor, the 2-fold cross validation was the best choice. Under another programming paradigm (other than MapReduce), the construction of a single model with such large amount of data would have been impossible. The algorithms used in this work for data-preparation are: (1) Feature standardization, (2) Normalization, (3) Principal Component analysis, (4) Shift and scale and (5) Discretization. For feature selection, the algorithms are: (1) Joint Mutual Information, (2) Minimum Redundancy Maximum Relevance, (3) Interaction Capping, (4) Conditional Mutual Information Maximization and (5) Informative Fragments. Finally the classification algorithms are: (1) Support Vector Machine (SVM), (2) Logistic Regression (LR), (3) Nave Bayes (NB), (4) Decision Tree (DT), (4) Random Forest (RF) and (5) Gradient-Boosted Trees (GBT).

5   Experiments and Results

With the purpose to evaluate the proposed algorithm performance, we experimented with the datasets shown in Table 1. The datasets "Synthetic 1" and "Synthetic 2" were created using the tool for synthetic datasets generation in the context of ordinal regression: "Synthetic Datasets Nspheres" provided in [15]. Despite of have been developed for ordinal regression, the tool can be properly adjusted for traditional binary or multi-class problems and provides the mechanism to control the overlaps and classes balance.

Table 1. Datasets used in the experiments.

Datasets	Data points	Attributes	Samples by class	Type of variables	File size
RLCP	5749111	11	(5728197; 20915)	Real	261.6 MB
KDD	4856150	41	(972780; 3883369)	Categorical	653 MB
Synthetic 1	200000000	3	(100000000; 100000000)	Real	5.5 GB
Higgs	11000000	28	(5170877; 5829123)	Real	7.5 GB
Synthetic 2	49000002	30	(24500001; 24500001)	Real	12.7 GB
Epsilon	500,000	2000	(249778; 250222)	Real	15.6 GB

Another major feature of the aforementioned datasets is its intrinsic dimension. The intrinsic dimension (ID) is the minimum number of parameters needed to represent the data without information loss [12]. The id of the employed datasets was estimated with the "Minimum neighbor distance estimator" (MNDE) [12] and the "Dimensionality from angle and norm concentration" (DANCO) estimator [4]. The importance of the estimation of the id of each dataset is ensure that each dataset represent a different computational problem and, therefore, that the proposed algorithm have the capability to deal with a wide range of problems and in the context of this work also with datasets of different sizes. In the next table the calculated intrinsic dimension using the aforementioned estimators is shown.

Table 2. Intrinsic dimension of the datasets.

Datasets	MNDE	DANCO
RLCP	2	2
KDD	1	1
Synthetic 1	3	3
Higgs	12	15
Synthetic 2	22	28
Epsilon	160	78

We compared the performance of our algorithm against the "Kernel" K Nearest-Neighbour algorithm (K-NN) present in [19] and the Apache Spark MLlibs tool for tuning machine learning algorithms [1]. This tool allows users to optimize hyper-parameters via Cross-Validation and employs a grid search mechanism. In order to make adequate comparisons, we set our algorithm to complete 47 iterations as stopping criterion and the swarm size was set to 30, therefore 1,410 models were evaluated during the search step. Referring to the tool of the Apache Spark (AST) we set the number of models to be evaluated to 1,412 (the nearest number to ours). As PSMS is a population based algorithm, we take advantage of that fact and the final model is an ensemble of all the best particles found. This ensemble is performed by a weighted voting scheme. The aforementioned algorithms were tested in the datasets of Table 1 and, in order to obtain an statistical power of 90% in an ANOVA test, 20 replications were performed. Each replication was performed with a particular random sample of the data points with different random samples among replications. For each experiment, the dataset was divided into two disjoint datasets with 60% of the data samples for the training set and 40% for the test set. The obtained results (mean error) in the datasets over 20 replications are shown in Table 3.

Table 3 shows that the best performance was obtained for the AST algorithm in three datasets (RLCP, KDD and Epsilon), and in the remaining datasets (Synthetic 1, Higgs and Synthetic 2) AST obtained a greater error than PSMS (the best method in those remaining datasets). From Table 2 it can be seen that datasets RLCP and KDD are the easiest problems from the perspective of its intrinsic dimension compared to remaining datasets. Regarding to dataset Epsilon, it is plain to see that is the hardest problem in the comparison and it is necessary to refine more the MapReduce-based PSMS version. With the purpose to find statistical differences, an ANOVA test was performed and the results are shown in Table 4.

Table 3. Mean classification error obtained in the test dataset by PSMS and the obtained by K-NN (K = 9,999) and AST, over 20 replications. The best results are in **bold**

Dataset	PSMS	AST	K-NN (k = 9,999)
RLCP	0.052 ± 0.001	**0.001 ± 0.000**	0.500 ± 0.098
KDD	0.156 ± 0.134	**0.001 ± 0.000**	19.535 ± 0.261
Synthetic 1	**15.862 ± 0.004**	17.011 ± 0.120	50.088 ± 0.028
Higgs	**28.299 ± 0.057**	30.955 ± 0.228	46.916 ± 0.408
Synthetic 2	**6.681 ± 0.005**	22.152 ± 0.541	50.126 ± 0.115
Epsilon	54.008 ± 0.925	**29.664 ± 0.174**	50.673 ± 3.323

Table 4. F-statistic obtained from the ANOVA test and q-values from the Tukey HSD test for performing all possible pairwise comparisons among the proposed strategies for the final model construction. The critical values at the 95% confidence level for the ANOVA test are 3.16 (F(2,57)) for all datasets. The critical values at the 95% confidence level for the Tukey HSD test are 3.44 (57 degrees of freedom). Cases that exceed the critical value are considered as a difference that is statistically significant at the fixed level and are marked with an asterisk (*)

Dataset	ANOVA F	PSMS vs AST	PSMS vs K-NN
RLCP	470.340*	4.000*	35.400*
KDD	87594.480*	4.100*	510.560*
Synthetic 1	1482334.540*	71.950*	2143.800*
Higgs	27501.970*	43.750*	306.600*
Synthetic 2	95223.560*	216.800*	608.820*
Epsilon	875.596*	54.58*	7.476*

The statistical test shown that there are differences in those datasets where PSMS and AST got their respective best results. From these results it can be seen that PSMS and AST are very even with the best performance in three datasets each one, on the other hand regarding the ID of each dataset, PSMS got the best performance in three datasets with a higher ID than AST, except in the Epsilon dataset. A possible explanation of the low performance of PSMS in Epsilon is the vast search space that the FMS problem on Big Data involves. It is necessary for PSMS to perform a better exploration within the execution time provided and avoiding wasting time on those particles that will not lead to a good model. Reducing the time employed in the construction and evaluation of that non-promissory models could lead to a better focused search and therefore to a better performance.

6   Conclusions and Future Work

In this work we proposed an adaptation of the PSMS algorithm to the MapReduce paradigm to deal with the full model selection problem for datasets that belongs to BigData. Experimental results shown that applying a model selection algorithm in order to analyze large and average size datasets is feasible as well as with different intrinsic dimensions. Our results show a significant predictive power improvement of the employed search algorithms compared with those in the base line (also designed for big data). However it is necessary to refine our algorithm in order to make a better exploration of the search space within the provided execution time and to focus on the promissory particles. As a future work, the use of the proxy models and meta-learning techniques will analyzed in order to accomplish the aforementioned goal and to obtain a better performance.

References

1. Apacheorg: ML tuning: model selection and hyperparameter tuning, August 2016. http://spark.apache.org/docs/latest/ml-tuning.html
2. Bansal, B., Sahoo, A.: Full model selection using bat algorithm. In: 2015 International Conference on Cognitive Computing and Information Processing (CCIP), pp. 1–4. IEEE (2015)
3. Bergstra, J., Bengio, Y.: Random search for hyper-parameter optimization. J. Mach. Learn. Res. **13**, 281–305 (2012)
4. Ceruti, C., Bassis, S., Rozza, A., Lombardi, G., Casiraghi, E., Campadelli, P.: DANCo: dimensionality from angle and norm concentration. arXiv preprint arXiv:1206.3881 (2012)
5. Chatelain, C., Adam, S., Lecourtier, Y., Heutte, L., Paquet, T.: A multi-model selection framework for unknown and/or evolutive misclassification cost problems. Pattern Recogn. **43**(3), 815–823 (2010). https://doi.org/10.1016/j.patcog.2009.07.006
6. Escalante, H.J., Montes, M., Sucar, L.E.: Particle swarm model selection. J. Mach. Learn. Res. **10**(Feb), 405–440 (2009)
7. Goodrich, M.T., Sitchinava, N., Zhang, Q.: Sorting, searching, and simulation in the MapReduce framework. In: Asano, T., Nakano, S., Okamoto, Y., Watanabe, O. (eds.) ISAAC 2011. LNCS, vol. 7074, pp. 374–383. Springer, Heidelberg (2011). https://doi.org/10.1007/978-3-642-25591-5_39
8. Guller, M.: Big Data Analytics with Spark: A Practitioners Guide to Using Spark for Large Scale Data Analysis. Apress, New York (2015). http://www.apress.com/9781484209653
9. Guo, X., Yang, J., Wu, C., Wang, C., Liang, Y.: A novel LS-SVMs hyper-parameter selection based on particle swarm optimization. Neurocomputing **71**(16), 3211–3215 (2008)
10. Kaneko, H., Funatsu, K.: Fast optimization of hyperparameters for support vector regression models with highly predictive ability. Chemom. Intell. Lab. Syst. **142**, 64–69 (2015). https://doi.org/10.1016/j.chemolab.2015.01.001, http://linkinghub.elsevier.com/retrieve/pii/S0169743915000039
11. Lessmann, S., Stahlbock, R., Crone, S.F.: Genetic algorithms for support vector machine model selection. In: 2006 International Joint Conference on Neural Networks. IJCNN 2006, pp. 3063–3069. IEEE (2006)

12. Lombardi, G., Rozza, A., Ceruti, C., Casiraghi, E., Campadelli, P.: Minimum neighbor distance estimators of intrinsic dimension. In: Gunopulos, D., Hofmann, T., Malerba, D., Vazirgiannis, M. (eds.) ECML PKDD 2011. LNCS (LNAI), vol. 6912, pp. 374–389. Springer, Heidelberg (2011). https://doi.org/10.1007/978-3-642-23783-6_24

13. Rosales-Pérez, A.: Surrogate-assisted multi-objective model selection for support vector machines. Neurocomputing **150**(2015), 163–172 (2015)

14. Rosales-Pérez, A., Gonzalez, J.A., Coello Coello, C.A., Escalante, H.J., Reyes-Garcia, C.A.: Multi-objective model type selection. Neurocomputing, **146**, 83–94 (2014). https://doi.org/10.1016/j.neucom.2014.05.077, http://linkinghub.elsevier.com/retrieve/pii/S0925231214008789

15. Sánchez-Monedero, J., Gutiérrez, P.A., Pérez-Ortiz, M., Hervás-Martínez, C.: An n-spheres based synthetic data generator for supervised classification. In: Rojas, I., Joya, G., Gabestany, J. (eds.) IWANN 2013. LNCS, vol. 7902, pp. 613–621. Springer, Heidelberg (2013). https://doi.org/10.1007/978-3-642-38679-4_62

16. Thornton, C., Hutter, F., Hoos, H.H., Leyton-Brown, K.: Auto-WEKA: combined selection and hyperparameter optimization of classification algorithms. In: Proceedings of the 19th ACM SIGKDD International Conference on Knowledge Discovery and Data Mining, pp. 847–855. ACM (2013)

17. Tlili, M., Hamdani, T.M.: Big data clustering validity. In: 2014 6th International Conference of Soft Computing and Pattern Recognition (SoCPaR), pp. 348–352. IEEE (2014)

18. Wu, X., Zhu, X., Wu, G.Q., Ding, W.: Data mining with big data. IEEE Trans. Knowl. Data Eng. **26**(1), 97–107 (2014)

19. Yu, K., Ji, L., Zhang, X.: Kernel nearest-neighbor algorithm. Neural Process. Lett. **15**(2), 147–156 (2002)

20. Zaharia, M., et al.: Apache spark: a unified engine for big data processing. Commun. ACM **59**(11), 56–65 (2016)

A Case-Based Reasoning Framework for Clinical Decision Making

Ivett E. Fuentes Herrera[1(✉)], Beatriz Valdés Pérez[1],
María M. García Lorenzo[1], Leticia Arco García[1],
Mabel M. Herrera González[2], and Rolando de la C. Fuentes Morales[2]

[1] Computer Science Department,
Universidad Central "Marta Abreu" de Las Villas,
Carretera a Camajuaní Km 5 ½, Santa Clara, Cuba
{ivett, bvaldes}@uclv.cu,
{mmgarcia, leticiaa}@uclv.edu.cu
[2] Medicine Department, Universidad de Ciencias Médicas de Villa Clara Dr.
"Serafín Ruíz de Zarate Ruiz",
Carretera Circunvalación Km 3½, Santa Clara, Cuba
{mabelmhg, rolandocfm}@infomed.sld.cu

Abstract. The information is increasing in hospital centers due to the widespread use of Electronic Medical Records, which make it necessary to develop new methods capable of processing information and ensuring its productive use. In this paper is proposed a framework of case-based reasoning for systems of clinical decision making by using the complete linkage hierarchical algorithm. Next, it is shown the series of steps that involve the pre-processing performed in this work and how to calculate a similarity measure between the new problem and each case based on textual features. The presented retrieve and adaptation mechanisms allow a better case retrieval and they can support clinical diagnosis.

Keywords: Clustering · Knowledge discovering · Case base reasoning
Electronic medical records

1 Introduction

Due to the exponential increase in the organizations of stored information, the Information Society is being overtaken by the need for new methods capable of processing information and ensuring productive use. This is logically extended to the hospitals, from the widespread use of clinical histories in electronic format. In addition, there is the need for standards to support the exchange information and knowledge among health institutions; specifically, Health Level Seven (HL7 [1]) has become one of the most widely used because it implements XML.

Hospital Information Systems (HIS) provide a common source of information about a patient's health history. These systems enhance the ability of health care professionals to coordinate care by providing a patient's health information and visit

---

[1] www.hl7.org/.

© Springer Nature Switzerland AG 2018
F. Castro et al. (Eds.): MICAI 2017, LNAI 10632, pp. 290–301, 2018.
https://doi.org/10.1007/978-3-030-02837-4_24

history at the place and time that it is needed. Consequently, the information flow in these organizations is continuously increasing, due to the use of EMR, as a principal component of HIS [1].

EMR may also improve prevention by providing doctors and patients' better access to test results, identifying missing patient information, and offering evidence-based recommendations for preventive services [2]. The adoption of tools to support decision-making in clinical practice is necessary to provide better working conditions that contribute to evidence-based medicine, and ensure productive use of the information stored, while protecting the health information of patients [3].

Among the Artificial Intelligence (AI) techniques used in the solution of making decisions problems are: rule-based systems, neuronal networks, fuzzy systems and case-based systems [4]. Specifically, the Case-Based Reasoning (CBR) is induced by the role of memory in man's reasoning capacity. Memory allows linking the present with the past. It can organize, generalize and use experience in solving problems. In general, the second time intended to solve some problem is easier than the first, because the former solution is reminded and repeated. In AI, this way of solving problems has been modelled by analogical reasoning [5].

CBR is a type of analogical reasoning. Analogy and case-based are two sides of the same proverbial coin: both rely on encapsulating episodic knowledge to guide complex problem solving, while the former emphasizes the process of modifying, adapting and verifying past derivations (cases), the latter emphasizes the organization, hierarchy, indexing and retrieval of case memory [6]. The CBR systems have two main components, a case base and the problem solver. The case base contains the description of the solved and not solved before problems, and the problem solver has two modules, the retriever and the reasoner. The retriever has the function of searching and retrieving the similar cases from the case base using a similarity or dissimilarity function [6]. The CBR systems have been employed in different diagnosis tasks [7, 8].

The opinions that have medical experts about the correct treatment and conduct to fallow for a new patient is reflected in the EMR documents. This information can be used to give a better practice in the admission of new patient, and these opinions are especially useful for offering support to a process of clinical decision making. This process is complex. For that reason, the experts find out a series of possible diagnosis in the practice of clinical method. These diagnosis should be considered or discarded. Another aspect of high importance in these CBR systems is to achieve a quick and efficient way to share and retrieve the information. Then, the expert opinions and the linguistic terms used for retrieving the more similar cases to a new problem must have been treated for reducing the space of search in this step. This work proposes a new case-based reasoning framework for clinical decision making where the clustering and classification are integrated.

The paper is organized as follows. In Sect. 2 the model used is described. In Sect. 3 a case-based reasoning framework for clinical decision making from the EMR is presented. Finally, in Sects. 4 and 5 the experimental results and conclusions are shown respectability.

2 A Model for Discovery Implicit Knowledge in EMR

Clustering algorithms discover a group structure from the dataset, achieving homogeneity within groups and heterogeneity among them. It is an alternative to automatically describe the scientific and clinical significance of biomedical information from large volumes of data. A clustering algorithm tries to find groups primarily based on similarity and relations among objects, for obtaining internal distribution. Specifically, the element distribution in an EMR implementing Clinical Document Architecture (CDA), defines a specification of EMR as a XML document. The model presented in [9] establishes some steps for clustering XML documents, where it is more natural to process them as a set of parts or series of sections than considering a bag of words model (each document can be divided into several subsections, etc.) [9]. Consequently, the EMR can be seen as a collection of documents $D = \{D_1,..., D_m\}$, where each D_i contains a set of Structural Units (SU) $SU = \{SU_1,..., SU_n\}$ [10]. Thus, the concept of document disappears as an indivisible unit [11]. Specifically, the SU semantically identified in chronological EMR based on expert criteria are SU = (Antecedents (AP), Toxic Habits (TH), Symptoms (ST), Sings (SG), History of Current Disease (HCD), Differential Diagnosis (DD), Final Diagnosis (FD), Tests, Treatments, Recovery, Prognostic) [12, 13].

The model proposed in [9], for obtaining a final XML clustering, combines both structure and content of XML document, based on the existent structural relationship among them. It can contribute to better clustering results when the content is used in function of the relation between their SU. The general procedure for obtaining *OverallSimSUX* similarity matrix, starts from a collection of EMR documents. This similarity matrix [10] facilitates to capture the similarity degree among documents. It is calculated by considering the clustering results carried out for the k-collections and the similarity matrix based on the calculation of the similarity measure. Three steps are necessary: (1) pre-processing the whole collection, by identifying each SU; (2) textual representation and (3) final clustering processing.

The original document collection is divided in k-collections. The k-collection concept [11] reflects the correspondence between collection and SU. In this model the representation for each SU is the classic Vector Space Model (VSM) [14]. *OverallSimSUX* similarity measure calculation [9] begins with the clustering results carried out for the k-collections, based on the calculation of the Cosine measure [15].

3 A Case-Based Reasoning Framework

In this paper, a case-based reasoning framework for clinical decision making from the EMR in the CDA standard is presented. Given a repository of EMR with SU in Spanish, let us suppose that a new case arrives. At this moment, the expert applies the clinical method taking into account both, the interrogation and physical exploration, as a result only the first five SU of EMR have been complete. Given an EMR for a new patient, the five features (i.e. AP, TH, ST, SG and HCD) are known. The proposed CBR is to retrieve the records whose similarity with the given patient is maximum by using a similarity function, taking into account that features have different weights. So, the CBR proposed in this work, uses the textual information associated with each SU defined as predictor characteristic. Having described the cases and information that is used as predictor features in the inference, it is described the schema for the case base organization in order to improve the access and the recovery of similar cases to solve a new problem (Fig. 1).

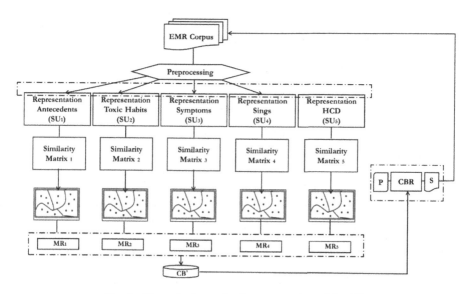

Fig. 1. General scheme for the construction of the CB

The schema of case base organization is conceived from the clusters of EMR semi-structured documents. These clusters are obtained by grouping the SU corresponding to the k-collections for each predictor feature. Subsequently the typical element of the remaining group at a higher level is determined. Figure 2 shows an overview of the steps developed to organize the Case Base (CB).

Pre-processing EMR for CBR

The pre-processing stage must be ensured by filtering the information and unifying the medical terminology. This step includes some common linguistic-related processing for preparing features, such as lexical analysis, stop word removal and stemming. In addition, others linguistic aspects have been developed, for handling negation, modification (intensification and attenuation) and synonymy. If these features are not considered previously into the analysis, then inconsistencies in the representation and the clustering process appear, due to these terms are stops words, and consequently they are avoided. In addition, synonym consideration allows to reduce the number of terms and improve the quality of representation.

This work, like the proposals presented in [16, 17], considers other elements such as the negation words: *"tampoco"*, *"nadie"*, *"jamás"*, *"ninguno"*, *"ni"* and *"nada"*, taking into account that this framework starts from a EMR collection in Spanish.

```
Input: EMR Corpus
Output: CB(Set of clusters, cluster quality, the
more representative documents by cluster)
Begin
Step 1. Preprocessing
Step 2. Build all the k-collections (EMR Corpus)
Step 3. For each DSUₖ
        -To create the representation
        -To calculate a similarity matrix
        -To apply clustering method
        -To compute prototype for each cluster
        End For
end
```

Fig. 2. General procedure for the CB construction

Each negating word is identified, then the modified term is negated. In [18] a heuristic that assumes that negation is scoped to the three tokens next to the negating word is used. This work is based on this heuristic to identify the noun or the verb, which is modified by a negation term. The identified term is treated as a different term. For example, in the sentences "*El paciente no tuvo fiebre*" and "*El paciente presentó fiebre alta*" the term "*fiebre*", despite being the same, is in two different contexts, appears in the first sentence denied and in the second not. In the case of the first sentence, by applying the general procedure for handling the negation terms, the model obtains "*no_fiebre*", which is different from the term "*fiebre*" obtained in the second sentence.

Modifying words may be either intensifiers or attenuators. The intensifications can be adjectives or adverbs. Adjectives modify nouns and adverbs of intensification commonly modify verbs, adjectives adjustable, and other adverbs. In this work, only adjectival intensifiers are handled, due to EMR are documents with short and slightly complex sentences. To do this, two lists of terms were built, one for intensifiers and the other one for attenuators, by analyzing the existing list of modifier words and consulting dictionaries. For intensification, like as negation, three terms on the right are the ones to be modified in [18]. Based on this idea, to treat these modifier words, the intensifier terms are considered as different terms. For example, in the sentence "*el paciente tuvo mucha fiebre*", by applying the general procedure "*mucha_fiebre*" was obtained. All modifier terms are considered in the representation stage and depending on if the modifier term is an intensifier or it is an attenuator, the frequency value of the modified term in the document is increased or decreased, respectively. This paper proposes to increase the quality of the terms modified by intensifier in 25% and subtract the same percentage equitably to all other terms, by guaranteeing the total sum of the term quality in the document to be 1. In the case of the presence of attenuating words it is exactly the opposite.

A thesaurus of Medical Terms from Referencing Manual of Medical Terminology [19] was built for handling synonymy. This thesaurus is composed by synonym groups; each group consists of a term representative group and members. This dictionary has the structure of an XML document, which facilitates indexing and searching about it.

As following step, the representation is obtained for each SU. For each representation is calculated a similarity matrix using the cosine similarity as shown in Eq. (1), which computes the cosine of the angle between two documents vectors. As next step a clustering for each SU are generated from the calculated similarity, using the complete linkage hierarchical algorithm [20]. The S-*Space Package*[2] [21] was used to perform clustering tool.

$$S_{Cosine}(d_i, d_j) = \frac{\sum_{r=1}^{s}(d_{ir} \times d_{jr})}{\sqrt{\sum_{r=1}^{s} d_{ir}^2 \times \sum_{r=1}^{s} d_{jr}^2}} \tag{1}$$

For each obtained cluster, the "representative" case or "prototype", which corresponds to the more similar case to the remaining documents in this cluster, is determined. The membership of each document is calculated based on the average of the cosine similarity between documents that are included in the same cluster. Equation (2) shows how obtaining a document membership to a cluster C, where m represents the number of documents in the cluster.

$$SC(d_k, C) = \frac{\sum_{\substack{i=1 \\ i \neq k}}^{m} S_{Cosine}(d_i, d_k)}{m - 1} \tag{2}$$

Components of Case-Based System
Two fundamental components of the case-based system are the retriever and adaptation modules. The retriever process allows obtaining the K most similar cases to the current problem. In many practical problems, it is necessary to reduce the group of cases to obtain the most excellent solution. In this work, an alternative via for the retriever process is proposed based on considering the most representative cases. The two key aspects of this process are the access algorithm to cases and the similarity measure among cases. To determine the most similar case several other techniques have been developed. The simplest technique to do that, consists of the use of a heuristic that allows us to determine which characteristics have greatest relevance (or weight) and to formulate a similarity function that involves the similarity among each one of the features keeping in mind the weight [4]. Since features of this problem are textual units, it is proposed a mathematical formulation that compute an overall similarity as a result of the weighted sum of the similarities for each SU between a new problem P and a case X of the base. Equation (3) shows this similarity function where m is the number of predictor features (i.e., number of SU) and w_i represents the weight or relevance of the feature i (in this work it is defined by expert criteria), $SCosine$ is the cosine similarity between the cases P and X according to the SU_i.

---

[2] https://github.com/fozziethebeat/S-Space/wiki/GettingStarted.

$$OverallSim(P, X) = \sum_{i=0}^{m} W_i * S_{Cosine\,i}(P_{UE_i}, X_{UE_i})/m \qquad (3)$$

The prototypical cases are accessed by using a hierarchical, and a prototype is in a high level in its cluster. An important result of this research is the capacity of performing the inference of values for the set of objective features without needing to search over the repository for each demand. The comparison in the retriever process is done only between the case problem and the prototypical cases.

Figure 3 shows the procedure used in the retriever process of the K most similar cases to a new patient, based on the calculation of the $OverallSim$ similarity. The adaptation process should infer values for the objective features from the assigned values to the predictive features, by considering the cases retrieved in the previous step to make a solution, which is a set of possible diagnoses to consider at the admission of a new patient. In addition to the suggested diagnosis, the system proposes a first diagnosis (*Hypothesis or FD*) as possible diagnosis considering diagnoses presented for the most similar cases to the new problem P, and a set of differential diagnoses (*DD*) to be analyzed by the expert through the test. To present the set of differential diagnoses the most similar cases and their differential diagnoses are given. In the adaptation process is obtained the diagnostic or differential diagnosis by occurrence of these in the retrieved cases as more similar. Figure 4 shows the procedure used in the adaptation process from the k most similar cases to a new patient recovered in the previous process.

```
Input: case problem P, CB' = {cb'₁, cb'₂, ..., cb'ₙ}
Output: MS={oᵢ|i = 1,m}
Begin
    1. G = {(cb'ᵢ, sᵢ)|sᵢ = OverallSim(cb'ᵢ, P), cb'ᵢ ∈ CB'}
    2. MS = ∅
    3. KS=maxₖ{(cb'ᵢ, sᵢ) ∈ G|sᵢ ∈ kₘₐₓ}
    4. cᵢ_max = max{SC(cbᵢ, cᵢ)| ∀cᵢ, cbᵢ ∈ cᵢ}
    5. γᵢ = (Σⱼ₌₁ⁿ ASCosine(dⱼ,cᵢ))/n
    6. For each (cb'ᵢ, sᵢ) ∈ KS
        -If sᵢ > γᵢ
            MS=MS∪ cb'ᵢ
        -Else
            MS=MS∪ cᵢ_max
        -End If
    7. End For
end
```

Fig. 3. General procedure for retriever process

The revision is done when in the retriever process any case was recovered as the most similar to a new problem, due to the retriever process cannot discriminate considering the similarity. In this process, a selection step based on the predictor features and the importance of the recovery is done in order to obtain the most similar case to a new problem.

Input: $MS=\{o_i | i = \overline{1,m}\}$
Output: *Hypothesis*, DD
Begin

    1. $\forall\ o_i \in MS, LD=\{ld_k=\{FD_i \cup DD_i\ \}\}.\ k = \overline{(1,m)}$

    2. $R(i,j) = \begin{cases} 1 & , ld_i \cap ld_j \neq \emptyset \\ 0 & , e.o.c. \end{cases}$

    3. $D = MAJORITY\ (o_{i\ FD \cup DD}, R)$

    4. Build MS´ ⊆ MS
       - **If** $o_i \in D$
           MS´= MS´ ∪ o_i
       - **End If**

    5. **For each** $o_i \in MS$´
       $-D_1 = \{d_i | d_i \in FD(o_i)\}.$
       $-FD = \max\{OCCUR(d_i), d_i \in D_1\}$
       $-D_2 = \{d_j | d_j \in DN(ci) \cup List(DD(ci)\ ) \wedge d_j \notin D_1\}.$
       $-DD = List(\max_k \{OCCUR(d_i), d_i \in D_2\})$

    6. **End For**
end

Fig. 4. General procedure for reuse process

Figure 5 describes how the *FD* is obtained in the process of revising from the adaptive weights the features.

Input: $MS=\{o_i | i = \overline{1,m}\},\ W=\{w_i | i = \overline{1,5}\}$
Output: *FD*
Begin

    1. $SortDescending(W)$

    2. $\forall\ o_i \in MS\ \forall\ w_j \in W$

    3. $FD = FD_{\max_{i=1,k}}\left\{S_{Cosine_i}\left(o_{i_{SU_j}}, P_{i_{SU_j}}\right)\right\}$

end

Fig. 5. General procedure for revise process

4   Experimental Setup

Case Study

EMR collections which belong "Celestino Hernández Robau" Admissions Service Hospital in Villa Clara-Cuba, are associated with different diseases are used. We are conformed 15 EMR document corpora (which are named with a number from 1 to 15). Each corpus is made up of a quantity of EMR documents ranging between 270 and 320. The data considered for conforming our corpora set are not public, and they were used only for the validation of the model inside the margins of the center, according to norms of privacy and security of the information.

Experiment' Results and Analysis

The Java programming language was used to perform the experimentation. Due to the facilities offered by several libraries for pre-processing and textual analysis. Specifically, TreeTagger is a useful tool for labeling texts with grammatical and lexical information.

We consider two classical representation models VSM and Latent Semantic Analysis (LSA) [22], due to the need of performing both: lexical and semantic analysis of information. In order to develop a comparative study, one experiment has been designed applied to the dataset, with the purpose of carrying out a statistical analysis that allows showing the result of both, VSM and LSA representation for a clustering. It is important to remark that the precise values for the clustering only differ in two SU. To evaluate the results, we consider the external measure Overall F-Measure (OFM) [23] for showing the quality of the clusters obtained in each clustering.

Figure 6 shows the graphical results for SU, Toxic Habits and History of Current Disease, which have different values of OFM using both representation models. The Wilcoxon's test [24] using a significance level of 0.05 suggests not reject the null hypothesis (p value > 0.05), therefore there not exist significant different between both representations. Although, VSM was selected because it is a model that is not computationally expensive as with probabilistic models, and it can be adapted to the context of the shortest opinions emitted by specialists in EMR about the patients.

An experiment was designed to measure the accuracy of CBR by using the Leave One Out Cross Validation (LOOCE) [25], such that in each iteration is considered a test case and the rest training cases. The test case is taken as a new problem to solve and training cases from the case base using the framework to retrieve the most similar cases and infer a response with the highest similarity degree. The literature suggests the following values of $K = 1$, $K = 3$, $K = 5$ or $K = 7$, so we experienced with these values [26]. Table 1 shows the obtained results for each K-value. The better precision is obtained with $K = 1$ in the experimentation. In this paper we propose to use the value in the recovery $K = 3$, because this value reported good results too. Besides, experts suggest that for completing EMR, the possible diagnostics should not limit further verification, so for $K = 1$ the set of retrieved cases for adaptation is very small and could be ignored other cases.

The overall similarity calculation depends on the predictor feature weights. Experts were consulted to calculate these feature weights. They concluded that the History of Present Illness, Signs and Symptoms are the most important features, which provide about 75% of the information required for diagnosis in the most cases. The sum of

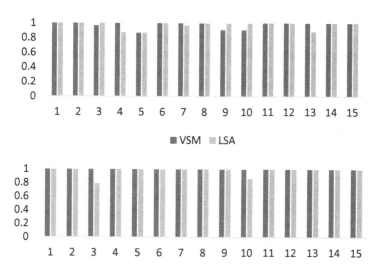

Fig. 6. Values of OFM using VSM and LSA representation model for SU Toxic Habits and History of Current Disease respectively

Table 1. Accuracy for fixed threshold values

k-value	1	3	5	7
Correct classifications (%)	100	99.77	99.54	98.62

Table 2. Weight values for predictor features

HCD	SG	ST	AP	TH
0.25	0.25	0.25	0.12	0.13
0.30	0.25	0.20	0.13	0.12
0.35	0.20	0.20	0.15	0.10

weights assigned to these features should be 0.75, and the total sum of all weights must be 1. So, using different settings, as shown in Table 2, for calculating the importance of features, the correct classification percent is the same 99.77.

5 Conclusions

In this paper we have presented a framework to implement a CBR for clinical decision making. The retriever process uses a similarity function taking into account the fact that the features can have different importance from the expert criteria. Besides, the retriever process allows to combine the similarity among textual units using the cosine similarity measure. The manager of linguistic resources allows to obtain better results in the representation and clustering steps, which contributes to case base organization and retrieve similarity cases to a new problem. The pre-processing makes to decrease the number of comparisons ostensibly in the retriever process. It facilitates in a significant way the adaptation process. CBR proposes a complete set of features that involves the diagnosis of early hypotheses from the effective retrieving of recovered cases. Some linguistic resources were applied when the information related to cases are not sufficient and consequently it is not possible to detect differences between cases.

Acknowledgements. The authors acknowledge the support of the Department of Propaedeutics and Internal Medicine of the Provincial Hospital "Celestino Hernández Robau" in Villa Clara, Cuba. We are especially grateful to the doctors of the Internal Medicine Service.

References

1. Gunter, T.D., Terry, N.P.: The emergence of national electronic health record architectures in the United States and Australia: models, costs, and questions. J. Med. Internet Res. **7**(1), 3 (2005)
2. Fiks, A.G., et al.: Electronic medical record use in pediatric primary care. J. Am. Med. Inform. Assoc. **18**(1), 38–44 (2010)
3. Fernández, A., et al.: Analysis of health professional security behaviors in a real clinical setting: an empirical study. Int. J. Med. Inf. **84**(6), 454–467 (2015)
4. Martínez, I.G., Pérez, R.E.B.: Making decision in case-based systems using probabilities and rough sets. Knowl.-Based Syst. **16**(4), 205–213 (2003)
5. Lorenzo, M.M.G., Pérez, R.E.B.: A model and its different applications to case-based reasoning. Knowl.-Based Syst. **9**(7), 465–473 (1996)
6. De Mantaras, R.L., et al.: Retrieval, reuse, revision and retention in case-based reasoning. Knowl. Eng. Rev. **20**(3), 215–240 (2005)
7. Kriegsman, M., Barletta, R.: Building a case-based help desk application. IEEE Expert **8**(6), 18–26 (1993)
8. Simoudis, E.: Using case-based retrieval for customer technical support. IEEE Expert **7**(5), 7–12 (1992)
9. Magdaleno, D., et al.: Clustering XML documents using structure and content based on a new similarity function OverallSimSUX. Comput. y Sist. **19**(1), 151–161 (2015)
10. Fuentes, I.E., et al.: Methodology for discovery of implicit knowledge in medical records. In: Paper Presented at the Fifth International Workshop on Knowledge Discovery, Knowledge Management and Decision Support, EUREKA 2015, Universidad Autónoma Metropolitana. Ciudad México (2015)
11. Magdaleno, D.G., et al.: Comparative study of clustering algorithms using OverallSimSUX similarity function for XML documents. Intel. Artif.: Rev. Iberoam. Intel. Artif. **18**(55), 69–80 (2015)
12. Fuentes, I.E., et al.: Toma de decisiones inteligente a partir de registros médicos almacenados en CDA-HL7. Rev. Cuba. Informática Médica **8**(1), 109–124 (2016)
13. Fuentes, I.E., et al.: Metodología para asistir la toma de decisiones diagnóstica a partir del descubrimiento del conocimiento implícito en Historias Clínicas. Rev. Cienc. Matemáticas **29**(2), 99–106 (2015)
14. Salton, G., Wong, A., Yang, C.-S.: A vector space model for automatic indexing. Commun. ACM **18**(11), 613–620 (1975)
15. Frakes, W., Baeza-Yates, R.: Information Retrieval. Data Structure and Algorithms. Prentice Hall, New York (1992)

16. Fernández, A., et al.: Sentiment analysis and topic detection of Spanish tweets: a comparative study of NLP techniques. Proces. Del Leng. Nat. **50**, 45–52 (2013)
17. Amores, M., et al.: Efectos de la Negación, Modificadores, Jergas, Abreviaturas y Emoticonos en el Análisis de Sentimiento. In: Proceedings of the 2nd International Workshop on Semantic Web (IWSW). CEUR, La Habana (2016)
18. Zafra, J., et al.: Tratamiento de la Negación en el Análisis de Opiniones en Español. Proces. Del Leng. Nat. **54**, 37–44 (2015)
19. Beers, M.H., et al.: The Merck Manual of Medical Information. Pocket Books, New York (2003)
20. Manning, C.D., et al.: Introduction to Information Retrieval, vol. 1. Cambridge University Press, Cambridge (2008)
21. Jurgens, D., Stevens, K.: The S-Space package: an open source package for word space models. In: Proceedings of the ACL 2010 System Demonstrations. Association for Computational Linguistics, pp. 30–35 (2010)
22. Aggarwal, C.C., Zhai, C.: Mining Text Data. Springer, Berlin (2012). https://doi.org/10.1007/978-1-4614-3223-4
23. Steinbach, M., et al.: A comparison of document clustering techniques. In: Proceedings of 6th ACM SIGKDD World Text Mining Conference, Boston. ACM Press (2000)
24. Wilcoxon, F.: Individual comparisons byranking methods. Biom. Bull. **1**(6), 80–83 (1945)
25. Cawley, G.C.: Leave-one-out cross-validation based model selection criteria for weighted LS-SVMs. In: Paper Presented at the Neural Networks 2006. IJCNN 2006 (2006)
26. Wess, S., Althoff, K.-D., Derwand, G.: Using k-d trees to improve the retrieval step in case-based reasoning. In: Wess, S., Althoff, K.-D., Richter, Michael M. (eds.) EWCBR 1993. LNCS, vol. 837, pp. 167–181. Springer, Heidelberg (1994). https://doi.org/10.1007/3-540-58330-0_85

The Use of Artificial Intelligence
for the Intrusion Detection System
in Computer Networks

Santiago Yip Ortuño[1], José Alberto Hernández Aguilar[1,3]([✉]),
Blanca Taboada[2], Carlos Alberto Ochoa Ortiz[3],
Miguel Pérez Ramírez[3], and Gustavo Arroyo Figueroa[3]

[1] Autonomous University of Morelos State, Ave. University 1001,
62209 Cuernavaca, Morelos, Mexico
jose_hernandez@uaem.mx
[2] IBT-UNAM, Ave. University 1001, Cuernavaca, Morelos, Mexico
[3] National Institute of Electricity and Clean Energies (INEEL), Reforma 113,
Palmira, 62490 Cuernavaca, Morelos, Mexico

Abstract. We discuss the application of Artificial Intelligence for the design of
intrusion detection systems (IDS) applied on computer networks. For this purpose, we use J48 rand Clonal-G [5] immune artificial system Algorithms, in
WEKA software, with the purpose to classify and predict intrusions in KDD-
Cup 1999 and Kyoto 2006 databases. We obtain for the KDD-Cup 1999
database 92.69% for ClonalG and 99.91% of precision for J48 respectively. For
the Kyoto University 2006 database, we obtain 95.2% for ClonalG and 99.25%
of precision for J48. Finally, based on these results we propose a model to detect
intrusions using AI techniques. The main contribution of the paper is the
adaptability of the CLONAL-G Algorithm and the reduction of database attributes by using Genetic Search.

Keywords: Artificial immune system · ClonalG · J48
Intrusion detection system · Security model

1 Introduction

1.1 Information Technologies and Security

The growth of information technology has generated a change in the world; currently,
the use of technology is an obligation to achieve competition, both for companies and
organizations of all kinds. However, despite all the benefits that these technologies
offer there are many threats, which? Among all those who manipulate ICTs, which
once materialized cause irreparable damage, ranging from damage to the image of an
entity or person, millionaire losses and even loss of freedom or endangering human
lives. Some of the best-known cases include Sony Pictures, Home Depot [13], Cele-
bgate, Stuxnet [12] and Ransomware [14].

For these reasons, technologies have emerged to help reduce the risks of using
these; within these tools are the intrusion detection systems. This research proposes the

© Springer Nature Switzerland AG 2018
F. Castro et al. (Eds.): MICAI 2017, LNAI 10632, pp. 302–312, 2018.
https://doi.org/10.1007/978-3-030-02837-4_25

evaluation of the intrusion detection system with a bio-inspired heuristic known as the artificial immune system.

Problem at Hands

Can artificial intelligence (AI) techniques detect and report intrusions in an institution?
Hypotheses:

H. through AI techniques is possible to detect and report intrusions in an institution.
H0. Through AI techniques is not possible to detect and report intrusions in an institution.

Structure of the document, in Section two, we discuss the theoretical framework, in section three we present the methodology as well as the description of the algorithms used in this research (CLONALG and J48), later are shown the experiment design, and the results of an experiment using the KDD cup 1999 database [18] and Kyoto University 2006 database [28]. Finally, we present our conclusions, future work, and references.

2   Review of Literature

2.1   Information Technologies and Security

Whitman and Herbert in his work "Principles of information security" define information security as: "The Protection of Information and its critical elements including the systems and the hardware that use stored and transmitted information" [15].

For that reason, security of the information includes all those mechanisms, controls, devices, best practices, etc. That ensures the 3 basic aspects of the information [8]:

- Availability: The information is available when it is required.
- Integrity: the information should not suffer any type of alteration; the modifications shall be solely done by known processes or mechanisms for the treatment of it.
- Confidentiality: the information will be available to the persons entitled to it.

At the same time, according to [15], an intrusion is defined as:
"The satisfactory accesses to an information system in order to disrupt, modify, remove or damage the information or its integrity".

2.2   Intrusion Detection System

Due the exponential growth of the threats have emerged different types of tools that allow their detection and mitigation, among these, are the physical and logical tools; within the physical tools are: Firewalls, content filtering, intrusion prevention systems (IPS), among others; within the logic are: Antivirus, Intrusion Detection Systems (IDS), etc. Why have the IDS had enough popularity in the companies? An IDS consists of procedures that react to detect patterns of intrusion, this includes all those actions taken by an organization when an intrusion is detected [15] due it is difficult to know what an attacker will do [24]. For this reason, the security of the information includes all those mechanisms, controls, devices, good practices, etc. that ensure the three basic aspects of the information [8] which as mentioned in [25] represents a challenge for cyber law in Mexico and abroad.

2.3   Artificial Intelligence Techniques Applied to Computer Security

Figure 1 is a summary obtained from [4] that shows the different techniques of artificial intelligence that have been used in recent years applied to computer security. This figure shows that the detection of intruders and attacks is a current research problem of interest, to both the scientific community and security professionals, which has been approached with artificial intelligence techniques such as neural networks, genetic algorithms and artificial immune systems (AIS). Bayesian networks have been used mainly for attack detection and a combination of fuzzy logic and genetic algorithms for the generation of adaptive IDS. In this work, we will focus on (AIS).

1. Artificial vision
   a. Biometrics
   b. Handwritten recognition
2. Bayesian networks
   a. Spam
   b. Attack detection
3. Artificial Neuronal Networks
   a. **Intrusion Detection Systems**
4. Artificial Immune Systems
   a. **Intrusion Detection Systems**
5. Intelligent Agent Systems
   a. Network security systems
   b. Safe architecture
   c. Auditing
   d. File integrity checking systems
6. Expert Systems
   a. Auditing
7. Genetic Algorithms
   a. **Intrusion Detection Systems**
8. Fuzzy logic & Genetics
   a. Adaptive **Intrusion Detection Systems**

Fig. 1.   Artificial intelligence techniques applied to computer security adapted from [4]

2.4   Artificial Immune System

The biological immune system is a collection of molecules with highly evolved procedures that allow the identification and elimination of any substance foreign to the body that protects [2, 3], the artificial immune system is a simulation of the biological functioning of the immune system to perform specific tasks [5, 6]. The artificial immune system [10, 11] has three main theories:

Clonal Selection

- According to the work reported by [1], the clonal selection theory was proposed by Frank Macfarlane Burnet in 1959 in his work "The clonal selection theory of acquired immunity", the main idea of this theory states that cells are able to recognize antigens will be those that will proliferate.

Negative Selection

- Kim and Bentley in their work "An Evaluation of Negative Selection in an Artificial Immune System", quoted that the theory of negative selection was proposed by Stephanie Forrest in the year 1994 in his work "Self - no self-Discrimination in a Computer", where the antibodies generated by the immune system reacts only against the antigens by omitting any action against its own cells [16].

Network Theory

- According to [1] the theory of networks in the artificial immune systems was proposed by Niels K. Jerne in 1974 in his work: "Toward a Network Theory of the Immune System", in establishing a network of antibodies that recognize antigens.

3   Methodology

The proposed methodology for this research is called KDD (knowledge data discovery); is based on the works of [7, 17] and it is briefly explained in the following figure (Fig. 2).

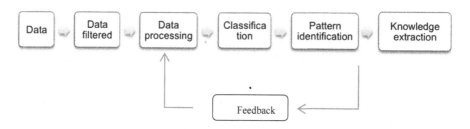

Fig. 2. Cycle of generic data mining [7]

(1) Data. The test databases used in this research are:
   (a) The available on the Internet for the KDD CUP 1999 tournament [18] (10% of 4 million records, 42 features).
   (b) Kyoto University data base 2006 [28] (116,307 records, 24 features).
(2) Data filtered. Data was reviewed in order to contain a value for the field class, for a proper intrusion detection to distinguish between "good" and "bad" connections. For this purpose, databases were imported and filtered in Excel tool. Data was exported to comma-delimited format (.CSV extension) for further processing.

(3) Data processing. Data was imported into Weka ClassAlgoss version 3.6.4, working under Linux environment, for data validation and preliminary data visualization in graphs and tables; basic statics (minimum, maximum, mean and standard deviation) for each attribute were analyzed.

(4) Classification. From Fig. 1, is possible to identify three bio inspired techniques for (IDS): Artificial Neuronal Networks (ANN), Artificial Immune Systems (AIS) and Genetic Algorithms (GA). We decide to use AIS technique because of the Similarity between an intruder and a germ or virus, a network of computers and a body, the attack on the network and an infection or illness, that is to say, the problem of intrusions in a natural way is matching a disease [1, 3, 5], meanwhile the detection and control of the attack is carried out by a system that functions as the natural immune system [10]. For this stage, we used CLONAL-G Artificial Immune System [5] and J48 [26, 27] algorithms available in the WEKA 3.6.4. [19].

Clonal Selection theory has been used as a base for AIS that performs optimization and pattern recognition tasks, so we select CLONAL-G because is the most popular and used AIS clonal selection algorithm that performs pattern matching [29]. To compare the precision of classification we compare the performance of this adaptive AIS classification system versus a well-known and powerful decision tree in our case J48. Pseudo codes of CLONAL-G and J48 and a brief explanation of them are shown next:

Algorithm ClonalG [5]

```
1. Beginning: Initial population created in a random way
(P)
2. Antigen presentation: for each pattern, do:
  a. Fitness function: present to the P population and
     determine its affinity for each element in the P
     population;
  b. Clonal Selection: select n1 elements with high-
     est fitness function of P and generate clones of
     these individuals in a proportional way according to
     affinity to antigen: highest the fitness, the great-
     est number of copies and vice versa;
  c. Maturity of fitness: mutate all these copies with a
     ratio inversely proportional regarding its fitness
     function according to an initial pattern: More fit-
     ness, mutation ratio is lesser and vice versa. Add
     these mutated individuals to P and select the best
     individual to preserve him as the memory "m" of an-
     tigen.
  d. Dynamic goal: replace n2 number of individuals with
     less fitness function (randomly generated) by the
     newest;
3. Cycle: Repeat the step 2 until a certain criterion is
obtained.
```

When CLONAL-G is applied to Pattern matching, a set of patterns "S" are considered to be antigens, the task of the algorithm is producing a set of memory antibodies "M" that matched the members in S [30].

Algorithm J48 [26, 27]:

```
INPUT:D //Training data. OUTPUT T //Decision tree
DTBUILD (*D)
Beginning
   T=φ;
   T= Create root node and label with splitting attribute;
   T= Add arc to root node for each split predicate and
   label;
   For each arc do
   D= Database created by applying splitting predicate to
   D;
   If stopping point reached for this path, then
   T'= create leaf node and label with appropriate class;
   Else
   T'= DTBUILD(D);
   T= add T' to arc;
End
```

J48 is the implementation of Algorithm ID3 (Iterative dichotomized 3) that allows predicting the target variable of a new dataset, based on a list of predictors and a list of targets. The algorithm requires as input a set of training data and produces a decision tree [26, 27].

(5) Pattern identification. According to [1], we use 80% of data, cross-validation 10 folds, for training and model generation, and 20% of the database for testing.
(6) Knowledge extraction. Based on the comparison of the performance (precision and execution time) of algorithms, working over two different databases, we will determine which algorithm is better.

Experiment Design

We design an experiment to analyze databases of the KDD cup (1999) and Kyoto University (2006), for each database we compared the performance of CLONALG and J48 Algorithms, without and with feature selection using genetic algorithmic search. We will measure precision (in percentage) on classifications and speed on execution time for each database.

Feature selection Process

The KDD Cup (1999) database initially had 42 features meanwhile Kyoto (2006) had 24 features. In order to optimize the execution time and improve the accuracy, a selection feature process was applied; the filter that reached a better accuracy was the GeneticSearch CfsSubsetEval, which allows discarding 34 attributes and improving the accuracy of 77% to 92%, with a running time of 34.18 s per model. We used the same process for the Kyoto University (2006) database and features were reduced to 9. Results of feature selection process are shown in Table 1.

Table 1. Results of feature selection process

Database	Number of original attributes	Number of attributes after F.S.	Resulting attributes
KDD cup 1999 (494,021 records)	42	8	duration, protocol, flag, dst_bytes, land, is_guest_loggings, same_srv_rate, dst_host_diff_srv_rate
Kyoto University (116,307 records)	24	9	duration, service, source_bytes, destination_bytes, same_srv_rate, dst_host_srv_count, dst_host_srv_serror_rate, flag, label

4   Results and Discussion

This section is summarized in two tables, a comparative analysis of the experiments carried out in this research, Table 1 for the performance of CLONALG algorithm and Table 2 for the performance of J48 Algorithm applied to KDD cup (1999) and Kyoto University (2006) databases respectively. In Tables 2 and 3: Column 1 describes precision, column 2 processing time, column 3 precision using feature selection, column 4 execution time by using feature selection, columns 5 and 6 show improvement in precision and improvement of execution time respectively.

As is shown in Table 2 when processing KDD Cup (1999) database and feature selection, processing time decrease, and precision increase substantially. The use of artificial immune system through the use of the ClonalG algorithm for classification of traffic in a network yielded very good results 92.69% of accuracy. In another hand, when processing Kyoto University precision decrease from 95.35% to 95.22% when using J48 and feature selection, but processing time decrease 5.64 s.

Table 2. Comparative analysis for the two models of classification generated using CLONAL G algorithm

Database	Precision clonal G (CG)	Time CG (s)	Precision CG + FS	Time CG + FS (s)	Improvement precision	Improvement time (s)
KDD cup 1999 (494,021 records)	77.92%	90.8	92.69%	40.7	**14.77%**	**50.1**
Kyoto University (116,307 records)	95.35%	16.2	95.22%	10.56	**-0.13%**	**5.64**

As is shown in Table 3, the performance of the J48 algorithm is good, obtains high precisions in both databases, despite improvement on precision is negative, improvement in time is substantial by using feature selection in both databases. KDD cup precision decrease from 99.96% to 99.91% when using feature selection, but processing time decrease 129.95 s. Kyoto University precision decrease from 95.35% to 95.22% when using J48 and feature selection, but processing time decrease 6.03 s.

Table 3. Comparative analysis for the two models of classification generated using J48 algorithm

Database	Precision J48	Time (s)	Precision J48 + FS	Time J48 + FS (s)	Improvement precision	Improvement time (s)
KDD cup 1999 (494,021 records)	99.96%	138.5	99.91%	8.55	-0.05%	129.95
Kyoto University (116,307 records)	99.46%	8.43	99.25%	2.4	-0.21%	6.03

Yan and Yu in his work "AINIDS: an immune-based network intrusion detection system" obtained 88% of accuracy in classification [20]. Xiaojie and Jinquan et al. in their work "A self-adaptive negative selection algorithm used for anomaly detection" obtained 88% of correct classification [21]. Levin in the KDD-99 Classifier Learning Contest [18] obtained 92% of classification [22]. Our approach using feature selection provides a better performance than these related works.

4.1 Proposed Model

Based on our preliminary results we propose a model for the creation of an Intrusion Detection System (IDS) using artificial intelligence (IA), see next figure.

Figure 3 shows the conceptual model of the IDS using IA. The data acquisition module captures information coming and going from a computer network. The intelligent heuristic inference module contains the IDS analysis engine responsible for processing the collected information. This uses the heuristic model stored in the knowledge base, which is generated in the learning module. Finally, the response module generates the alarms and actions to be performed once an intrusion is detected; this is fed by the diagnosis generated by the inference module. The upper part shows the process of obtaining the heuristic model through information obtained from the database and a learning module that feedback the responses of the inference module. At the moment, to obtain the heuristic model, research and tests are performed with two intelligent algorithms: one based on an artificial immune system and one based on J48 or other artificial intelligence technique, i.e. a Bayesian network.

310   S. Y. Ortuño et al.

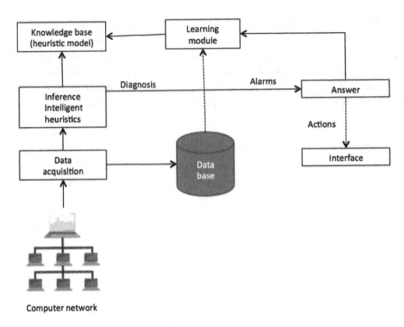

Fig. 3. Model for the intrusion detection systems using artificial intelligence

5 Conclusions And Future Work

Artificial Immune System and the particularly CLONAL-G algorithm, is a promising technology to identify malware and intrusions in computer networks, therefore our hypothesis is true. Artificial Immune System is very important due to its adaptive nature regarding other available technologies like J48.

Preliminary results show AIS provides an acceptable technology to identify intrusions regarding similar technologies. Feature selection by means of genetic algorithms reduces substantially the time to carry out classification process and increase (CLONAL G) or maintains (J48) level of precision.

The results presented here are not in any way final, they represent only the first steps for the generation of a robust model for intrusion detection system. We want to increase the capabilities of this approach to detect intrusion in smart grids. We would like to compare different SIA algorithms available in literature and with respect traditional algorithms like naïve Bayes or a priori. As future work, we plan to apply the methodology described above with actual instances of an institute that experience IDS and include comparisons with other well-known techniques like Bayesian Networks [23]. We would like to implement a prototype system in R Language as described in [9].

References

1. Al-Enezi, J.R., Abbod, M.F., Alsharhan, S.: Artificial Immune Systems - Models, Algorithms and Applications. Academic Research Publishing Agency (2010)
2. Bachmayer, S.: Artificial Immune Systems. Department of Computer Science, University of Helsinki (2008)
3. Dasgupta, D., Ji, Z., González, F.: Artificial immune system (AIS) research in the last five years. IEEE Congr. Evol. Comput. **1**, 123–130 (2003)
4. Dario Duke, N., Chavarro Porras, J.C., Moreno Laverde, R.: Smart security. Scientia Et Technica 1(35) (2007)
5. Castro, L.N., Timmis, J.: Artificial Immune Systems: A New Computational Intelligence Approach. Springer, London (2002)
6. Farmer, J.D., Packard, N.H., Perelson, A.S.: The immune system, adaptation, and machine learning. Elsevier Science Publishers B.V., pp. 197–204 (1986)
7. Han, J., Pei, J., Kamber, M.: Data Mining: Concepts and Techniques. Elsevier, Amsterdam (2011)
8. ISO: The portal of ISO 27001 in Spanish. What is an ISMS? (2012). http://www.iso27000.es/sgsi.html
9. Torgo, L., Torgo, L.: Data Mining with R: Learning with Case Studies. Chapman & Hall/CRC, Boca Raton (2011)
10. Zum Herrenhaus, M., Schommer, C.: Security analysis in internet traffic through artificial immune systems. In: INTERREG IIIC/e-Bird, Workshop "Trustworthy Software", pp. 1–9 (2006)
11. Zum Herrenhaus, M., Schommer, C.: Healthy-security analysis in Internet traffic through artificial immune systems. arXiv preprint arXiv:0805.0909 (2008)
12. Symantec: El gusano Stuxnet. (2010). http://www.symantec.com/es/mx/page.jsp?id=stuxnet
13. Neal, D.: Home Depot confirms 53 million email addresses stolen in recent hack, 7 November 2014. http://www.v3.co.uk/v3-uk/news/2380100/home-depot-confirms-53-million-email-addresses-stolen-in-recent-hack
14. Kaspersky Security Network Report: Ransomware in 2014–2016 (2016)
15. Whitman, M.E., Herbert, M.J.: Principles of Information Security. Cengage Learning, Boston (2011)
16. Kim, J., Bentley, P.J.: An evaluation of negative selection in an artificial immune system. In: Proceedings of GECCO, pp. 1330–1337 (2001)
17. Hernández Aguilar, J.A., Burlak, G., Lara, B.: Diseño e Implementación de un Sistema de Evaluación Remota con Seguridad Avanzada para Universidades Utilizando Minería de Datos. Comput. y Sist. **13**(4), 463–473 (2010)
18. KDD Cup: Dataset, 72 (1999). http://kdd.ics.uci.edu/databases/kddcup99/kddcup99.html
19. Weka (2017). https://sourceforge.net/projects/weka/files/weka-3-6/3.6.4/
20. Yan, Q., Yu, J.: AINIDS: an immune-based network intrusion detection system. In: International Society for Optics and Photonics Defense and Security Symposium, p. 62410U, April 2006
21. Jinquan, Z., Xiaojie, L., Tao, L., Caiming, L., Lingxi, P., Feixian, S.: A self-adaptive negative selection algorithm used for anomaly detection. Prog. Nat. Sci. **19**(2), 261–266 (2009)
22. Levin, I.: KDD-99 classifier learning contest: LLSoft's results overview. SIGKDD Explor. **1**(2), 67–75 (2000)
23. Rojas Gonzalez, I., García Gallardo, J.: Bayesian network application on information security. Res. Comput. Sci. **51**, 87–98 (2010). (I.P. Nacional, Ed.)

24. Pimentel, J.C.L., Monroy, R.: Formal support to security protocol development: a survey. Comput. y Sist. **12**(1), 89–108 (2008)
25. Argüelles Arellano, M.D.C.: Challenges of Cyber Law in Mexico. Comput. y Sist. **20**(4), 827–831 (2016)
26. Danham, M.H., Sridhar, S.: Data mining, Introductory and Advanced Topics, 1st edn. Person education, London (2006)
27. Patil, T.R., Sherekar, S.S.: Performance analysis of Naive Bayes and J48 classification algorithm for data classification. Int. J. Comput. Sci. Appl. **6**(2), 256–261 (2013)
28. Kyoto: Kyoto data (1999). http://www.takakura.com/kyoto_data/
29. Cutello, V., Narzisi, G., Nicosia, G., Pavone, M.: Clonal selection algorithms: a comparative study using effective mutation potentials. In: Jacob, C., Pilat, M.L., Bentley, P.J., Timmis, J. I. (eds.) Artificial Immune Systems, ICARIS 2005. LNCS, vol. 3627, pp. 13–28. Springer, Berlin (2005). https://doi.org/10.1007/11536444_2
30. AISWEB: The Online Home of Artificial Immune Systems (2017). http://www.artificial-immune-systems.org/algorithms.shtml#clonal-alg
31. Data Mining with R: J48 decision tree (2017). http://data-mining.business-intelligence.uoc.edu/home/j48-decision-tree

Jeffrey Divergence Applied to Docking Virtual

Mauricio Martínez-Medina[1(✉)], Miguel González-Mendoza[1(✉)],
and Oscar Herrera-Alcántara[2]

[1] Instituto Tecnológico y de Estudios Superiores de Monterrey,
Lago de Guadalupe Km 3.5, Margarita Maza de Juárez, Atizapán de Zaragoza,
52926 Mexico, Mexico
{A00964166,mgonza}@itesm.mx
[2] Universidad Autónoma Metropolitana, San Pablo 180, Reynosa Tamaulipas,
Azcapotzalco, 02200 Mexico, Mexico
oha@correo.azc.uam.mx

Abstract. Data analysis with high dimensionality and few samples
implies a set of problems related with the *Curse of dimensionality* phenomenon. Molecular Docking faces these kind problems to compare
molecules by similarity. LBVS-Ligand-Based Virtual Screening conducts
studies of docking among molecules using their common attributes registered in specialized databases. These attributes are represented by high
dimensionality boolean vectors where an bit set indicates the presence
of an specific attribute in the molecule, whereas a zero bit, its absence.
The discovering of new drugs through the comparison of these vectors
involves exhaustive processes of matching among the vectors. In this
work, it is proposed the use of *Jeffrey divergence* as a similarity measurement in order to find the best approximate virtual docking between
distinct molecules, to reduce the computation time, and offset some of
Curse of dimensionality effects. The results suggest the application of
Jeffrey divergence on discovering of candidates to drugs allow to identify
the best approximate matching among them.

Keywords: Molecular docking · Ligand-based virtual screening
Curse of dimensionality · Jeffrey divergence · Approximate matching
Drug discovering

1 Introduction

The analysis of high dimensionality vectors is a common activity in fields such
as e-commerce, Molecular biology, Time series, Drug design, among others. Frequently, this kind of data sets have a lower number of samples than the number
of attributes in them. What presents challenges to the algorithms used in their
analysis. The results of *high dimensionality* in them is known as *Curse of dimensionality* and this phenomenon covers a set of effects as *Hypervolume of cubes*

© Springer Nature Switzerland AG 2018
F. Castro et al. (Eds.): MICAI 2017, LNAI 10632, pp. 313–324, 2018.
https://doi.org/10.1007/978-3-030-02837-4_26

and spheres, Volume of thin hypersphere shell, and *Concentration of norms and distances* [1,2]. Depending upon the activity carried out by algorithms such as data clustering, classification, regression data; one or more of the Curse of dimensionality effects will impact its performance and quality of its analysis.

Several techniques have been designed to mitigate these problems, what improves the algorithms performance and their results; these techniques are based on the feature reduction, and in the extraction and construction of new attributes [3–5]. They are pre-processing techniques for identifying a minimum subset of features which captures the relevant properties of a dataset [6]. Unfortunately, some problems requires an exhaustive comparison among vectors, component by component, as is the case of Drug design based in silico methods as *Virtual screening.* In the drug design, the docking process concerns to find the binding site between a pair of molecules named *Ligand* and *Receptor,* in accordance with their structural, electrostic properties and the position between them. Additionally to Drug design, molecular docking is applied in bioremediation processes, fatty acid biosynthesis, and nanomaterial interactions [7].

The docking methods are based on *in vitro* techniques but they are expensive and require large time periods of researching. Nowadays, there exists databases that store the activity and inactivity relationship between molecules, physical properties, chemical, structural, and functional of millions of compounds from which new molecules can be discovered by their similarity, in order to discover potential drugs, compounds with chemical characteristic specific, or with certain affinity between them [8]. The techniques designed for docking molecular under this standpoint are called *in silico* that they reduce the spent time and their costs for discovering new molecules [9].

1.1   Virtual Screening

Virtual screening in Docking molecular brings together a set of procedures based on computational algorithms that identify new molecules using *Similarity* concept, where the information contained in the databases of molecular compounds is represented with high dimensionality vectors and examined with Heuristic search and Optimization algorithms, including Machine learning methods [10–12]. The goal is to identify those compounds that have a high degree of similarity with a molecule objective. The challenges for these algorithms lie in reducing the complexity computational and the computing time to discover them. There exists two areas in Virtual screening: *Structure-based virtual screening* (SBVS) and *Ligand-based virtual screening* (LBVS). SBVS methods search for the best 3D binding between a ligand and a receptor molecule using Optimization algorithms which are computationally intensive. The LBVS methods use chemical databases to find compounds with the best matching by similarity with a objective molecule comparing their common attributes and structure-activity relationships [10,13].

1.2   Vector Comparison

Many problems in the real-world involve the matching of pairs of objects according to a set of common attributes, in order to determine whether two entities are enough similar between them to represent the same object [14]. The application of a *Brute Force Matching Algorithm*, in the vectors comparison by similarity is the least effective method, mainly due to the high dimensionality of them. The algorithms that identify these coincidences increase their temporal complexity when the vectors increase their dimensionality as well as the cardinality of their alphabet. Thus, depending on the data representation, the number of comparisons to be recognized in the matchings will increase. Methods such as *Blocking*, *Matchers* and *Matcher ensembles* are just some of the more efficient algorithms employed to specify the similarity between two entities [15].

1.3   Related Works

The similarity functions that are classified in three types: *character-based, token-based*, and *hybrid similarity functions*. In these methods there are a tradeoff between the accuracy and the processing speed to match a pair of strings [16]. *Character-based* methods measure the similarity between two strings through operations of insertion, deletion, and substitution, to calculate the distance between them at the least number of edit operations needed to transform one string in to other string. *Token-based* methods transform strings into sets either as tokenization, or as q-grams and then quantify their similarity. *hybrid similarity functions* combine the aforementioned methods. In this sense, we are focused in character-based similarity functions.

1.4   Problem Statement and Research Questions

Molecular docking involves the design and implementation of optimization functions and efficient searches that explore the solutions space, to match a set of molecules in an appropriate way or to discover similarity among them. Molecular similarity is based on the idea that globally similar molecules should have similar chemical or biological activities, but it is also known that small changes in an molecule may nearly or completely affect these activities [13].

The algorithms aimed to docking tasks appeal to schemes of Machine Learning such as *Supervised learning*, that require a number of specific instances for being trained and validated, which implies large learning processes. *Curse of dimensionality* affects these algorithms due to high dimensionality of vectors coming from the databases and their reduced number of samples. Additionally, the *Unsupervised learning methods* use *Relevance measurements* to evaluate the similarity between vectors. These methods are faster than the supervised counterpart, since their implementation is simple although imprecise due to their dependency in parameters, Statistical distributions, Scale factors, presence of outliers, and incomplete data.

The existence of large databases of chemical compounds demand fast and scalable algorithms to discover compounds whose attributes have the maximum level of similarity with other useful molecules such as drugs. An alternative to similarity functions are the *Divergence measures* based on *Shannon Entropy* which can compensate many of the shortcomings above mentioned. The comparison of data distributions through these Divergence measurements use the randomness contained in them for quantifying their dissimilarity [16,17], examples of them are *Kullback-Leibler divergence*, *Jeffrey divergence*, and *Jensen-Shannon divergence* amongst others.

According to the above several research questions are proposed: Is it possible to implement *Approximate matching algorithms* through *Divergence measures* based on *Shannon Entropy?*, Can these algorithms identify the best matchings between vectors without a exhaustive comparison? Could matching algorithms based on *Divergence measures* to achieve an acceptable performance to identify the best matchings validated with results of force brute matching algorithms?

1.5   Hypothesis and Objectives

The high dimensionality of vectors and low number of instances in a problem of *Ligand-Based Virtual Screening* can be posed in matters of Divergence entropy as an alternative to force brute matching algorithms. The objective of this work is to propose an algorithm which emphasizes dissimilarity among compounds through Divergence entropy, by expressing the similarity as the lowest magnitude of dissimilarity between a pair of vectors. Note that, low magnitudes of divergence indicate a high degree of similarity between a pair of vectors otherwise, they will have a high dissimilarity. Divergence entropy based algorithms will avoid expensive exploration of the solution space and the design of complex optimization functions.

2   Materials and Methods

DuPont Pharmaceuticals released by KDD Cup 2001 competition a dataset composed of 1908 compounds[1] which match with Thrombin molecule. Each one vector consists of 139,351 attributes with binary representation, such attributes are inactive when they have a value of zero, and active when they have a one value. These vectors are divided into two sets: 42 are classified as *Drugs* or *Active Compounds*, 1886 vectors to be proposed as *Candidates to drug*, given the similarity that they have with the active compounds. The duty is to determine which inactive compounds are the best candidates to drug once they were compared with the active vectors. For the aforementioned, it will be employed the Algorithm 1 which adopts the *Jeffrey divergence* (see Subsect. 2.1) as dissimilarity measure among vectors.

---

[1] We are grateful to DuPont Pharmaceuticals Research Laboratories and KDD Cup 2001 by provided this data set through UCI Machine Learning Repository.

Algorithm 1 is divided in two sections: the first as a preprocessing section, and the second for the dissimilarity calculation with the *Jeffrey divergence*. The preprocessing seeks to identify those inactive and active vectors which components be zeros in all they. Subsequently, these vectors will be labelled to avoid additional comparisons. A counting process of ones is carried out on the rest of the vectors.

Once the preprocessing stage was carried out, it calculates the dissimilarity among the *Inactive*; Candidates to drugs, and *Active* vectors; Drugs. This process will carry out as many comparisons as combinations there exist between the active and inactive vectors. The *Jeffrey divergence* needs only the counting of zeros and ones in each one the vectors to be compared. Once that divergence magnitudes have been calculated for all Inactive-Active pairs, they are ordered according to their divergence magnitudes in decreasing way. On the top of the data structure will be the best matchings. Hence it arises the inactive compounds which can be postulated as drugs by having the lowest Jeffrey divergence magnitudes.

2.1 Jeffrey Divergence

The basic concept to define the different Divergence measures is the *Kullback-Leibler divergence*, its mathematical expression is showed in Eq. 1 [18]. Such concept represents the difference of information between two distributions which is expressed in bits.

$$D_{KL}(P \parallel Q) = \sum_{i=1}^{n} p_i Log_2 \frac{p_i}{q_i} \tag{1}$$

$$J(P,Q) \;=\; D_{KL}(P \parallel Q) + D_{KL}(Q \parallel P) \tag{2}$$

In this expression, the variables P and Q are two distributions obtained from the vectors with boolean data. For each one identified event in them, it must be obtained separately its counting (frequencies) to evaluate Eq. 1. *Kullback-Leibler divergence* is not symmetrical, in order to obtain the dissimilarity between two distributions that are not symmetrical, it must be considered to evaluate the Divergence from P to Q and also from Q to P. The mathematical expression to calculate such variant is showed in Eq. 2 (Jeffreys Divergence).

2.2 Events of Matching Between Two Vectors

The matching between two vectors with binary data implies to recognize four events: *True Positives*, *False Positives*, *True Negatives* and *False Negatives*. Although these events will not be determined by direct matching, it will be expressed in the Jeffrey Divergence as follows (see Eq. 3).

Input: $P[N, M]\ Q[N, L]$
Output: $D[M, 3]$

begin

    $f_1 \leftarrow 0,\ f_P[1 \ldots M] \leftarrow 0,\ f_Q[1 \ldots L] \leftarrow 0$

    $D[1 \ldots M, 1] \leftarrow null,\ D[1 \ldots M, 2] \leftarrow null,\ D[1 \ldots M, 3] \leftarrow null$

    $DivMag \leftarrow null,\ latch \leftarrow 1$

    1's Frequency in each P distribution

    for $j \leftarrow 1$ **to** M **do**

        for $i \leftarrow 1$ **to** N **do**

            if $P[i, j] == 1$ **then**

                $f_1 \leftarrow f_1 + 1$

            end

        end

        $f_{P1}[j] \leftarrow f_1/N$

        $f_1 \leftarrow 0$

    end

    1's Frequency in each Q distribution

    for $j \leftarrow 1$ **to** L **do**

        for $i \leftarrow 1$ **to** N **do**

            if $Q[i, j] == 1$ **then**

                $f_1 \leftarrow f_1 + 1$

            end

        end

        $f_{Q1}[j] \leftarrow f_1/N$

        $f_1 \leftarrow 0$

    end

    Calculation of D_{KL}

    for $i \leftarrow 1$ **to** M **do**

        for $j \leftarrow 1$ **to** L **do**

            $D[i, 1] \leftarrow i,\ D[i, 2] \leftarrow j$

            Trivial Cases

            if $(f_{P1}[i] == 0\ \wedge\ f_{Q1}[j] == 0)$ **then**

                $DivMag \leftarrow null$

            else if $(f_{P1}[i] == 0 \wedge f_{Q1}[j] \leq N)$ **then**

                $DivMag \leftarrow null$

            else if $(f_{P1}[i] \leq N \wedge f_{Q1}[j] == 0)$ **then**

                $DivMag \leftarrow null$

            else if $(f_{P1}[i] == N \wedge f_{Q1}[j] == N)$ **then**

                $DivMag \leftarrow 0$

            Approximate Matching

            else

                $DivMag \leftarrow D_{kl}(f_{P1}/N, f_{Q1}/N)$

            end

            it chooses the minimum

            if $(DivMag \neq null)$ **then**

                if $(latch == 1)$ **then**

                    $D[i, 3] \leftarrow DivMag$

                    $latch \leftarrow 0$

                else

                    $D[i, 3] \leftarrow \min(D[i, 3], DivMag)$

                end

            else

                null

            end

        end

        $latch \leftarrow 1$

    end

    return(D[M,3])

end

Algorithm 1: Approximate Matching through Jeffrey divergence

$$J(P,Q) = D_{KL}(P \parallel Q) + D_{KL}(Q \parallel P) \tag{3}$$

$$= p_0 Log_2 \frac{p_0}{q_0}$$

$$+ p_0 Log_2 \frac{p_0}{q_1}$$

$$+ p_1 Log_2 \frac{p_1}{q_0}$$

$$+ p_1 Log_2 \frac{p_1}{q_1}$$

$$+ q_0 Log_2 \frac{q_0}{p_0}$$

$$+ q_0 Log_2 \frac{q_0}{p_1}$$

$$+ q_1 Log_2 \frac{q_1}{p_0}$$

$$+ p_1 Log_2 \frac{q_1}{p_1}$$

Note that, it is sufficient to know the simple counting of zeros and ones in distributions P and Q to calcule their *Jeffrey divergence*.

3 Results

The searching of best matching between an Inactive vector; Candidate to medicament, and an Active vector or Drug to discover new medicaments imply to compare a serie of common characteristics between them. Such comparison must take into account that the considered characteristics can be present or absent in both vectors. For that reason, the vectors' Boolean representation is the simplest way to compare them, with a minimal of events to be considered. These events can be divided in *True Positives*, *False positives*, *True Negatives* and *False negatives*.

The degree of similarity between an Inactive vector and an Active is determined by the number of *True Positives* during their comparison. This characteristic was used in the construction of graphics (Figs. 1 and 2) that show the performance of *Jeffrey divergence* concept on *Docking Virtual*. Previously, it was used the *Brute Force Algorithm* to identify the True Positives events for each Inactive-Active pair in the dataset. A second characteristic used to show the *Jeffrey divergence* performance was the counting of ones for each one active vector ordered in an incremental way. So, each time that a Active vector was compared with the Inactives, a decreasing behavior of the *Jeffrey divergence's* was appreciated (see Fig. 1).

Finally, the *Jeffrey divergence's* performance was exemplified through the Inactive vectors whose frequency of ones have the lowest, the median and the highest countings in the dataset. These vectors are indexed as 105, 901 and 438 rows respectively in the dataset, respectively. The Fig. 1 shows the corresponding vectors with 3, 691 and 17022 ones, and they are compared with 40 (of 42) active vectors since 2 are completely zeros.

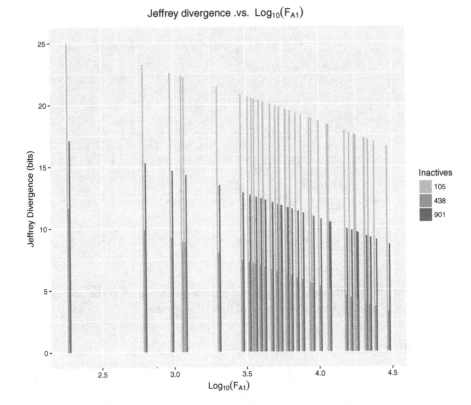

Fig. 1. Similarity of inactive compounds with active vectors by *Jeffrey divergence*

In Fig. 1 is shown the decreasing behavior of *Jeffrey divergence's* as the number of ones on the inactive vectors increases. In the same way, in the x-axis, where the active vectors were ordered incrementally by their counting of ones, it can be appreciated the same behaviour, i.e. the *Jeffrey divergence's* magnitude decreases.

Figure 2 shows a comparison between *True Positives* identified by the *Brute Force Algorithm* and also identified with the *Jeffrey divergence*. Note that, *Jeffrey divergence* decreases when Inactives and Actives increases their frequency of ones simultaneously. In this case, the *True Positives* means the true coincidences of ones for each comparison.

A global incremental sorting of all compared pairs by the number of ones was developed, and the *Jeffrey divergence* shows a decremental behaviour (see Table 1).

Table 1 shows the best top-ten matchings on the Dupont dataset based on the *Jeffrey divergence* (columns 2, 4 and 6).

See for example that the lowest Jeffreys divergence in Table 1 is 3.228575, that compares the Active 1642 with Inactive 438 and True Positives equals to

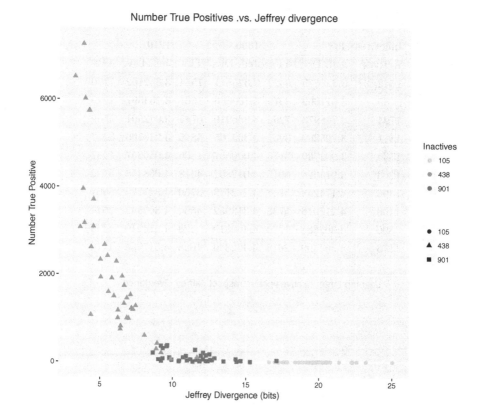

Fig. 2. TP coincidences between inactive with active vectors by *Jeffrey divergence*

6522. The next Jeffreys divergence in Table 1 is 3.611069 corresponding to Active 85 and Inactive 438 with True Positives equals to 3073. In this way, the highest Jeffreys divergence is 4.364409 that compares Active 1173 with Inactive 438 with True Positives equals to 2618.

Now, in an horizontal reading, we observed the same behaviour for inactive 1090 and 1210. Both vectors compared with the inactive 438 decrease their divergence, and in their columns too. A broader view of this we can see it in the Fig. 3.

4   Discussion

The similarity analysis between two vectors through *Jeffrey divergence*'s measurement allow to identify the best approximate matching between them. For the virtual docking problem this concept is appropriate when the dimensionality of the vectors is very high. A ranking process over the calculated divergence magnitudes will outline these matchings showing the most promising, which does not ensure the maximum number of True Positives.

Table 1. Top ten best dockings through *Jeffrey divergence*

Inactives	438		1090		1210	
Actives	Jeff. Div.	TPs	Jeff. Div.	TPs	Jeff. Div.	TPs
1642	3.228575	6522	3.326511	7554	3.382102	7190
85	3.611069	3073	3.709006	1601	3.764597	1529
1794	3.788973	7262	3.886910	6785	3.942501	5559
1311	3.795269	3951	3.893205	3845	3.948796	3297
1533	3.902730	3173	4.000667	1506	4.056257	1467
1203	3.914926	6015	4.012862	4318	4.068453	3792
1496	4.174243	5737	4.272179	3750	4.327770	3067
1408	4.216016	5738	4.313952	4564	4.369543	3641
896	4.362883	1070	4.460819	428	4.516410	348
1173	4.364409	2618	4.462346	1028	4.517936	1114

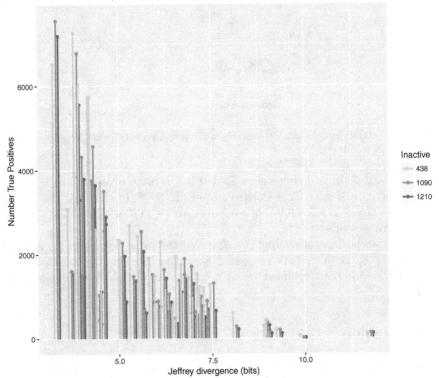

Fig. 3. Last top three inactive in terms of TPs vs. *Jeffrey divergence*

We must take into account that a comparison of two probabilistic distributions does not make one exhaustive matching, but nevertheless under *Jeffrey divergence*'s measurement as comparator is a good indicator of the potential True Positives between them.

5   Conclusion

The application of Jeffrey divergence concept to Docking Virtual on high dimensionality boolean vectors offers a good first approximation to the matching problem between vectors. Only counting the frequency of ones between two vectors to compare, it avoids initially an exhaustive comparison. Some of the effects of *Curse of dimensionality* be avoided as *Concentration of norms and distances* [1,2]. The unbalanced between distributions with respect to the counting of ones and zeros is not in itself a problem since *Jeffrey divergence* ensures a measure for them.

References

1. Bellman, R.: On the theory of dynamic programming. Proc. Natl. Acad. Sci. **38**(8), 716–719 (1952)
2. Clarke, R., et al.: The properties of high-dimensional data spaces: implications for exploring gene and protein expression data. Nat. Rev. Cancer **8**(1), 37 (2008)
3. Lan, F.: The discriminate analysis and dimension reduction methods of high dimension. Open J. Soc. Sci. **3**(03), 7 (2015)
4. Motoda, H., Liu, H.: Feature selection, extraction and construction. In: Communication of IICM (Institute of Information and Computing Machinery, Taiwan), vol. 5, pp. 67–72 (2002)
5. Khalid, S., Khalil, T., Nasreen, S.: A survey of feature selection and feature extraction techniques in machine learning. In: Science and Information Conference (SAI), pp. 372–378. IEEE (2014)
6. Phyu, T.Z., Oo, N.N.: Performance comparison of feature selection methods. In: MATEC Web of Conferences, vol. 42. EDP Sciences (2016)
7. Kim, S.-K., Goddard III, W.A.: Molecular-docking-based drug design and discovery: rational drug design for the subtype selective GPCR ligands. In: Applied Case Studies and Solutions in Molecular Docking-Based Drug Design, pp. 158–185. IGI Global (2016)
8. Sheridan, R.P., Kearsley, S.K.: Why do we need so many chemical similarity search methods? Drug Discov. Today **7**(17), 903–911 (2002)
9. Nicolaou, C.A., Brown, N.: Multi-objective optimization methods in drug design. Drug Discov. Today: Technol. **10**(3), e427–e435 (2013)
10. Lavecchia, A.: Machine-learning approaches in drug discovery: methods and applications. Drug Discov. Today **20**(3), 318–331 (2015)
11. Lill, M.: Virtual screening in drug design. In: Kortagere, S. (ed.) In Silico Models for Drug Discovery, pp. 1–12. Humana Press, Totowa (2013). https://doi.org/10.1007/978-1-62703-342-8_1
12. Danishuddin, M., Khan, A.U.: Virtual screening strategies: a state of art to combat with multiple drug resistance strains. MOJ Proteomics Bioinform. **2**(2), 00042 (2015)

13. Eckert, H., Bajorath, J.: Molecular similarity analysis in virtual screening: foundations, limitations. Drug Discov. Today **12**(5), 225–233 (2007)
14. SaiKrishna, V., Rasool, A., Khare, N.: String matching and its applications in diversified fields. Int. J. Comput. Sci. Issues **9**(1), 219–226 (2012)
15. Köpcke, H., Rahm, E.: Frameworks for entity matching: a comparison. Data Knowl. Eng. **69**(2), 197–210 (2010)
16. Minghe, Y., Li, G., Deng, D., Feng, J.: String similarity search and join: a survey. Front. Comput. Sci. **10**(3), 399–417 (2016)
17. Garrid, A.: About some properties of the Kullback-Leibler divergence. Adv. Model. Optim. **11**, 571–578 (2009)
18. Cichocki, A., Amari, S.: Families of alpha-beta-and gamma-divergences: flexible and robust measures of similarities. Entropy **12**(6), 1532–1568 (2010)

Towards a Classification of Binary Similarity Measures

Ivan Ramirez Mejia and Ildar Batyrshin[(✉)]

Centro de Investigación en Computación, Instituto Politécnico Nacional,
Av. Juan de Dios Bátiz, Esq. Miguel Othón de Mendizábal S/N,
Nueva Industrial Vallejo, 07738 Ciudad de México, Mexico
ramirez.alvarez.ipn@gmail.com, batyr1@gmail.com

Abstract. Similarity measures for binary variables are used in many problems of machine learning, pattern recognition and classification. Currently, the dozens of similarity measures are introduced and the problem of comparative analysis of these measures appears. One of the methods used for such analysis is clustering of similarity measures based on correlation between data similarity values obtained by different measures. The paper proposes the method of comparative analysis of similarity measures based on the set theoretic representation of these measures and comparison of algebraic properties of these representations. The results show existing relationship between results of clustering and the classification of measures by their properties. Due to the results of clustering depend on the clustering method and on data used for measuring correlation between measures we conclude that the classification based on the proposed properties of similarity measures is more suitable for comparative analysis of similarity measures.

Keywords: Similarity measure · Binary data · Contingency table
Clustering

1 Introduction

Similarity measures for binary variables play important role in machine learning, data mining, pattern recognition, classification, etc. At this moment, several tens of similarity measures are introduced [2–10, 13, 14, 17, 19–24] and the problem of comparative analysis of these measures appears. Different approaches have been proposed in order to detect similarity between similarity measures and to group them into the classes of similar measures: comparison of measures by their properties, by the results of their application, by the possibility of transformation of one measure into another one, by clustering etc. [2–4, 7, 9, 12–14, 16, 19, 21, 22, 24]. These approaches compare similarity measures from different points of view.

In this paper, we propose new approach to analysis of similarity measures based on set theoretic representation of these measures. Such representation of similarity measures gives possibility to formulate and easily verify different algebraic properties fulfilled for them. The set of properties fulfilled for similarity measures can be used for classification of these measures. Here we make such analysis for most popular

© Springer Nature Switzerland AG 2018
F. Castro et al. (Eds.): MICAI 2017, LNAI 10632, pp. 325–335, 2018.
https://doi.org/10.1007/978-3-030-02837-4_27

similarity measures and classify them based on their properties. We compare this classification with the clustering structure obtained for these measures by hierarchical clustering algorithm and found existing relationship between results of clustering and the classification of measures by their properties. Because the clustering results highly depend on the clustering method and on data used for measuring correlation between similarity measures, we can consider the classification based on the properties of similarity measures as more suitable for comparative analysis of similarity measures. The obtained results can be extended on all known similarity measures.

The rest of this paper is structured as follows. Section 2 introduces the similarity measures of binary vectors. Section 3 considers the set theoretic representation of 2×2 tables and popular similarity measures. Section 4 considers algebraic properties of similarity measures and presents the Hasse diagram of similarity measures. Section 5 proposes the method of computation of distances between similarity measures and depicts results of hierarchical clustering of these measures. Section 6 concludes the paper.

2 Similarity Measures of Binary Data

Consider the objects characterized by n binary attributes. Each object A is given by a binary vector $A = (a_1, \ldots, a_n)$ where $a_i = 1$ means that the objet possesses the attribute i and $a_j = 0$ means that it does not possesses the attribute j, where $i, j \in \{1, \ldots, n\}$. The similarity between two objects $A = (a_1, \ldots, a_n)$ and $B = (b_1, \ldots, b_n)$ is calculated using four values a, b, c and d defined as follows:

- a is the number of attributes i possessed by both objects, such that $a_i = 1$ and $b_i = 1$, the number of *positive matches*;
- b is the number of attributes i possessed by A but not by B, such that $a_i = 1$ and $b_i = 0$;
- c, the number of attributes i possessed by B but not by A, such that $a_i = 0$ and $b_i = 1$;
- d, the number of attributes i do not possessed by both objects, i.e. such that $a_i = 0$ and $b_i = 0$, the number of *negative matches*.

For these numbers it is fulfilled: $a + b + c + d = n$.

These numbers usually represented as 2×2 contingency table, see Table 1.

Table 1. 2×2 contingency table.

	B	$\bar{B}$
A	a	b
$\bar{A}$	c	d

The similarity measures are defined by numbers from this table, e.g.

$$S(A,B) = \frac{a}{a+b+c}, \quad \text{(Jaccard)} \tag{1}$$

$$S(A,B) = \frac{a+d}{a+2(b+c)+d}. \quad \text{(Roger and Tanimoto)} \tag{2}$$

The survey and analysis of similarity measures as functions of values a, b, c, d can be found in [2, 3, 5, 13, 14, 19, 21].

3 Set Theoretic Representation of 2×2 Contingency Tables and Similarity Measures

In this paper, we study algebraic properties of similarity measures as functions of arguments A and B. In this case A and B will be considered as subsets of the set of attributes $U = \{1,\ldots,n\}$ possessed by objects given by vectors $(a_1,\ldots,a_n)$ and $(b_1,\ldots,b_n)$, respectively. The binary vector $(a_1,\ldots,a_n)$ determines the set of attributes A that contains the attribute i if and only if $a_i = 1$. In such set theoretic interpretation, the values a, b, c, d defined above will be equal to: $a = |A \cap B|$, $b = |A \cap \bar{B}|$, $c = |\bar{A} \cap B|$, $d = |\bar{A} \cap \bar{B}|$, where $\bar{A}$ and $\bar{B}$ are the complements of the sets A and B, correspondingly, and $|A|$, $|B|$ are the numbers of elements in these sets, see Table 2.

Table 3 shows some popular similarity measures taking values in interval $[0,1]$ in traditional and set representation forms. Take into account that $a + b + c + d = n = |U|$. In measures 9 and 10 the values σ, σ' are defined as follows: $\sigma = \max(a,b) + \max(c,d) + \max(a,c) + \max(b,d)$ and $\sigma' = \max(a+c, \ b+d) + \max(a+b,c+d)$. In set notation we obtain: $\sigma = \max(|A \cap B|, |A \cap \bar{B}|) + \max(|\bar{A} \cap B|, |\bar{A} \cap \bar{B}|) + \max(|A \cap B|, |\bar{A} \cap B|) + \max(|A \cap \bar{B}|, |\bar{A} \cap \bar{B}|)$, and $\sigma' = \max(|B|, |\bar{B}|) + \max(|A|, |\bar{A}|)$.

Table 2. Set representation of the contingency table

	B	$\bar{B}$
A	$|A \cap B|$	$|A \cap \bar{B}|$
$\bar{A}$	$|\bar{A} \cap B|$	$|\bar{A} \cap \bar{B}|$

4 The Properties of Similarity Measures

Below we consider possible properties of similarity measures formulated for all subsets $A, B \subseteq U$:

- P1. $S(A,B) = S(B,A)$, (symmetry)
- P2. $S(A,A) = 1$, (reflexivity)

- P3. $S(A,B) < S(A,A)$, if $A \neq B$,
- P4. $S(A,\bar{A}) < 1$,
- P5. $S(A,\bar{A}) = 0$.
- P6. $S(\bar{A},\bar{B}) = SIM(A,B)$ (co - symmetry).

Table 3. Some popular similarity measures in traditional notation and in set representation

	Name	a,b,c,d form	Set representation
1	Sokal and Michener	$\frac{a+d}{a+b+c+d}$	$\frac{|A \cap B| + |\bar{A} \cap \bar{B}|}{|U|}$
2	Sokal and Sneath–II	$\frac{2(a+d)}{2a+b+c+2d}$	$\frac{2(|A \cap B| + |\bar{A} \cap \bar{B}|)}{2|A \cap B| + |\bar{A} \cap B| + |A \cap \bar{B}| + 2|\bar{A} \cap \bar{B}|}$
3	Roger and Tanimoto	$\frac{a+d}{a+2(b+c)+d}$	$\frac{|A \cap B| + |\bar{A} \cap \bar{B}|}{|A \cap B| + 2(|\bar{A} \cap B| + |A \cap \bar{B}|) + |\bar{A} \cap \bar{B}|}$
4	Gower and Legendre	$\frac{a+d}{a+0.5(b+c)+d}$	$\frac{|A \cap B| + |\bar{A} \cap \bar{B}|}{|A \cap B| + 0.5(|\bar{A} \cap B| + |A \cap \bar{B}|) + |\bar{A} \cap \bar{B}|}$
5	Ochai–II	$\frac{ad}{\sqrt{(a+b)(a+c)(b+d)(c+d)}}$	$\frac{|A \cap B||\bar{A} \cap \bar{B}|}{\sqrt{(|A|)(|B|)(|\bar{B}|)(|\bar{A}|)}}$
6	Cosine	$\frac{a}{\sqrt{(a+b)(a+c)}}$	$\frac{|A \cap B|}{\sqrt{(|A|)(|B|)}}$
7	Jaccard	$\frac{a}{a+b+c}$	$\frac{|A \cap B|}{|A \cap B| + |\bar{A} \cap B| + |A \cap \bar{B}|}$
8	Faith	$\frac{a+0.5d}{a+b+c+d}$	$\frac{|A \cap B| + 0.5|\bar{A} \cap \bar{B}|}{|U|}$
9	Goodman and Kruskal	$\frac{\sigma - \sigma'}{2n - \sigma'}$	$\frac{\sigma - \sigma'}{2|U| - \sigma'}$
10	Anderberg	$\frac{\sigma - \sigma'}{2n}$	$\frac{\sigma - \sigma'}{2|U|}$
11	Kulczynski–II	$\frac{\frac{a}{2}(2a+b+c)}{(a+b)(a+c)}$	$\frac{\frac{|A \cap B|}{2}(2|A \cap B| + |A \cap \bar{B}| + |\bar{A} \cap B|)}{(|A|)(|B|)}$

Table 4. The fulfillment (Y) or not (N) of properties P1–P6 for 11 similarity measures.

		P1	P2	P3	P4	P5	P6	Class
1	Sokal and Michener	Y	Y	Y	Y	Y	Y	1
2	Sokal and Sneath-II	Y	Y	Y	Y	Y	Y	1
3	Roger and Tanimoto	Y	Y	Y	Y	Y	Y	1
4	Gower and Legendre	Y	Y	Y	Y	Y	Y	1
5	Ochai–II	Y	Y	Y	Y	Y	Y	1
6	Cosine	Y	Y	Y	Y	Y	N	2
7	Jaccard	Y	Y	Y	Y	Y	N	2
11	Kulczynski–II	Y	Y	Y	Y	Y	N	2
8	Faith	Y	N	Y	Y	Y	N	3
9	Goodman and Kruskal	Y	Y	N	N	N	Y	4
10	Anderberg	Y	N	Y	Y	N	Y	5

The representations of similarity measures in Table 3 give a simple way to check the fulfillment of the considered above properties P1–P6. The results are presented in Table 4 where the letters Y and N denote respectively "fulfillment" and "not fulfillment" of property in the corresponding column for the method given in the string. For example, from the set representation of similarity measures we can easy to see that the first 5 measures in the Table 3 satisfy co-symmetry property P6, Faith similarity measure does not satisfy reflexivity property P1 etc.

Based on Table 4 we can see that the first five measures compose the class of similarity measures with similar properties. The following 3 measures with numbers 6, 7, 11 are joined in the second class: they satisfy the first five properties P1–P5 and do not satisfy the property P6. These three methods use only information about the positive matching of attributes given by the parameter a but they do not take into account negative matches given by the parameter d. The *pro* and *contra* for inclusion negative matches into the similarity measure can be found in [6, 13, 21]. The properties P1–P6 or P1–P5 can be considered as rational requirements on similarity measures in many applications. But the last three similarity measures 8, 9 and 10 from Table 4 do not satisfy two or more properties from P1–P6. By its properties the Faith similarity measure is more similar to the measures from the class 2 but this measure does not satisfy reflexivity P2 that is usually considered as a necessary requirement on any similarity measure. The Goodman and Kruskal measure satisfies the reflexivity property P2 but one can check that for this measure it is fulfilled the very unnatural property:

- P7. $S(A, \bar{A}) = 1$.

May be for some specific application one of the three similarity measures 8, 9 and 10 can be useful but generally these methods should be used with precautions due to their non-rational properties.

Figure 1 depicts the Hasse diagram of the considered similarity measures partially ordered by the inclusion of the sets of properties fulfilled for them.

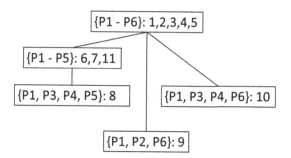

Fig. 1. Hasse diagram of considered similarity measures

5   Computing Distances Between Similarity Measures

Distances between measures and calculated using a modification of algorithms considered in [3, 7, 11, 15, 16, 18, 21] under the following circumstances:

1. 10 synthetic random binary vectors with $n = 100$ are generated with different number of ones.
2. Parameter p controls such number of ones. Number p is selected in $(0, 1)$ with the step 0.1. For example, $p = 0.3$ in order to get a proportion of 30 percent of ones, $p = 0.5$ for a proportion of 50 ones and so on.
3. Distance between similarities is measured by using the correlation coefficient.
4. Aggregation of the correlation matrix is performed by getting a mean value.

The clustering of similarity measures have been implemented as follows:

- For each value p in $(0,1)$ obtained with the step 0.1
  generate 10 synthetic objects each containing 100 features with proportion p of ones.
- For each generated pair of objects (O_i, O_j), $i, j = 1, 2,...,10$
  calculate similarity measure k from Table 4 and save in a matrix of similarities.
- For each column in previously generated matrix use correlation coefficient between similarity values obtained for each measure and save it in correlation matrix.
  Use obtained correlation matrix of correlation as a squared representation of distance values.
- Apply complete linkage clustering method.
- Generate dendrogram.

Figures 2, 3 and 4 depict scatterplots for each similarity measure taken from its cluster versus different measures both in the same and different clusters.

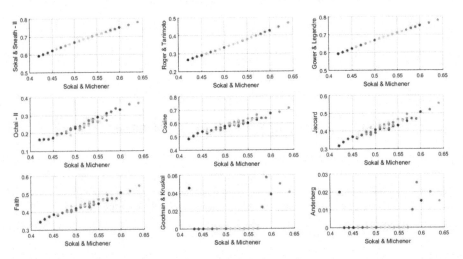

Fig. 2. Scatterplot of Sokal and Michener similarity measure versus other similarity measures.

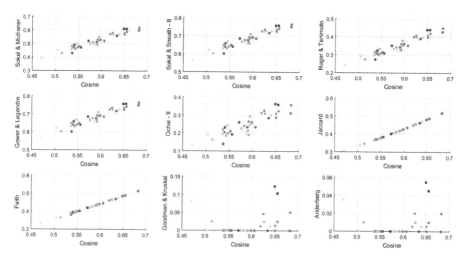

Fig. 3. Scatterplot of Cosine similarity measure versus other similarity measures.

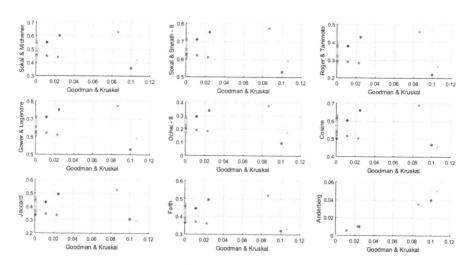

Fig. 4. Scatterplot of Goodman and Kruskal similarity measure versus other similarity measures.

Note from Table 5 that positive and almost perfect correlation is obtained for similarity measures D1, D2, D3, D4, D5, D6, D7, D8, and D11 and in the meantime measures D9 and D10 produce those values that reflects negative values and no association with other similarity measures. A relationship cannot be clearly shown just by these raw values. Recall that this table is generated for different proportions p in $(0, 1)$. It is necessary to aggregate such correlation values in just one value that reflects the whole analysis. A mean value is obtained along every correlation matrix for all analyzed proportions.

Clustering of similarity measures is made using complete linkage and with a small change in scale to every value in the final correlation matrix.

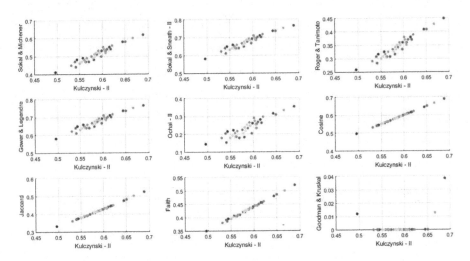

Fig. 5. Scatterplot of Kulczynski - II similarity measure versus other similarity measures.

Table 5. Example of correlation values obtained from the matrix of similarity measurements for measures D1 to D11 as was stated in Table 4 for a proportion $p = 0.9$.

	D1	D2	D3	D4	D5	D6	D7	D8	D9	D10	D11
D1	1.000	0.999	0.999	0.999	0.975	0.974	0.975	0.982	− 0.267	− 0.272	0.974
D2	0.999	1.000	0.997	1.000	0.969	0.976	0.976	0.983	− 0.299	− 0.305	0.977
D3	0.999	0.997	1.000	0.997	0.979	0.970	0.973	0.979	− 0.235	− 0.241	0.971
D4	0.999	1.000	0.997	1.000	0.969	0.976	0.976	0.983	− 0.299	− 0.305	0.977
D5	0.975	0.969	0.979	0.969	1.000	0.901	0.905	0.916	− 0.150	− 0.156	0.902
D6	0.974	0.976	0.970	0.976	0.901	1.000	0.999	0.999	− 0.346	− 0.351	1.000
D7	0.975	0.976	0.973	0.976	0.905	0.999	1.000	0.999	− 0.314	− 0.319	0.999
D8	0.982	0.983	0.979	0.983	0.916	0.999	0.999	1.000	− 0.323	− 0.328	0.999
D9	− 0.267	− 0.299	− 0.235	− 0.299	− 0.150	− 0.346	− 0.314	− 0.323	1.000	1.000	− 0.345
D10	− 0.272	− 0.305	− 0.241	− 0.305	− 0.156	− 0.351	− 0.319	− 0.328	1.000	1.000	− 0.350
D11	0.974	0.977	0.971	0.977	0.902	1.000	0.999	0.999	− 0.345	− 0.350	1.000

One can see close relationship between structure of classes shown in Figs. 1 and 6. Cluster {1, 2, 3, 4, 5} is presented in both classifications. It is interesting that the measure 5 having quite different formula in comparison with similarity measures 1–4 was joined with them in one cluster (Fig. 5). From Fig. 1 we see that all 5 similarity measures have the same properties P1–P6 and this is the reason why then joined in one cluster in Fig. 6. The similarity measures 6, 7, 11 are joined in both classifications in the same cluster. In Fig. 6 they joined together with similarity measure 8 which is on periphery on this cluster. The similarity measures 9 and 10 are quite different by properties from other measures and clustering joined them in one cluster. The classification of similarity measures on Fig. 1 based on similarity of their properties gives more useful information about classes than hierarchical clustering based on correlation of data. Note also that the hierarchical clustering can give different results of clustering depending on clustering method and data used in calculation of correlation of measures.

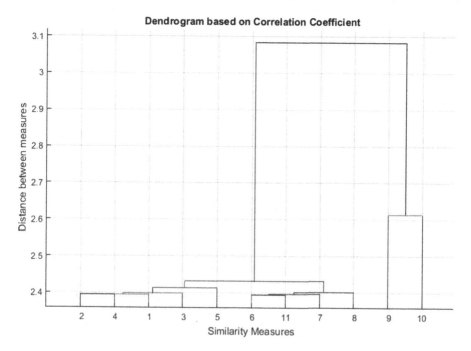

Fig. 6. Dendrogram that shows different groups of similarity measures by using correlation coefficient as distance measure with $1 + \log(3 - r\_value)$.

6 Conclusions

At this moment, there are proposed more than 40 different similarity measures for binary data [5]. Different methods of mutual comparison of them are considered in the literature. In this paper, we propose to compare similarity measures by algebraic properties fulfilled for them. For simplifying such analysis, it is proposed to give set representation of these measures. The Hasse diagram of partial ordering of the considered similarity measures defined by partial ordering of the sets of properties fulfilled for them is constructed. This diagram includes classes of similarity measures with similar properties. This classification was compared with the clustering of similarity measures based on correlation of values obtained by different similarity measures on the same data. It was surprising that the obtained clusters are very similar to the classes of similarity measures with the same properties. However, we trust more in classification based on similarity of properties than in clustering based on correlation of similarity values. The obtained results can be used in different manner. We plan to extend our comparative analysis on all known similarity measures of binary data. The set presentation of similarity measures will be helpful in such analysis. The classification of similarity measures by their properties can be helpful in excluding of similarity measures with "strange" properties from the list of "rational" similarity measures. In data exploration and classification one can use similarity measures from different classes to analyze possible data structures.

Acknowledgements. The work is partially supported by the projects SIP 20171344, BEIFI of IPN and 283778 of CONACYT.

References

1. Batyrshin, I.: On definition and construction of association measures. J. Intell. Fuzzy Syst. **29**, 2319–2326 (2015)
2. Batyrshin, I.Z., Kubysheva, N., Solovyev, V., Villa-Vargas, L.A.: Visualization of similarity measures for binary data and 2 × 2 tables. Computación y Sistemas **20**(3), 345–353 (2016)
3. Batagelj, V., Bren, M.: Comparing resemblance measures. J. Classif. **12**(1), 73–90 (1995)
4. Baulieu, F.B.: A classification of presence/absence based dissimilarity coefficients. J. Classif. **6**(1), 233–246 (1989)
5. Choi, S.S., Cha, S.H., Charles, C.T.: A survey of binary similarity and distance measures. J. Syst. Cybern. Inf. **8**, 43–48 (2010)
6. Clifford, H.T., Stephenson, W.: An Introduction to Numerical Classification, vol. 229. Academic Press, New York (1975)
7. Duarte, J.M., Santos, J.B.D., Melo, L.C.: Comparison of similarity coefficients based on RAPD markers in the common bean. Genet. Mol. Biol. **22**(3), 427–432 (1999)
8. Goodman, L.A., Kruskal, W.H.: Measures of association for cross classifications. J. Am. Stat. Assoc. **49**, 732–764 (1954)
9. Gower, J. C. (1971). A general coefficient of similarity and some of its properties. Biometrics, 857–871
10. Gower, J.C., Legendre, P.: Metric and Euclidean properties of dissimilarity coefficients. J. Classif. **3**(1), 5–48 (1986)
11. Hassanat, A.B.: Dimensionality invariant similarity measure. J. Am. Sci. 221–226 (2014)
12. Johnston, J.W.: Similarity indices I: what do they measure? In: Energy Research and Development Administration, vol. 136 (1976)
13. Legendre, P., Legendre, L.F.: Numerical Ecology, 2nd edn. Elsevier, Amsterdam (1998)
14. Lesot, M.-J., Rifqi, M., Benhadda, H.: Similarity measures for binary and numerical data: a survey. Int. J. Knowl. Eng. Soft Data Paradig. **1**(1), 63–84 (2009)
15. Meilă, M.: Comparing clusterings: an information based distance. J. Multivar. Anal. **98**, 873–895 (2007)
16. Meyer, A.D.S., Garcia, A.A.F., Souza, A.P.D., Souza Jr., C.L.D.: Comparison of similarity coefficients used for cluster analysis with dominant markers in maize (Zea mays L). Genet. Mol. Biol. **27**(1), 83–91 (2004)

17. Pearson, K., Blakeman, J.: Mathematical contributions to the theory of evolution. In: 13th on the Theory of Contingency and Its Relation to Association and Normal Correlation. Dulau & Co., London (1912)
18. Pfitzner, D., Leibbrandt, R., Powers, D.: Characterization and evaluation of similarity measures for pairs of clusterings. Knowl. Inf. Syst. **19**, 361–394 (2009)
19. Rodríguez-Salazar, M.E., Álvarez-Hernández, S., Bravo-Núñez, E.: Coeficientes de asociación. Plaza y Valdés Editores, México (2001)
20. Sidorov, G., Gelbukh, A., Gómez-Adorno, H., Pinto, D.: Soft similarity and soft cosine measure: similarity of features in vector space model. Computación y Sistemas **18**(3), 491–504 (2014)
21. Sokal, R.R., Sneath, P.H.A.: Principles of Numerical Taxonomy. WH Freeman, New York (1963)
22. Tan, P.N., Kumar, V., Srivastava, J.: Selecting the right interestingness measure for association patterns. In: Proceedings of the 8th ACM SIGKDD International Conference on Knowledge Discovery and Data Mining, pp. 32–41 (2002)
23. Tversky, A.: Features of similarity. Psychol. Rev. **84**, 327–352 (1977)
24. Warrens, M.J.: A comparison of multi-way similarity coefficients for binary sequences. Int. J. Res. Rev. Appl. Sci. **16**(1), 12 (2013)

Ranking Association Rules by Clustering Through Interestingness

Veronica Oliveira de Carvalho[1(✉)], Davi Duarte de Paula[1],
Mateus Violante Pacheco[1], Waldeilson Eder dos Santos[1], Renan de Padua[2],
and Solange Oliveira Rezende[2]

[1] Instituto de Geociências e Ciências Exatas,
UNESP - Univ Estadual Paulista, Rio Claro, Brazil
veronica@rc.unesp.br, davi_duarte@outlook.com,
mateusvpacheco@gmail.com, wwesantos@gmail.com
[2] Instituto de Ciências Matemáticas e de Computação,
USP - Universidade de São Paulo, São Carlos, Brazil
{padua,solange}@icmc.usp.br

Abstract. The association rules (ARs) post-processing step is challenging, since many patterns are extracted and only a few of them are useful
to the user. One of the most traditional approaches to find rules that
are of interestingness is the use of objective measures (OMs). Due to
their frequent use, many of them exist (over 50). Therefore, when a user
decides to apply such strategy he has to decide which one to use. To
solve this problem this work proposes a process to cluster ARs based on
their interestingness, according to a set of OMs, to obtain an ordered list
containing the most relevant patterns. That way, the user does not need
to know which OM to use/select nor to handle the output of different
OMs lists. Experiments show that the proposed process behaves equal
or better than as if the best OM had been used.

Keywords: Association rules · Post-processing · Objective measures
Clustering

1 Introduction

Association rules is a very used technique due to its simplicity of interpretation
and, so, have been applied to solve a variety of problems in many domains. An
association rule, $A \Rightarrow B$, expresses the existing relation, in a given data set,
between a set of the items in antecedent A with a set of items in consequent B.
However, a problem associated with the technique is the number of rules that
are obtained, making the post-processing step a difficult task. The most common
solution for this problem is to apply objective evaluation measures, or simply
objective measures (OMs), to retrieve the patterns that will be of interest to
the users (in thesis, to select the most relevant rules of the domain). An OM,
as support ($P(AB)$) and confidence ($P(B|A)$) [11], computes the relevance of a

© Springer Nature Switzerland AG 2018
F. Castro et al. (Eds.): MICAI 2017, LNAI 10632, pp. 336–351, 2018.
https://doi.org/10.1007/978-3-030-02837-4_28

rule based on the information available in the data set. Based on this relevance value, an ordered list of interestingness patterns is generated, sorting the rules from the most important/relevant to the least. In general, the first top rules of the list are those that are considered the most interestingness to the user.

As many OMs exist, over 50, the first problem the user will encounter is to decide which OM to use. Many works have been proposed for that [1,7,8,11]. The idea of these works is to minimize the number of OMs to be chosen. In this way, only a small number of OMs will have to be handled. In general, a way of doing this is to cluster OMs so that measures behaving as similarly as possible, in terms of sorting the patterns, will be grouped together. Therefore, by selecting one measure from each group it is possible to obtain a small list of measures that minimizes the number of OMs to be chosen. Although the user's effort is minimized, the problem remains: (i) which measure, from a previous selection, to use? (ii) As some measures can be selected from (i), how to handle the output of each OM ordered list considering that each one will rank the patterns in a different way? The problem becomes more difficult since the user does not know which of them is the best to his problem, i.e., which measure will place the "true" (real) interestingness rules in the top of the list. Finally, it is important to mention that selecting a good association rule through a suitable OM is an important issue in many areas, as in recommender systems [2].

Based on what stated above, this work proposes to cluster the association rules based on their interestingness. This is done according to a set of OMs to obtain an ordered list containing the most interestingness/relevant patterns of the domain. For that, this work's hypothesis are:

(a) since it is not known which measure is the most suitable to the problem, all the interestingness rules are spread over the clusters, since each cluster represents a subset of similar interestingness rules suffering the impact of a subset of OMs more than the rules on the other clusters;

(b) as each cluster will contain a set of similar interestingness rules, only a small number of them is enough to represent the other rules in the cluster;

(c) the rules within each cluster to be selected and added to the list are the ones better evaluated by the set of all OMs, since each measure provides a different semantic for the rules;

(d) the order the rules are added to the list is determined not only by their relevance (item (c)), but also by the interestingness of the clusters, since each one can contain, on average, more rules better classified.

That way, the problems above stated ((i), (ii)) can be solved: (i) it is not necessary to know which OM to use/select nor (ii) to handle the output of different lists to obtain an ordered list of the interestingness rules. It is expected that the proposed process, named RAR_{C_tI} (Ranking Association Rules by Clustering through Interesting), behaves equal or better as if the best OM had been used. To the best of our knowledge, this is the first work that discusses the current problem as presented here. An initial proposal was made in [3]; however, the one presented here works differently (see Sect. 2). It is important to mention that works that clusters association rules exist, as in [4,5]. However, their aim is to organize the rules to provide the user with a better understanding of the domain.

The paper is structured as follows: Sect. 2 presents some related works; Sect. 3 the RAR_{C_tI} process; Sect. 4 the settings used in experiments; Sect. 5 the results and discussion; Sect. 6 the conclusions.

2   Background and Related Works

As mentioned before, the use of objective measures (OMs) is a common approach to post-process association rules. An OM computes the relevance of a rule based on the information available in the data set. An example of such measures is support, which expresses the frequency of a pattern in the data set, being defined as $P(AB)$ for a given rule $A \Rightarrow B$. 61 OMs are defined and discussed in [11], which contains a good review of them, so we will not describe any of them here. The measures are usually computed for each rule in a given rule set. Based on these values, the rules can be ranked considering their relevance to obtain a list of rules ordered by their degree of interestingness. In general, the higher the value the better the rule. For example, the rules with the highest support will be placed at the top of the list. However, looking at the ordered list of rules, we note that what matters is the order the rules will be explored. Therefore, each rule can receive a ranking value, so that the first rule in the list receives a value of 1, the second a value of 2, and so on. In this alternative view, the lower the value, the better the rule – this is the view we use in this work (see Sect. 3). In general, given an ordered list of rules, only the first top rules of the list are the ones considered the most interestingness to the user; otherwise, we would have to explore all the exploration space which would be meaningless given that an OM aims to minimize the user effort. In other words, when using OMs to post-process association rules, the goal is to reduce the exploration space to minimize the user's effort by exploring only the most interestingness rules.

Although OMs are widely used, the problem with it is to decide which OM to use/select since many of them exist. To solve this issue, some works were proposed. The aim of these works is to minimize the number of OMs to be chosen by the user. In general, a way of doing this is to cluster OMs so that measures behaving as similarly as possible are grouped together. By selecting one measure of each group it is possible to obtain a small list of measures. [8] propose to cluster OMs using a matrix R x M (Rules by Measures), where each cell $[r][m]$ stores, for a given rule rl, its value in each measure m ($|M| = 36$). To compute the similarity between the measures the user can choose Pearson, Spearman or Kendall (correlation coefficients). Groups of similar OMs are obtained by cutting a graph. The approach is available within a tool, named ARQAT, which provides other resources. The work does not specifically focus on analyzing OMs and, so, must be executed for each rule set. However, the number of OMs can be minimized with the tool.

Other works focus specifically on analyzing the behavior of many OMs. [11] propose to cluster OMs also using a matrix R x M (Rules by Measures). Here, different from the previous work, each cell $[r][m]$ stores, for a given rule rl, its rankings associated with all measures M ($|M| = 61$). To compute the similarity between the measures the Spearman's correlation coefficient is used. Groups of similar OMs are obtained by applying the Complete Linkage algorithm. The behavior of the measures is studied using 110 data sets and the work finishes showing that the initial set of 61 OMs can be reduced to 21 groups of measures containing 50 OMs (however, two of them can be disregard). Since OMs within each cluster are similar, it is sufficient to select one measure from each one – the same idea holds for the other works.

Using a different analysis, the works of [1] and [7] use a matrix M x P (*Measures by Properties*), where each cell $[m][p]$ stores 0 or 1 (contains (1) or not (0) the property). Regarding the work of [1], the clusters obtained by their approach are overlapped, i.e., one OM can belong to more than one cluster. To do the clustering, a boolean factor analysis is used (in their work $|M| = 52$). The work of [7] also uses a matrix M x P to do the clustering, using as similarity the Euclidean distance (in their work $|M| = 52$). The groups of similar OMs are obtained by computing a mean between the results of the Ward Linkage algorithm with the K-means algorithm.

The idea of the presented works is to cluster the measures in a manner that since OMs within each obtained group are similar, it is enough to select one measure from each one. The problem related to it is that the user can select one OM from each cluster and, so, many OMs can still remain. Although the user's effort is minimized, a question arises: which measure, from a previous selection, to use? Besides, as some measures are selected, at least one from each cluster, how to handle the output of each OM ordered list? The only work that presents a simple solution to this last issue is the one of [8], which provides the user with some operators, as union and intersection, to support the identification of the most interestingness rules. The others only discuss the reduction of the measures set.

To overcome the exposed problems, a initial proposal to cluster the rules based on their interestingness was done in [3]; however, the one presented here works differently: (i) the output of the process is an association rules list; (ii) the rules within the clusters are ranked to determine the order the rules will be placed on the list, as well to determine the relevance of the clusters; (iii) the parameter Cut that controls the size of the list to be explored; (iv) the use of a more efficient clustering algorithm, which had the parameters automatized. Therefore, this work can be seen as an extension of the one presented by [3]. It is important to mention that the presented works, which clusters OMs in spite of rules, are relevant since they demonstrate that we do not need to use a large set of measures – only a subset of them is sufficient, once OMs within a group are considered redundant. Therefore, this current work can benefit from this information only using all the non-redundant OMs to identify the interestingness rules of the domain.

3 RAR_{C_tI} Process

The process Ranking Association Rules by Clustering through Interesting (RAR_{C_tI}) is presented in Algorithm 1. The process receives as input an association rules set R, a set M of OMs to compute the interestingness of each rule in R and a parameter Cut to establish the percentage of rules to be selected within each cluster to compose an ordered list L of interestingness rules (output). In Algorithm 1, $|X|$ stands for the number of elements in vector X, where X can be a set of measures ($|M|$), rules ($|R|$), clusters ($|C|$), etc.

The general idea of the process is (a) to compute a matrix Mat: R x M, where each row contains the rule's ranking in all OMs in M; (b) to cluster the rules based on Mat; (c) to compute an average rank value for each rule, which will be used to select the rules within each cluster; (d) to compute an average rank value for each cluster, which will be used to determine the order the rules, selected in each one of the clusters, will be placed in the list L; (e) build the list L of interestingness association rules. As seen, the process can be divided into five steps, which are described below:

Step 1. (lines 1–6) A matrix "Rules" by "Measures" is computed (Mat: R x M) (line 1) to store for each rule rl in R its relevance according to each OM in M. That way, a rule can be evaluated in different views – one for each OM. However, since each OM contains a different range value (some of them vary from $[0, 1]$, for example, while others from $[0, \infty[$), a normalization process is done (lines 2 to 6): first, the rules are ranked in descending order considering each measure at a time (line 3) – the higher the value the better the rule. After that, as in [11], the values are changed by their ranking's values, because what matters is the order the rules will be explored (line 4) – here, as values are changed by a ranking value, the lower the value, the better the rule. Finally, each ranking's value is normalized by min-max (line 5) – the rules' values in all OMs will range between $[0, 1]$, providing equal weighting for each one of the OMs, since each of them can have different values for rv_n (the highest ranking in a given OM). In fact, this block of code processes the data as presented in [9] regarding how to handle ordinal variables.

Step 2. (line 7) Based on Mat, the rules are clustered using the DBSCAN algorithm considering the existing agreement among the rules regarding their interestingness: the rules that behave similarly according to all OMs are grouped together. Therefore, it is possible to obtain groups of rules that agree with their classifications considering different semantics (one for each OM). DBSCAN[1] [6] was chosen because it is an algorithm that can find clusters of arbitrary shape, can find the number of clusters automatically and, depending on the implementation, has a complexity time of $O(n\ log\ n)$. It is an algorithm based on density that clusters the points considering that a group is a dense region of objects that is surrounded by a region of low density [10]. Two

---

[1] The algorithm won the "2014 SIGKDD Test of Time Award" (http://www.kdd.org/News/view/2014-sigkdd-test-of-time-award).

Algorithm 1. The $RAR_{Ct}I$ process (extended from [3]).

Input: R: an association rules set; M: a set of OMs; Cut: percentage of rules to be selected inside a cluster
Output: L: An association rules list ordered by their degree of interest

1: Compute Mat: $R \times M$
2: **for** $OM := 1$ to $|M|$ **do**
3:     Rank $Mat[][OM]$ in descending order
4:     Assign $Mat[][OM]$ a ranking value ranging from 1 to rv_n
5:     Normalize $Mat[][OM]$ by min-max: $rv = \frac{rv - rv_{min}}{rv_{max} - rv_{min}}$
6: **end for**

7: Apply DBSCAN to cluster the rules using Mat (C stores the result)

    //each rule receives an average rank value based on all OMs
8: **for** $rl := 1$ to $|R|$ **do**
9:     $RR[rl] = \sum_{OM=1}^{|M|} Mat[rl][OM]$
10:     $RR[rl]/|M|$
11: **end for**

    //each cluster receives an average rank value based on all its rules considering their average rank values
12: **for** $cl := 1$ to $|C|$ **do**
13:     $RR_{cl} = cl_{rules}(RR)$ //select from RR the rules inside cluster cl
14:     $CR[cl] = \sum_{NR=1}^{|RR_{cl}|} RR_{cl}[NR]$
15:     $CR[cl]/|RR_{cl}|$
16: **end for**

17: Sort(CR)
18: BuildList(L,CR,RR,Cut)
19: Output L

20: **procedure** Sort($Vector$)
    //Modify $Vector$ to store the order objects (clusters or rules) must be accessed considering their average rank values
21:     $Aux = Vector$
22:     **for** $i := 1$ to $|Vector|$ **do**
23:         $Vector[i] = O_{id}(min(Aux))$ //select the number (id) of an object (O)
                //among the current ones that present the lowest average rank value
24:         Remove($min(Aux)$)   //delete from Aux the object already selected
25:     **end for**
26: **end procedure**

27: **procedure** BuildList(L,CR,RR,Cut)
    //Select within each cluster a percentage of rules based on Cut parameter to produce L. The rules to be selected are accessed considering their average rank value. In addition, the order the clusters are accessed also depends on their interest
28:     **for** $cl := 1$ to $|CR|$ **do**
29:         $RR_{cl} = cl_{rules}(RR)$ //select from RR the rules inside cluster cl
30:         Sort(RR_{cl})   //idem Sort(CR) for the vector RR_{cl}
31:         $L = L \cup$ Select(RR_{cl},Cut)   //select from RR_{cl}, from the most
                //interestingness ones, a set containing "$|RR_{cl}| * Cut$" rules
32:     **end for**
33: **end procedure**

parameters have to be defined: Eps and $MinPts$. Eps, which determines the neighborhood of a point, using a distance function (in this case, Manhattan), can be computed automatically through the knee of the curve of a k-dist plot (see [10]). Therefore, only $MinPts$, which specifies the minimum number of points within an *Eps* radius, has to be set. To make the whole process automatically, it was considered that $MinPts$ should be equal to 0.5% of the total number of rules (which represents the number of points in the data set). The idea behind this value is to specify a minimum frequency (as support) that a point relates with its neighborhood. Because the number of rules can be large, the percentage is low to keep a small value for $MinPts$ as the data set becomes larger.

Step 3. (lines 8–11) Each rule rl receives a value that expresses its overall interestingness. This value is computed considering its rankings obtained in each OM. Adding the row of rl in Mat, which contains all of its evaluations (line 9), and dividing by the number of measures (line 10), rl receives an average rank value based on all OMs. The values are stored in vector RR and are used to decide which rules within each cluster will be selected and added to the list L – the lower the average rank value the better is the rule's interestingness.

Step 4. (lines 12–16) Each cluster cl receives a value that expresses its overall interestingness. This value is computed considering the rankings of the rules belonging to it (line 13), which was computed in the previous step. Adding the average rank value of each rule rl within the cluster cl (line 14) and dividing by the number of rules in cl (line 15), each cluster cl receives an average rank value based on all its rules considering their average rank values. The values are stored in vector CR and are used to decide the order the rules will be added to the list L, since this will be determined not only by their relevance (Step 3), but also by the interestingness of the clusters, since each one can contain, on average, more rules better classified – as above, the lower the average rank value the better is the cluster's interestingness.

Step 5. (lines 17–18) Based on the overall performance of the clusters, as of the rules, the list L can be built, which contains a subset of the rules ordered by their degree of interestingness. For that, this step is divided in two:

>**Step 5.1.** (lines 17; 20–26) First, it is necessary to know the order the clusters must be accessed to know in which order the rules will be placed in L. For that, the clusters are sorted in ascending order considering their average rank values (lines 20–26). The lower the value the more interestingness the cluster, since it means that, on average, its rules were well classified by all OMs, and so, its rules must be placed previously in L.

>**Step 5.2.** (lines 18; 27–33) Knowing the order clusters must be accessed (line 28), the rules within each cluster (line 29) are also sorted in ascending order considering their average rank values (lines 30; 20–26). The lower the value the more interestingness the rule is, as it was better classified by all OMs, and so, must be placed in L. After sorting the rules of a certain cluster, a percentage of them are placed in L (line 31). The number of rules to be stored in L is determined by the Cut parameter, which specifies the percentage of rules to be selected within a cluster. As each cluster contains a different number of rules, setting a percentage causes each cluster to contribute to L equally. Cut ranges from [0,1], where 0 equals to 0% and 1 equals to 100%.

Note that L is composed of rules belonging to all clusters. As we do not know which is the best measure for the problem, it is considered that all the interestingness rules are spread over the clusters – each cluster represents a subset of similar interestingness rules suffering the impact of a subset of OMs more than the rules on the other clusters. Also, note that each cluster contributes with a subset of rules. It is considered that as each cluster will contain a set of similar interestingness rules, only a small number of them is enough to represent the other rules in the cluster.

As seen, the list L is outputted to the user (line 19), who will explore only the rules considered as interestingness, minimizing his effort. It is important to mention that the output, as in the traditional post-processing approach regarding the use of OMs, is the same, i.e., an association rules list ordered by their degree of interestingness. That way, it is possible to compare these two approaches to demonstrate the feasibility of the proposed process. However, note that with $RAR_{C_t I}$ (i) it is not necessary to know which OM to use/select nor (ii) how to handle the output of different lists to obtain an ordered list of interestingness rules.

4   Experiments

To demonstrate the feasibility of the $RAR_{C_t I}$ process, experiments were carried out. For that, a real data set was used. The data set was provided by the Civil Defense of Rio Claro city, São Paulo state, and contains the occurrences attended by them from 2008 to 2012. The pre-processed data contains 1043 transactions, each one composed of 9 items. The set was converted to a transactional format, where each transaction was composed of pairs with the form "attribute = value". Due to privacy, specific details about the data will not be provided. Using the pre-processed data, association rules were extracted using 5% of minimum support, 0% of minimum confidence (not to bias the results when using this OM to cluster the rules), rules with a minimum of 2 and a maximum of 5 items considering only one item in the consequent. A total of 2215 rules were obtained. However, to analyze the impact the size of the rules has on the results, 4 different rule sets were considered: the first one, R_2, containing only the extracted rules with 2 items; the second one, R_3, containing the extracted rules with a minimum of 2 and a maximum of 3 items; the third one, R_4, containing the extracted rules with a minimum of 2 and a maximum of 4 items; the last one, R_5, containing all the extracted rules. The number of rules contained in each set is shown in Table 1.

As seen in Algorithm 1, in addition to R, it is also necessary to specify a set M of OMs. Although the works described in Sect. 2 present some problems ((i) to know which OM to use/select; (ii) to handle the output of different lists), they show an interesting result: as in [11] (details in Sect. 2), they have already analyzed a large number of OMs, in a variety of data sets, and discussed which of them may be grouped together, which of them are similar, equivalent, etc.

Table 1. Configurations used in the experiments.

Rule sets (R)	$\|R_2\| = 408, \|R_3\| = 1317, \|R_4\| = 1985, \|R_5\| = 2215$
Gold sets (G)	$\|G_2\| = 45, \|G_3\| = 116, \|G_4\| = 160, \|G_5\| = 181$
M	Support, Prevalence, K-measure, Least Contradiction, Confidence, EII1, Leverage, Directed Information Ratio, Loevinger, Odds Ratio, Dilated Chi-square, Added Value, Cosine, Lift, J-measure, Recall, Specificity, Conditional Entropy, Coverage
Cut	10% to 100%, counting every 10

Therefore, it does not make sense to use a large set of measures if there are studies that demonstrate that only a subset of them are needed. That way, we evaluated the RAR_{C_tI} process using one representative measure of each group described in [11], using for M the 19 OMs presented in Table 1. The choice, within each group, was made considering the computational cost of an OM; in this case, the simplest ones were selected.

As mentioned before, it is expected that RAR_{C_tI} behaves equal or better as if the best OM had been used, i.e., if the best solution had been applied. To find the best measure it is necessary to know which are the true interestingness rules among the ones in R. For that, a "gold standard" rule set (named here as G set) was construct: the expert analyzed all the 2215 extracted rules and identified the ones he considered as interestingness, reaching a total of 181 ($\|G\| = 181$). Since 4 different rule sets were considered, to analyze the impact the size of the rules has on the results, 4 different gold sets were taken into account: G_2 containing the gold rules with only 2 items, G_3 containing the gold rules with a minimum of 2 and a maximum of 3 items, G_4 containing the gold rules with a minimum of 2 and a maximum of 4 items and G_5 containing all the gold rules. The number of rules contained in each set is shown in Table 1.

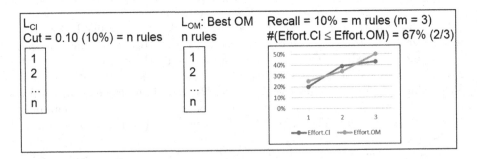

Fig. 1. Evaluation process.

Considering the configurations presented in Table 1, RAR_{C_tI} was executed for each rule set R_x. The Cut parameter was ranged from 10% to 100%, counting every 10. It is important to mention that the higher the Cut the lower the reduction regarding the exploration space considering all the patterns in the list. For example, a $Cut = 20\%$ implies in a list containing 20% of the patterns to be explored, which implies in an exploration space reduction of 80% ($1\text{-}Cut = 1\text{-}0.20$). When $Cut = 100\%$, it means the list will contain all the extracted patterns – even though it is expected that only the top first rules will be of interestingness to the user. However, we tested all the specified range to analyze the effect of the parameter on the results when compared to the best OM (details below). Therefore, Sect. 5 discusses the results considering the entire range and, after that, only those related with a $Cut \leq 50\%$, which means the exploration space was reduced by half or more.

To evaluate the results, the methodology shown in Fig. 1 was applied. As we want to compare the feasibility of RAR_{C_tI} with the best OM, first of all, two lists are considered: L_{Cl} and L_{OM}. L_{Cl} is obtained by applying Algorithm 1 to a R_x, considering the set M and a specific Cut value. In Fig. 1, for example, it is supposed that L_{Cl} contains n rules. To compare this list, with the one that would be obtained by applying the best measure, L_{OM} is generated. For that, it is first necessary to discover which is the best measure. Applying each one of the 19 OMs considered in Table 1, one at a time, 19 different rankings are obtained for a given rule set R_x. The ranking that would provide better results is the one that finds all the G_x rules with less effort, i.e., that reaches a recall of 100% without having to explore all the list. For example: suppose R_x contains 5 rules ($R_x = \{r_1, r_2, r_3, r_4, r_5\}$). Suppose 2 OMs are available, generating two different lists: $OM_1 = \{r_2, r_3, r_1, r_5, r_4\}$ and $OM_2 = \{r_4, r_3, r_5, r_2, r_1\}$. Also suppose that $G_x = \{r_1, r_3\}$. Note that by exploring only the first 3 rules in OM_1 list the user would reach a recall of 100% with an effort of 60% (3/5); on the other hand, a recall of 100% with an effort of 100% (5/5) regarding OM_2 list – in the first case, 60% of the exploration space is analyzed, leading to a reduction of 40% (1-0.60); in the second case, 100%, leading to a reduction of 0% (i.e., the user will have to explore everything). Therefore, OM_1 would be the best measure to consider – the user can find all the "true" interestingness patterns without having to explore the whole list. Note that the user's effort is equal to the space he explored, despite the size of the space available – "User's Effort $\leq = \%$ Space to be Explored" (in case 1: 60% $\leq$ 100% (all rules are available); in case 2: 100% $\leq$ 100% (all rules are available)). In addition, the size of the space will be determined by Cut, which determines the list's size. Once the best measure is discovered, the same number of rules obtained in L_{Cl} is taken from the best measure list, obtaining L_{OM} – in Fig. 1, it is supposed that L_{OM} also contains n rules. It is necessary that both of them contain the same number of rules to compare the lists considering a maximum user's effort regarding a certain recall.

Since the two lists are available, L_{Cl} and L_{OM}, the following analysis can be done: since it is known the number of rules within a G_x set, if we specify a recall $= 10\%$, we know the number of m rules that must be found to reach this respective recall. For example, for a $|G_x| = 10$, to get a recall $= 20\%$, it is necessary to find, in a certain list L_x, 2 rules belonging to G_x. Therefore, we can compare the user's effort regarding L_{Cl} and L_{OM} until a specific recall is reached. Supposing $m = 3$, as in Fig. 1 for a recall $= 10\%$, we can plot the user's effort to find these m rules, as in the plot shown in Fig. 1. In the figure's example, since $m = 3$, it is possible to compare, point by point, the user's effort to discover, in each one of the lists, the 3 gold rules. As seen in the example, the user's effort to find one gold rule in L_{Cl} is 20%, while in L_{OM} 25% (axis $x =$ the number of gold rules found (recall); axis $y =$ the user's effort to reach a certain recall). This means the user would see fewer rules in L_{Cl}, in relation to L_{OM}, until finding the first gold rule. The percentages are calculated by exploring rule by rule in a given list L_x and checking if the current rule is a gold rule. If so, it is checked the number of rules seen until up to that point and the percentage calculated (as in the example of the paragraph above). The process continues until all the m gold rules are found.

Based on what stated above, it is expected that $RARC_tI$ behaves equal or better as if the best OM had been used. If we compute the number of times the user's effort in L_{Cl} (Effort.Cl) performed equal or better than the user's effort in L_{OM} (Effort.Cl $\leqslant$ Effort.OM) we can evaluate the feasibility of $RARC_tI$. In Fig. 1, for example, Effort.Cl presents equal or better results in 2 of the 3 cases (67% (2/3)) – the lower the effort the better the result. That way, what is being analyzed is the user's effort until reaching a specific recall (in Fig. 1, recall $= 10\%$ implies until finding 3 gold rules). Therefore, it is possible to compare the results, i.e., those obtained by $RARC_tI$ with those obtained by the best OM. However, it is important to remember that in a real case we do not know that measure, since we do not know which are the interestingness patterns. For that reason, it is expected that the proposed process behaves equal or better than the traditional one. Finally, it is important to mention that although the lists present the same number n of rules, which indicates a maximum user's effort, they may not provide the same recall, since a list can have more gold rules than another. In this case, the lists can not be comparable, since the plot is built point by point for a specific recall.

5   Results and Discussion

The results obtained from the experiments are presented in Tables 2, 3, 4 and 5. The evaluation process described in Fig. 1 was applied to each R_x set, considering all Cut values and analyzing the recall from 10% to 100%, counting every 10. Each table contains 10 columns, one for each Cut value, and 10 rows, one for each recall. Each cell stores the number of times Effort.Cl presented equal or better results than Effort.OM until reaching a certain recall (as explained before through Fig. 1). When one of the lists reaches a certain recall and the other not, the cell has an indication (i.e., one list contains a number of gold rules corresponding to a particular recall and the other not); in addition, if both are unable to reach a specific recall, a "-" indication is found. For example, in Table 2, regarding R_2, used to generate an L_{Cl} considering a $Cut = 10\%$, it can be seen that: (a) comparing L_{Cl} with the corresponding L_{OM}, both reached a recall of 10% and, until this recall, Effort.Cl presented equal or better results than Effort.OM, i.e., the user's effort considering L_{Cl} was $\leq$ than L_{OM} in 80% of the cases; (b) in relation to a recall of 20%, only L_{Cl} reached this value; in this case, no comparison could be done – this is why the cell is indicated with a "CL"; (c) for recall values above 30%, none of the lists reached the respective values.

Table 2. Obtained results regarding R_2 considering the user's effort in all Cut values and specified recalls.

Recall	Cut									
	10%	20%	30%	40%	50%	60%	70%	80%	90%	100%
10%	80%	80%	80%	80%	80%	80%	80%	80%	80%	80%
20%	Cl	89%	89%	89%	89%	89%	89%	89%	89%	89%
30%	-	93%	93%	93%	93%	93%	93%	93%	93%	93%
40%	-	-	89%	94%	94%	94%	94%	94%	94%	94%
50%	-	-	OM	96%	96%	96%	96%	96%	96%	96%
60%	-	-	-	OM	96%	96%	96%	89%	93%	85%
70%	-	-	-	-	OM	97%	91%	75%	78%	72%
80%	-	-	-	-	-	97%	92%	72%	69%	64%
90%	-	-	-	-	-	-	OM	OM	63%	56%
100%	-	-	-	-	-	-	-	OM	OM	53%

As can be observed, each table provides an overview of the $RAR_{C_t I}$ performance over the traditional OM approach, i.e., if the user can, with the proposed process, recover the same interestingness patterns as if the best OM had been used. Remember that the information about the best OM to use is not known during real applications and, so, the proposed process is expected to behave equal or better than the traditional one. Evaluating the results, presented in Tables 2, 3, 4 and 5, it can be noted that:

– each cell of Tables 2, 3, 4 and 5, with a valid value (X%), can be considered as a test case, from which we can evaluate the overall performance of $RAR_{C_t I}$. Table 2, for example, has 62 test cases, in which on 12 of them ($19\% = 12/62$) L_{Cl} presented a performance $\geq 95\%$ in relation to L_{OM}. In other words, in 19% of the test cases, the user's effort considering L_{Cl} was equal or better than L_{OM} in 95% of the times regarding a certain recall. Observing the results as a whole, i.e., considering all recall and cut values, it can be seen, as summarized in Table 6, that in almost all test cases, regarding all R_x sets (exception for R_2), L_{Cl} presented a performance $\geq 90\%$ in relation to L_{OM}: $\geq 95\%$ in 91% of the test cases in R_3, $\geq 90\%$ in 94% of the test cases in R_4 and $\geq 90\%$ in 90% of the test cases in R_5 (highlighted values). In R_2, in 92% of the test cases L_{Cl} presented a performance $\geq 70\%$ in relation to L_{OM}, which is a

Table 3. Obtained results regarding R_3 considering the user's effort in all *Cut* values and specified recalls.

Recall	Cut									
	10%	20%	30%	40%	50%	60%	70%	80%	90%	100%
10%	Cl	100%	100%	100%	100%	100%	100%	100%	100%	100%
20%	-	100%	100%	100%	100%	100%	100%	100%	100%	100%
30%	-	Cl	100%	100%	100%	100%	100%	100%	100%	100%
40%	-	-	Cl	100%	100%	100%	100%	100%	100%	100%
50%	-	-	-	-	100%	100%	100%	100%	100%	100%
60%	-	-	-	-	-	100%	100%	100%	100%	100%
70%	-	-	-	-	-	-	94%	100%	100%	100%
80%	-	-	-	-	-	-	OM	100%	92%	97%
90%	-	-	-	-	-	-	-	-	91%	90%
100%	-	-	-	-	-	-	-	-	-	84%

Table 4. Obtained results regarding R_4 considering the user's effort in all *Cut* values and specified recalls.

Recall	Cut									
	10%	20%	30%	40%	50%	60%	70%	80%	90%	100%
10%	-	94%	94%	94%	94%	94%	94%	94%	94%	94%
20%	-	97%	97%	97%	97%	97%	97%	97%	97%	97%
30%	-	-	98%	98%	98%	98%	98%	98%	98%	98%
40%	-	-	-	Cl	98%	98%	98%	98%	98%	98%
50%	-	-	-	-	99%	99%	99%	99%	99%	99%
60%	-	-	-	-	-	OM	99%	99%	99%	99%
70%	-	-	-	-	-	-	OM	97%	99%	98%
80%	-	-	-	-	-	-	-	93%	90%	91%
90%	-	-	-	-	-	-	-	-	83%	85%
100%	-	-	-	-	-	-	-	-	-	80%

reasonable result, since in real cases we do not know which is the best OM; however, observe that 50% of the test cases presented a performance $\geq 90\%$. Finally, it can be noted that R_2 is the only one that affects a little more the results; the others showed really good results.

- as mentioned before, the lower the *Cut* the greater the reduction of the exploration space, which implies less effort from the user, since fewer rules must be explored (details in Sect. 4). As seen in Tables 2, 3, 4 and 5, with some highlighted values, with a *Cut* between 40% and 60% it is possible to reach a recall of 50% with a performance in relation to $L_{OM} \geq 95\%$, which is also a really good result. Considering an analysis with *Cut* values $\leq 50\%$, it is possible to observe that in all test cases, regarding all R_x sets (exception for

R_2), L_{Cl} presented a performance $\geq 90\%$ in relation to L_{OM} (Table 7): $\geq$ 95% in 100% of the test cases in R_3, $\geq 90\%$ in 100% of the test cases in R_4 and $\geq 95\%$ in 100% of the test cases in R_5 (highlighted values) (the table was constructed as Table 6, but only considering Cut values $\leq 50\%$). In R_2, 100% of the test cases presented a performance $\geq 80\%$ in relation to L_{OM}, which is a good result, since in real cases we do not know which is the best measure. Cut values $\leq 50\%$ were chosen since they represent the situations where the exploration space is reduced by half or more. Looking at these situations we see that the results are very good.

– observing Tables 2, 3, 4 and 5, it can be seen that, in most of the cases, when one of the lists do not reach a specific recall, avoiding the lists comparison, this occurs with L_{Cl}: in R_2, in 88% of the times OM reaches a recall and CL not (7/8); in R_4 and R_5, in 67% of the times OM reaches a recall and CL not (2/3) – exception in R_3, where the opposite occurred, i.e., in 75% of the times Cl reaches a recall and OM not (3/4). In cases where these situations occurred, a minimum number of times, one list performed only one range above the other. For example, in Table 2, for $Cut = 10\%$, CL presented a better performance until a recall range of 20%, while both of them until 10% (exception in R_2, $Cut = 80\%$). This means that in some cases ($18/218 = 8\%$), OM performed one range above CL; however, the user does not know which is the best measure to use to retrieve the best patterns.

Table 5. Obtained results regarding R_5 considering the user's effort in all Cut values and specified recalls.

Recall	Cut									
	10%	20%	30%	40%	50%	60%	70%	80%	90%	100%
10%	-	95%	95%	95%	95%	95%	95%	95%	95%	95%
20%	-	97%	97%	97%	97%	97%	97%	97%	97%	97%
30%	-	-	98%	98%	98%	98%	98%	98%	98%	98%
40%	-	-	-	99%	99%	99%	99%	99%	99%	99%
50%	-	-	-	-	Cl	99%	99%	99%	99%	99%
60%	-	-	-	-	-	OM	94%	99%	99%	99%
70%	-	-	-	-	-	-	OM	95%	99%	99%
80%	-	-	-	-	-	-	-	83%	87%	90%
90%	-	-	-	-	-	-	-	-	77%	82%
100%	-	-	-	-	-	-	-	-	-	77%

As seen, the $RAR_{Cl I}$ process presents very good results compared to the traditional OM approach, exhibiting equal or better results, in most cases, as if the best OM had been used. That way, it can be said that the proposed process provides a reasonable way to reduce the user's effort in finding the relevant patterns. Therefore, through the real case study that was done, the importance of the work can be visualized.

Table 6. L_{Cl}'s performance, summarized from Tables 2, 3, 4 and 5, considering all Cut values.

L_{Cl}'s Performance	R_2	R_3	R_4	R_5
$\geq 95\%$	19%	**91%**	71%	86%
$\geq 90\%$	**50%**	98%	**94%**	**90%**
$\geq 85\%$	69%	98%	96%	92%
$\geq 80\%$	85%	100%	100%	96%
$\geq 75\%$	89%	100%	100%	100%
$\geq 70\%$	**92%**	100%	100%	100%
$\leq 70\%$	8%	0%	0%	0%

Table 7. L_{Cl}'s performance, summarized from Tables 2, 3, 4 and 5, considering Cut values $\leq 50\%$.

L_{Cl}'s Performance	R_2	R_3	R_4	R_5
$\geq 95\%$	16%	**100%**	69%	**100%**
$\geq 90\%$	47%	100%	**100%**	100%
$\geq 85\%$	74%	100%	100%	100%
$\geq 80\%$	**100%**	100%	100%	100%

6   Conclusion

This work proposed a process, named $RAR_{Ct I}$ (*R*anking *A*ssociation *R*ules by *C*lustering *t*hrough *I*nteresting), to cluster association rules based on their interestingness, according to a set of OMs. The process obtain an ordered list containing the most interestingness/relevant patterns of the domain. The goal was to solve the problems related to the difficulty (i) in knowing which OM to use/select and (ii) in handling the output of different lists to obtain an ordered list of the interestingness rules.

Experiments were done using a real data set and we could observe that the proposed process behaves as equal or better than as if the most suitable OM had been used. However, as stated before, in real cases we do not know this measure. Therefore, we consider that the presented work contributes to the state of the art. As a future work, we intend to apply $RAR_{Ct I}$ in different data sets to evaluate the impact of the proposal on other domains.

Acknowledgments. We wish to thank FAPESP (2015/08059-0) and CAPES for the financial support.

References

1. Belohlavek, R., Grissa, D., Guillaume, S., Nguifo, E.M., Outrata, J.: Boolean factors as a means of clustering of interestingness measures of association rules. Ann. Math. Artif. Intell. **70**(1), 151–184 (2014)
2. Bong, K.K., Joest, M., Quix, C., Anwar, T.: Automated interestingness measure selection for exhibition recommender systems. In: Nguyen, N.T., Attachoo, B., Trawiński, B., Somboonviwat, K. (eds.) ACIIDS 2014. LNCS (LNAI), vol. 8397, pp. 221–231. Springer, Cham (2014). https://doi.org/10.1007/978-3-319-05476-6_23

3. de Carvalho, V.O., de Padua, R., Rezende, S.O.: Solving the problem of selecting suitable objective measures by clustering association rules through the measures themselves. In: Freivalds, R.M., Engels, G., Catania, B. (eds.) SOFSEM 2016. LNCS, vol. 9587, pp. 505–517. Springer, Heidelberg (2016). https://doi.org/10.1007/978-3-662-49192-8_41
4. de Carvalho, V.O., dos Santos, F.F., Rezende, S.O., de Padua, R.: PAR-COM: a new methodology for post-processing association rules. In: Zhang, R., Zhang, J., Zhang, Z., Filipe, J., Cordeiro, J. (eds.) ICEIS 2011. LNBIP, vol. 102, pp. 66–80. Springer, Heidelberg (2012). https://doi.org/10.1007/978-3-642-29958-2_5
5. Djenouri, Y., Drias, H., Habbas, Z., Chemchem, A.: Organizing association rules with meta-rules using knowledge clustering. In: 11th International Symposium on Programming and Systems, pp. 109–115 (2013)
6. Ester, M., Kriegel, H., Sander, J., Xu, X.: A density-based algorithm for discovering clusters in large spatial databases with noise. In: 2nd International Conference on Knowledge Discovery and Data Mining, pp. 226–231 (1996)
7. Guillaume, S., Grissa, D., Mephu Nguifo, E.: Categorization of interestingness measures for knowledge extraction. CoRR abs/1206.6741 (2012)
8. Huynh, X.H., Guillet, F., Blanchard, J., Kuntz, P., Briand, H., Gras, R.: A graph-based clustering approach to evaluate interestingness measures: a tool and a comparative study. In: Guillet, F.J., Hamilton, H.J. (eds.) Quality Measures in Data Mining. Studies in Computational Intelligence, vol. 43, pp. 25–50. Springer, Heidelberg (2007). https://doi.org/10.1007/978-3-540-44918-8_2
9. Kaufman, F., Rousseeuw, P.J.: Finding Groups in Data: An Introduction to Cluster Analysis. Wiley, Hoboken (2005)
10. Tan, P., Steinbach, M., Kumar, V.: Introduction to Data Mining (2006)
11. Tew, C., Giraud-Carrier, C., Tanner, K., Burton, S.: Behavior-based clustering and analysis of interestingness measures for association rule mining. Data Min. Knowl. Discov. **28**(4), 1004–1045 (2014)

An Approach for Automatic Discovery, Composition and Invocation of Semantics Web Services for Data Mining

Társis Marinho[1,2]([✉]), Michel Miranda[3], Heitor Barros[1], Evandro Costa[3], and Patrick Brito[3]

[1] Federal Institute of Alagoas - IFAL,
Rua Mizael Domingues, 75 - Centro, Maceió, Alagoas, Brazil
`heitor.barros@ifal.edu.br`
[2] Federal University of Campina Grande - UFCG,
Rua Aprígio Veloso, 885, Bairro Universitário, Campina Grande, Paraíba, Brazil
`tarsis@copin.ufcg.edu.br`
[3] Federal Univeristy of Alagoas - UFAL,
Av. Lourival de Melo Mota, Tabuleiro do Martins, Maceió, Alagoas, Brazil
`{msm,evandro,patrick}@ic.ufal.br`

Abstract. Nowadays, several educational institutions make use of e-Learning environments and other technologies to support the teaching and learning process. As a consequence, a large amount of data is generated from the many interactions of students, tutors, teachers and other actors involved in these environments. These data can be a great and important source of information, however, analyzing them is a complex and expensive task. One way to analyze such data properly is to apply Educational Data Mining (EDM) techniques, and thus to use the information obtained in decision making support. There are, however, several challenges in the application of mining in educational data. In particular, the integration challenge is complex because it involves different tools developed in different programming languages. Thus, we propose an approach for automatic discovery, composition and invocation of Semantic Web Services (SWS) for data mining based on a new semantic model. With this, we hope to contribute to a greater flexibility in the integration between data mining tools and e-Learning environments. In order to evaluate, we adopted a scenario-based method to evaluate quality attributes of performance and reliability of the proposed solution in these scenarios.

Keywords: Semantic web services · Data mining
Educational data mining

1 Introduction

Nowadays, several educational institutions make use of e-Learning environments and other technologies to support the teaching and learning process. Moodle, for example, gathers large amounts of information about students' interactions [5].

© Springer Nature Switzerland AG 2018
F. Castro et al. (Eds.): MICAI 2017, LNAI 10632, pp. 352–364, 2018.
https://doi.org/10.1007/978-3-030-02837-4_29

As a consequence, a large amount of data generated by these environments from the many interactions of students, tutors, teachers and other actors involved in these environments. Faced the need to analyze the large mass of data generated, new research area emerged, called Educational Data Mining (EDM). Educational Data Mining is an emerging discipline, concerned with developing methods for exploring the unique types of data that come from educational settings, and using those methods to better understand students, and the settings which they learn in [4]. Thus, to awaken opportunities in the development of EDM research, studies carried out by Romero e Ventura point out challenges for EDM [10–12]:

- **Standardization of methods and data** current tools for mining data from a specific course may be useful only to its developers. There are no general tools or re-using tools or techniques that can be applied to any educational system. So, a standardization of data, and the preprocessing, discovering and postprocessing tasks is needed.
- **Integration with the e-learning system** the data mining tool has to be integrated into the e-learning environment as another author tool. All data mining tasks (preprocessing, data mining and post-processing) have to be carried out into a single application. Feedback and results obtained with data mining can be directly applied to the e-learning environment.
- **Mining tools more easy to use by educators or not expert users in data mining** Data mining tools are normally designed more for power and flexibility than for simplicity. Most of the current data mining tools are too complex to use for educators and their features go well beyond the scope of what an educator may want to do. So, these tools must have a more intuitive and easy to use interface, with parameter-free data mining algorithms to simplify the configuration and execution, and with good visualization facilities to make their results.

In particular, the integration challenge is complex because it involves different tools developed in different programming languages. An alternative to the integration problem is the Service-oriented architecture (SOA). According to [3] Web services are the next-generation of applications that will provide functionalities and interoperability ranging from the basics to the more complex processes required by different platform-independent applications. In this context, several authors have presented solutions in order to solve this challenge for EDM domain, such as: Zorilla [15], Podpecan [9], Barros [1] and Marinho [14]. However, the presented solutions have some limitations, including: addition of a new algorithm; discovery and composition of services; costs to create and integrate new services the current base; among others.

This paper presents an approach for automatic discovery, composition and invocation of Semantic Web Services (SWS) for Data Mining based on a new semantic model. Our approach provides Web services that encapsulate algorithms and data mining techniques, performs an automatic service discovery, composition and invocation; and promotes reuse of algorithms and solutions.

The remainder of this paper is structured as follows: Initially, we present related work, in particular work similar to the approach proposed in this work; In Sect. 2, we present the proposed solution, including the architectural project and the semantic model adopted; Sect. 5 presents the results of evaluation carried out using a scenario-based evaluation method; Finally, In Sect. 5, we present the main conclusions and future work.

2 Related Work

In this Section, we present the main works related to the proposed approach. These works are presented below, as well as their disadvantages in relation to the proposed approach.

Zorilla [15] proposes a service-oriented architecture for EDM. This paper has as objective to assist non-specialists to use mining techniques and algorithms through Web services in data mining domain. However, the proposed approach has some limitations: (i) The Web service discovery and composition process are totally manual; (ii) Use of SOAP-based services - the Simple Object Access Protocol (SOAP) protocol has poor performance, because it uses XML (EXtensible Markup Language) as a common syntax for the message exchange and the problems of processing XML files are well known [15].

Podpečan [9] presents an framework for Knowledge discovery in Databases (KDD) process based on Web services. In its development, the authors used the Orange4WS environment. The Orange4WS is a visual environment that provides a data mining toolkit. This paper present some limitations: (i) The service composition is performed manually; (ii) Orange4WS dependency; (iii) This propose also adopt the SOAP protocol.

Marinho [14] proposes a framework based on semantic web services for educational data mining. This framework is composed of SWS that encapsulate mining algorithms and provides an automatic discovery, composition and invocation of SWSs. For this, the Authors adopt a middleware, called GRINV [1]. The GRINV uses OWL-S [6] to describe the Semantic Web Services. This is the main disadvantage of the proposed approach, because the use of OWL-S is very complex and has several problems, such as: Technology with low level of maturity; Performance problems; Creating a service using Web Ontology Language (OWL) is very complex; The service invocation process also is very complex; among others. Thus, using the proposed solution is very complex, making the process unviable for users without experience in SWS domain.

3 Proposed Approach

3.1 Overview

Our approach aims to offer automatic discovery, composition and invocation of Semantic Web Services with focus on Data Mining domain in an extensible and transparent way. In this way, the proposed solution presents a flexible structure allowing developers to make modifications in the techniques and algorithms used in the process of discovery, composition and automatic invocation of services without causing major impacts to the rest of the solution. In this context, as an application for the Data Mining domain, the proposed solution provides Semantic Web Services that encapsulate preprocessing and post-processing algorithms of the Weka tool's data mining API. In addition, developers can perform the instantiation of the proposed solution for the development of new applications based on the use of semantic Web services for the mining domain. Another feature of the solution is to enable the developer to insert new services to allow the addition of unplanned features. These services can perform the steps of data mining, preprocessing and/or post-processing.

3.2 Semantic Model

An important step in the development of applications based on the use of Semantic Web Services (SWS) is the definition of the semantic approach that will be used to describe services. In this context, there are different approaches to provide semantic description of services such as: OWL-S (Web Ontology Language for Services), WSMO (Web Service Modeling Ontology), WSDL (Web Service Definition Language) and SAWSDL (Semantic Annotations for WSDL and XML Schema). However, these templates do not provide support for developing Web services that use messages in the JSON (JavaScript Object Notation) format to communicate with other services, for example, applications developed with REST (Representational State Transfer). In this work we used a semantic model that was proposed by Barros [2] to describe Semantic Web Services, since it is an application based on the REST paradigm and, consequently, to provide automatic discovery, composition and innovation of Semantic Web Services that implement the REST paradigm and use JSON to exchange messages.

The service ontology created by Barros [2] is an adaptation of the OWL-S language aiming at the semantic representation of Web services implemented with the REST paradigm. For the construction of this service ontology, a subset of the OWL-S descriptions was chosen in order to provide compatibility with this language and to add support to features that are not present in OWL-S language. The Fig. 1 displays the entities that are part of the service ontology, with their respective attributes and relationships. The Service class represents the Web services. This class has as attributes a label, description and location. For each service, its parameter set is defined, which can be either Input or Output.

In this service ontology is defined a schema for the input parameters and another for the output parameters of each service. These schemas define the format that the input parameters should be sent to the services and how the output parameters of the services will be returned. These schemas follow a JSON Schema-based definition.

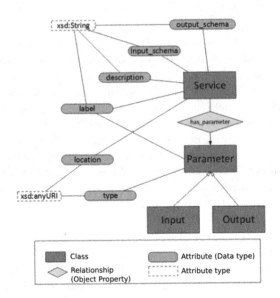

Fig. 1. Graphical representation of service ontology

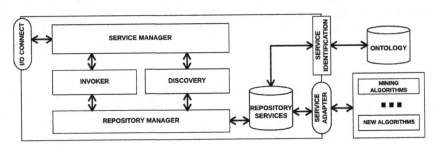

Fig. 2. Approach architecture

3.3 Approach Architecture

The Fig. 2 presents the architecture's logical view of the proposed solution includ-ing its main components. The solution follows a Service Oriented (OA) approach to facilitate the extension and integration with other Web applications. In this sense, this architectural project aims at contemplating the proposed solution to automatically discover, compose and invoke semantic services that encapsu-late algorithms of the Weka API. Sections 3.4 to 3.8 present details about the components architectures.

3.4 I/O Connect

This component contains the communication standards adopted in the proposed solution to enable the integration of other Web applications. In addition to the communication standards, this component allows other client applications to make use of services and/or composition of mining services. Another function of this component is to provide the input of different types of data that will be used in data mining. To ensure that the data submitted by other applications obey the formats accepted by the mining algorithms, this component has access to services that receive the data sent from the application and transform it into formats supported by the algorithms.

3.5 Service Manager Mechanism

The **ServiceManager** Mechanism is considered the kernel of the proposed solution. It is responsible for controlling the flow of processes that must be performed to meet one or more requests made by client applications. Through the component **Connect I/O** (presented in more detail in the Sect. 3.4) the service manager provides access to all available functionality in the proposed solution. In addition, ServiceManager is responsible for controlling the flow of processes that must be performed to discover, compose, and dynamically invoke compatible data mining services to service requests sent by client applications. The requests can be one of following types: request of service discovery, request of service discovery and invocation and request of service invocation.

Service Discovery Request: the client informs as input the descriptions of the service that he wants to invoke. Through this request, the Service Manager searches for the service that best serves the client needs, making service compositions if necessary, and returning as a response to the user the service found or the composition of services so that he can analyze, if he wants to, and in the future to make the invocation.

Discovery and Invocation Request: The user defines the semantic descriptions of the service to be invoked and the input parameters of the desired service. Through this request, the proposed solution makes the discovery of services that best meets, making service compositions if necessary, and invoking the chosen services in an automatic and dynamic way, and, after that, returns the result of the invocation to the user.

Service Invocation Request: The user informs as input the URI of the service that he wants to invoke and the input parameters to invoke the service. Through the URI and the parameters reported, the proposed solution automatically and dynamically invokes the service, and returns the invocation result to the user as a response.

3.6 Service Adapter

This component provides an abstraction of the encapsulation of mining algorithms provided by other tools, allowing the integration of techniques and algorithms of mining available by them in this approach.

3.7   Discovery and Invocation Strategies

The discovery process starts with the service description (input and output parameters) that the user needs and aims to identify the service in the repository that best fits with this description. In some scenarios there is no single service that meets the needs of the user, but instead the solution can be found in a set of services can be used in a composition. The Discovery process have a *Direct Matching* when this process finds a unique service as a result and an *Indirect Matching* when the result of the process is a service composition.

To perform the service discovery and composition tasks, the BCMatchMaker algorithm was implemented. This algorithm is responsible for controlling the entire process of discovery and composition of services. This algorithm consists of two methods, direct match and indirect match. The algorithm implements the cosine metric of similarity [13] to calculate the Semantic Matching that exists between each service and the user's request. Thus, the cosine metric calculates the similarity between the user-defined parameters and the repository services.

Through the user-defined parameters, the algorithm executes the direct match method, this method verifies that in the service repository there is some saved composition that meets the parameters defined in the matching request with 100% similarity between the parameters. If there is composition in the repository, the BCMatchMaker algorithm returns that composition to the Service Manager, which will start the invocation process. However, when there are no compositions saved in the service repository, direct match performs the services search in the service repository to check if there is a service with input and output parameters that has Matching with 100% similarity. Given that service exists, the BCMatchMaker algorithm returns the service to the Service Manager.

When the direct match method does not find a service that meets the request, the indirect match method is invoked to perform the search for service compositions that meet the user's request. The search for service composition is performed in a backward chaining strategy using the input and output parameters defined in the request. Thus, the method returns the composition that maintains the highest level of similarity, with a minimum threshold of 80%.

If no service composition with sufficient similarity is found, the algorithm does not return any service to the Service Manager, which will alert the user that there is no service that meets his needs and, then, interrupt the system execution. When the algorithm finds a service or composition, Service Manager activates the service invocation engine. The workflow performed by the proposed approach to discover, compose, and invoke services is illustrated in Fig. 3.

3.8   Repositories

This section aims to describe the components of repositories used in the proposed approach.

Repository Manager: This component controls the access to the service repository by the other components of the application. The component defines the

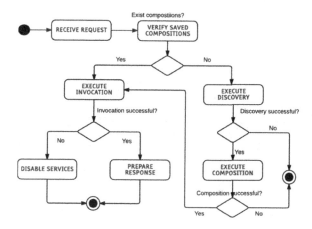

Fig. 3. Execution flow of the approach.

set of operations that can be performed to meet the requests requested by the application components, such as: adding service, fetching a service, listing all services, removing service, and updating.

Repository Services: When the proposed approach is executed, the information of the Semantic Web Services defined by the service ontology (Fig. 1), such as: service inputs and outputs parameters, URI to access these parameters, service description, Label, URI to access the service, service inputs and outputs json schemas are stored in this component. In this context, the MongoDB database was adopted in order to improve of the performance of the processes of service discovery, composition and automatic invocation in order to allow educational environments to execute these processes at run time. MongoDB [7] is an open-source, high-performance, schema-free, document-oriented database application.

Repository Ontology: This component stores the domain ontologies used in the proposed approach. In this component, we have the services and mining ontologies. According to Payne et al. [8], ontologies provide semantic annotation, allowing for greater automation of the Web services discovery, composition, and invocation process.

This service ontology defines all aspects of the services that are relevant to automate the discovery, composition and automatic innovation of Semantic Web services that encapsulate algorithms and mining techniques for the Data Mining domain, such as: URI to access the parameters, service description, label, URI to access the service, json schema of inputs and outputs of the service. The semantic description of the mining services available in this work was carried out according to the structure defined in the service ontology given in [2], as stated in Fig. 1 of Sect. 3.2. Listing 1.1 shows the OWL individual that represents the Semantic Web Service that implements J48 classifier algorithm.

Listing 1.1. Service J48 Data Mining presented in the Manchester OWL syntax. Input and Output Json Schemas are hidden for better attributes visualization and length constraints.

```
1   Individual: <domain.owl#J48_Service>
2     Types:
3       <domain.owl#Service>
4     Facts:
5       <domain.owl#hasInput><domain.owl#Arff_Input>,
6       <domain.owl#hasOutput><domain.owl#J48_Model>,
7       <domain.owl#URI> "http://172.20.9.39/framework/j48",
8       <domain.owl#input_schema> "INPUT_JSON_SCHEMA",
9       <domain.owl#label> "J48 Service",
10      <domian.owl#descrition> "retorna o modelo Classify",
11      <domain.owl#output_schema> "OUTPUT_JSON_SCHEMA"
```

Mining ontology describes tasks and data mining techniques, specifying the input and output parameters of the Weka tool's data mining algorithms. Subsequently, this ontology has been extended to include the input and output parameters of the available mining services in the proposed solution. It is also possible for the user to include in the mining ontology the specification of input parameters and outputs of the algorithms provided by other tools. In Listing 1.2 a fragment of the mining ontology is displayed in the Manchester OWL syntax, as well as the distribution of classes and subclasses. Below, we find in more detail, the description of some classes of the ontology.

Listing 1.2. Ontology of Mining presented in the Manchester OWL syntax

```
1
2   Ontology: <Onto_Mining.owl>
3   Class: <Onto_Mining.owl#BayesNet>
4       SubClassOf:
5           <Onto_Mining.owl#Bayes>
6   Class: <Onto_Mining.owl#EM>
7       SubClassOf:
8           <Onto_Mining.owl#Clusterers>
9   Class: <Onto_Mining.owl#EM_MODEL>
10      SubClassOf:
11          <Onto_Mining.owl#TrainClusteres>
12  Class: <Onto_Mining.owl#FPGrowth>
13      SubClassOf:
14          <Onto_Mining.owl#Associations>
```

– **MiningAlgorithms:** is the parent class of all data mining techniques and algorithms. In the ontology, the techniques and algorithms of mining are separated by type, like: preprocessing, classification, grouping and association.
  • **Preprocess:** Algorithms and techniques that perform preprocessing must be subclasses of this class. For example: Filters algorithm of Weka tool.

- **Classifiers:** is a parent subclass of all classification techniques and algorithms. In the ontology, the algorithms and classification techniques are divided by types, such as: trees, functions, rules, association, Bayesian, among others.
  * **Trees:** Algorithms and techniques that perform tree-based classification should be subclasses of this class. For example: J48 algorithm of the Weka tool.
  * **Functions:** The algorithms and techniques that perform function-based classification should be subclasses of this class. For example: SimpleLogistic algorithm of the Weka tool.
  * **Bayes:** The algorithms and techniques that perform classification based on Bayesian probability must be subclasses of this class. For example: NaiveBayes algorithm of the Weka tool.
  * **Rules:** Algorithms and techniques that perform rule-based classification must be subclasses of this class. For example: OneR algorithm of the Weka tool.
- **Clusters:** The algorithms and techniques that perform clustering must be subclasses of this class. For example: SimpleKMeans algorithm of the Weka tool.
- **Associetes:** The algorithms and techniques that perform association must be subclasses of this class. For example: Apriori algorithm of the Weka tool.
- **Parameters:** Represents the input and output parameters of the algorithms and data mining techniques defined in the ontology.

The mining ontology used in the proposed solution provides the flexibility to include and/or modify input and output parameters of mining techniques and algorithms. Therefore, the developer can adapt the mining services according to the needs required in the application.

3.9   Services Identification

This component is responsible for mapping the services available in the service repository with its semantic description available in the ontology repository, that is, it is a component that makes the interconnection of the repositories.

4   Evaluation

This Section has as objective to present the evaluation process of the proposed approach. For this, we adopt an scenario-based evaluation was aimed at evaluating the proposed approach in scenarios as close to the real as possible. The scenarios were constructed to evaluate the quality attributes of performance and reliability. Thereby, based on the real cases, we defined 07 scenarios and, during the scenarios execution, observe the response time and the behavior of the proposed approach.

[01] Unsuccessful composition execution - The system has received input and output parameters reported in the user request do not correspond to any of the services available in the service repository.

[02] Direct Match - Based o the user's request, the proposed approach needs to find a service that matches the user's request.

[03] Simple Indirect Match - Based o the user's request, the proposed approach needs to find a simple composition of services that matches the user's request.

[04] Indirect Match - The proposed approach must perform the services composition with 02 or more services in a scenario with multiple composition options available.

[05] Indirect Match in a recovery scenario - Given that a service has been disabled, the proposed approach must perform the services composition with 02 or more services in a recovery scenario with multiple composition options available.

[06] Indirect Match in a recovery scenario - Given that a service has been disabled, the proposed approach must perform the services composition with 03 or more services in a recovery scenario with multiple composition options available.

[07] Complex Indirect Match - The proposed approach must perform the services composition with 04 or more services in a scenario with multiple composition options available.

The selected scenarios were executed in a notebook with Intel Core i7 processor with 8 GB RAM memory and Windows 10 operating system. Each scenario has been executed 30 times and the scenario execution results are presented in Table 1. Thus, we measured the following indicators: Mean Response Time, Standard Deviation and Confidence Interval.

Table 1. Experiment results.

	C01	C02	C03	C04	C05	C06	C07
SD	15,12	62,41	74,07	40,14	51,5	62,49	92,49
Lower CI	145,52	959,73	1050,99	1027,20	1031,10	1077,94	1150,67
M	151,00	982,00	1078,0	1042,00	1050,00	1100,00	1184,00
Upper CI	156,34	1004,40	1104,01	1055,93	1067,97	1122,66	1216,86

Legend: SD: *Standard Deviation* and CI: *Confidence Interval*, M: *Mean Response Time in milliseconds*

The proposed approach responded well to all scenarios. No errors were reported. The results demonstrated that the proposed approach has executed the discovery, composition and invocation of services quickly and efficiently. Besides that, with the semantic model adopted, the process of creating and adding new services is more simple. Therefore, our propose can be viable in real scenarios.

5 Conclusion and Future Work

This paper proposes an approach to discovery, composition and invocation of SWS for data mining based on new semantic model [2]. This approach offers advantages, such as: (i) Reuse of mining algorithms and solutions that can be integrated to the approach proposed through services; (ii) Integration of mining tools and educational environments in a simple way; (iii) Addition of new mining algorithms and/or techniques at runtime; (iv) With the REST adoption and a new semantic model, the creation of new services is facilitated; (v) Performance in the process of discovering, composing and invoking services; among others. Based on the scenarios evaluated, the results demonstrated the feasibility in adopting the proposed approach in scenarios close to the real scenarios.

As future work, we intend to carry out other assessments with different scenarios, integrate other mining tools and couple the proposed solution to an educational environment in order to evaluate the proposal in a real use scenario.

Acknowledgments. Authors would like to thank Fundação de Amparo à Pesquisa do Estado de Alagoas (FAPEAL) for financial support.

References

1. Barros, H.J.S.: Um middleware adaptável para descoberta, composição e invocação automática de serviços web semântico. Master's thesis, Federal University of Alagoas (2011)
2. Barros, H.J.S.: Um Modelo Semântico para Compartilhamento de Recursos Educacionais. Ph.D. thesis, Federal University of Campina Grande (2016)
3. IBM. Standards and web services (2017). Accessed 6 Jan 2017
4. IEDMS. What is EDM? (2016). Accessed 10 Oct 2016
5. Luna, J.M., Castro, C., Romero, C.: MDM tool: a data mining framework integrated into moodle. Comput. Appl. Eng. Educ. **25**(1), 90–102 (2017)
6. Martin, D., et al.: OWL-S: semantic markup for web services. W3C Member Submission **22**, 2007–04 (2004)
7. MongoDB. What is MongoDB (2017). Accessed 6 Jan 2017
8. Payne, T., Lassila, O.: Guest editors' introduction: semantic web services. IEEE Intell. Syst. **19**(4), 14–15 (2004)
9. Podpečan, V., Zemenova, M., Lavrač, N.: Orange4WS environment for service-oriented data mining. Comput. J. **55**, 82–98 (2011). https://doi.org/10.1093/comjnl/bxr077
10. Romero, C., Ventura, S.: Educational data mining: a survey from 1995 to 2005. Expert Syst. Appl. **33**(1), 135–146 (2007)
11. Romero, C., Ventura, S.: Educational data mining: a review of the state of the art. IEEE Trans. Syst. Man Cybern. Part C: Appl. Rev. **40**(6), 601–618 (2010)
12. Romero, C., Ventura, S.: Data mining in education. Wiley Interdiscip. Rev.: Data Min. Knowl. Discov. **3**(1), 12–27 (2013)

13. Schwarz, M., Lobur, M., Stekh, Y.: Analysis of the effectiveness of similarity measures for recommender systems. In: 2017 14th International Conference on Experience of Designing and Application of CAD Systems in Microelectronics (CADSM), pp. 275–277. IEEE (2017)
14. Souza, T.M.: Um framework para mineração de dados educacionais baseado em serviços semânticos. Master's thesis, Federal University of Alagoas (2011)
15. Zorrilla, M., García-Saiz, D.: A service oriented architecture to provide data mining services for non-expert data miners. Decis. Support. Syst. **55**(1), 399–411 (2013)

Author Index

Printed in the United States
By Bookmasters